Designed to be read on a variety of devices, the ebook includes a number of exciting enhancements.

◀ RECORDINGS of every example in the book are just a tap away.

The ebook is also the launch pad for online KNOW IT? SHOW IT! pedagogy. You'll find links to Know It? Show It! activities in every chapter.

At the beginning of each chapter, ▶ a FORMATIVE QUIZ—powered by Norton InQuizitive—helps you learn and prepares you for workbook assignments. A variety of question types—many featuring musical notation—offer a range of ways to practice skills, while robust feedback helps you understand mistakes. With InQuzitive, you can answer questions until you've mastered fundamental skills.

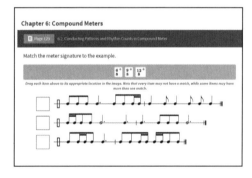

◀ Finally, you can complete WORKBOOK assignments in print or online. The new online workbook includes nearly the same exercises that appear in print and offers instant feedback.

The Musician's Guide to Fundamentals

THIRD EDITION

The Musician's Guide to Fundamentals

THIRD EDITION

Jane Piper Clendinning

Florida State University College of Music

Elizabeth West Marvin

Eastman School of Music

Joel Phillips

Westminster Choir College of Rider University

W. W. NORTON & COMPANY · NEW YORK · LONDON

W. W. NORTON & COMPANY has been independent since its founding in 1923, when William Warder Norton and Mary D. Herter Norton first published lectures delivered at the People's Institute, the adult education division of New York City's Cooper Union. The firm soon expanded its program beyond the Institute, publishing books by celebrated academics from America and abroad. By midcentury, the two major pillars of Norton's publishing program—trade books and college texts—were firmly established. In the 1950s, the Norton family transferred control of the company to its employees, and today—with a staff of four hundred and a comparable number of trade, college, and professional titles published each year—W. W. Norton & Company stands as the largest and oldest publishing house owned wholly by its employees.

Editor: Justin Hoffman
Editorial Assistant: Julie Kocsis
Associate Project Editor: Michael Fauver
Managing Editor, College: Marian Johnson
Media Project Editor: Meg Wilhoite
Managing Editor, College Digital Media: Kim Yi
Production Manager: Andy Ensor
Media Editor: Steve Hoge
Assistant Editor, Emedia: Stephanie Eads
Copyeditor: Jodi Beder
Proofreader: Debra Nichols
Art Director: Jillian Burr
Designer: Lisa Buckley
Marketing Manager, Music: Trevor Penland
Composition: Six Red Marbles, Inc.
Music Engraving: Six Red Marbles, Inc.
Manufacturing: LSC Communications—Kendallville

Splanky by Neal Hefti. Copyright © 1958 (renewed) WB Music Corp. All rights reserved. Used by permission of Alfred Publishing, LLC.

Library of Congress Cataloging-in-Publication Data

Names: Clendinning, Jane Piper, author. | Marvin, Elizabeth West, 1955-
    author. | Phillips, Joel, 1958- author.
Title: The musician's guide to fundamentals / Jane Piper Clendinning,
    Elizabeth West Marvin, Joel Phillips.
Description: Third edition. | New York : W. W. Norton & Company, [2018] |
    Includes index.
Identifiers: LCCN 2017027563 | ISBN 9780393616576 (pbk.)
Subjects: LCSH: Music theory.
Classification: LCC MT6 .C5677 2018 | DDC 781—dc23 LC record available at
    https://lccn.loc.gov/2017027563

ISBN 978-0-393-61657-6

W. W. Norton & Company, Inc., 500 Fifth Avenue, New York, NY 10110
wwnorton.com
W. W. Norton & Company, Ltd., 15 Carlisle Street, London W1D 3BS

2 3 4 5 6 7 8 9 0

To our teachers, colleagues, and students—
with whom we have shared the joy of music, and from
whom we continue to learn—and, with thanks,
to our families for their patience and support

Brief Contents

CHAPTER 1   Pitch Notation and the Grand Staff   1

CHAPTER 2   Accidentals and Half and Whole Steps   25

CHAPTER 3   Simple Meters   47

CHAPTER 4   Beat Subdivisions and Syncopation   73

CHAPTER 5   Major Scales and Keys   97

CHAPTER 6   Compound Meters   127

CHAPTER 7   Minor Scales and Keys   157

CHAPTER 8   Intervals   193

CHAPTER 9   Triads and Seventh Chords   233

CHAPTER 10   Melody Harmonization and Cadences   267

MAKE MUSIC A   Write a Folk Song   301

MAKE MUSIC B   Write a Blues Song   313

MAKE MUSIC C   Write a Popular Song   325

Anthology   339

Appendix 1   Try It Answers   A-1

Appendix 2   Reading Review Answers   A-16

Appendix 3   Glossary   A-18

Appendix 4   The Overtone Series   A-28

Appendix 5   The Diatonic Modes   A-29

Appendix 6   More on Seventh Chords   A-32

Appendix 7   Basic Guitar Chords   A-34

Appendix 8   Piano Fingerings for Selected Scales   A-39

Appendix 9   Connecting Chords   A-42

Contents

Preface   xiii

CHAPTER 1   Pitch Notation
and the Grand Staff   1

Musical Contour   1
Introduction to Pitch Notation: Letter Names   2
The Piano Keyboard: Naming White Keys   3
Staff Notation   3
Treble and Bass Clefs   4
Naming Pitches with Octave Numbers   6
Ledger Lines   6
The Grand Staff   7
Writing Music in a Score   9
Explore Further: C-clefs   12

Did You Know? 13 ▪ Terms You Should Know 13
▪ Questions for Review 14 ▪ Reading Review 14
▪ Apply It 15 ▪ Listen and Write 17 ▪ Workbook 19

CHAPTER 2   Accidentals and Half
and Whole Steps   25

Sharps, Flats, and Naturals   25
Writing Pitches with Accidentals   28
Half Steps and Whole Steps   29
Hearing Half and Whole Steps   32
Double Sharps and Flats   32
Explore Further: More on Enharmonic Spellings   34

Did You Know? 35 ▪ Terms You Should Know 35
▪ Questions for Review 36 ▪ Reading Review 36
▪ Apply It 37 ▪ Listen and Write 39 ▪ Workbook 41

CHAPTER 3   Simple Meters   47

Duple, Triple, and Quadruple Meters   47
Tempo Markings and Conducting Patterns   48
Rhythmic Notation   50
Meter Signatures   52
Counting Rhythms in Simple Meters   54
Rests   56
Explore Further: Meters with ♪ or ♪ Beat Units   57

Did You Know? 59 ▪ Terms You Should Know 59
▪ Questions for Review 60 ▪ Reading Review 60
▪ Apply It 61 ▪ Listen and Write 65 ▪ Workbook 67

CHAPTER 4   Beat Subdivisions
and Syncopation   73

Beat Subdivisions   73
Ties and Slurs   76
Syncopation   77
Triplets   79
Explore Further: Rhythmic Variations in Performance   80

Did You Know? 81 ▪ Terms You Should Know 82
▪ Questions for Review 82 ▪ Reading Review 82
▪ Apply It 83 ▪ Listen and Write 89 ▪ Workbook 91

CHAPTER 5   Major Scales and Keys   97

Scales   97
Major Scales   98
Scale Degrees   98
Writing Major Scales   100
Major Key Signatures   102
The Circle of Fifths   106
Explore Further: Chromatic Scales   107

Did You Know? 108 ▪ Terms You Should Know 108
▪ Questions for Review 109 ▪ Reading Review 109
▪ Apply It 110 ▪ Listen and Write 115 ▪ Workbook 119

CHAPTER 6   Compound Meters   127

Compound Meters   127
Meter Signatures   129
Subdivisions   131
Duplets and Syncopation   133
Other Compound Meters   134
Explore Further: Asymmetrical Meters and Changing
Meter   137

Did You Know? 139 ▪ Terms You Should Know 139
▪ Questions for Review 140 ▪ Reading Review 140
▪ Apply It 141 ▪ Listen and Write 147 ▪ Workbook 149

CHAPTER 7 Minor Scales and Keys 157

Parallel Keys 157

Natural Minor 159

Harmonic Minor 160

Melodic Minor 162

Comparing Scale Types 164

Relative Keys 165

Minor Key Signatures and the Circle of Fifths 168

Identifying the Key from a Score 170

Explore Further: Major and Minor Pentatonic Scales 171

Did You Know? 173 ▪ Terms You Should Know 173
▪ Questions for Review 174 ▪ Reading Review 174
▪ Apply It 175 ▪ Listen and Write 181 ▪ Workbook 185

CHAPTER 8 Intervals 193

Intervals 193

Interval Quality 195

Spelling Intervals Method 1: Using the White Keys 197

Inverting Intervals 201

Spelling Intervals Method 2: Scale and Key-Signature Method 203

Augmented and Diminished Intervals 207

Compound Intervals 210

Consonance and Dissonance 211

Explore Further: Doubly Augmented and Doubly Diminished Intervals 212

Did You Know? 213 ▪ Terms You Should Know 213
▪ Questions for Review 213 ▪ Reading Review 213
▪ Apply It 214 ▪ Listen and Write 221 ▪ Workbook 225

CHAPTER 9 Triads and Seventh Chords 233

Triads 233

Triad Qualities in Major Keys 234

Triad Qualities in Minor Keys 236

Spelling Triads 237

Triad Inversion 241

The Dominant Seventh Chord 244

Spelling the Dominant Seventh Chord 244

Seventh Chord Inversion 245

Explore Further: Other Seventh Chords 246

Did You Know? 248 ▪ Terms You Should Know 249
▪ Questions for Review 249 ▪ Reading Review 249
▪ Apply It 250 ▪ Listen and Write 257 ▪ Workbook 259

CHAPTER 10 Melody Harmonization and Cadences 267

Triads on $\hat{1}$, $\hat{4}$, and $\hat{5}$ and the Seventh Chord on $\hat{5}$ 267

Melody, Motive, and Phrase 270

Harmonizing Major Melodies with the Basic Phrase Model 271

Cadence Types 272

The Subdominant in the Basic Phrase 274

Melodic Embellishments and Melody Harmonization 276

Harmonizing Minor-Key Melodies 276

Writing Chord Progressions 279

Explore Further: Writing Keyboard Accompaniments 281

Did You Know? 283 ▪ Terms You Should Know 283
▪ Questions for Review 284 ▪ Reading Review 284
▪ Apply It 285 ▪ Listen and Write 289 ▪ Workbook 293

MAKE MUSIC A Write a Folk Song 301

Quaternary Song Form 301

Writing Folk Melodies 304

Terms You Should Know 305 ▪ Apply It 306
▪ Workbook 309 ▪ Project A: Write a Folk Song 311

MAKE MUSIC B Write a Blues Song 313

The Blues Scale 313

12-Bar Blues 316

Terms You Should Know 317 ▪ Apply It 318
▪ Workbook 321 ▪ Project B: Writing a Song in Blues Style 323

MAKE MUSIC C Write a Popular Song 325

Form 325

Harmonic Loops 327

Terms You Should Know 329 ▪ Apply It 330
▪ Workbook 335 ▪ Project C: Writing a Song in a Recent Popular Style 337

Anthology 339

"The Ash Grove" 340

Johann Sebastian Bach, Invention in D Minor 342

Bach, "Wachet auf" (Chorale No. 179) 344

Joseph Brackett, "Simple Gifts" 347

"Come, Ye Thankful People, Come" ("St. George's Windsor") 348

Stephen Foster, "Oh! Susanna" 349

Patrick S. Gilmore, "When Johnny Comes Marching Home" 350

"Greensleeves" 351

"Home on the Range" 353

Scott Joplin, "Solace" (excerpt) 354

Wolfgang Amadeus Mozart, String Quartet in D Minor, K. 421, third movement 357

Mozart, *Variations on "Ah, vous dirai-je Maman,"* (excerpts) 360

"My Country, 'Tis of Thee" ("America") 363

John Newton, "Amazing Grace" 364

Joel Phillips, "Blues for Norton" 365

Franz Schubert, Waltz in B Minor, Op. 18, No. 6 369

Robert Schumann, "Wild Rider" 371

Hart A. Wand and Lloyd Garrett, "Dallas Blues" 372

Appendix 1 Try It Answers A-1

Appendix 2 Reading Review Answers A-16

Appendix 3 Glossary A-18

Appendix 4 The Overtone Series A-28

Appendix 5 The Diatonic Modes A-29

Appendix 6 More on Seventh Chords A-32

Appendix 7 Basic Guitar Chords A-34

Appendix 8 Piano Fingerings for Selected Scales A-39

Appendix 9 Connecting Chords A-42

Index of Musical Examples A-44

Index of Terms and Concepts A-48

Preface

We hope you have chosen this course because you have an interest in—even a love for—music. Perhaps you want to learn to read music, write your own songs, or just listen to music with more understanding. This book can help you do all three.

Have you ever tried to explain something but didn't know the right words? Our study begins with the vocabulary that will help you communicate your musical ideas. You'll learn musical terms and symbols and how to read and write pitches and rhythms, scales, intervals, and chords. We'll build on these basics and consider how music is constructed, what musical elements are being used, and why it sounds the way it does.

When you finish this book, you'll have all the tools you need to compose a song, and we hope you'll perform it in class. What better way to demonstrate what you have learned than to write your own music!

In this course, you will study classical music, as well as rock, jazz and blues standards, and folk songs. We encourage you to explore music of other cultures and styles, too; much of what you'll learn is useful in thinking about any type of music. We hope that you will enjoy using this book, and that the concepts you learn will enrich the ways you think about music for many years to come.

The online features in this new edition—an ebook with streaming recordings, formative assessments, and an online workbook—make it easier than ever to learn, and offer resources for both traditional and online classes.

Using This Text

This book offers a comprehensive set of materials for learning music fundamentals through repertoire, hands-on music making, and creative music writing. The ten chapters introduce everything you need to know to compose and notate a song of your own. The Make Music activities at the end of the book guide you to write a folk song, a blues song, or a popular song.

The *Musician's Guide to Fundamentals* is organized to make it as easy as possible for you to learn. It includes many useful features, described here, that will facilitate your study.

- **Key Concept** and **Summary** boxes highlight new ideas and gather essential information.

> **KEY CONCEPT** A **half step** (or **semitone**) is the interval between any pitch and the next closest pitch on the keyboard in either direction. The combination of two half steps forms a **whole step** (or **whole tone**). A whole step always has a note that could be inserted in the middle.

- **Try It** exercises are scattered throughout chapters to provide opportunities to practice new concepts. They give you immediate feedback on your understanding and prepare you for the assignments at the end of the chapter. When you see one of these exercises, try it, then check your answer. Only then will you know that you understand the concept and can apply it in your music making.

TRY IT #4

Identify the key of "Simple Gifts" by answering these questions.

- The key signature suggests what key? _____
- What are the first six scale degrees? _____
- What are the last six scale degrees? _____
- Key of piece _____

Brackett, "Simple Gifts"

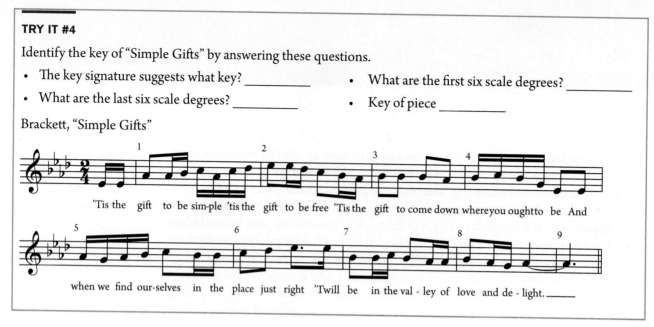

- Since many concepts can be learned in more than one way, **Another Way** boxes offer alternative explanations. Use the method that works best for you.

ANOTHER WAY A common mnemonic (memory) device to help you remember the first four flats is the word "bead." One handy sentence to remember for the order of both sharps and flats is "Father Charles Goes Down And Ends Battle." When you read it forward, the first letter of each word gives the order of sharps; when you read it backward ("Battle Ends And Down Goes Charles's Father"), you get the order of flats.

- **Explore Further** features in each chapter go beyond the basics to introduce more-sophisticated concepts.
- Every chapter ends with a list of **Terms You Should Know, Questions for Review**, and a **Reading Review**. The **Questions for Review** are open-ended questions about chapter content; formulate answers to them in your own words. **Reading Reviews** are short, matching quizzes; answers are in Appendix 2. These tools will help you test your mastery of the material covered before you move on to the next chapter.
- A **Did You Know?** box also appears at the end of each chapter to explain historical background for featured composers and pieces.

Did You Know?

William "Smokey" Robinson (Examples 6.9 and 6.10) was inducted into the Rock and Roll Hall of Fame in 1987, in honor of his extended career as singer-songwriter with the Miracles and his role as talent scout and record producer. During his long association with Detroit-based Motown Records—once the largest black-owned company in the United States—and its founder, Berry Gordy, Robinson worked as songwriter and producer with the Miracles, the Temptations, and Marvin Gaye. Gordy took Robinson under his wing when the young artist was still a teenager, and he released the Miracles' first single when

Robinson was eighteen. The group became a hit during the 1960s and early 70s, with such songs as "You've Really Got a Hold on Me," "I Second That Emotion," and "The Tears of a Clown." With Ronnie White of the Miracles, Robinson wrote "My Girl," which became a #1 hit for the Temptations. After splitting from the Miracles in 1972, Robinson enjoyed a strong solo career. In 1999, he received a Grammy Lifetime Achievement Award.

End-of-chapter activities and assignments invite you to practice what you've learned:

- **Apply It** activities emphasize the skills you need to understand and recall musical patterns. Activities include singing and rhythm reading, keyboard practice, short listening and writing activities, and more. So that you can assess your progress, answers to written Apply It exercises appear in the back of the book, and recordings of many melodies and rhythms are available online, with the ebook. Each Apply It section ends with a **Listen and Write** assignment that may be assigned for homework or completed during class.

- Three or four double-sided, tear-out-and-turn-in **Workbook Assignments** give you the opportunity to master the concepts presented in each chapter; each assignment is also available in the online workbook. These assignments, which include abundant practice, reinforce concepts in the order that they appear in the chapter; headings indicate when you are ready to complete each assignment.

Using Know It? Show It! Pedagogy

The Musician's Guide to Fundamentals now features **Know It? Show It!** pedagogy, a revolutionary new set of resources for learning music fundamentals. Students can access a fully interactive online ebook, with recordings just a click away. Within the ebook, students can launch these online resources:

- *Know It?* Formative quizzes (by Sarah Sarver of Oklahoma City University), powered by Norton InQuizitive, to help students develop fundamental skills. InQuizitive activities feature a wide range of question types, including many in which students interact with musical notation.

- *Show It!* An automatically graded Online Workbook (adapted by Michael McClimon of Furman University) with the exercises that appear in the text.

Using the Anthology

As part of this text, we have included a short **Anthology** with musical scores for 20 pieces. Our spiral-learning approach revisits the anthology's core repertoire from chapter to chapter as you learn new concepts—a single piece might illustrate pitch, meter, scales, and triads. By the second or third time you "visit" a particular work, it will seem like an old friend. We hope that you will listen to the music until you know each work well enough to hear it in your head, the same way you can hear familiar songs from the radio, television, or movies just by thinking about them.

We have chosen music for study that we like and that our students have enjoyed. Some of the works should be familiar to you, and other pieces may be new. The anthology includes pieces for varied performing ensembles in contrasting musical styles—from

American popular songs to classical string quartets, from a piano rag to a piano waltz, from a folk song to a choral hymn. Complete recordings of all the anthology pieces are available online.

To the Instructor

The *Musician's Guide to Fundamentals* is a comprehensive teaching and learning package for online and in-person music fundamentals classes. We have designed the package with numerous support mechanisms to help you efficiently prepare for class.

- The online **Answer Key** includes answers to all exercises in the same format and pagination as the text, plus instructions and resources for Apply It activities.
- The **Instructor's Manual** by Peter Martens (Texas Tech University) offers a wealth of materials, including chapter overviews, teaching strategies, class activities, supplemental repertoire, additional exercises, and test questions.
- New online resources—including **InQuizitive** and the online workbook—are self-grading. Grades can report automatically to your campus LMS or be accessed via the Norton website.

Our Thanks to . . .

A work of this size and scope requires the help of many people. We are especially grateful for the support of our families—Elizabeth A. Clendinning and David Stifler; Rachel Armstrong Bowers and Rocky Bowers; and Allen, Bao, and Jin Joseph; Glenn, Russell, and Caroline West; and Elizabeth Scheiber and Tom Phillips. Our work together as coauthors has been incredibly rewarding, and we are thankful for that collaboration and friendship. While working on the project, we received encouragement and useful ideas from music fundamentals teachers across the country. We thank these teachers for their willingness to share their years of experience with us.

For subvention of the recordings that accompany the text, and for his support of strong music theory pedagogy, we thank Jamal Rossi (Dean of the Eastman School of Music). For performance of many of the short examples in the text, we thank Richard Masters and Edward Rothmel, whose sight-reading abilities, flexibility, and good grace are all appreciated. For pedagogical discussions over the years, we are grateful to our colleagues at Florida State University, the Eastman School of Music, and Westminster Choir College, and to the College Board's AP Music Theory Test Development Committee members and AP readers. Thanks also to Peter Martens (Texas Tech University) for his work on the Instructor's Manual, to Sarah Sarver (Oklahoma City University) for writing InQuizitive questions, and to Michael McClimon (Furman University) for adapting the workbook activities for online use. Alissa Guntren (Indiana University) class tested the book and media in the summer of 2017.

We are indebted to the thorough and detailed work of our prepublication reviewers, whose careful reading of the manuscript inspired many improvements large and small. For the third edition, reviewers included P. Catherine Card (Glendale Community College), Edward J. Ercilla (Doral Academy), Matt Falker (MiraCosta College), Jeffrey Gillespie (Butler University), Richard Plotkin (University at Buffalo), Adam Ricci (University of North Carolina at Greensboro), Louie Silvestri (Fossil Ridge High School), and Lori Wacker (East Carolina University). Reviewers of the second edition included Joel Galand (Florida International University), Courtenay Harter (Rhodes College), Barbara Murphy (University of Tennessee), Mark Richardson (East Carolina University), and Amelia Triest (University of California at Davis). First edition reviewers were Lyn Ellen Burkett (University of North Carolina at Asheville), Robert Carl (Hartt School, University of Hartford), Don Fader (University of Alabama), Taylor Greer (Pennsylvania State University), Judy Cervetto Hedberg (Portland Community College), Rebecca Jemian (University of Louisville), Joan F. Jensen (Tulane University), Laura L. Kelly (The University of Texas at San Antonio), Laila R. Kteily-O'Sullivan (Indiana State University), Linda Apple Monson (George Mason University), Kathy Murray (Missouri State University), Shaugn O'Donnell (The City College of New York), Malia Roberson (California Lutheran University), Peter J. Schoenbach (Curtis Institute of Music), Paul Sheehan (Nassau Community College), Jason Roland Smith (Ohio University School of Music), Jennifer Snodgrass (Appalachian State University), and Stephen Zolper (Towson University). Feedback from Alyssa Barna (Eastman School of Music), Bryn Hughes (University of Lethbridge), Rebecca Jemian (University of Louisville), Cora Palfy (Elon University), Richard Plotkin (University at Buffalo), Keith Salley (Shennandoah Conservatory), Loretta Terringo (The Juilliard School), and Benjamin Wadsworth (Kennesaw State University) helped shape the media that accompanies this text. James Palmer (University of British Columbia) and Steven Reale (Youngstown State University) error checked the InQuizitive exercises and online workbook. We also acknowledge that the foundation of this book rests on writings of the great music theorists of the past and present, from the sixteenth to the twenty-first century, from whom we have learned the tools of the trade and whose pedagogical works have inspired ours.

For the production of the recordings, our thanks go to recording engineers Mike Farrington and John Ebert, who worked tirelessly with Elizabeth Marvin at Eastman on recording and editing sessions, as well as to Helen Smith, director of Eastman's Office of Technology and Media Production. We finally thank the faculty and students of the Eastman School who gave so generously of their time to make these recordings. The joy of their music making contributed mightily to this project.

We are indebted to the W. W. Norton staff for their commitment to *The Musician's Guide to Fundamentals* and their painstaking care in producing this volume. Our editor, Justin Hoffman, launched this new edition with the help of editorial assistants Grant Phelps and Julie Kocsis. Project editor Michael Fauver and production manager Andy Ensor worked with copy editor Jodi Beder and proofreader Debra Nichols to see the manuscript through production. Media editor Steve Hoge helped refine our ideas for the book's online components and made them a reality with the help of assistant editor Stephanie Eads. Myles Boothroyd handled the recordings with a great eye and ear for detail. Trevor Penland developed marketing strategies. Our gratitude to one and all.

Jane Piper Clendinning
Elizabeth West Marvin
Joel Phillips

Pitch Notation and the Grand Staff

1

KNOW IT? **Take the quiz to focus your studies.**

TOPICS

- Musical contour
- Introduction to pitch notation: letter names
- The piano keyboard: naming white keys
- Staff notation
- Treble and bass clefs
- Naming pitches with octave numbers
- Ledger lines
- The grand staff
- Writing music in a score
- Explore further: C-clefs

MUSIC

- Johann Sebastian Bach, Prelude, from Cello Suite No. 2 in D Minor
- Elton John and Tim Rice, "Circle of Life," from *The Lion King*
- Scott Joplin, "Solace"
- John Lennon, "Imagine"
- John Newton, "Amazing Grace"
- Joel Phillips, "Blues for Norton"
- Lalo Schifrin, Theme from *Mission: Impossible*

Musical Contour

Listen to the hymn "Amazing Grace," shown in musical notation in Example 1.1. Follow the shape of the musical line or **melody** as you listen.

EXAMPLE 1.1   Newton, "Amazing Grace," mm. 1–8

The musical notation—or **score**—shows various symbols that represent musical sounds. The most basic symbol is the **note**. Each note, written as a small oval (either black or hollow) attached to a **stem** going either up or down, represents a single musical sound, or **pitch**. Notes are written higher or lower on the five horizontal lines of a musical **staff**; this shows graphically the "shape," or **contour**, of a melody. Notes 5 to 9 of "Amazing Grace" represent a **descending contour** and the notation on the staff

1

likewise moves downward from left to right, each note lower than the previous one. The next three pitches move upward in an **ascending contour**. Most music—like this melody—moves both up and down, with melodic contours forming arches and waves, often with a single high point, as marked at the end of this example. The vertical lines on the staff, called **bar lines**, mark off equal amounts of time, called **measures**.

Introduction to Pitch Notation: Letter Names

Drawing a melody's contour may give a general idea of its shape, but you need more-precise information to play the tune correctly.

> **KEY CONCEPT** In a musical score, each note has a **letter name**—A, B, C, D, E, F, or G—which is determined by its position on the staff. These letters are known as the **musical alphabet**.

To count up beyond G, start over with A; to count down below A, start over again with G, as shown in Example 1.2. You can also think of the seven letter names around a circle, like a clock. Think of the movement as upward when you count forward or clockwise, and downward when you count backward or counterclockwise. For example, five notes above E is B: E–F–G–A–B. Six notes below E is G: E–D–C–B–A–G. When counting, be sure to include the first and last letter names of the series: three above F is A (count F–G–A, not G–A–B). These distances between pitches, counted in letter names, are called **intervals** (Chapter 8).

EXAMPLE 1.2   Letter names

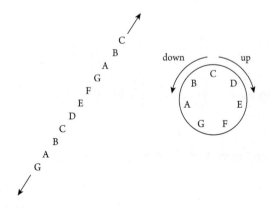

In this seven-name system, each letter name reappears every eighth position (eight above or below D is another D).

> **KEY CONCEPT** Pitches separated by eight letter names are an **octave** apart. The repetition of letter names reflects the way we hear: pitches an octave apart sound similar. This principle is called **octave equivalence**.

TRY IT #1

Find the letter name requested.

(a) 7 above D: __C__   (b) 5 above A: _____   (c) 3 below B: _____

(d) 6 below C: _____   (e) 2 below E: _____   (f) 5 above F: _____

(g) 3 above C: _____   (h) 8 below D: _____   (i) 4 below E: _____

(j) 6 above G: _____   (k) 2 above G: _____   (l) 4 above B: _____

(m) 6 below D: _____   (n) 5 below F: _____   (o) 7 above E: _____

The Piano Keyboard: Naming White Keys

Look at the diagram in Example 1.3 to identify pitch locations on the keyboard. The white key immediately to the left of any group of two black keys is a C, and the white key immediately to the left of any three black keys is an F; each is indicated by an arrow. Write in the remaining letter names for the white keys in the example, using the black-key groupings to find your place.

KEY CONCEPT **Middle C** is the C closest to the middle of the keyboard. No black key appears between E and F or between B and C.

EXAMPLE 1.3   Piano keyboard

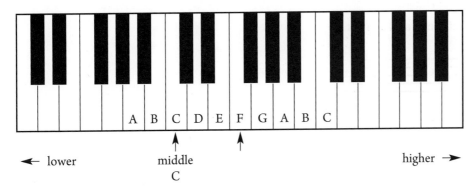

Staff Notation

As shown in Example 1.4, the staff (plural is staves) consists of five lines and four spaces, which are generally read from bottom to top, with the bottom line called the first and the top line the fifth. As a first step in writing pitches, ovals called notes or **note heads** are drawn on the lines or in the spaces of the staff (most notes will also require stems, as we'll see later). Filled note heads are played for a shorter duration than hollow ones. Higher pitches are notated toward the top of the staff, lower pitches toward the bottom.

EXAMPLE 1.4   Note heads on a staff

Treble and Bass Clefs

The letter names of the notes in Example 1.4 can't be identified without a **clef**, the symbol that appears on the far left of every staff. The clef shows which line or space represents which pitch (and in which octave). In Example 1.5, notes are written on the staff with a **treble clef**, sometimes called the G-clef. Its shape somewhat resembles a cursive capital G, and the end of its curving line (in the center) rests on the staff line for G. All the other pitches can be read from G by counting up or down in the musical alphabet. The note above the highest staff line (F) is G. The note below the lowest staff line (E) is D, and the note below that, with the short line through it, is middle C. The treble clef represents the higher notes.

As soon as possible, memorize the note names for each line and space. Learn the "line notes" together and the "space notes" together, as in Example 1.6.

EXAMPLE 1.5   Treble clef (G-clef)

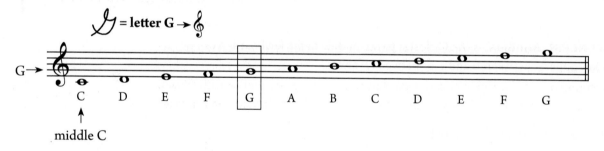

EXAMPLE 1.6   Treble-clef lines and spaces

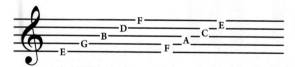

> **ANOTHER WAY** To remember note names of the lines (E–G–B–D–F), you might make up a sentence whose words begin with these letters, like "Every Good Bird Does Fly." The spaces simply spell the word F–A–C–E.

TRY IT #2

(a) Write the letter name of each pitch in the blanks provided.

(1) **B** (2)___ (3)___ (4)___ (5)___ (6)___ (7)___ (8)___ (9)___ (10)___ (11)___ (12)___

(b) Write the letter names in the blanks provided, then circle the highest and lowest pitches.

Lennon, "Imagine," mm. 28–30

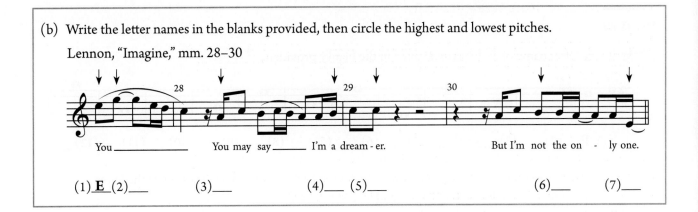

(1) __E__ (2)___ (3)___ (4)___ (5)___ (6)___ (7)___

Now listen to Example 1.7, the beginning of Bach's Cello Suite No. 2, while looking at the musical notation shown in the example. This lower-sounding melody is written in the **bass clef**.

EXAMPLE 1.7   Bach, Prelude, from Cello Suite No. 2 in D Minor, mm. 1–4

The bass clef, used for lower notes, is also known as the F-clef: it somewhat resembles a cursive capital F, and its two dots surround the line that represents F. Other pitches may be counted from F, or memorized according to their positions on the staff, shown in Example 1.8. Example 1.9 shows the lines and spaces labeled with their letter names; memorize these.

EXAMPLE 1.8   Bass clef (F-clef)

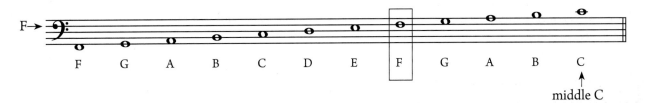

EXAMPLE 1.9   Bass-clef lines and spaces

ANOTHER WAY Two ways to remember the bass-clef spaces (A–C–E–G) are "All Cows Eat Grass" and "All Cars Eat Gas." The bass-clef lines (G–B–D–F–A) might be "Great Big Doves Fly Away."

(a) Write the letter name of each bass-clef pitch in the blanks provided.

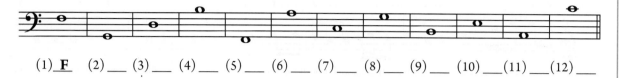

(1) __F__ (2) ___ (3) ___ (4) ___ (5) ___ (6) ___ (7) ___ (8) ___ (9) ___ (10) ___ (11) ___ (12) ___

(b) Listen to the beginning of "Blues for Norton." The lowest part is shown here. Then write the letter names for each pitch in the blanks. Circle the highest and lowest pitches.

Phillips, "Blues for Norton" (bass line), mm. 2–3

(1) __F__ (2) ___ (3) ___ (4) ___   (5) ___ (6) ___ (7) ___ (8) ___

SHOW IT! Assignment 1.1

Naming Pitches with Octave Numbers

As seen in the previous examples, letter names reappear in different octaves in the bass and treble clefs. To specify exactly in which octave a pitch appears, use **octave numbers**.

> **KEY CONCEPT** As Example 1.10 shows, the lowest C on a standard piano keyboard is designated C1, and the highest is C8; middle C is C4. The number for a particular octave includes all the pitches from C up to the following B.

The B above C4, for example, is B4; the B below C4 is B3. The white keys below C1 on the piano are A0 and B0.

EXAMPLE 1.10   Piano keyboard with octave numbers

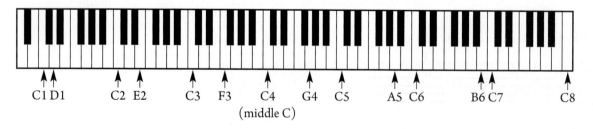

Ledger Lines

Some of the pitches on the piano keyboard, including middle C, cannot be notated on the five lines and four spaces of the treble or bass staff.

> **KEY CONCEPT** When music extends above or below the staff, extra lines—called **ledger lines**—are drawn to accommodate these notes (Example 1.11). Read ledger lines (and the spaces between them) just like other staff lines and spaces: by counting forward or backward in the musical alphabet.

The Grand Staff

Pitches for keyboards, and other instruments that play very high and low notes, are written on a grand staff like the one in Example 1.11.

> **KEY CONCEPT** A treble staff and a bass staff connected by a curly brace and a line make a **grand staff**.

Ledger lines may extend above and below the grand staff. Notes that fill in the middle, between the two staves, may be written in either clef, as shown in Example 1.11a. Memorize landmark pitches above and below the staves to help you read ledger lines quickly—as in Example 1.11b, which gives the first three lines above and below each staff.

EXAMPLE 1.11   Pitches on a keyboard and grand staff

(a) Ledger lines above and below the grand staff

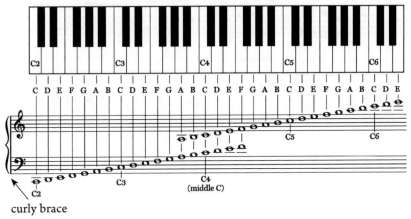

(b) Landmark ledger-line pitches

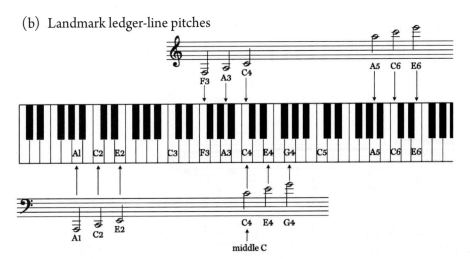

> **KEY CONCEPT** The ledger-line notes below the treble staff are F–A–C; those above the staff are A–C–E. The ledger-line notes below the bass staff are A–C–E; those above the staff are C–E–G.

Listen to the opening of Joplin's "Solace" while following the score in Example 1.12. This passage shows ledger lines between the staves. In measure 5, the bass-clef F written with ledger lines is F4. This note could also have been written in the treble clef on the bottom space. In piano music with ledger lines written between the staves, the ranges of the two hands overlap; the clef shows which hand is supposed to play a particular note. Treble clef generally indicates the right hand, bass clef the left hand.

EXAMPLE 1.12   Joplin, "Solace," mm. 5–12

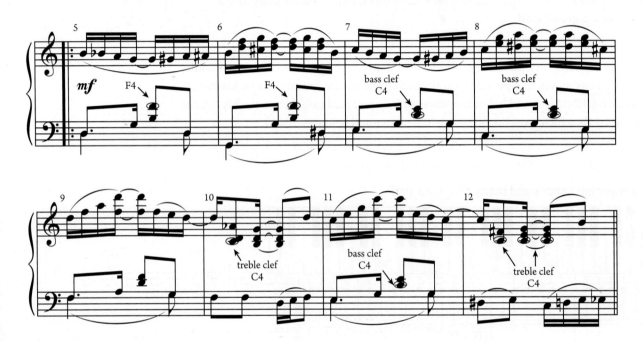

> **TRY IT #4**
>
> The example on the following grand staff includes many notes written with ledger lines. For each note with a blank beneath it, write the letter name and octave number. Then locate these pitches on a keyboard.
>
> Schifrin, Theme from *Mission: Impossible*, mm. 1–2
>
>

KEY CONCEPT The highness or lowness of a pitch (in other words, the octave in which it lies) is called its **register**.

Instruments and singing voices sound in different registers, which can be used to create certain moods and effects. In Example 1.13, from "Circle of Life," the low register of the melody is important in setting the mood. Some pitches are marked with their octave numbers; try identifying others.

EXAMPLE 1.13   John and Rice, "Circle of Life," from *The Lion King*, mm. 1–8

TRY IT #5

Write the letter name and octave number for each pitch shown.

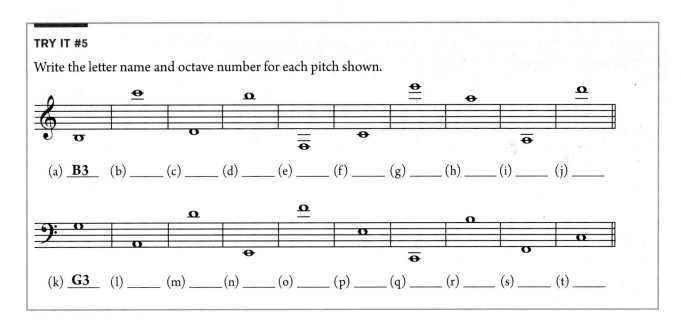

(a) __B3__ (b) _____ (c) _____ (d) _____ (e) _____ (f) _____ (g) _____ (h) _____ (i) _____ (j) _____

(k) __G3__ (l) _____ (m) _____ (n) _____ (o) _____ (p) _____ (q) _____ (r) _____ (s) _____ (t) _____

SHOW IT! Assignment 1.2

Writing Music in a Score

Writing music correctly (and neatly) helps those performing it to read fluently and without errors. You can draw a treble clef in a single continuous curved line, or in two strokes as shown in Example 1.14: (1) first draw a wavy line from top to bottom, like an elongated S, then (2) draw a second line that starts at the top and curves around it (ending on the G line). The bass clef is drawn in two steps as well: (1) draw an arc that looks a bit like a backward C, then (2) add two dots that surround the F line.

EXAMPLE 1.14   Drawing clefs

When you draw note heads on the staff, make them oval-shaped rather than round; they should not be so large that it's hard to tell whether they sit on a line or in a space (Example 1.15a).

> **KEY CONCEPT** Most notes have thin vertical lines, called stems, that extend above or below the note head. If a note lies below the middle line of the staff, its stem usually goes up, on the right side of the note head (♩); if a note lies on or above the middle line, its stem goes down, on the left side (♩).

The stem of a note on the middle line can, however, go up if the notes around it have stems up (both stem directions are shown in Example 1.15b). The length of the stem from bottom to top spans about an octave.

EXAMPLE 1.15   Notation guidelines

(a)

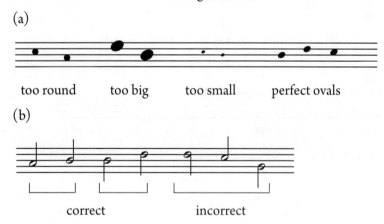

(b)

Example 1.16 shows ledger lines drawn correctly and incorrectly. When you write notes above the staff, draw ledger lines through the note heads or beneath them, but never above them. Note heads below the staff have ledger lines through them or above them, but never beneath. Draw ledger lines the same distance apart as staff lines.

EXAMPLE 1.16   Ledger-line pitches

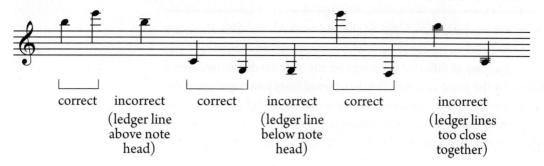

correct   incorrect   correct   incorrect   correct   incorrect
           (ledger line   (ledger line   (ledger lines
           above note   below note   too close
           head)   head)   together)

TRY IT #6

Write each of the specified notes in the correct octave, using hollow note heads and correctly notated stems and ledger lines.

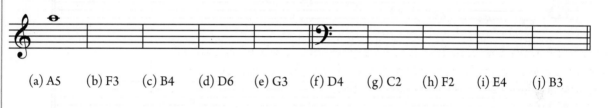

(a) A5   (b) F3   (c) B4   (d) D6   (e) G3   (f) D4   (g) C2   (h) F2   (i) E4   (j) B3

SUMMARY

When notating music, write neatly so that others can read your score easily and accurately.

- Draw a clef at the beginning of each staff.
- To indicate a grand staff, draw a long line and curly brace to connect the treble and bass staves on the left side.
- Draw both black and hollow note heads as neat ovals on or between staff lines.
- For ledger-line notes, draw ledger lines parallel to staff lines, the same distance apart, and between the note head and the top or bottom staff line.
- Draw straight, thin stems that span about an octave and follow the guidelines for stem direction.

You will learn more notational guidelines for rhythm and other topics in later chapters.

SHOW IT! Assignment 1.3

Although music reading starts with knowledge of the treble and bass clefs, there are other clefs as well that are standard for some band and orchestra instruments. A C-clef is a "movable" clef: it can appear at different positions on the staff. Its distinctive shape (𝄡) identifies middle C by the point at which the two curved lines join together in the middle. The most common C-clefs in modern practice are the alto clef and tenor clef (Example 1.17), but you may come across other clefs in older scores. To read these clefs, practice counting the lines and spaces from C (as in the example), then memorize them.

EXAMPLE 1.17   C-clefs

(a) Alto clef

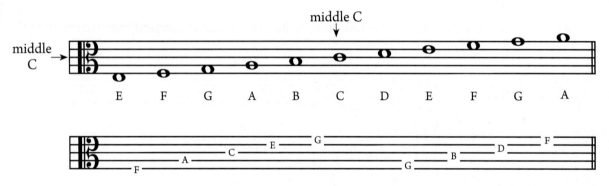

(b) Tenor clef

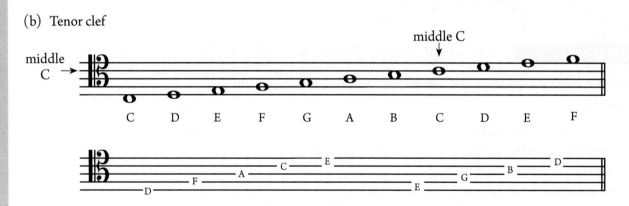

Musicians read different clefs because each one corresponds to the range of pitches needed for a particular instrument or voice type. The higher instruments, like flute and violin, read treble clef. Lower instruments, like cello and bass, generally read bass clef, while violas use the alto clef. Music for higher voices is notated in treble clef, while lower voices are notated in bass clef. Piano music is notated in both bass and treble clefs, while trombone, bassoon, and cello parts are written in both bass and tenor clefs. You will encounter all of these clefs in an orchestral score.

Write the letter name of each pitch in the blanks provided.

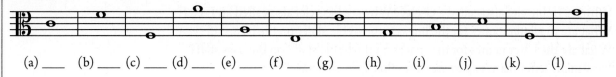

(a) ___ (b) ___ (c) ___ (d) ___ (e) ___ (f) ___ (g) ___ (h) ___ (i) ___ (j) ___ (k) ___ (l) ___

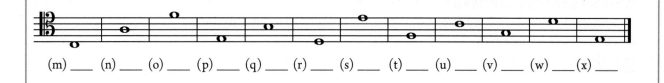

(m) ___ (n) ___ (o) ___ (p) ___ (q) ___ (r) ___ (s) ___ (t) ___ (u) ___ (v) ___ (w) ___ (x) ___

Did You Know?

Sir Elton John was born Reginald Kenneth Dwight in 1947. The child of a musician, he began studying piano at age four and won a scholarship to the Royal Academy of Music at age eleven. By the 1970s, John had become a pop superstar, and he had a Top 40 single every year from 1970 to 1996. Among his most famous songs are "Your Song," "Goodbye Yellow Brick Road," songs from *The Lion King* (including "Circle of Life," Example 1.13), and "Candle in the Wind." This last song, originally a tribute to Marilyn Monroe, John rerecorded as a tribute to Princess Diana after her untimely death in 1997. "Candle in the Wind" became his biggest hit ever, selling over three million copies in the United States in its first week. John contributed royalties from this recording to Princess Diana's favorite charities.

Terms You Should Know

bar line	ledger line	octave
clef	letter name	octave equivalence
bass	measure	octave numbers
treble	melody	pitch
contour	middle C	register
ascending	musical alphabet	score
descending	note	staff
grand staff	note head	stem
interval		

Questions for Review

1. Which letters represent pitches?
2. Why are clefs necessary?
3. Why is a treble clef also called a G-clef? Why is a bass clef also called an F-clef?
4. What are the letter names for the lines on the treble staff? on the bass staff?
5. What are the letter names for the spaces on the treble staff? on the bass staff?
6. How many letter names apart are notes that span an octave?
7. What is the purpose of ledger lines?
8. When is a grand staff used? What does it consist of?
9. To which side of the note head do ascending stems connect? To which side do descending stems connect?
10. How do you decide whether stems should go up or down?

Reading Review

Match the term on the left with the best answer on the right.

_____ (1) E–G–B–D–F	(a) 𝄞
_____ (2) score	(b) five lines and four spaces on which music is notated
_____ (3) ledger lines	(c) notation of a piece of music
_____ (4) octave equivalence	(d) letter names for treble-clef spaces
_____ (5) clef	(e) attached to note heads above the middle line
_____ (6) contour	(f) similarity in sound of notes with the same letter name
_____ (7) F–A–C–E	(g) the shape of a musical line
_____ (8) treble-clef symbol	(h) letter names for treble-clef lines
_____ (9) G–B–D–F–A	(i) used to notate pitches above or below the staff lines
_____ (10) A–C–E–G	(j) ovals written on a staff to represent pitches
_____ (11) bass-clef symbol	(k) attached to note heads below the middle line
_____ (12) notes	(l) specifies the octave register of a pitch
_____ (13) octave number	(m) middle C
_____ (14) grand staff	(n) treble- and bass-clef staves joined with a curly brace
_____ (15) stems down	(o) letter names for bass-clef lines
_____ (16) C4	(p) letter names for bass-clef spaces
_____ (17) stems up	(q) symbol that gives notes on a staff their letter names
_____ (18) staff	(r) 𝄢

Apply It

Because singing and playing piano can help you understand and remember musical concepts, these performing activities will make up a significant part of your study.

When singing:
- Don't be shy; sing out with enthusiasm!
- Don't worry about the quality of your voice. Sing every chance you get. Everything improves with practice.
- Sing a warm-up pattern first (like the ones given on p. 16) to orient your voice and ear.

When playing on a keyboard:
- Keep your fingers curved.
- Don't depress any pedals for now.
- Typically, play different notes with different fingers.

If you don't have access to a piano:
- Practice on any keyboard app.
- Practice on the foldout keyboard in the front of the book.

A. Sing at Sight

1. Point and sing

When your teacher or a partner points to a note, sing the pitch with any of the "lyrics" shown beneath the staff. If you have a keyboard, sing and play using the left-hand (L.H.) and right-hand (R.H.) finger numbers.

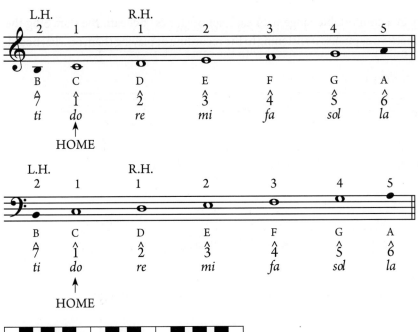

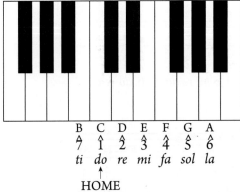

2. Warm-ups

For each warm-up, sing in a comfortable range on the "lyrics" beneath the staff. Try to achieve an open, free sound. If you have a keyboard, sing and play using the finger numbers.

Warm-up 1

Warm-up 2

3. Melodies

Play the first pitch, then sing each melody in a comfortable range with each set of "lyrics" beneath the staff. Sing the hollow notes longer than the filled notes. Check your pitches by listening to the recording or playing them on a keyboard.

Melody 1

Melody 2

Melody 3

Melody 4

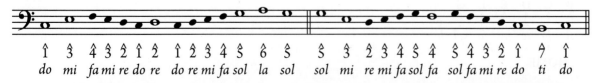

Listen and Write 1.1

A. Hearing and writing melodies

Listen to each example. Then write letter names and/or "lyrics" in the blanks beneath the staff, as directed. Finally, notate the pitches with open note heads.

1.

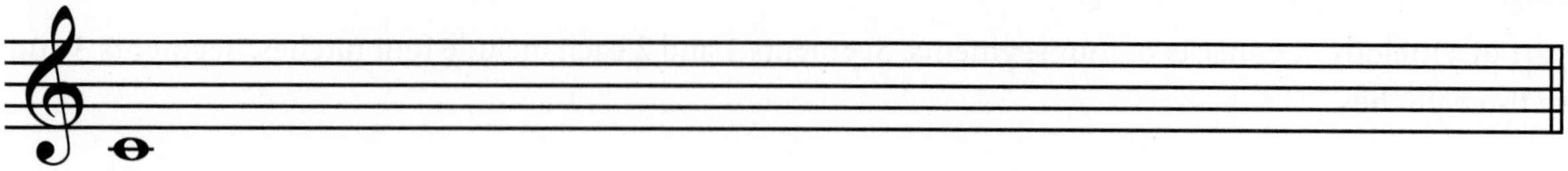

C
1̂
do

2.

C
1̂
do

3.

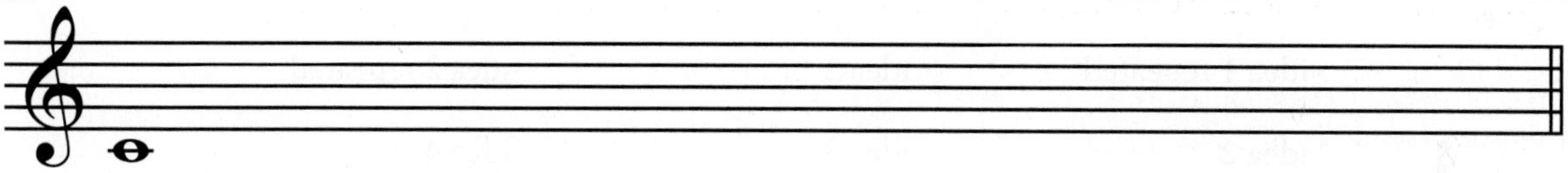

C
1̂
do

4.

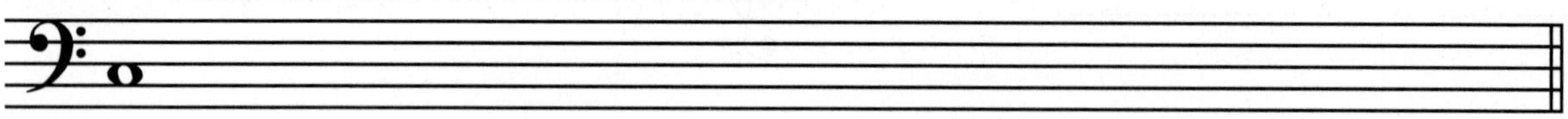

C
1̂
do

5.

C
1̂
do

B. Hearing and writing a folk song

Listen to part of a melody. It consists of four segments. Segments 1 and 2 each include four pitches. Segments 3 and 4 each have three pitches.

1. Focus on segment 1, the first four pitches. Which of the following best diagrams the contour of the segment?

(a) /   (b) \   (c) /\   (d) \/

2. Focus on the ending. Which of the following best diagrams the contour of segment 4?

(a) /   (b) \   (c) /\   (d) \/

3. Which of the following best describes how the segments are organized?

Segment 1	Segment 2	Segment 3	Segment 4
(a) idea 1	idea 1 repeated	idea 2	idea 1 returns
(b) idea 1	idea 1 repeated	idea 2	idea 2 repeated
(c) idea 1	idea 2	idea 3	idea 4

4. On the staff to the left, notate segment 1 (four notes) with the pitches C, D, and E. On the staff to the right, notate segment 4 (the final segment of three notes) with the pitches E, F, and G.

5. On the following staff, notate the pitches of the *entire* melody.

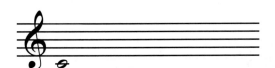 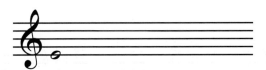

Workbook ASSIGNMENT 1.1

A. Letter names

Fill in the letter name requested. Remember to count the letter you begin with.

(1) 6 above C: **A**

(2) 3 above G: ____

(3) 2 below F: ____

(4) 7 below A: ____

(5) 4 above D: ____

(6) 2 above E: ____

(7) 4 below D: ____

(8) 5 below E: ____

(9) 7 above C: ____

(10) 5 below B: ____

(11) 7 above G: ____

(12) 3 below A: ____

B. Identifying notes on the keyboard

On the following keyboards, write each letter name on its corresponding key.

(1) C, D, G, B

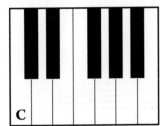

(2) E, F, A, B

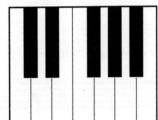

On the following keyboards, write each letter name on *every* key with that name (in three octaves).

(3) C, E, A

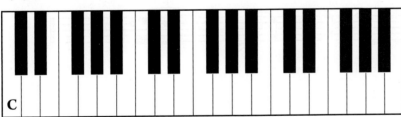

(4) G, B, D

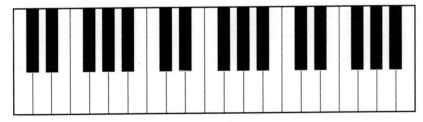

C. Drawing clefs

(1) Trace the treble clefs given as dotted lines, then draw additional clefs.

(2) Trace the bass clefs given in dotted lines, then draw additional clefs.

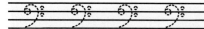

D. Reading notes in treble and bass clefs

Write the letter name of each pitch in the blank provided.

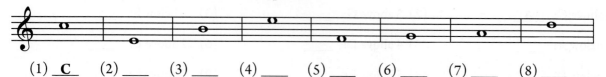

(1) __C__   (2) ___   (3) ___   (4) ___   (5) ___   (6) ___   (7) ___   (8) ___

(9) __B__   (10) ___   (11) ___   (12) ___   (13) ___   (14) ___   (15) ___   (16) ___

E. Reading notes in music

In each blank, write the letter name of the note above.

(1) Stevie Wonder, "You Are the Sunshine of My Life," mm. 5–11

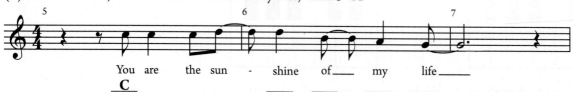

(2) Lennon and McCartney, "Hello, Goodbye," mm. 17–21

Workbook ASSIGNMENT 1.2

A. Identifying pitches with ledger lines

For each pitch notated on the staff, write its number on the correct key of the keyboard in the correct octave. Write the letter name on the blank beneath the staff.

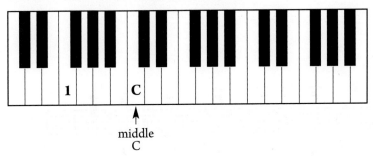

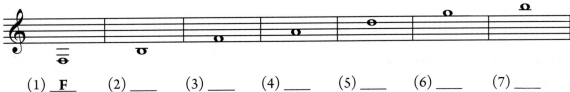

(1) **F**   (2) ___   (3) ___   (4) ___   (5) ___   (6) ___   (7) ___

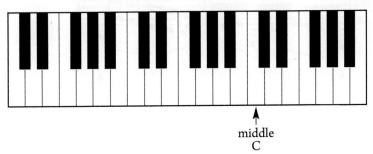

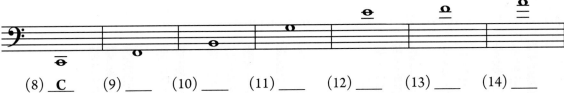

(8) **C**   (9) ___   (10) ___   (11) ___   (12) ___   (13) ___   (14) ___

Beneath each pitch, write its letter name and octave number.

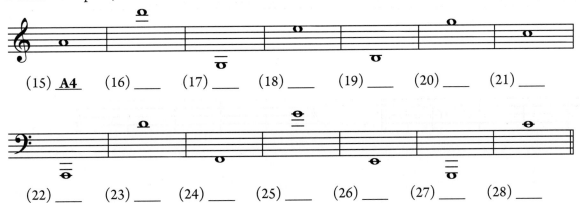

(15) **A4**   (16) ___   (17) ___   (18) ___   (19) ___   (20) ___   (21) ___

(22) ___   (23) ___   (24) ___   (25) ___   (26) ___   (27) ___   (28) ___

B. Identifying pitches with ledger lines and octave numbers in music

In the following passages, write the letter name and octave number for any ledger-line note marked by an arrow.

(1) Mozart, *Variations on "Ah, vous dirai-je Maman,"* mm. 1–8

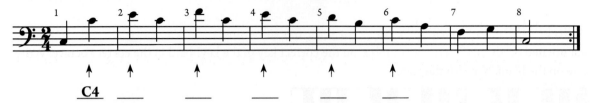

C4 ___   ___   ___   ___   ___

(2) Mozart, *Variations,* Var. VII, mm. 187–192

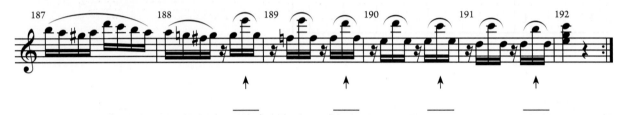

(3) Mozart, *Variations,* Var. XII, mm. 293–296

C. Writing pitches with ledger lines and octave numbers

For each number on the keyboard, write the corresponding note on the staff below it in the correct octave.

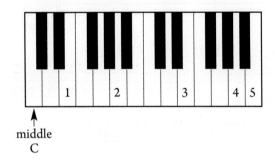

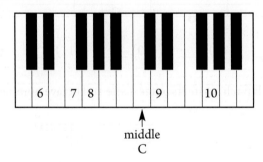

Workbook ASSIGNMENT 1.3

A. Writing pitches with ledger lines, stems, and octave numbers

For each note requested, neatly write a hollow note head on the correct line or space of the staff, then add a stem that extends in the correct direction.

(1)

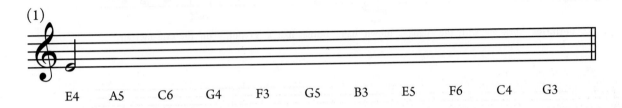

E4   A5   C6   G4   F3   G5   B3   E5   F6   C4   G3

(2)

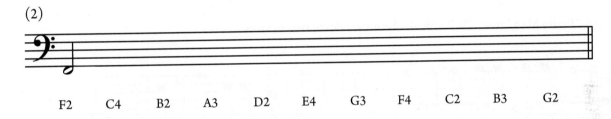

F2   C4   B2   A3   D2   E4   G3   F4   C2   B3   G2

For each pitch given, rewrite in the octave specified.

(3) Rewrite exactly two octaves lower.

(4) Rewrite exactly two octaves higher.

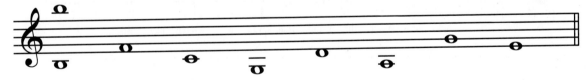

B. Arranging: Changing clef and octave

Rewrite the pitches of each melody down one or two octaves as specified, on the staff provided. Copy the original notation (even the symbols that are unfamiliar to you) but change stem direction as needed. You do not need to copy the lyrics.

(1) Stephen Foster, "Jeanie with the Light Brown Hair," mm. 5–8. Write the music down one octave.

(2) Billy Joel, "Piano Man," mm. 72–78. Write the music down two octaves.

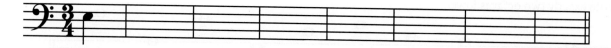

(3) Rewrite the beginning of "Amazing Grace" up one octave, as though scored for violin or flute. You'll need to use ledger lines.

Accidentals and Half and Whole Steps

2

TOPICS

- Sharps, flats, and naturals
- Writing pitches with accidentals
- Half steps and whole steps
- Hearing half and whole steps
- Double sharps and flats
- Explore further: more on enharmonic spellings

MUSIC

- John Barry and Tim Rice, "All Time High"
- Scott Joplin, "Solace"
- Mel Leven, "Cruella de Vil," from *101 Dalmatians*
- Willie Nelson, "On the Road Again"
- Ed Sheeran and John McDaid, "Photograph"

Sharps, Flats, and Naturals

Listen to the melody from Joplin's "Solace" while looking at Example 2.1. The first four notes in each line are labeled on the keyboard that follows.

EXAMPLE 2.1   Joplin, "Solace," mm. 1–8 (right hand only)

(a) Mm. 1–4

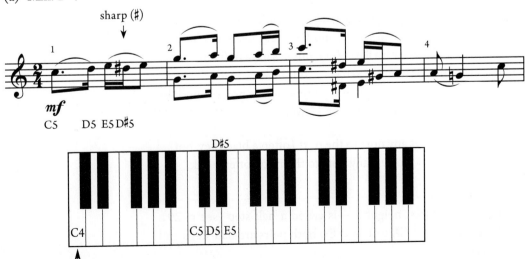

25

(b) Mm. 5–8

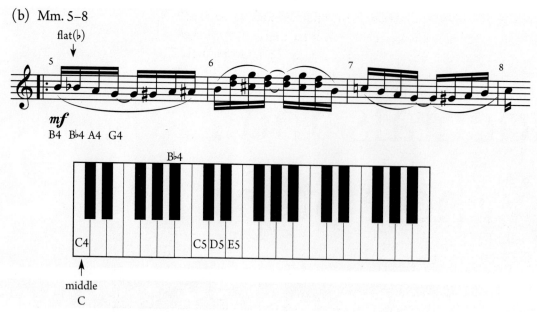

The fourth note of Example 2.1a is D♯5 (D-sharp 5), which is played on the black key between D5 and E5. In Example 2.1b, the second note is B♭4 (B-flat 4), played on the black key between B4 and A4.

The black keys are named in relation to the white keys next to them, as shown in Example 2.2. The black key immediately *above* (to the right of) any white key takes the white key's name plus a **sharp** (♯). The two black keys grouped together are C♯ (C-sharp) and D♯, and the three black keys grouped together are F♯, G♯, and A♯.

EXAMPLE 2.2   Names for white and black keys

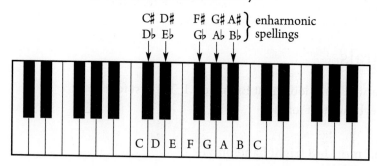

The black key immediately *below* (to the left of) any white key takes the white key's name plus a **flat** (♭). The group of two black keys may also be called D♭ (D-flat) and E♭, and the three black keys may also be called G♭, A♭, and B♭. Every black key has two possible names: one with a sharp and one with a flat. When pitches have different names but make the same sound and are played with the same key on the keyboard (D♭ = C♯), their spellings are called **enharmonic** (see Example 2.2). Enharmonic notes sound the same but are spelled differently—like the words "too" and "two."

> **KEY CONCEPT** A sharp sign (♯) raises any note to the next (often a black key, but sometimes a white key). A flat sign (♭) lowers any note to the next (often black, but sometimes white).

This span—from a note to its closest neighbor—is called a half step (see p. 29). Look again at Example 2.2 to see C and C♯, or E and E♭: both pairs are half steps and include a white then a black key.

Sharp and flat symbols are called **accidentals**, though there is nothing "accidental" about their use or placement. A third common accidental, called a **natural** (♮), is shown in Example 2.3, from later in Joplin's piano rag. A natural returns a pitch to its "natural" state. In the left hand (bass clef) of Example 2.3, you would first play F♯ followed by F♮, and in the right hand (treble clef) D♯ followed by D♮—in both cases, a black key followed by a white one.

EXAMPLE 2.3   Joplin, "Solace," mm. 17–20

"Solace" has many accidentals. If a note with an accidental is repeated before the bar line, the accidental still applies. The bar line cancels an accidental.

As Example 2.4 shows, there is no black key immediately to the right of E; the next note up is F. E♯ is therefore played on a white key and is enharmonic with F. B♯ is also a white key, and is enharmonic with C. On the flat side, C♭ is enharmonic with B, and F♭ is enharmonic with E. These enharmonic spellings for white keys are summarized in the example.

EXAMPLE 2.4   Enharmonic spellings for white keys

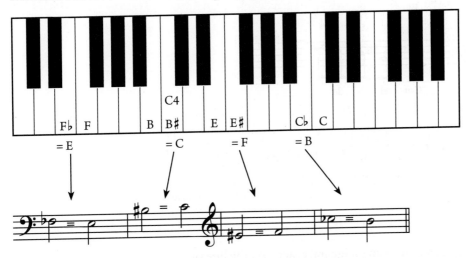

To see how composers use enharmonic notes in pieces of music, look back at the beginning of Example 2.1b. Joplin has considered the musical context in which pitches appear, and written a B♭ as the musical line travels down, but an A♯ as the line moves up (see measure 5). These pitches (B♭ and A♯) sound the same, but their spelling denotes their function.

TRY IT #1

Name the enharmonic equivalent.

(a) G♭ is enharmonic with **F♯**

(b) B♯ is enharmonic with ____

(c) A♯ is enharmonic with ____

(d) E♯ is enharmonic with ____

(e) D♭ is enharmonic with ____

(f) B is enharmonic with ____

(g) A♭ is enharmonic with ____

(h) E♭ is enharmonic with ____

KEY CONCEPT

Accidentals:

♯ (sharp)	raises the pitch a half step
♭ (flat)	lowers the pitch a half step
♮ (natural)	cancels a sharp or flat

Enharmonic notes: sound the same but are spelled differently

Writing Pitches with Accidentals

As you can see in Example 2.5, the beginning of "Cruella de Vil," an accidental is positioned before (to the left of) the note head in a musical score.

EXAMPLE 2.5   Leven, "Cruella de Vil," mm. 1–2

When you write or say note names, however, the accidental goes after (to the right of) the note name; for example, C♯ (C-sharp). For an accidental on a space (see the A♭ and F♯ in Example 2.5), the middle of the accidental is centered within the space, not on the line above or below. For an accidental on a line (see the B♭ and D♭), the line passes through its middle.

KEY CONCEPT   Always be careful to notate an accidental exactly on the line or space you intend, not floating above or below the note, and to place the accidental before the note.

Write the letter name in the space beneath each note given. Then write the enharmonically equivalent note in the blank measure to the right, and that note's name beneath.

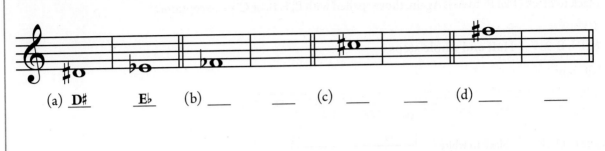

(a) **D♯**   **E♭**   (b) ___   ___   (c) ___   ___   (d) ___   ___

(e) ___   ___   (f) ___   ___   (g) ___   ___   (h) ___   ___

Half Steps and Whole Steps

The distance between any two notes is called an **interval**. Look at the melody of Ed Sheeran's "Photograph" (Example 2.6). Most of the intervals between its pitches are related by **steps**. Steps span any two adjacent keys on a keyboard, which may be white-to-black keys (A to B♭ on the word "closer") or white-to-white (A to G on "eyes meet"). Steps are spelled with two adjacent letter names (A–B♭ or A–G) or with a letter name that is repeated with an accidental (B–B♭). This type of motion between pitches—called **stepwise motion**—is easy to sing and play. There are two types of steps: whole steps and half steps.

EXAMPLE 2.6   Sheeran and McDaid, "Photograph," mm. 36–39

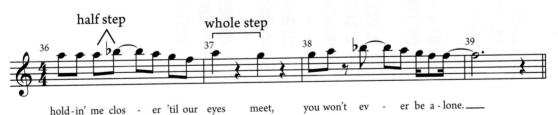

hold-in' me clos - er 'til our eyes   meet,   you won't ev - er be a - lone.____

> **KEY CONCEPT** A **half step** (or **semitone**) is the interval between any pitch and the next closest pitch on the keyboard in either direction. The combination of two half steps forms a **whole step** (or **whole tone**). A whole step always has a note that could be inserted in the middle.

Example 2.7 shows half and whole steps on the keyboard. Usually a half step (Example 2.7a) spans a white key to a black key (like B to A♯) or black to white (like G♭ to G). The only exceptions are B to C and E to F, which naturally span a half step. Whole steps (Example 2.7b) usually span two keys of the same color: white to white (like C to D) or black to black (like B♭ to A♭). Again, those spelled with E, F, B, or C are exceptions.

EXAMPLE 2.7   Half and whole steps

(a) Half steps

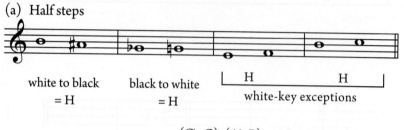

white to black   black to white
    = H   = H
                    white-key exceptions

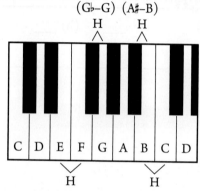

(b) Whole steps

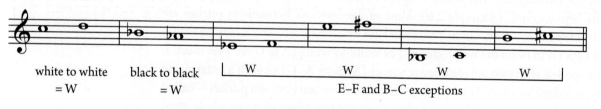

white to white   black to black
    = W   = W
                    E–F and B–C exceptions

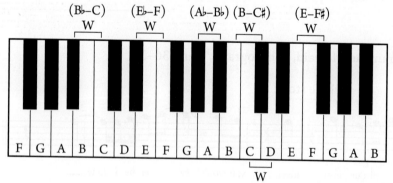

Half steps that are spelled with two adjacent letter names (G–A♭) are called **diatonic half steps**. Half steps that are spelled with the same letter name (G–G♯) are called **chromatic half steps**. Both spellings are correct—they are enharmonic equivalents—but are used in different contexts, as we will see. Both types of half steps are found in Example 2.7: B–A♯, E–F, and B–C are diatonic half steps; G♭–G♯ is a chromatic half step.

- Half steps usually span keys of different colors: white to black or black to white. The exceptions are E–F and B–C, the white-key half steps (Example 2.7a).
- Whole steps usually span keys the same color: white to white or black to black. The exceptions are E♭–F, E–F♯, B♭–C, and B–C♯ (Example 2.7b).
- Double-check the spelling of any half or whole step that includes E, F, B, or C.

TRY IT #3

(a) Name the pitch requested, then for the half steps, identify an enharmonically equivalent pitch.

A half step:

(1) above G: **G♯** or **A♭**

(2) below C♯: ___ or ___

(3) below B: ___ or ___

(4) above E: ___ or ___

(5) above D: ___ or ___

A whole step:

(6) above F♯: ___

(7) below C: ___

(8) above D: ___

(9) above C♯: ___

(10) below B♭: ___

(b) Identify whether each pair of pitches spans a whole step (W), half step (H), or neither (N).

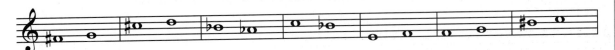

(1) **H** (2) ___ (3) ___ (4) ___ (5) ___ (6) ___ (7) ___

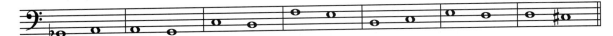

(8) ___ (9) ___ (10) ___ (11) ___ (12) ___ (13) ___ (14) ___

(c) Identify each pair of bracketed pitches as a whole step (W), half step (H), or neither (N).

Leven, "Cruella de Vil," mm. 1–2

Cru - el - la de Vil,___   Cru - el - la de Vil,___

H ___   ___ ___

Hearing Half and Whole Steps

Listen to Example 2.8 to hear the difference in sound between half and whole steps. When you hear a whole step (C–D), you can imagine a note in the middle on the keyboard (C♯). When you hear a half step, you can't. Practice playing whole and half steps at the keyboard. For each whole step, insert the note between to hear how it divides the whole step in half.

EXAMPLE 2.8   Whole steps divided in half

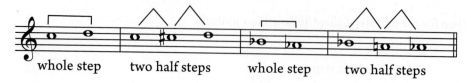

whole step   two half steps   whole step   two half steps

SHOW IT! Assignment 2.2, 2.3

Double Sharps and Flats

Examples 2.9 and 2.10 show two other accidentals: the **double sharp** (×) and **double flat** (♭♭). A double sharp (×) raises a pitch two half steps (a whole step; see p. 29) above its letter name. A double flat (♭♭) lowers a pitch two half steps below its letter name. A double sharp (F×4) appears on the first note of Willie Nelson's melody and in the second line. A double flat (B♭♭3) appears as marked in the bass-clef piano part of "All Time High."

EXAMPLE 2.9   Nelson, "On the Road Again," mm. 8–14

Just can't   wait to   get   on   the   road   a - gain.

The life   I   love   is   mak - ing   mu - sic   with   my   friends.

EXAMPLE 2.10   Barry and Rice, "All Time High," mm. 34–37

So hold on tight, let the flight be - gin._____

Most double-sharped or double-flatted notes are played on the white keys of the piano. For example, the F×4 in the Nelson song is enharmonic with G, and the B♭♭ in "All Time High" is enharmonic with A. Example 2.11 shows other examples.

EXAMPLE 2.11   Enharmonic pitches with double sharps and flats

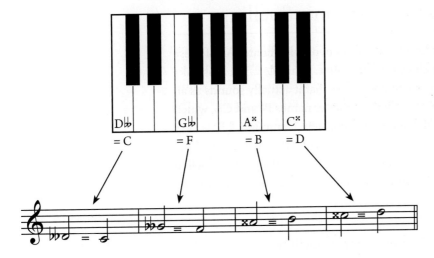

SUMMARY

Accidentals:

♯ (sharp)	raises the pitch a half step
♭ (flat)	lowers the pitch a half step
× (double sharp)	raises the pitch a whole step
♭♭ (double flat)	lowers the pitch a whole step
♮ (natural)	cancels a sharp, double sharp, flat, or double flat

Identify whether each pair of pitches spans a whole step (W), half step (H), or neither (N).

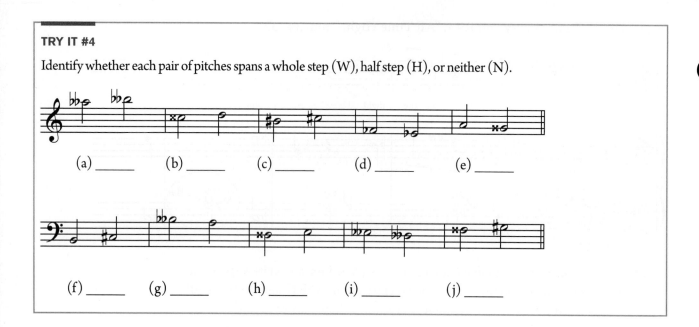

(a) _____　　(b) _____　　(c) _____　　(d) _____　　(e) _____

(f) _____　　(g) _____　　(h) _____　　(i) _____　　(j) _____

EXPLORE FURTHER More on Enharmonic Spellings

Look at the intervals in Example 2.12 and listen or find them on a keyboard. All of these sound like half or whole steps, but the spellings are deceptive. Example 2.12a looks like a descending interval, but its enharmonic respelling shows that it actually sounds as an ascending half step. In 2.12b, the interval is spelled with letter names B♯ and C♭♭, which seems to be ascending, but sounds as a descending whole step. Example 2.12c is very hard to read with a double sharp and double flat, but sounds like the ascending whole step. Likewise 2.12d sounds like a whole step, but it does not look like it when spelled C♯–F♭♭. Using the correct spelling for the context will be important as we learn more about scales, intervals, and triads.

EXAMPLE 2.12　　Intervals and their enharmonic respelling

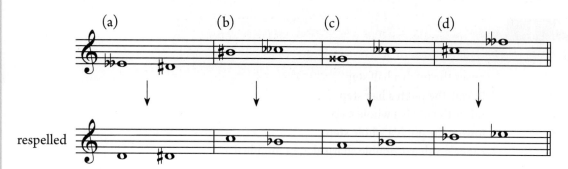

respelled

Enharmonically respell each pair of given pitches, using adjacent letter names. Play them on a keyboard to be sure your respelled interval sounds the same as the original.

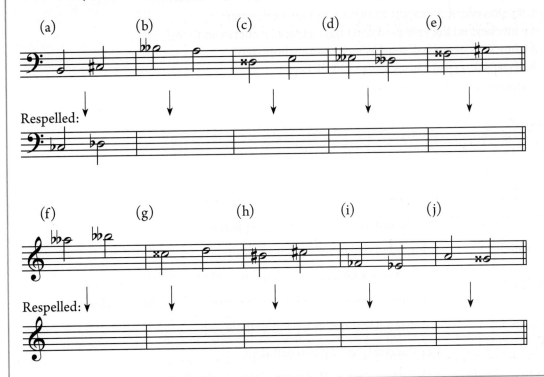

Did You Know?

Scott Joplin's father was a former slave. One of Joplin's most famous compositions, "The Maple Leaf Rag" (published in 1899), earned him one penny for every sheet-music copy sold. His opera *Treemonisha* (composed in 1911) won an award for being the "most American opera" ever written, yet Joplin never saw it fully staged. Joplin's music was played in bars, dance halls, and other popular gathering places from the 1890s to the 1910s. It became popular once again in the 1970s after it was featured in the movie *The Sting* (1973), with Paul Newman and Robert Redford. Joplin's rags (Example 2.1) have remained among the best-known American music of the early twentieth century.

Terms You Should Know

accidentals
   flat (♭)
   sharp (♯)
   natural (♮)
   double flat (♭♭)
   double sharp (𝄪)

enharmonic
interval
half step (semitone)
   chromatic half step
   diatonic half step
whole step (whole tone)

Questions for Review

1. What is the effect of adding a sharp to a note? Adding a flat? Adding a natural?
2. What is an example of an enharmonic spelling?
3. Does an accidental precede or follow a note's letter name when spoken or written? Does an accidental precede or follow the note head in a musical score?
4. Which pairs of white keys on the keyboard don't have a black key between them?
5. Which pairs of white keys span a half step? Which span a whole step?
6. Are there any half steps that span a black key to a black key?
7. How can you distinguish whole and half steps by ear?

Reading Review

Match the term on the left with the best answer on the right.

_____ (1) half step	(a) symbol that raises a pitch a whole step
_____ (2) interval	(b) the distance between any two pitches
_____ (3) enharmonic	(c) symbol that raises a pitch a half step
_____ (4) ♯	(d) half step with a different letter name for each note
_____ (5) ♭	(e) interval between any key on the keyboard and the next closest key
_____ (6) whole step	(f) symbol that lowers a pitch a whole step
_____ (7) 𝄫	(g) interval spanning two half steps
_____ (8) 𝄪	(h) notes written with different letter names that sound the same
_____ (9) accidentals	(i) half step with the same letter name but different accidentals
_____ (10) chromatic half step	(j) symbols that indicate how much to raise or lower a pitch
_____ (11) ♮	(k) symbol that cancels a sharp or flat
_____ (12) diatonic half step	(l) symbol that lowers a pitch a half step

Apply It

A. Sing at sight

Mark the half steps with brackets, as shown in Melody 1. Then perform the melodies with the lyrics shown. Sing the hollow notes longer than the filled notes. Vary your performance in the following ways:

- Echo melodies after your teacher or the recording.
- Play on a keyboard and sing along.

Melody 1

Melody 2

Melody 3

Melody 4

Melody 5

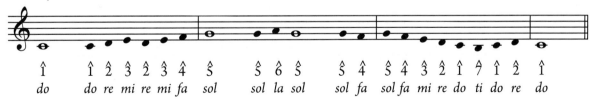

B. Play and sing

1. For each of the following pitches, first play on a keyboard, then sing in a comfortable range:
   - the pitch and a half step above and below
   - the pitch and a whole step above and below

   C♯, A♭, E♭, F♯, B, E♯, D♭

2. Start with the given pitch, then move your finger on a keyboard (or keyboard diagram), following the pattern of whole and half steps indicated. Write the name of the pitch at the end of the sequence.

   (a) Begin on C: down W, down H, down W, up H, up H =   **A**

   (b) Begin on E: up W, up H, up W, down H, up W, up W = _____

   (c) Begin on F♯: down W, down W, up H, down W, down H, up W = _____

   (d) Begin on A♭: up W, up W, up W, down H, up W, up W = _____

C. Identify half and whole steps

Listen to the following pairs of notes (played in class or on the recording). The pitches make either a half step (H) or whole step (W). Write H or W in the blank, and ↑ for ascending or ↓ for descending.

(a)   **W ↑**   (b) _____   (c) _____   (d) _____

(e) _____   (f) _____   (g) _____   (h) _____

(i) _____   (j) _____   (k) _____   (l) _____

D. Create a melody with whole and half steps

On your own or with a partner, write a short melody in bass clef.
   - Choose a "home" pitch for your melody. Start and end your melody on this pitch.
   - Include 10–12 pitches in your melody. Make a pleasing contour.
   - Keep most pitches on the staff, with few ledger lines. Use only adjacent letter names (e.g., F–G–A–G).
   - Notate an accidental for every pitch.
   - Notate with note heads only. Mix hollow and filled note heads.
   - Prepare to sing or play your melody in class.

Sample melody

Bb = home

Your melody

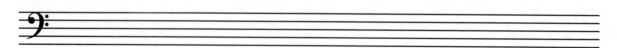

Listen and Write 2.1

A. Hearing half steps

1. Contour

Listen to the following pairs of notes (played in class or on your recording). First a pitch will be played, then raised or lowered one half step. Circle the arrow that shows the pitches' contour; ascending or descending, ↑ or ↓.

(a) ↑   ↓

(b) ↑   ↓

(c) ↑   ↓

(d) ↑   ↓

(e) ↑   ↓

(f) ↑   ↓

2. Accidentals

The same pairs of notes will be played again. This time, for each pair the accidental of the first note is given; circle the accidental of the second note.

(a) ♯ →   ♭   ♮   ♯
(b) ♮ →   ♭   ♮   ♯
(c) ♭ →   ♭   ♮   ♯
(d) ♯ →   ♭   ♮   ♯
(e) ♮ →   ♭   ♮   ♯
(f) ♮ →   ♭   ♮   ♯

B. Hearing half and whole steps

Listen to the recording. For each two-pitch pattern, write H (half), W (whole), or N (neither).

1. _____   2. _____   3. _____   4. _____   5. _____

6. _____   7. _____   8. _____   9. _____   10. _____

11. _____   12. _____   13. _____   14. _____   15. _____

Beginning with the given pitch, a two-pitch pattern will be played and then repeated. In the blank beneath each exercise, write the interval between the two pitches, W or H. Notate the second pitch with an adjacent note name and with its accidental—♭, ♮, or ♯.

C. Hearing and writing a melody

- Listen to the melody until you can sing it from memory.
- Sing again, then find and play it on a keyboard.
- On the following staff, write the notes of the melody with filled and hollow note heads. (The beginning of each segment of the melody is provided.)

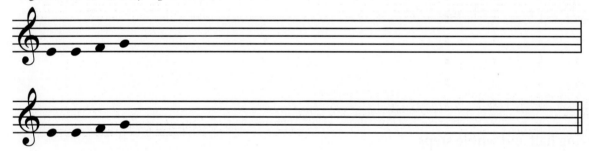

Workbook ASSIGNMENT 2.1

A. Identifying pitches with accidentals

(1) Write one letter name for each white key marked with an arrow below the keyboard; then write two possible enharmonic names for each black key marked with an arrow above the keyboard.

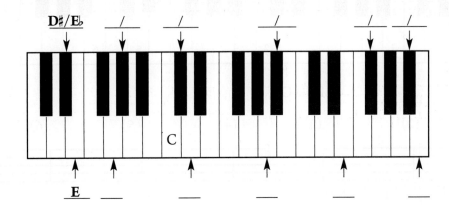

(2) Write the name of each pitch, together with its octave number, in the blank beneath the staff.

C♯3   ___   ___   ___   ___   ___   ___   ___

___   ___   ___   ___   ___   ___   ___   ___

B. Writing accidentals

Use the following staves to practice writing accidentals.

Write flat signs before each pitch.   Write natural signs.

Write sharp signs before each pitch.   Write natural signs.

C. Writing pitches with accidentals

Notate each numbered keyboard pitch on the staff in the correct octave, using a hollow note head, below the corresponding number. (Choose either enharmonic spelling for black keys.)

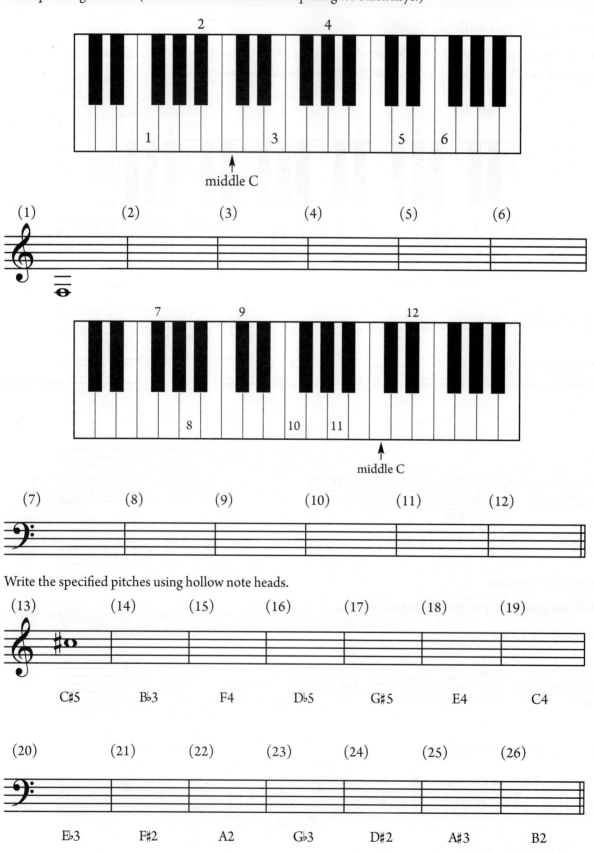

Workbook ASSIGNMENT 2.2

A. Identifying and writing whole and half steps

Label each pair of notes as a whole step (W), half step (H), or neither (N).

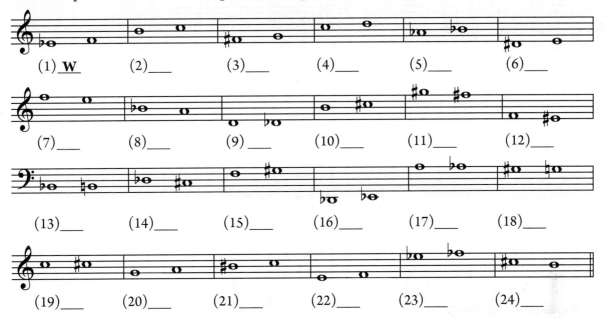

(1) __W__   (2) ___   (3) ___   (4) ___   (5) ___   (6) ___

(7) ___   (8) ___   (9) ___   (10) ___   (11) ___   (12) ___

(13) ___   (14) ___   (15) ___   (16) ___   (17) ___   (18) ___

(19) ___   (20) ___   (21) ___   (22) ___   (23) ___   (24) ___

Write the specified whole or half step above the given note. For half steps, write the chromatic spelling (same letter names).

(25)   (26)   (27)   (28)   (29)   (30)

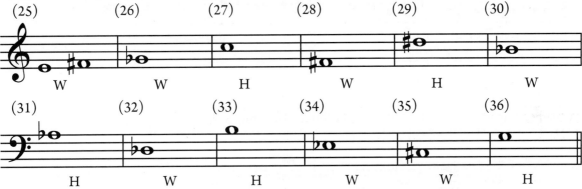

   W   W   H   W   H   W

(31)   (32)   (33)   (34)   (35)   (36)

   H   W   H   W   W   H

Write the specified whole or half step below the given note. For half steps, write the diatonic spelling (different letter names).

(37)   (38)   (39)   (40)   (41)   (42)

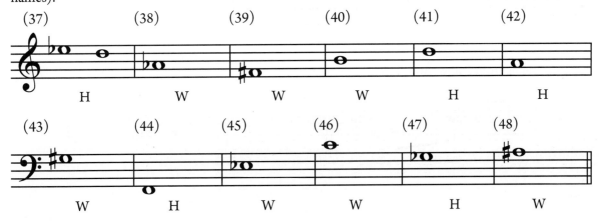

   H   W   W   W   H   H

(43)   (44)   (45)   (46)   (47)   (48)

   W   H   W   W   H   W

B. Identifying whole and half steps in music

Each of the following melodies features whole and half steps. Beneath each bracketed interval, write W or H in the blank. Listen to the recorded examples to hear how the whole and half steps sound, or play the pitches on a keyboard.

(1) Sousa, "The Stars and Stripes Forever," mm. 1–4

(2) Phillips, "Blues for Norton," mm. 20–24 (bass line)

(3) Joplin, "Pine Apple Rag," mm. 1–4

(4) John Williams, "Imperial March," from *The Empire Strikes Back*, mm. 5–8

(5) Bruce Miller, Theme from *Frasier*, mm. 2–5

Workbook ASSIGNMENT 2.3

A. Reading and writing enharmonic pitches

(1) In the first row of blanks below the staff, write the letter name for each pitch. In the second row, give the letter name of one possible enharmonic equivalent.

Letter
name: G♭   ___ ___ ___ ___ ___ ___ ___ ___

Enharmonic
equivalent: F♯   ___ ___ ___ ___ ___ ___ ___ ___

Letter
name: ___ ___ ___ ___ ___ ___ ___ ___

Enharmonic
equivalent: ___ ___ ___ ___ ___ ___ ___ ___

(2) Notate an enharmonic equivalent for each pitch.

B. Identifying and writing half and whole steps

For each pair of pitches, write W (whole step), H (half step), or N (neither) in the blank.

(1) G♯–A **H**

(2) E♭–F♯ ____

(3) A♭–B♭ ____

(4) B–C ____

(5) F♯–G♯ ____

(6) D♯–C♯ ____

(7) A–G♯ ____

(8) C–B♭ ____

(9) E♯–F ____

Write a whole step above the given note, on the next line or space, so that it has the adjacent letter name.

(10)   (11)   (12)   (13)   (14)   (15)

Write a whole step below the given note. Use adjacent letter names.

(16)   (17)   (18)   (19)   (20)   (21)

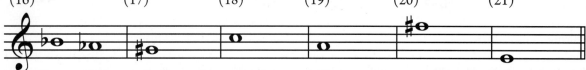

Write a half step above the given note. When you write black-key pitches, choose either enharmonic spelling. Remember to write a natural sign, if needed, to cancel a sharp or flat.

(22)   (23)   (24)   (25)   (26)   (27)

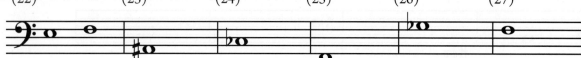

Write a half step below the given note. For black-key pitches, use either enharmonic spelling. Remember to write a natural sign, if needed, to cancel a sharp or flat.

(28)   (29)   (30)   (31)   (32)   (33)

Simple Meters

TOPICS

- Duple, triple, and quadruple meters
- Tempo markings and conducting patterns
- Rhythmic notation
- Meter signatures
- Counting rhythms in simple meters
- Rests
- Explore further: meters with ♪ or ♪ beat units

MUSIC

- Johann Sebastian Bach, Invention in D Minor
- Johann Sebastian Bach, Prelude in C Major, from *The Well-Tempered Clavier*, Book I
- "Come, Ye Thankful People, Come"
- Stephen Foster, "Jeanie with the Light Brown Hair"
- Foster, "Oh! Susanna"
- John Lennon and Paul McCartney, "Hey Jude"
- Wolfgang Amadeus Mozart, Piano Sonata in C Major, K. 545
- Mozart, *Variations on "Ah, vous dirai-je Maman"*
- "My Country, 'Tis of Thee"
- John Newton, "Amazing Grace"
- Joel Phillips, "Blues for Norton"
- John Philip Sousa, "The Stars and Stripes Forever"

Duple, Triple, and Quadruple Meters

Listen to an excerpt from "Oh! Susanna" by Stephen Foster and tap your foot in time to the music. This tap represents the work's primary pulse, or **beat**. Now listen for a secondary pulse moving faster than your foot tap. Tap the secondary pulse in one hand, while your foot continues with the beat. This secondary pulse is the **beat division**.

Beats typically divide into two or three parts. When you tap the beat division in your hand, you'll notice that there are two hand taps to one foot beat: the beat divides into two.

> **KEY CONCEPT** Pieces with beats that divide into two are in **simple meter**.

Listen again while tapping the primary beat and division as shown in Example 3.1. Because the beat divides into twos, the song is in simple meter.

EXAMPLE 3.1 Meter in "Oh! Susanna"

Counts	1		2		1		2		1		2		1		2	
Beats	tap		tap		tap		tap		tap		tap		tap		tap	
Divisions	tap	tap	tap	tap	tap	tap	tap	tap	tap	tap	tap	tap	tap	tap	tap	tap
Lyrics	Oh!		Su-		san-	na,		Oh!	don't	you	cry	for	me			

Besides dividing, primary beats also group into twos, threes, or fours. As you listen to a piece, try saying "1-2-1-2" aloud (one number per primary beat); if the piece doesn't seem to fit that pattern, try "1-2-3-1-2-3." Listen now to "My Country, 'Tis of Thee," which groups into threes. Tap while following Example 3.2.

EXAMPLE 3.2 Meter in "My Country, 'Tis of Thee"

Counts	1		2		3		1		2		3	
Beats	tap		tap		tap		tap		tap		tap	
Divisions	tap	tap	tap	tap	tap	tap	tap	tap	tap	tap	tap	tap
Lyrics	My		coun-		try,		'tis			of	thee	

> **KEY CONCEPT** A work's **meter** tells (1) how its beats are divided, and (2) how they are grouped. When beats group into twos, the meter is called **duple**. When they group into threes, the meter is **triple**. When they group into fours, the meter is **quadruple**.

To determine the meter of a composition by ear:

1. listen for the beat and tap it with your foot,
2. listen for the beat division (simple meters will divide beats in two parts), and
3. listen for the groupings of the beat.

Try conducting (see the patterns in Example 3.3) or counting to determine whether the meter is duple, triple, or quadruple.

Tempo Markings and Conducting Patterns

When only a few musicians are playing together, one may "count off" "1-2-1-2," "1-2-3," or "1-2-3-4" to help everyone start together at the same time and at the same speed, or **tempo** (plural is either "tempos" or "tempi"). Selecting the correct tempo for a performance is important to conveying the character or mood of a piece. The most common **tempo indications** (in Italian) are:

Slower tempos: *grave, largo, larghetto, adagio*

Medium tempos: *andantino, andante, moderato, allegretto*

Faster tempos: *allegro, vivace, presto, prestissimo*

Increasing in tempo (gradually faster): *accelerando* (abbreviated *accel.*)

Decreasing in tempo (gradually slower): *ritardando* (abbreviated *rit.*)

With larger groups, such as a band or choir, a conductor sets the tempo and maintains the beat for the musicians. Conductors outline specific patterns for each duple, triple, or quadruple meter, as shown in Example 3.3. Conduct the duple pattern with the recording of "Oh! Susanna"; for "My Country," use the triple pattern. For a quadruple pattern, conduct "Come, Ye Thankful People, Come."

EXAMPLE 3.3   Conducting patterns

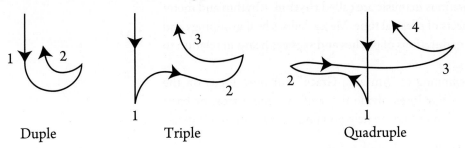

Duple   Triple   Quadruple

The following chart summarizes the meters of the pieces heard so far.

Piece	Meter type
"Oh! Susanna"	simple duple
"My Country, 'Tis of Thee"	simple triple
"Come, Ye Thankful People, Come"	simple quadruple

As you practice **conducting patterns**, you may feel a physical weight on the **downbeat**—the downward motion of the hand on beat 1. You may also feel anticipation on the **upbeat**—the upward lift of the hand for the final beat of each pattern. The "weight" of the downbeat and the "lift" of the upbeat reflect the strong and weak beats of each measure.

> **KEY CONCEPT** In duple meters, the first beat is strong and the second is weak, making an alternating pattern of strong-weak. In triple meters, the pattern is strong-weak-weak (the relative strengths of beats 2 and 3 may vary), and in quadruple meters, strongest-weak-strong-weak. Strong beats in a meter are heard as **metrical accents**.

An **accent** adds weight, emphasis, or loudness to a musical element. Notated accents (>) instruct the performer to play with a sudden burst of loudness. Metrical accents are not necessarily louder; their emphasis comes from a strong beat.

In addition to showing the beat, a conductor's gestures and expressions may also convey the mood of the music, coordinate breaths, and indicate the volume, or **dynamic level**. As with tempo markings, dynamic marking are often in Italian, and are typically abbreviated.

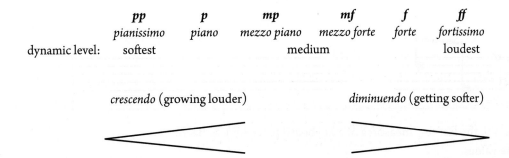

Rhythmic Notation

When you listened to the music at the beginning of the chapter, you probably noticed that some pitches lasted longer and others were shorter—these are **durations**. The patterns of longer and shorter durations in music are called **rhythm**. Rhythm and meter are two different, but related, aspects of musical time. Meter defines beat groupings and divisions, while rhythm consists of durations of pitches and silences heard in relation to the underlying meter.

Look at Example 3.4, the beginning of "Amazing Grace." For now, focus on the labeled parts of the notation. The **bar lines** divide the staff into **measures**, or bars; numbers above the staff are measure numbers, to help you find your location in a piece.

EXAMPLE 3.4   Newton, "Amazing Grace," mm. 1–4

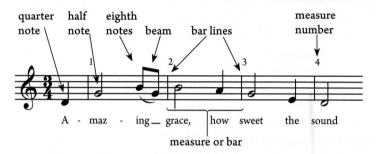

The example features three of the most common note values in music: **quarter**, **half**, and **eighth notes**. A half note lasts twice as long as a quarter; a quarter note lasts twice as long as an eighth. Eighth notes can be written two ways: **beamed** together as in the example, or with a **flag** attached to the right of the stem, as in Example 3.5. Write flags on the right side of the stem, whether the stem goes up or down. If eighth notes are beamed together, take the stem direction of the second note, as in the first measure of Example 3.4. For more than two beamed notes, choose the stem direction based on the majority of the pitches; don't change direction within the beamed group.

EXAMPLE 3.5   Parts of a note

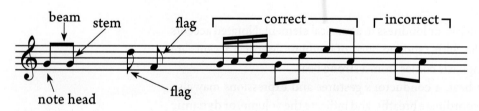

TRY IT #1

Circle the incorrectly notated stems, flags, and beams.

Notate them correctly here.

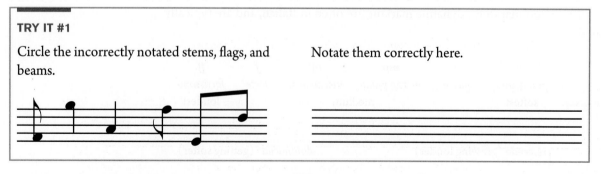

Now consider Example 3.6, the last few measures of a keyboard piece by J. S. Bach, to learn two additional note values.

EXAMPLE 3.6   Bach, Prelude in C Major, from *The Well-Tempered Clavier,*
Book I, mm. 34–35

The notes with two beams are **sixteenth notes**. They may be written with either two
beams or two flags, and they last half as long as eighth notes. The last measure contains
whole notes—hollow note heads with no stem. A whole note lasts four times as long as
a quarter note and twice as long as a half note.

The chart in Example 3.7 sums up the basic note durations in simple meter and how
these notes relate to each other: a whole note divides into two half notes, a half note
divides into two quarters, and so on. You can create even smaller note values by adding
beams or flags to the stem; a thirty-second note, for example, has three flags or beams
and a sixty-fourth note has four.

EXAMPLE 3.7   Chart of rhythmic durations

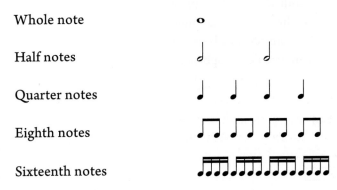

Whole note

Half notes

Quarter notes

Eighth notes

Sixteenth notes

SUMMARY

- A o is equivalent to ♩♩ or ♩♩♩♩
- A ♩ is equivalent to ♩♩ or ♫ ♫
- A ♩ is equivalent to ♫ or ♬

TRY IT #2

In each blank, write the value of the note above: W (whole), H (half), Q (quarter),
E (eighth), or S (sixteenth).

(a) Foster, "Jeanie with the Light Brown Hair" mm. 13–14

Ma - ny   were   the   wild   notes   her   mer - ry   voice   would   pour,

 E   ___   ___   ___   ___

(b) Lennon and McCartney, "Hey Jude," mm. 3–6

SHOW IT! Assignment 3.1

Meter Signatures

Listen again to the melody of "Amazing Grace," shown in Example 3.8, and tap or conduct along with the music. The meter is simple triple; this is indicated on the staff by the symbol $\frac{3}{4}$—called the **meter signature** (or time signature). The 3 means that there are three beats in a measure, and the 4 indicates that the quarter note gets one beat—it is the **beat unit**. The quarter note before the first bar line is an **anacrusis** (or upbeat or pickup)—a weaker beat that precedes the first strong one.

EXAMPLE 3.8   Newton, "Amazing Grace," mm. 1–4

> **KEY CONCEPT** In simple meters: the top number of the meter signature—2, 3, or 4—shows the number of beats in a measure (duple, triple, or quadruple); the lower number represents the type of note that gets one beat (2 = half note, 4 = quarter note, 8 = eighth note, 16 = sixteenth note). In sum, the meter signature shows "how many" (top number) of "what" (bottom number) constitutes a measure.

Examples 3.9 and 3.10 show simple duple ($\frac{2}{4}$) and simple quadruple ($\frac{4}{4}$) meters. In Example 3.9, a familiar melody ("Twinkle, Twinkle, Little Star") used by Mozart, both hands play the beat unit—the quarter note. In Example 3.10, the rhythm moves primarily in quarter notes in a $\frac{4}{4}$ meter. On the grand staff or on multiple staves, the meter signature appears on each staff, as shown.

Both examples share another rhythmic device: a dot. Notes with dots are circled in Examples 3.9 and 3.10.

> **KEY CONCEPT** A **dot** beside a note adds to that note half of its own value.
>
>

EXAMPLE 3.9   Mozart, *Variations on "Ah, vous dirai-je Maman,"* mm. 1–8

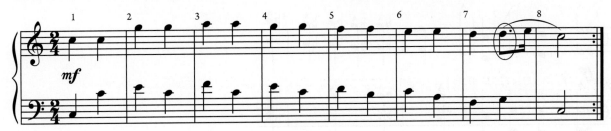

EXAMPLE 3.10   "Come, Ye Thankful People, Come," mm. 1–4

Come, ye thank - ful peo - ple, come, Raise the song of har - vest home:

In Example 3.9, the dotted-eighth note in measure 7 lasts three-quarters of a beat. In Example 3.10, the dotted-quarter notes last a beat and a half.

You will often see meter signatures that consist of symbols other than numerals. For example, the symbol 𝐂, called "common time," is sometimes written instead of $\frac{4}{4}$, as in Example 3.11.

EXAMPLE 3.11   Mozart, Piano Sonata in C Major, K. 545, mm. 1–4

The quarter note is the most common beat unit, but it's not the only possibility. For example, "The Stars and Stripes Forever," shown in Example 3.12, is a march in a quick tempo with half notes felt as the beat unit and pairs of quarter notes as the beat division (see m. 3). The meter signature could be written as $\frac{2}{2}$—two beats to the measure, with a half note receiving the beat—but more often we find $\frac{2}{2}$ written as ₵, called *alla breve* or "cut time." We will focus for now on these two beat units (♩ and ♪).

EXAMPLE 3.12   Sousa, "The Stars and Stripes Forever," mm. 1–4

There are various reasons why composers choose a particular beat unit. Sometimes it's to remind the performer of a particular compositional type—such as *alla breve* for marches. A piece may be notated with a longer beat unit for ease of reading, to avoid notating quick-moving rhythms with sixteenth or thirty-second notes. The meter may also suggest a tempo: an eighth-note beat unit might indicate a faster tempo and a lively motion.

SUMMARY

Simple-meter signatures with 𝅗𝅥 or ♩ beat units:

Simple duple	$\frac{2}{2}$	¢	$\frac{2}{4}$
Simple triple	$\frac{3}{2}$	$\frac{3}{4}$	
Simple quadruple	$\frac{4}{2}$	$\frac{4}{4}$	C

Counting Rhythms in Simple Meters

To count rhythms in a simple-meter piece, you first need to look at the meter signature and identify the beat unit and beat division. For example, if the beat unit is a quarter note, the beat division is two eighths; if the beat unit is a half note, the beat division is two quarters. Example 3.13 shows how to interpret various simple-meter signatures; the first three are the most common.

EXAMPLE 3.13   Beat units and divisions in simple meters with ♩ and 𝅗𝅥 beat units

Meter signature	Beats per measure	Beat unit	Beat division
$\frac{2}{4}$	2	♩	♫
$\frac{3}{4}$	3	♩	♫
$\frac{4}{4}$ (C)	4	♩	♫
$\frac{2}{2}$ (¢)	2	𝅗𝅥	♩ ♩
$\frac{3}{2}$	3	𝅗𝅥	♩ ♩
$\frac{4}{2}$	4	𝅗𝅥	♩ ♩

We will count a rhythm in simple triple meter. The first step is to locate the beats and divisions in the music.

> **KEY CONCEPT** In $\frac{3}{4}$, a measure of all quarter notes is counted 1-2-3; a measure of all eighth notes is counted 1 & 2 & 3 &.

In "Amazing Grace," shown in Example 3.14, the beat unit is the quarter note, but the melody mixes quarter notes with half notes and eighths. To count measure 1, write: 1 (2) 3 &, as shown in the example. The (2) indicates that the first half note extends through beat 2. The eighth-note division of beat 3 is written with an ampersand (3 &) and counted aloud as "three and."

EXAMPLE 3.14   Newton, "Amazing Grace," mm. 1–4

The first quarter note of the melody, the anacrusis (or upbeat), counts as the final beat (3) of an incomplete measure. When an anacrusis begins a whole piece, as in this song, the measure numbering (above the staff) starts with the first *complete* measure. The last measure of the score is often incomplete, in order to "balance" the anacrusis.

Example 3.15 shows the counts for the same rhythm, notated in two different ways: with a quarter-note beat unit (a) and a half-note beat unit (b). Both rhythms are counted in the same way and sound the same. While you may find the first easier to read, you may also encounter the second in music you play or sing. Practice reading rhythms with the less typical half-note beat unit, as well as the more familiar quarter-note unit.

The rhythms in Example 3.15 are notated with a **rhythm clef**: two vertical lines preceding the meter signature. The rhythm clef is typically placed on a single line instead of a staff for percussion parts that play only rhythm, not specific pitches. The stems of notes on a rhythm clef typically point upward.

EXAMPLE 3.15   Equivalent rhythmic notation

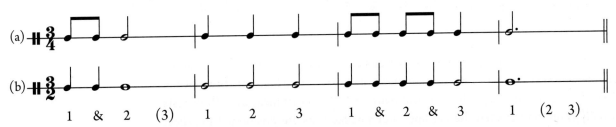

At each arrow, add one note value to complete the measure in the meter indicated.
Write the counts beneath each rhythm.

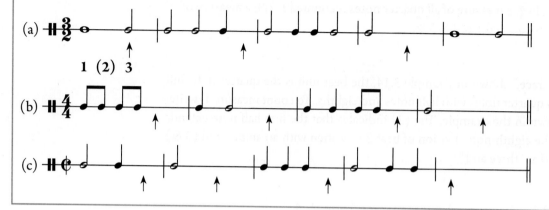

Rests

Listen to the beginning of "Blues for Norton," shown in Example 3.16, to hear the effect
of **rests**, or durations of silence. Here, the saxophone begins with a solo line while all
the other instruments wait in silence for their first entrance. This silence is notated with
rests.

EXAMPLE 3.16   Phillips, "Blues for Norton," mm. 1–3

Example 3.17 shows each type of rest with its corresponding note value in simple
meter. A **whole rest** may represent four quarter-note beats or two half-note beats; it can
also last a whole measure, regardless of how many beats are in that measure. Whole rests
are usually centered between the bar lines, but smaller rests are positioned to reflect
where the beats occur, as shown in Example 3.16. To write shorter rests, like the thirty-
second ($\mathcal{y}$), just add additional flags to the sixteenth. Like other rhythmic values, rests
may be dotted.

EXAMPLE 3.17   Note values and rests

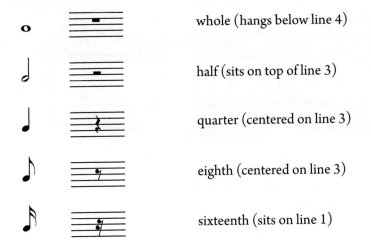

whole (hangs below line 4)

half (sits on top of line 3)

quarter (centered on line 3)

eighth (centered on line 3)

sixteenth (sits on line 1)

SHOW IT! Assignment 3.2, 3.3

Counts for rests are written in parentheses to show that there are no sounding pitches for these durations. Listen to Example 3.18 and practice counting the rhythms along with the bass line. Measure 2 begins with a pitch on a weak part of the beat, or **offbeat**. We will consider the rhythms of the upper lines in Chapter 4.

EXAMPLE 3.18   Phillips, "Blues for Norton," mm. 1–4

EXPLORE FURTHER Meters with ♪ or ♫ Beat Units

In addition to the beat units introduced to this point, meters with ♪ or ♫ beat units may be found—though they are far less common. Listen, for example, to the opening of Bach's Invention in D Minor (Example 3.19). In this simple triple meter, the beat unit is the ♪ and the beat division is ♫.

EXAMPLE 3.19   Bach, Invention in D Minor, mm. 1–5

To read a simple meter with a less common beat unit, the same general principles apply. Example 3.20 provides a summary of some of these meters.

SUMMARY

In simple meters,

- The upper number of the meter signature tells how many beats are in a measure; this number is 2, 3, or 4, to represent simple duple, simple triple, or simple quadruple meter.

- The lower number indicates the beat unit; this number may be 2 (♩), 4 (♩), 8 (♪), or 16 (♬).

EXAMPLE 3.20   Simple meters with ♪ and ♬ beat units

Meter signature	Beats per measure	Beat unit	Beat division
3/8	3	♪	♫
4/8	4	♪	♫
3/16	3	♬	♬
4/16	4	♬	♬

TRY IT #4

Write the counts for each rhythm. Then rewrite in the meter indicated.

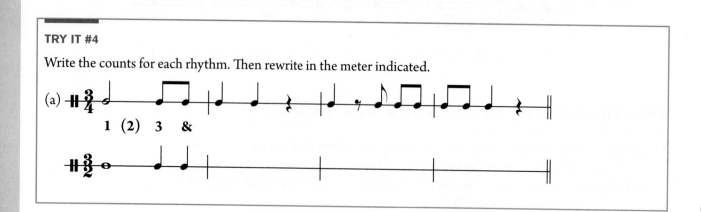

(b)

SHOW IT! Aural Skills 3.1

Did You Know?

Much of the time when we think about music, we focus on sounds and don't pay much attention to silences. Twentieth-century composer John Cage (1912–1992) forced us to do just the opposite when he composed his famous 4'33" (1952)—a three-movement work where each movement has a duration selected by the performer, but is marked "Tacet" (a term usually used to tell certain instrumentalists not to play in one movement of a multimovement work). The title, 4'33", refers to the duration of the whole piece. The performers indicate the start and end of each movement in some way—by lifting their instruments up and down or by opening and closing the piano keyboard cover—but make no sounds. The piece is not completely silent, however; normally people in the audience make some sound by moving, coughing, shuffling program pages, and so forth. Through this work and his writings, including *Silence* (1961), Cage inspired musicians and listeners to think about what happens between the sounds—in the silences.

Terms You Should Know

accent
anacrusis
bar line
beam
beat
beat division
beat unit
conducting patterns
dot
downbeat
duration
dynamic level
flag

measure
meter
  simple
  duple
  triple
  quadruple
meter signature
metrical accent
note
  whole
  half
  quarter
  eighth

sixteenth
offbeat
rest
  whole
  half
  quarter
  eighth
  sixteenth
rhythm
rhythm clef
tempo
tempo indication
upbeat

Questions for Review

1. How do you decide if a piece is in duple, triple, or quadruple meter?
2. How do you decide which conducting pattern to use?
3. Where do the stronger metrical accents fall in simple triple meter? In simple duple meter? In simple quadruple meter?
4. Explain the difference between rhythm and meter.
5. Draw an eighth note on a staff. Draw one above the middle staff line and another below it.
6. On which side of a note are stems drawn? On which side of the stem are flags drawn?
7. What are the most common simple-meter signatures?
8. What do the upper and lower parts of a meter signature represent in simple meters?
9. Which numbers may appear in the upper and lower positions of the meter signature in simple meters?
10. What is the beat unit in **C**? In **₵**?

Reading Review

Match the term on the left with the best answer on the right.

_____ (1) quarter note

_____ (2) beat unit

_____ (3) rhythm

_____ (4) whole note

_____ (5) **C**

_____ (6) simple meter

_____ (7) duple meter

_____ (8) dot

_____ (9) meter signature

_____ (10) triple meter

_____ (11) ¾

_____ (12) sixteenth note

_____ (13) dynamic marking

_____ (14) rhythm clef

_____ (15) anacrusis

_____ (16) ₵

_____ (17) half rest

_____ (18) tempo

(a) meter with beats that divide into two

(b) equal in duration to two quarter rests

(c) the type of note that gets one beat

(d) ♪

(e) the sequence of pitches and silences in music

(f) indicates how loud or soft the music should be

(g) ³₂ and ³₄

(h) ♩

(i) counted the same as ⁴₄

(j) ²₂ and ²₄

(k) the speed of the beats

(l) notation symbol that shows the beat unit and the number of beats in a bar

(m) has three quarter-note beats per measure

(n) *alla breve*, or cut time

(o) upbeat

(p) adds half its value to a note or rest

(q) used to notate unpitched percussion parts

(r) duration equal to two half notes

Apply It

A. Listen and compare meters

Listen to the beginning of each of the following pieces. Focus on the grouping of the beats to decide whether the meter is simple duple, simple triple, or simple quadruple. Conduct along as you listen.

1. Bach, Passacaglia in C Minor _____

2. "Michael Finnegan" _____

3. "Come, Ye Thankful People, Come" _____

4. Chopin, Prelude in C Minor, Op. 28, No. 20 _____

5. Mozart, String Quarter in D Minor, K. 421, third movement _____

B. Read rhythms

Perform the following rhythms as musically as possible, following the dynamic markings. As you perform, tap or conduct the beats. Speak with rhythm syllables or counts (if instructed to do so) or a neutral syllable such as "ta," and give a slight emphasis to each downbeat.

Rhythm 1

Rhythm 2

Rhythm 3

Rhythm 4

Rhythm 5

Rhythm 6

Rhythm 7

Rhythm 8

C. Make a simple-meter rhythm

- Compose an eight-measure rhythm or rhythmic duet that features only the following patterns. If you're working as a group, each person should notate one or two measures.
- Add dynamic and tempo markings.
- Write in simple quadruple, simple duple, or simple triple meter. For simple triple, add one ♩ to every pattern.
- Have another person or group perform your rhythm and critique it in class.

Patterns

D. Sing at sight

- Before singing always warm up your voice. Review Chapter 1, "Apply It" (p. 15).
- Practice rhythm alone. Tap or conduct with a steady beat. Chant on "ta" or rhythm syllables.
- Next, practice pitches alone. Perform the warm-up on a keyboard or another instrument immediately before each melody, then sing the melody with scale-degree numbers, solfège syllables, or a neutral syllable such as "la."
- Finally, combine pitch and rhythm and sing each melody.

Warm-up 1

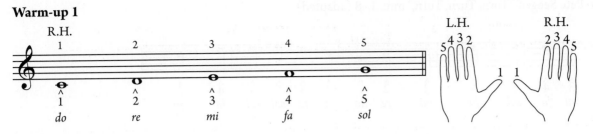

R.H.

1	2	3	4	5
$\hat{1}$	$\hat{2}$	$\hat{3}$	$\hat{4}$	$\hat{5}$
do	re	mi	fa	sol

L.H. 5 4 3 2 1   1 R.H. 2 3 4 5

Melody 1

$\hat{1}$ $\hat{2}$ $\hat{3}$ $\hat{4}$ $\hat{5}$ $\hat{5}$ $\hat{4}$ $\hat{2}$ $\hat{1}$ $\hat{2}$ $\hat{3}$ $\hat{4}$ $\hat{5}$ $\hat{4}$ $\hat{3}$ $\hat{2}$ $\hat{1}$ $\hat{3}$ $\hat{5}$ $\hat{3}$ $\hat{1}$

do re mi fa sol fa mi re do re mi fa sol fa mi re do mi sol mi do

Melody 2 "When the Saints Go Marching In," mm. 8–15 (traditional)

$\hat{3}$ $\hat{3}$ $\hat{2}$ $\hat{1}$ $\hat{1}$ $\hat{3}$ $\hat{5}$ $\hat{5}$ $\hat{4}$ $\hat{3}$ $\hat{4}$ $\hat{5}$ $\hat{3}$ $\hat{1}$ $\hat{2}$ $\hat{1}$

mi mi re do do mi sol sol fa mi fa sol mi do re do

Warm-up 2

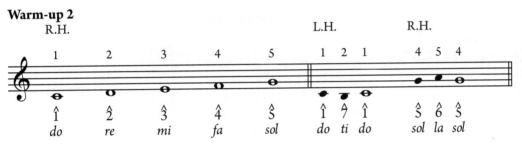

R.H.   L.H.   R.H.

1	2	3	4	5	1 2 1	4 5 4
$\hat{1}$	$\hat{2}$	$\hat{3}$	$\hat{4}$	$\hat{5}$	$\hat{1}$ $\hat{7}$ $\hat{1}$	$\hat{5}$ $\hat{6}$ $\hat{5}$
do	re	mi	fa	sol	do ti do	sol la sol

Melody 3

$\hat{1}$ $\hat{1}$ $\hat{7}$ $\hat{1}$ $\hat{2}$ $\hat{3}$ $\hat{4}$ $\hat{5}$ $\hat{5}$ $\hat{6}$ $\hat{5}$ $\hat{5}$ $\hat{6}$ $\hat{5}$ $\hat{4}$ $\hat{3}$ $\hat{2}$ $\hat{1}$ $\hat{1}$ $\hat{7}$ $\hat{1}$

do do ti do re mi fa sol sol la sol sol la sol fa mi re do do ti do

Melody 4

$\hat{1}$ $\hat{7}$ $\hat{1}$ $\hat{2}$ $\hat{3}$ $\hat{4}$ $\hat{5}$ $\hat{4}$ $\hat{3}$ $\hat{2}$ $\hat{3}$ $\hat{4}$ $\hat{3}$ $\hat{1}$ $\hat{7}$ $\hat{2}$ $\hat{1}$

do ti do re mi fa sol fa mi re mi fa mi do ti re do

Melody 5 Mozart, *Variations on "Lison dormait,"* mm. 1–8 (adapted)

$\hat{1}$ $\hat{2}$ $\hat{3}$ $\hat{4}$ $\hat{5}$ $\hat{5}$ $\hat{4}$ $\hat{3}$ $\hat{4}$ $\hat{5}$ $\hat{3}$ $\hat{5}$ $\hat{4}$ $\hat{2}$ $\hat{3}$ $\hat{1}$ $\hat{2}$ $\hat{7}$ $\hat{1}$

do re mi fa sol sol fa mi fa sol mi sol fa re mi do re ti do

Melody 6 Pete Seeger, "Turn, Turn, Turn," mm. 1–8 (adapted)

$\hat{1}$ $\hat{3}$ $\hat{4}$ $\hat{5}$ $\hat{4}$ $\hat{3}$ $\hat{2}$ $\hat{1}$ $\hat{3}$ $\hat{4}$ $\hat{5}$ $\hat{5}$ $\hat{4}$ $\hat{3}$
do mi fa sol fa mi re do mi fa sol sol fa mi

$\hat{2}$ $\hat{6}$ $\hat{6}$ $\hat{5}$ $\hat{5}$ $\hat{4}$ $\hat{3}$ $\hat{2}$ $\hat{1}$ $\hat{3}$ $\hat{2}$ $\hat{1}$
re la la sol sol fa mi re do mi re do

Warm-up 3

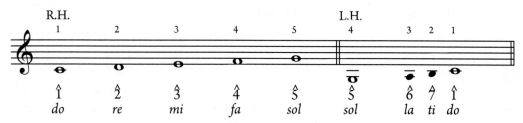

$\hat{1}$ $\hat{2}$ $\hat{3}$ $\hat{4}$ $\hat{5}$ $\hat{5}$ $\hat{6}$ $\hat{7}$ $\hat{1}$
do re mi fa sol sol la ti do

Melody 7 Curly Putman, "Green, Green Grass of Home," mm. 9–15 (adapted)

$\hat{1}$ $\hat{3}$ $\hat{5}$ $\hat{5}$ $\hat{4}$ $\hat{4}$ $\hat{3}$ $\hat{3}$ $\hat{2}$ $\hat{1}$ $\hat{1}$ $\hat{2}$ $\hat{1}$
do mi sol sol fa fa mi mi re do do re do

$\hat{1}$ $\hat{6}$ $\hat{5}$ $\hat{5}$ $\hat{5}$ $\hat{1}$ $\hat{1}$ $\hat{2}$ $\hat{2}$ $\hat{1}$ $\hat{7}$ $\hat{1}$
do la sol sol sol do do re re do ti do

Melody 8 Jacques Brel, "Seasons in the Sun," mm. 9–16 ("*Le Moribond*")

$\hat{3}$ $\hat{4}$ $\hat{5}$ $\hat{5}$ $\hat{5}$ $\hat{5}$ $\hat{4}$ $\hat{3}$ $\hat{2}$ $\hat{1}$ $\hat{2}$ $\hat{3}$ $\hat{6}$ $\hat{2}$ $\hat{3}$
mi fa sol sol sol sol fa mi re do re mi la re mi

$\hat{4}$ $\hat{4}$ $\hat{4}$ $\hat{4}$ $\hat{2}$ $\hat{1}$ $\hat{7}$ $\hat{6}$ $\hat{7}$ $\hat{2}$ $\hat{1}$
fa fa fa fa re do ti la ti re do

Listen and Write 3.1

A. Hearing simple meters

Listen to the beginning of each of the following pieces. Focus on the grouping of the beats to decide whether the meter is simple duple, simple triple, or simple quadruple. Try conducting along as you listen. Write the meter type in the blank (e.g., simple triple).

1. Bach, "O Haupt voll Blut und Wunden"   _____

2. Joplin, "Solace"   _____

3. Schubert, Waltz in B Minor   _____

4. Beethoven, *Pathétique* Sonata, second movement _____

5. Bach, Minuet II, from Cello Suite No. 1   _____

B. Writing short melodies

Listen to melodies composed with pitches C–D–E–F–G and four rhythm patterns from those numbered 1 though 5. Sing what you hear, then write it on the staff provided. You may want to work in two stages (rhythm alone, pitch alone) and then combine these elements on the staff.

These melodies use the following quadruple-meter patterns, combined with the pitches C–D–E–F–G. Each rhythm consists of four patterns. Sing what you hear, then write it on the staff provided.

Patterns

C. Listening to and writing simple-meter music

1. Listen to an English folk song and focus on its rhythm.
- While listening, tap the beat or conduct.
- Memorize the melody and sing it back. As you sing, tap or conduct.
- Finally, on the staff below, notate *only* the melody's rhythm.

2. Listen to a French folk song and focus on both its rhythm and its pitches.
- Focus first on the rhythm. While listening, tap the beat or conduct.
- Memorize the melody and sing it back while tapping or conducting.
- On the rhythm staff, notate the melody's rhythm.
- Musical challenge: Write the pitches of the melody on the staff beneath the rhythm using the notes found in Warm-up 3 (p. 64). A helpful way to identify the pitches of the melody is to sing them with the syllables or numbers in the Warm-up.

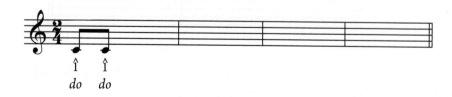

Workbook ASSIGNMENT 3.1

A. Identifying note values

In the examples that follow, write W (whole), H (half), Q (quarter), E (eighth), or S (sixteenth) in each blank to indicate the value of the note above.

(1) James Horner, "My Heart Will Go On," mm. 25–28

(2) Jonathan Larson, "Seasons of Love," from *Rent*, mm. 25–27

(3) Elton John and Bernie Taupin, "Your Song," mm. 9–10

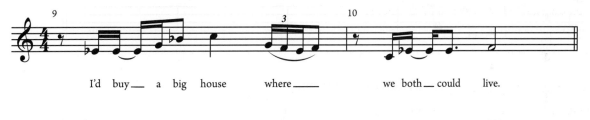

B. Understanding duration

Fill in the blanks with a number to show the equivalent duration. Some numbers may be fractions (♪ = ½ ♩).

C. Error detection in simple meters

In the following rhythmic examples, the quarter note receives one beat. Identify one measure in each example that has an incorrect number of beats for the meter specified. Circle the incorrect measure.

(1) simple triple

(2) simple duple

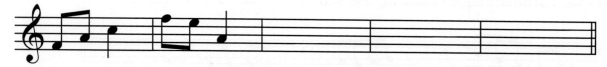

(3) simple quadruple

(4) simple triple

(5) simple quadruple

D. Notating quarter, half, and eighth notes with correct stem direction

Write the rhythms requested, using notes on a variety of lines and spaces. Choose notes so that roughly half require stems up and half stems down. Be sure that your stem direction, flags, and beaming follow correct musical notation guidelines.

(1) In each measure, write two beamed eighth notes and a quarter note.

(2) In each measure, write a quarter note, then two eighth notes with flags.

(3) In each measure, write a half note, then two quarter notes.

(4) In each measure, write a quarter note, two beamed eighth notes, four beamed sixteenth notes, and a quarter note.

Workbook ASSIGNMENT 3.2

A. Reading meters with quarter-note beats

For each of the following rhythms, write the appropriate meter signature at the beginning of the line. All of these examples are based on a quarter-note beat unit. Perform each rhythm.

(1)

(2)

(3)

(4)

At each position marked by an arrow, add one note to complete the measure in the meter indicated.

(5)

(6)

(7)

(8)

For each of the following rhythms, provide the missing bar lines that correspond with the meter signature given.

(9)

(10)

(11)

(12)

(13)

B. Understanding dots

Finish the following chart to show the equivalent durations.

𝅗𝅥.	=	𝅗𝅥	+ ♩
♩.	=	♩	+
	=	♪	+ ♪
𝅝.	=	𝅝	+
𝅗𝅥.	=		+ ♩
♩.	=		+ ♪

C. Writing rests

(1) On the following staff, write four whole rests, then four half rests.

Whole: Half:

(2) On the following staff, write four quarter rests, then four eighth rests.

Quarter: Eighth:

(3) Following each note, write a corresponding rest of the same duration.

Workbook ASSIGNMENT 3.3

A. Counting rhythms with quarter-note beats and rests

Write the counts (1 & 2 &) beneath each of the following rhythms and melodies. Put the counts that occur during sustained notes or rests in parentheses.

(1)

1　(2)　3　　1　&　2　&　3

(2)

(3)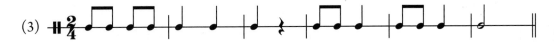

(4) Lionel Richie, "Three Times a Lady," mm. 11–14

Now　　that we've come　　　to the end　of　our　rain - bow

(5) Bono and U2, "Miracle Drug," mm. 29–32 (the last measure is incomplete)

Free - dom　has a scent　like the　top　of a new - born　ba - by's head.

(6) Richard Rodgers and Oscar Hammerstein, "If I Loved You," from *Carousel*, mm. 5–11

When I worked in the mill,　Weav-in' at the loom,　I'd gaze　ab-sent-mind-ed at the roof.

B. Counting rhythms with half-note beats

For each rhythm, provide the missing bar lines that correspond with the meter signature given. Then add the counts below each staff.

(1)

1　(2)　3　　4

(2)

(3)

C. Writing a rhythmic composition

Write a four-measure rhythmic duet in which the top part speaks the word "yes" and the bottom part says "no," in a musical argument. Use the sample composition as a model. Write durations and rests so that the two words always begin on a different beat or part of the beat, never together. Be ready to perform with a partner, or have the entire class read your composition as a musical argument. In performance, slowly *crescendo* to the final measure.

Sample

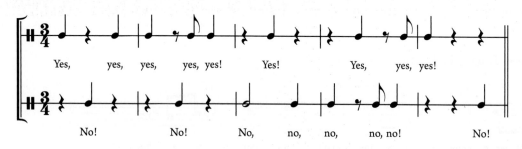

Space to work out your ideas

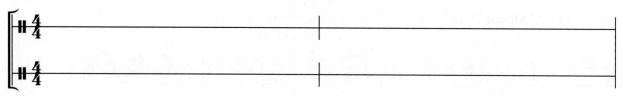

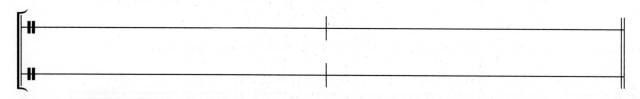

Final composition

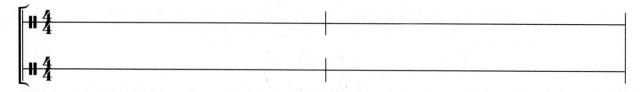

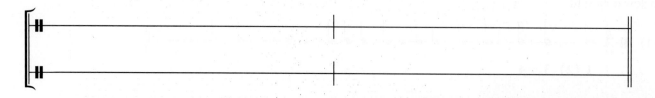

Beat Subdivisions and Syncopation

4

KNOW IT? **Take the quiz to focus your studies.**

TOPICS

- Beat subdivisions
- Ties and slurs
- Syncopation
- Triplets
- Explore further: rhythmic variations in performance

MUSIC

- Scott Joplin, "Pine Apple Rag"
- Joplin, "Solace"
- John Kander, Theme from *New York, New York*
- Jerome Kern, "Look for the Silver Lining"
- Don McLean, "American Pie"
- Wolfgang Amadeus Mozart, *Variations on "Ah, vous dirai-je, Maman"*
- John Newton, "Amazing Grace"
- Dolly Parton, "I Will Always Love You"
- Hart A. Wand and Lloyd Garrett, "Dallas Blues"
- Brian Wilson and Mike Love, "Girls on the Beach"

Beat Subdivisions

Listen to an excerpt from Mozart's *Variations on "Ah, vous dirai-je, Maman,"* following the score in Example 4.1. The left-hand melody (in the bass clef) moves primarily in quarter notes with a few eighth notes at the end of the excerpt. These durations represent the beat (♩) and beat divisions (♫) of this simple duple meter. The sixteenth notes in the right hand (♬) represent the **beat subdivision**—counted 1 e & a, as labeled in the example.

EXAMPLE 4.1   Mozart, *Variations on "Ah, vous dirai-je, Maman,"* Var. I, mm. 25–32

73

There are only seven basic rhythmic patterns made from divisions and subdivisions of a quarter-note beat; all are shown in Example 4.2 with counts written underneath. These patterns can be combined and recombined in many ways to create interesting and varied rhythms. Patterns 6 and 7 include dotted-eighth notes: since these last as long as three sixteenth notes, they are paired with a sixteenth note to complete the beat. A rest may be substituted for any duration in the following patterns; some examples are given in Example 4.3.

EXAMPLE 4.2   Rhythmic patterns for one quarter-note beat

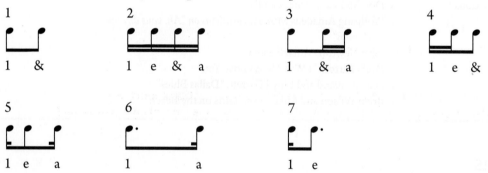

| 1 | 2 | 3 | 4 |
| 1   & | 1   e   &   a | 1   &   a | 1   e   & |

| 5 | 6 | 7 |
| 1   e   a | 1   a | 1   e |

EXAMPLE 4.3   Quarter-note beat patterns with rests

Original patterns:

Variants with one rest:

Variants with two rests:

Listen to the beginning of "Solace" while following the music in Example 4.4. Three of the seven patterns from Example 4.2 appear in these measures. The counts are written in for you.

EXAMPLE 4.4   Joplin, "Solace," mm. 1–4

> **KEY CONCEPT** The beaming of rhythmic patterns should reflect the beat unit, as in Example 4.4. Notes that sound within the same beat should be beamed together. Do not beam across the beat: ♩ ♫♫ ♩, not ♪♫♫ ♪.

Example 4.5 shows incorrect beaming, and illustrates how correcting the notation clarifies the beat units.

EXAMPLE 4.5   Beaming to reflect the quarter-note beat unit

> **TRY IT #1**
>
> Circle beats that are beamed incorrectly, then renotate the entire rhythm on the second line with correct beaming. Write the beat-level counts beneath the given line, as in (a).
>
>

Ties and Slurs

Listen to Example 4.6, the piano introduction to a blues song, which illustrates an element of rhythmic notation we have not yet considered: the tie.

> **KEY CONCEPT** **Ties** are arcs connecting the note heads of two identical pitches, which may have the same or different durations. A tie makes the first note sound as long as the two notes' durations added together; the second note is not played separately. If an accidental is applied to the first note of a tie, it continues through the tie's duration.

In the right hand of measure 1, Wand connects the final sixteenth notes of beat 1 to the beginning of beat 2 with ties—the small arcs that connect the E♭ and F across the beat. Additional ties appear from measure 2 to 3 (D and B♭), crossing the bar line. When ties extend across a beat, as here, write the "silent" count in parentheses to feel where the beat comes, even if no new note sounds on it. Do the same for dots that extend across a beat.

EXAMPLE 4.6 Wand, "Dallas Blues," mm. 1–4

The opening right-hand pitches of "Dallas Blues" are also notated with an arc below them. This time the arc connects *different* pitches. An arc that connects different pitches, whether just two (as in measure 4) or more (as in mm. 3–4), is called a **slur**. Slurs do not affect duration, but instead instruct the performer how to play the notes. In piano music, slurs indicate a smooth (or legato) line; in vocal music, slurred notes indicate one syllable or one breath. In music for wind and string instruments, slurs show tonguing and bowing.

TRY IT #2

Write the counts beneath each rhythm. When a dot or tie extends across a beat, write the count in parentheses (as shown).

SHOW IT! Assignment 4.1

Syncopation

Listen to Example 4.7, in cut time (¢), and tap along with the rhythm, using the counts underneath (think 1 e & a 2 e & a). This rhythm, one of the *clave* patterns from Afro-Cuban music, has been incorporated into many other popular styles. After the first note, all the notes are off the beat until the last one, which falls on beat 2. This rhythm is syncopated.

EXAMPLE 4.7 *Clave* pattern

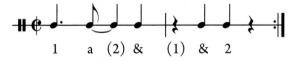

> **KEY CONCEPT** **Syncopations** are created when an expected accent is displaced—moved to another beat or part of a beat by dots, ties, rests, dynamic markings, or accent marks.

We've already seen two syncopated rhythm patterns (5 and 7) in Example 4.2 (both reproduced in Example 4.8). In each, the longest duration of the rhythm is on the "e" of 1 e & a instead of the stronger (expected) 1 or &. Other types of syncopation are shown by the arrows in Example 4.9.

EXAMPLE 4.8   Syncopated patterns within a quarter-note beat

l e a   l e

EXAMPLE 4.9   Types of syncopated rhythms

(a) created by ties

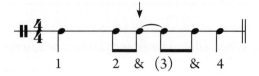

(b) created by rests

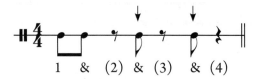

(c) created by accent marks

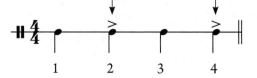

In Example 4.10, the arrows mark syncopations within the beat in measures 1 and 3 and across the beat in measures 2 and 4. Syncopations across the beat are usually notated with ties, like those in measures 2 and 4; here, the expected accent on beat 2 comes earlier, on the first of the tied notes. The arrows mark the offbeat accent.

EXAMPLE 4.10   Joplin, "Pine Apple Rag," mm. 1–4

In Example 4.11, from "American Pie," the syncopations span two beats in 𝄴 meter. The ♪ ♩ ♪ rhythm in measure 31, exactly doubles Joplin's ♬ ♩ pattern. The last syncopation in measure 31 of "American Pie" is created by the entrance of the word "love" on the offbeat.

EXAMPLE 4.11 McLean, "American Pie," mm. 30–31

Did you___ write the book of love___
(1)   2   &   (3) & (4) & 1   & (2) &   3

Syncopations require a strong sense of the underlying beat for the displaced accents to play against. When you read music with syncopations, look first for the common patterns, and use the counting syllables to count any unfamiliar ones. When performing, tap the steady beat to feel the metrical displacement of the syncopation.

TRY IT #3

The following rhythms are drawn from pieces discussed in this chapter. Write the counts beneath, and mark each syncopation with an arrow. All arrows should line up with e or a of the 1 e & a pattern. Perform the rhythm aloud.

(a) Joplin, "Solace," mm. 9–12

1 e & a

(b) Wand, "Dallas Blues," mm. 1–4

SHOW IT! Assignment 4.2

Triplets

In simple meters, it is possible to divide a beat into three parts instead of the usual two.

> **KEY CONCEPT** A **triplet** is a three-part division of the beat in a simple-meter piece.

Example 4.12 shows a passage from the Beach Boys' "Girls on the Beach." The piece is in ⁴⁄₄ meter, but in measures 11–12, three eighths are beamed together with a small 3 above the beam (♪♪♪). This indicates that three eighth notes make up the beat instead of two. We count the triplet here "2 la li" to emphasize the even division into three parts, and to avoid confusing it with the counts for division in two or four parts.

EXAMPLE 4.12   Wilson and Love, "Girls on the Beach," mm. 11–14

The   sun___ in her hair,   the warmth___ of the air,   on   a   sum - mer   day.

&   1   (2) la li 3 (4) &   1   (2) la li 3 (4)   1   2   3   4   1 (2   3   4)

You may also see triplets consisting of a quarter note and an eighth ($\sqcap^3$). The quarter substitutes for two eighths and is counted "1 li." The reverse ($\sqcap^3$) is counted "1 la." Example 4.13 summarizes the possibilities.

EXAMPLE 4.13   Notation of triplet divisions

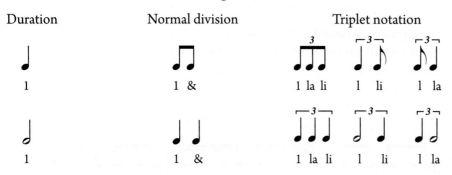

Duration	Normal division	Triplet notation		
1	1 &	1 la li	1 li	1 la
1	1 &	1 la li	1 li	1 la

In popular songs notated in $\frac{4}{4}$, you may encounter triplet patterns notated with quarter notes, as in Example 4.14. Because this type of triplet pattern spans two beats of the notated meter, these are called **two-beat triplets**. To count these triplets, you might imagine the passage in cut time, with the half note as the beat unit. Measure 22 of Example 4.14 would be counted as 1 la li 2 &.

EXAMPLE 4.14   Kander, Theme from *New York, New York*, mm. 20–23

I   wan - na   wake up   in   the   ci - ty that does - n't   sleep

(1)   &   2   &   1   &   2   &   1   la li   2   &   1   (2   3   4)

SHOW IT! Assignment 4.3

EXPLORE FURTHER
Rhythmic Variations in Performance

Blues, gospel, jazz, Broadway show tunes, and many other forms of popular music gain much of their character through their distinctive rhythm. A jazz improviser, for example, might take a simple but memorable melody and "jazz it up" by adding embellishments in rhythm and pitch. Gospel performance may also feature improvisation, and the pitches and rhythms you see on the score may differ substantially from what you hear. Listen to two versions of "Amazing Grace," while following the melody in your anthology (p. 364). In one performance, a verse sung by unaccompanied voice is followed by two verses with guitar. This arrangement is folk-like in its simplicity, and the singer performs the melody as shown in the score. In contrast, the other performance, by a lower voice and piano, is highly embellished. The singer freely improvises on the tune with additional pitches, variations in the rhythm, and repeated text to create a performance that is uniquely her own, while the pianist improvises an accompaniment to match.

> **KEY CONCEPT** In another common rhythmic variation, known as **swung eighths**, the score shows pairs of eighth notes in simple meter, but the performer plays or sings them unevenly, holding on to the first eighth a little too long and bringing in the second one after the &—as if they were notated as triplets (♩ ♪).

In jazz standards, such as "Look for the Silver Lining," shown in Example 4.15, rhythms notated in eighth notes may be performed swung, though performers may introduce other rhythmic variations as well. The exact lengths of swung eighth notes can vary; in a transcription (a score notated from a recorded performance), they may be notated as even eighth notes with the performance instruction "swung" or with triplet or dotted notation.

EXAMPLE 4.15   Kern, "Look for the Silver Lining," mm. 3–4

When you compose songs of your own, you might first create a simple melodic line with a basic rhythm, and then vary it—for example, delay a pitch or pull it ahead of the beat to make syncopations, or use triplets. When you analyze rhythmically elaborate music, be alert for the underlying simpler framework, and consider how the composer took something basic and made it memorable.

Did You Know?

Popular music includes many more syncopations than classical music. Syncopated and embellished melodies may imply a simpler underlying tune. Compare two published versions of a passage from "I Will Always Love You," shown next. The first represents the melody as sung by Dolly Parton, who composed this song; the second is a simpler version of the melody. For example, in Dolly's performance (a), she sings the word "I'll" early in measure 6, making it syncopated (coming in on the & of beat 3); in the simpler version (b), the same word lands squarely on beat 4. Parton also adds many embellishments that alternate between two pitches, such as in measure 8, and other variants intensifying the emotional expression of her performance. If you like, listen to Dolly Parton's performance and to another performance by Whitney Houston to compare how each embellishes the underlying simpler melodic outline.

Dolly Parton, "I Will Always Love You," mm. 7–8

(a) Published version 1:

I'll   think of   you   ev - 'ry   step   of   the __ way. _____

(b) Published version 2:

I'll   think   of   you   each   step _____   of the   way. _____

Terms You Should Know

beat subdivision	syncopation	triplet
slur	tie	two-beat triplet
swung eighths		

Questions for Review

1. What is the difference between a beat division and a beat subdivision?
2. Write seven rhythmic patterns that fill one quarter-note beat unit in simple meter.
3. In simple meter, what note value is generally paired with a dotted-quarter note to fill out the beat? What note value is generally paired with a dotted-eighth?
4. What guidelines are used to determine which notes to beam together?
5. What types of rhythmic patterns make syncopations?
6. How is a tie different from a slur?
7. How do you represent a three-part division of a beat in simple meters?
8. What note values represent a triplet division of a quarter-note beat unit? Of a half-note beat unit?

Reading Review

Match the term on the left with the best answer on the right.

_____ (1) 𝅘𝅥𝅯𝅘𝅥𝅯𝅘𝅥𝅯𝅘𝅥𝅯   (a) arc connecting the note heads of two identical pitches

_____ (2) tie   (b) arc connecting two or more different pitches

_____ (3) slur   (c) subdivision of a quarter-note beat

_____ (4) 1 e & a   (d) counting syllables for a common syncopation pattern

_____ (5) syncopation   (e) division of a quarter-note beat

_____ (6) 𝅘𝅥𝅮 𝅘𝅥   (f) counting syllables for a subdivided beat

_____ (7) triplet   (g) counting syllables for a triplet

_____ (8) 1 e a   (h) rhythmic displacement of accents

_____ (9) 1 la li   (i) beat division into three parts in simple meter

Apply It

A. Read rhythms

Perform the following rhythms on "ta" or counting syllables, as directed. Keep a steady beat by tapping the pulse or conducting, and follow the dynamic markings. Your teacher may ask you to write the counts below the rhythms.

Rhythm 1

Rhythm 2

Rhythm 3

Rhythm 4

Rhythm 10

Practice measure 3 by itself—first without, then with the ties. When performing the entire rhythm, make sure the quarter-note triplets sound identical to the tied eighth-note triplets.

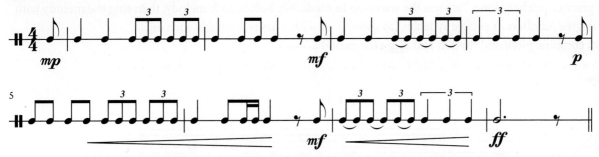

B. Read rhythms with a partner

Prepare each line of this duet. Perform it in class in groups with two different sounds (men vs. women, taps vs. claps, no vs. yes, etc.) so that the interplay between lines can be heard. Observe all dynamic markings. On your own, you can perform one part along with the recording of the other.

Duet

C. Sing at sight

- Before singing, always warm up your voice. Review Chapter 1, "Apply It" (p. 15).
- Practice rhythm alone. Tap or conduct with a steady beat. Chant on "ta" or rhythm syllables.
- Next, practice pitches alone. Perform the warm-up immediately before each melody, then sing the melody with scale-degree numbers or solfège syllables (as shown), or with a neutral syllable such as "la."
- Finally, combine pitch and rhythm and sing each melody.

Warm-up

Melody 1 Chris Kenner, "I Like It Like That," mm. 1–4

Melody 2 Frederick Loewe, "Wand'rin' Star," from *Paint Your Wagon* (adapted), mm. 1–4

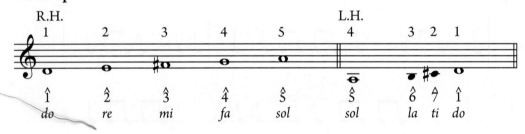

Warm-up

Melody 3 Erich Korngold, Theme from *King's Row*, mm. 1–4 (adapted)

Melody 4 Sid Wayne, "I Need Your Love Tonight," mm. 1–8

Warm-up

Melody 5 Isabella Leonarda, Credo, from *Messa Prima*, mm. 78–81

Melody 6 Clara Edwards, "Into the Night," mm. 3–6

Melodies 7 and 8 include quarter-note triplets. To perform these accurately, follow the strategy of Rhythm 10 (p. 85).

Melody 7 George David Weiss, Hugo Peretti, and Luigi Creatore, "Can't Help Falling in Love," from *Blue Hawaii*, mm. 5–12

Melody 8 Maurice Williams, "Stay," mm. 17–23

Listen and Write 4.1

A. Hearing and writing rhythms

Listen to rhythms made from two of the following numbered rhythmic patterns. Sing or tap what you hear, then write it on the staff provided.

1.
2.
3.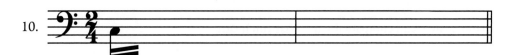
4.
5.
6.
7.
8.

Listen to the rhythms combined with pitches in the octave C to C. Sing what you hear, then write it on the staff provided.

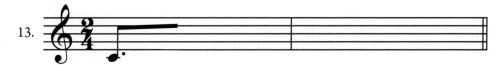

9.

10.

11.

12.

13.

14.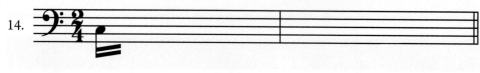

15.

B. Hearing and writing a melody

Listen to part of a melody by Thomas Bayly and complete the following exercises. The initial pitches and rhythm are given.

1. Memorize what you hear. In your mind you can replay it slower or faster.

2. Focus on the rhythm.
   - Tap your foot on the beat while singing the melody on a neutral syllable ("*la*").
   - Following the given pitches, write the remaining rhythm on the rhythm staff provided.

3. Musical Challenge: Write the pitches of the melody on the staff beneath the rhythm using the notes found in the Warm-up for Melody 1 on page 86. A helpful way to identify the pitches of the melody is to sing them with the solfège syllables or scale-degree numbers in the Warm-up.

4. Check your work. Perform your answer and compare it with what you heard.

Workbook ASSIGNMENT 4.1

A. Dots and ties

For each of the following rhythms, provide the missing bar lines that correspond with the meter signature given.

(1)

(2)

(3)

(4)

(5)

Rewrite the following rhythms with dots in place of tied notes. Be careful to beam your answers correctly. Write the correct counts beneath the rewritten rhythm, then perform it.

(6)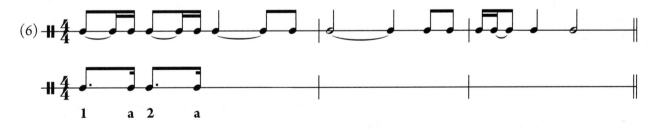

(7)

(8)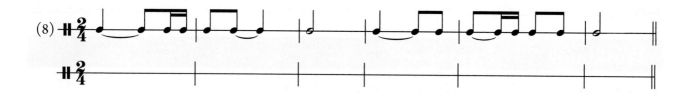

(9)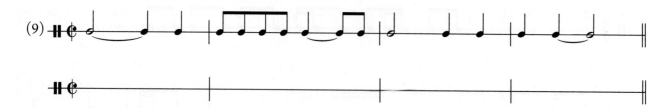

B. Beaming

Rewrite each of the following rhythms with correct beams to reflect the quarter-note beat unit. Add the proper counts beneath the rhythm and read the rhythm aloud on "ta" or with counting syllables.

(1)

1 & a 2 e &

(2)

(3)

Workbook ASSIGNMENT 4.2

A. Rhythms with divisions, subdivisions, dots, and rests

For each of the following rhythms, provide the missing bar lines that correspond with the meter signature given.

(1)

(2)

(3)

(4)

At each arrow, add one note to complete the measure in the meter indicated. For now, don't worry about beaming guidelines.

(5)

(6)

(7)

(8)

(9)

(10)

B. Counting rhythms with dots, ties, and syncopations

In the following melodies, write the appropriate counts beneath the notes. (Note: The final measure of a melody may be incomplete.) Place an arrow above each syncopation.

(1) Phillips, "Blues for Norton," mm. 1–3

(2) Carole King, "You've Got a Friend," mm. 5–8

When you're down ___ and trou - bled   And you need ___ some lov-ing care ___

(3) Antônio Carlos Jobim, "The Girl from Ipanema," mm. 13–19

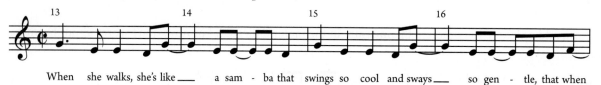

When she walks, she's like ___ a sam - ba that swings so cool and sways ___ so gen - tle, that when

___ she pass - es, each one ___ she pass - es goes "a–h–h!"

(4) Shania Twain, "You're Still the One," mm. 13–16

They said, "I bet ___ they'll ne-ver make it." But just look at ___ us hold-ing ___ on. ___

(5) James Horner, Barry Mann, and Cynthia Weil, "Somewhere Out There," mm. 27–28

it helps to think ___ we might ___ be wish - in' on the same ___ bright ___ star.

Workbook ASSIGNMENT 4.3

A. Syncopation and triplets

In each of the following examples, write an arrow above each syncopated rhythm. Then write in the appropriate counts below each rhythm.

(1) Frank Loesser, "Luck Be a Lady," from *Guys and Dolls,* mm. 3–6

They   call   you   La - dy   Luck   but   there   is   room   for   doubt   At

&   1   &   2   &   3   (4)   &

times   you   have   a   ver - y   un - la - dy - like   way   of   run - ning   out. ___

(2) Jim Weatherly, "Midnight Train to Georgia" mm. 6–12

L. A. ___   proved ___   too   hard   for the man,

so   he's   leav - in'   the life   he's   come   to   know.

B. Composition with dots, ties, and syncopations

Write a four-measure rhythm in $\frac{4}{4}$ that contains two syncopations (one using a tie), two dotted rhythms, and two rests.

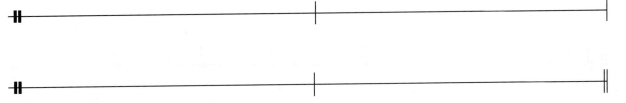

C. Triplets

Supply the missing bar lines corresponding to the meter shown in each of the following rhythms.

At each arrow, add one note to complete any measure with too few beats. Write the counts beneath your answer, then perform the rhythm you have written.

Major Scales and Keys

5

TOPICS

- Scales
- Major scales
- Scale degrees
- Writing major scales
- Major key signatures
- The circle of fifths
- Explore further: chromatic scales

MUSIC

- "The Ash Grove"
- Joseph Brackett, "Simple Gifts"
- Stephen Foster, "Oh! Susanna"
- John Philip Sousa, "The Stars and Stripes Forever"
- "Twinkle, Twinkle, Little Star"

Scales

Listen to the opening of a traditional Welsh folk song, "The Ash Grove" (Example 5.1). Following the melody (Example 5.1b) is a listing of its pitches, written from low to high, beginning and ending on E♭—an E♭ major scale.

EXAMPLE 5.1   "The Ash Grove," mm. 1–8

(a) Melody

(b) Pitches of the melody

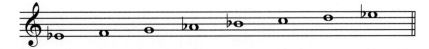

> **KEY CONCEPT** A **scale** is an ordered collection of pitches. When the primary pitches of a piece are written in ascending order without repetitions, they form a scale. Each note in a scale is separated from the next by a whole or half step. The first pitch is often repeated an octave higher at the end.

Major Scales

The ascending list of pitches in "The Ash Grove" (Example 5.1b) shows a mixture of whole (W) and half (H) steps.

> **KEY CONCEPT** The pattern of whole and half steps, W–W–H–W–W–W–H, forms an ascending **major scale**. If you play the scale starting at the top and descend, the pattern is H–W–W–W–H–W–W.

Because the scale in Example 5.1 begins and ends on E♭, we call it an E♭ major scale. Example 5.2 shows an ascending E♭ major scale with its whole and half steps labeled. Scales that are made up of half and whole steps, and include all seven letter names are **diatonic scales**. Half steps written with two different letter names (like those in diatonic scales) are called diatonic half steps.

EXAMPLE 5.2   E♭ major scale

Scale Degrees

Each pitch of the major scale is a **scale degree**, or scale step. The beginning, or tonic, scale degree is important in scales and musical works based on them, as a home base to which other pitches gravitate. When a piece is based on a scale with a particular tonic, we say it is "in the key of" that scale. For example, "The Ash Grove" is in the key of E♭ major.

> **KEY CONCEPT** When music is in a **major key**, its pitches come primarily from a major scale and its melody gravitates to the tonic of that scale.

Musicians often refer to scale degrees using numbers from $\hat{1}$ to $\hat{7}$, written with a caret (^) above. When singing music at sight, these scale-degree numbers can help you find your place in the scale. To keep track of tunes you hear or write, jot down the numbers as you sing or play, then translate the numbers into staff notation. Example 5.3 gives each scale step in C major and F Major, and Example 5.4 shows how to use these numbers to write the beginning of "Twinkle, Twinkle, Little Star." To write this melody in another key (F, for example)—known as **transposing** the melody—use the same degrees in that scale: F (= $\hat{1}$)–F–C (= $\hat{5}$)–C–D (= $\hat{6}$)–D–C, and so on, as Example 5.4b shows.

EXAMPLE 5.3   Scale-degree numbers and solfège syllables

(a) In C major

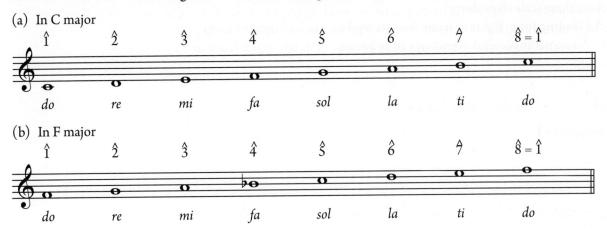

do   re   mi   fa   sol   la   ti   do

(b) In F major

do   re   mi   fa   sol   la   ti   do

EXAMPLE 5.4   "Twinkle, Twinkle, Little Star," mm. 1–4

(a) In C major

do do sol sol la la sol   fa fa mi mi re re do

(b) In F major

do do sol sol la la sol   fa fa mi mi re re do

Another method for sight-singing, **movable-do solfège** (or **solfège** for short), assigns each scale degree a syllable—*do, re, mi, fa, sol, la, ti, do*—as shown beneath the scale in Example 5.3. In the movable-*do* system, $\hat{1}$ is always *do*, $\hat{2}$ is always *re*, $\hat{3}$ is always *mi*, and so on—no matter which scale is used, as Example 5.4 shows.

> **ANOTHER WAY** A third method for sight-singing, called **fixed-do solfège**, always associates *do* with C, *re* with D, *mi* with E, *fa* with F, and so forth, regardless of the scale. Fixed-*do* solfège is analogous to singing letter names, while movable-*do* solfège is comparable to singing scale-degree numbers.

In addition to scale-degree numbers or solfège, musicians often refer to scale degrees by the names given in Example 5.5.

- $\hat{1}$ is called the **tonic**: it is the "tone" on which the scale is built.
- $\hat{2}$ is the **supertonic**: "super-" means "above" (as in "superhuman" or "superior"); its position is immediately above $\hat{1}$.
- $\hat{3}$ is the **mediant**: it falls midway between $\hat{1}$ and $\hat{5}$.
- $\hat{4}$ is the **subdominant**: "sub-" means "below" (as in "submarine"). $\hat{4}$ lies the same distance below the tonic as the dominant lies above. (Example 5.5b shows this relationship.)
- $\hat{5}$ is the **dominant**: its musical function "dominates" tonal music, as we will see.

- $\hat{6}$ is the **submediant**: it lies three scale steps below the tonic (mirroring the mediant, three scale steps above).
- $\hat{7}$ is the **leading tone**: it gets its name from its tendency to lead upward to the tonic; $\hat{7}$ is sometimes called a **tendency tone** because of its strong tendency to move up.

EXAMPLE 5.5   Scale-degree names

(a) Arranged $\hat{1}$ to $\hat{1}$

tonic   supertonic   mediant   subdominant   dominant   submediant   leading tone   tonic

(b) Arranged with $\hat{1}$ in the middle

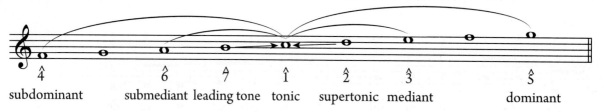

subdominant   submediant   leading tone   tonic   supertonic   mediant   dominant

Writing Major Scales

All major scales share the same pattern of whole and half steps between adjacent notes: W–W–H–W–W–W–H. An easy way to remember this pattern is to think of the position of half steps in a C major scale, which is made of the white keys from one C to the next. Another way to think of the scale's structure is to divide it into two four-note groups (or **tetrachords**) with a whole step between them, as shown in Example 5.6. These groups, each making the pattern W–W–H, are called **major tetrachords** because of their role in the major scale.

EXAMPLE 5.6   Major scale built from two major tetrachords

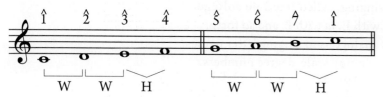

To write any major scale, follow the steps shown in Example 5.7, which builds the ascending D major scale.

1. Write $\hat{1}$ (which may or may not have an accidental).
2. Write the remaining seven notes (with no accidentals), one for each letter name, with $\hat{1}$ repeated at the top; these will fill one octave.
3. Write the interval pattern beneath the notes: W–W–H–W–W–W–H. (You could think of two major tetrachords, W–W–H, a whole step apart.)
4. Add accidentals if necessary to make the correct pattern of whole and half steps.

EXAMPLE 5.7   Steps to write an ascending D major scale

1. Write Î.

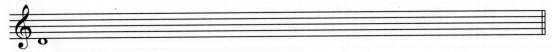

2. Add the remaining notes.

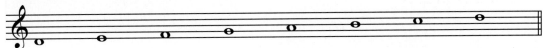

3. Write the interval pattern.

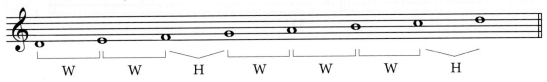

W   W   H   W   W   W   H

4. Add accidentals, if needed.

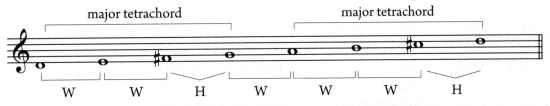

W   W   H   W   W   W   H

KEY CONCEPT Any major scale you write should include eight pitches—all seven letters plus the tonic repeated at the end—and the accidentals should be either all sharps or all flats, not a mixture.

In the B♭ major scale, for example, it would be incorrect to write D♯ instead of E♭ (Example 5.8a). This spelling would give both D and D♯ (a chromatic half step, instead of the diatonic D to E♭) and no E at all. Example 5.8b shows the correct spelling.

EXAMPLE 5.8   Notation of the B♭ major scale

(a) Incorrect:

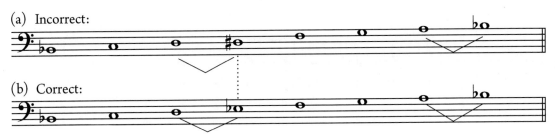

(b) Correct:

TRY IT #1

Write the ascending major scale beginning on each tonic pitch given.

(a)   (b)

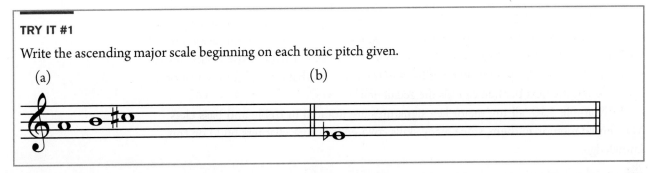

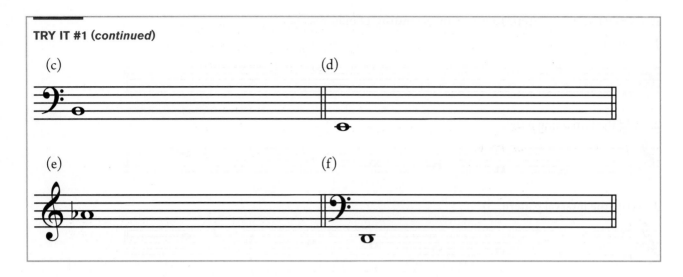

SHOW IT! Assignment 5.1

Major Key Signatures

Look at the melody of "Oh! Susanna," shown in Example 5.9, and examine the notation. This piece is in D major—whose scale includes two sharps—yet not a single accidental is notated next to any pitch. Instead, the **key signature** (circled) immediately following the clef sign instructs the performer to sharp every F and C throughout the song.

EXAMPLE 5.9   Foster, "Oh! Susanna," mm. 1–8

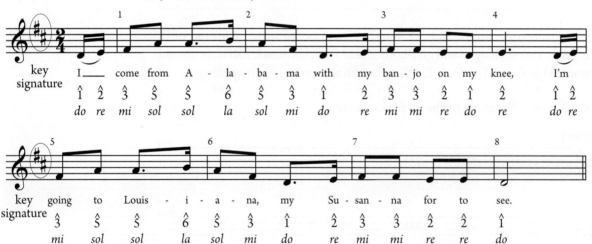

A key signature represents the sharps or flats of the scale on which the work is based, and applies to pitches in all octaves. The key signature, together with the scale-degree relationships between pitches, helps you determine the key of a piece. Occasionally, you may wish to alter a pitch by adding an accidental different from those in the key signature. Accidentals apply to all repetitions of the pitch (in that octave) for the rest of the measure; the next bar line cancels the accidental.

In Example 5.10, all the major key signatures are notated in treble and bass clefs. You should memorize them, since many skills covered in future chapters build on this knowledge.

In a musical score, the key signature appears on every staff and is always written between the clef sign and meter signature (in alphabetical order: clef, key, meter). In C major, the key signature has no sharps or flats.

EXAMPLE 5.10 Major key signatures

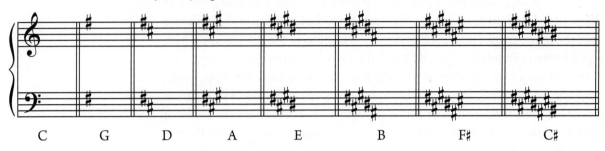

C   G   D   A   E   B   F♯   C♯

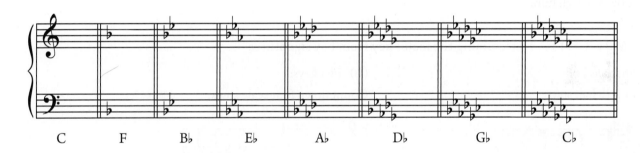

C   F   B♭   E♭   A♭   D♭   G♭   C♭

TRY IT #2

Write the key signature for the major keys specified, in both treble and bass clefs.

(a)

(b)

(c)

(d)

(e) 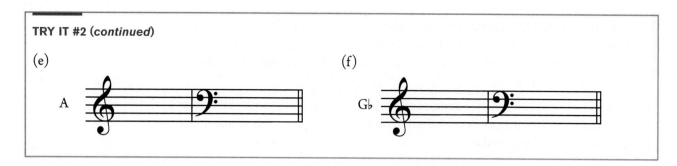 (f)

Although you should memorize which key signature goes with which key, you can also determine the key from the signature. For sharp keys, the last sharp of the signature is $\hat{7}$. To find the tonic, go up a diatonic half step. For example, in the key signature with four sharps (shown in Example 5.11a), if D♯ is $\hat{7}$, then E is $\hat{1}$, and the key is E major. For flat keys, the last flat of the signature is $\hat{4}$ of the key. Beginning with that note, count down four scale steps (as in Example 5.11b) to find the name of the key. As a shortcut (Example 5.11c), take the next-to-last flat of the signature: that will be the name of the key (for example, for B♭–E♭–A♭, the key is E♭). For F major, however, since there is only one flat (B♭), you have to count down four steps (Example 5.11d)—or better yet, memorize the signature.

EXAMPLE 5.11   Determining the major key from key signatures

(a) Sharp keys:

Count up a half step.

(b) Flat keys:

Count down four scale steps.

(c) Flat-key shortcut:

Next-to-last flat gives key name.

(d) F major:

Count down four scale steps.

In the blanks provided, identify the major key signature requested, using Examples 5.10 and 5.11 as your guide.

If a piece has two sharps in its key signature, you might assume it is in D major, but the key signature alone is not enough to identify the key. (Two sharps can also indicate B minor, as we will see in Chapter 7.) To tell the key of a piece, always check the beginning and end of the melody or bass line for scale-degree patterns like $\hat{3}$–$\hat{2}$–$\hat{1}$ or $\hat{5}$–$\hat{1}$. Look back at Example 5.9, the beginning of "Oh! Susanna," and at Example 5.12, the end of the song. The melody in Example 5.9 starts with a D, $\hat{1}$ in D major, and the first two measures emphasize $\hat{1}$–$\hat{2}$–$\hat{3}$ and $\hat{5}$–$\hat{3}$–$\hat{1}$. The end of the melody (mm. 15–16 of Example 5.12) is $\hat{3}$–$\hat{2}$–$\hat{1}$. These features indicate that the song is truly in D major.

EXAMPLE 5.12   Foster, "Oh! Susanna," mm. 13–16

TRY IT #4

Identify the key of "Simple Gifts" by answering these questions.

- The key signature suggests what key? _____
- What are the first six scale degrees? _____
- What are the last six scale degrees? _____
- Key of piece _____

Brackett, "Simple Gifts"

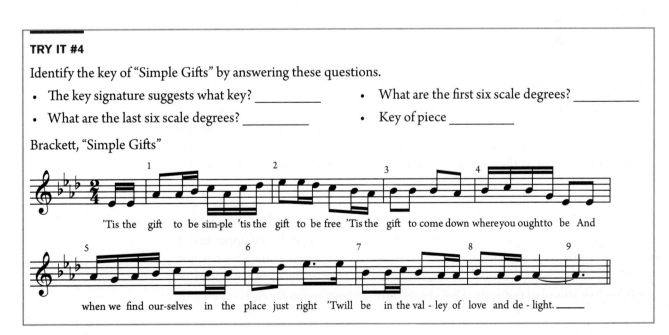

The Circle of Fifths

Example 5.13 is a handy aid for remembering the key signatures. On this diagram, each time a sharp is added, the new key is five steps higher than the last; and each time a flat is added, the key is five steps lower. C major has no sharps or flats. G major (five steps higher) one sharp, D major two sharps, and so on. This relationship between keys is represented by a circle, called the **circle of fifths**.

FCGDAEB

EXAMPLE 5.13   Circle of fifths

BEADGCF

The keys that require sharps appear around the right side, with each key (proceeding clockwise from C) a fifth higher. The keys that require flats appear around the left side of the circle, with each key (going counterclockwise from C) a fifth lower. After F (one flat), each key on the left side of the circle has a flatted note as the tonic (B♭, E♭, A♭, etc.).

Example 5.14 shows how the circle of fifths relates to scales when they are arranged by ascending or descending fifths. In Example 5.14a, each scale begins a fifth higher (C, then G, D, A). For each pair of scales related by ascending fifth, the upper major tetrachord of the first (e.g., for C major, G–A–B–C) is repeated as the lower major tetrachord of the next (G major), as the arrows show. Then an accidental is added to the upper tetrachord of this scale (D–E–F♯–G). This pattern recurs for each scale a fifth higher, adding one additional sharp for each scale. The flats follow a similar pattern, as scales are written a fifth lower. Follow the arrows in Example 5.14b to see which tetrachords remain the same and which have an added accidental.

EXAMPLE 5.14   Scales related by fifth

(a) Ascending by fifth

(b) Descending by fifth

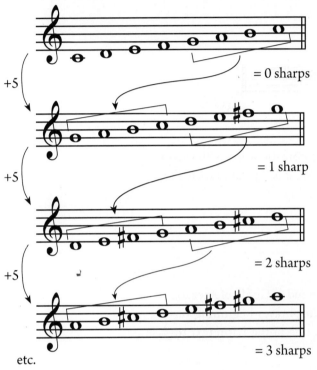

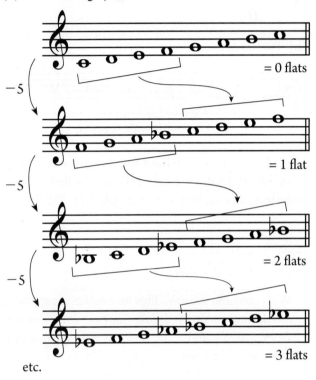

> **SHOW IT!** Assignment 5.3, 5.4

EXPLORE FURTHER Chromatic Scales

Scales in which all pitches are equally spaced a half step apart are called **chromatic scales**. Example 5.15 shows a complete chromatic scale, beginning on E♭, with all twelve possible pitches within an octave. Portions of this scale are often found in showy or virtuosic music, like the Sousa march of Example 5.16. Half steps written with the same letter name (like G♭–G♮) are called chromatic half steps because of their prevalence in the chromatic scale.

EXAMPLE 5.15   Chromatic scale, beginning on E♭

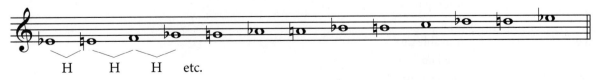

EXAMPLE 5.16   Sousa, "The Stars and Stripes Forever," mm. 1–4

(a) Melody

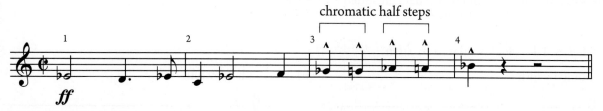

(b) Pitches of the melody

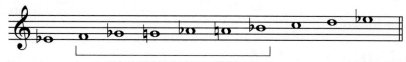

chromatic scale segment

Unless the first pitch has a flat, it is customary to spell chromatic scales with sharps ascending and flats descending. When the first note has a flat, it is typical to write flats and naturals ascending, as in Example 5.15, and flats descending.

Did You Know?

Who invented solfège? This innovation is usually attributed to Guido of Arezzo, an eleventh-century monk. Starting with a chant with phrases beginning on C, D, E, F, G, and A, he took the first syllable of each line of the Latin text to represent that note:

C: *Ut* queant laxis,
D: *Re*sonare fibris,
E: *Mi*ra gestorum,
F: *Fa*muli tuorum,
G: *Sol*ve polluti,
A: *La*brii reatum, Sancte Johannes

Since Guido's time, the system has been altered, changing *ut* to *do*, and adding a seventh syllable, *ti*, for the leading tone in major and minor keys.

Terms You Should Know

circle of fifths	mediant	tetrachord
key signature	subdominant	major tetrachord
major key	dominant	transpose
scale	submediant	
diatonic	leading tone	
major	solfège	
scale degree	movable *do*	
tonic	fixed *do*	
supertonic	tendency tone	

Questions for Review

1. What is the half- and whole-step pattern for an ascending major scale?
2. What systems can be used to label scale steps in a major scale? What are the characteristics of each?
3. What steps do you follow to write a major scale?
4. Why do we use specific spellings of pitches to notate a major scale? For example, why would an E♭ major scale include an A♭ and not a G♯?
5. List the order of sharps in the key signature for F♯ major.
6. List the order of flats in the key signature for C♭ major.
7. What major key has three sharps? Two flats? Five flats?
8. What do you need to consider besides the key signature to identify the key of a piece?
9. How is the circle of fifths organized, and what does it show?

Reading Review

Match the term on the left with the best answer on the right.

_____ (1) key signature	(a) has three flats in its key signature
_____ (2) circle of fifths	(b) order of sharps in a key signature
_____ (3) D major	(c) sharps or flats at the beginning of the staff (after the clef) that help determine the key
_____ (4) B–E–A–D–G–C–F	(d) order of flats in a key signature
_____ (5) fixed *do*	(e) pattern of half and whole steps in a major scale
_____ (6) W–W–H–W–W–W–H	(f) arrangement of key signatures by number of sharps or flats
_____ (7) major tetrachord	(g) has two sharps in its key signature
_____ (8) solfège syllables	(h) order of symbols at the beginning of the staff
_____ (9) E♭ major	(i) system where $\hat{1}$ is *do*; like reading scale-degree numbers
_____ (10) clef, key, meter	(j) *do–re–mi–fa–sol–la–ti*
_____ (11) F–C–G–D–A–E–B	(k) pattern of W–W–H in a major scale
_____ (12) movable *do*	(l) system where the note C is always *do*; like reading letter names

Apply It

A. Play and sing

1. Play the first five notes of a C major scale (with the W–W–H–W pattern), one note per finger, as shown in the diagram. Sing along with scale-degree numbers or solfège syllables, as shown below the example.

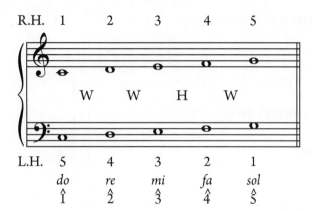
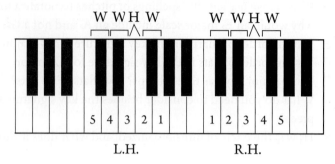

Beginning on each of the following pitches, play the five-finger pattern (W–W–H–W) in both hands at the same time in separate octaves. While playing, sing with letter names, solfège syllables, or scale-degree numbers.

a. A (A–B–C♯–D–E)　　b. F (F–G–A–B♭–C)　　c. G
d. E♭　　　　　　　　　e. B　　　　　　　　　 f. F♯
g. E　　　　　　　　　 h. C♯　　　　　　　　　i. A♭
j. B♭　　　　　　　　　k. D　　　　　　　　　 l. G♭

2. Beginning on each pitch specified in Exercise A.1, play a complete ascending major scale with the fingering shown. (Recall that each pitch must have a different letter name.) Play again and sing with solfège syllables or scale-degree numbers. Playing scales with this same fingering will help you remember the whole- and half-step "feel" of the pattern. (These fingers are only for remembering the pattern; they don't replace traditional scale fingerings used by keyboard players; see Appendix 8.)

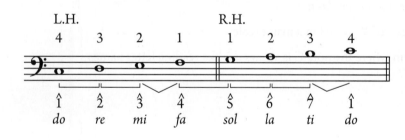
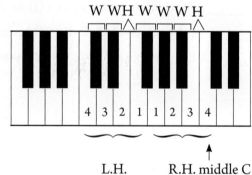

B. Sing at sight

Prior to singing a melody, perform the warm-up in its key. Sing each melody with scale-degree numbers or solfège syllables; the first few are given.

- Practice just the rhythm with counting syllables or a neutral syllable such as "*ta.*"
- Practice pitch alone, singing with a neutral syllable such as "*la.*"
- If you need help with a melodic skip, fill in the skip by singing the notes from the scale between the two notated pitches. Then sing only the skip without the filled-in notes.
- Practice singing the pitches with solfège syllables or scale-degree numbers.
- Combine pitch, solfège syllables, and rhythm.

Warm-up (Perform up and down.)

Melody 1 Richard Wagner, *Die Meistersinger,* Prelude to Act 3, mm. 16–20 (adapted)

Melody 2 Herman Hupfeld, "As Time Goes By," mm. 9–15

Warm-up (Perform up and down.)

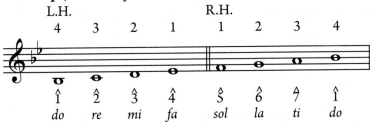

Melody 3 Harvey Worthington Loomis, "The Frog in the Bog," a round in three parts

To sing this melody as a round, divide into three groups. When group 1 reaches ②, group 2 begins the melody. When group 1 reaches ③, group 3 begins the melody.

f There once was a frog who lived in a bog and played a fid-dle in the
ŝ î 2̂ 3̂ 4̂ 5̂
sol do re mi fa sol

mid-dle of a pud-dle. What a mud-dle! Better go round! Better go round!

Melody 4 Traditional, "Come Follow Me," a round in three parts

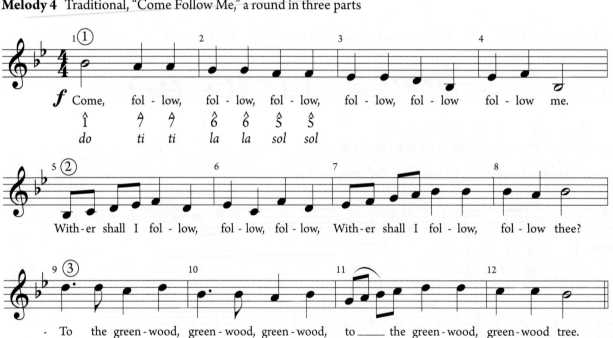

f Come, fol-low, fol-low, fol-low, fol-low, fol-low fol-low me.
î 7̂ 7̂ 6̂ 6̂ 5̂ 5̂
do ti ti la la sol sol

With-er shall I fol-low, fol-low, fol-low, With-er shall I fol-low, fol-low thee?

· To the green-wood, green-wood, green-wood, to ____ the green-wood, green-wood tree.

Warm-up

L.H.
4   3   2   1
R.H.
1   2   3   4

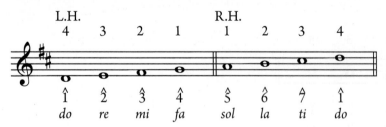

î 2̂ 3̂ 4̂ 5̂ 6̂ 7̂ î
do re mi fa sol la ti do

Melody 5 J. S. Bach, Musette, BWV Anh. 126, mm. 1–8 (adapted)

f 5̂ 4̂ 3̂ 2̂ 1̂
sol fa mi re do

p

f

p

Melody 6 Turlough O'Carolan, "Loftus Jones," mm. 1–8

1̂ 7̂ 6̂ 5̂ 4̂ 3̂ 4̂ 5̂ 3̂ 4̂ 3̂ 2̂ 3̂ 1̂
do ti la sol fa mi fa sol mi fa mi re mi do

Warm-up

R.H.
1   2   3   4   5   L.H.
                      4   3 2 1

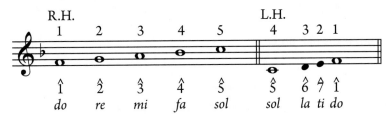

1̂   2̂   3̂   4̂   5̂   5̂   6̂ 7̂ 1̂
do re mi fa sol   sol la ti do

Melody 7 Clara Schumann, *Three Romances*, Op. 11, No. 3, mm. 1–8 (adapted)

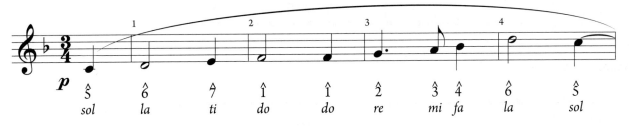

p 5̂   6̂   7̂   1̂   1̂   2̂   3̂ 4̂   6̂   5̂
sol   la   ti   do   do   re   mi fa   la   sol

C. Review rhythms

Perform the following rhythms on "ta" or counting syllables, as directed. Keep a steady beat by tapping the pulse or conducting, and follow the dynamic markings.

Rhythm 1

Rhythm 2

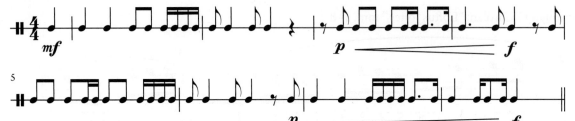

Rhythm 3

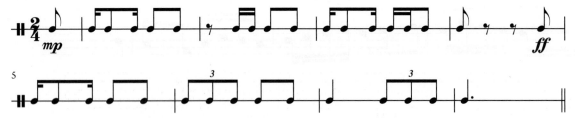

Cut time has two beats per measure and the beat unit is the half note.

Rhythm 4

Rhythm 5

Listen and Write 5.1

A. Review: Hearing half and whole steps

Listen to the recording. Beginning with the given pitch, a three-pitch melody will be played. In the blanks beneath each exercise, write W or H between pitches 1 and 2 and between pitches 2 and 3. Then notate pitches 2 and 3 with adjacent note names and the appropriate accidental.

B. Identifying whole and half steps in a melody

Listen to an excerpt from a carol, then identify the melody's whole and half steps. Write W or H in the blanks beneath the staff. Then use this information to write the appropriate accidental before the other notes.

C. Listening to and writing a major-key melody

Listen to an excerpt from a familiar melody, and complete the following exercises.

1. The excerpt consists of two five-note segments.
   - Notate segment 1's five-pitch melody with scale-degree numbers or solfège syllables above the staff provided. The melody begins on $\hat{1}$ (*do*) in C major.
   - Use this information to notate segment 1's pitches on the staff with open note heads. Don't worry yet about rhythm.
   - Between pitches, write W beneath whole steps and H beneath half steps.
   - Play your solution on a keyboard and compare with the recorded performance; correct any errors you hear.

Segment 1: $\hat{1}$ (*do*) _____ _____ _____ _____

2. Now notate segment 2's five-pitch melody with scale-degree numbers or solfège syllables above the staff provided.
   - The melody begins on $\hat{3}$ (*mi*).
   - Then notate segment 1's pitches on the staff with open note heads.
   - Between pitches, write W beneath whole steps and H beneath half steps.
   - Check your solution on a keyboard and correct any errors.

Segment 2: $\hat{3}$ (*mi*) _____ _____ _____ _____

3. On the following rhythm staff, write the rhythm of the entire melody (segments 1 and 2). Use correct notation, beaming, and bar lines. Then write the pitches and rhythm of the entire melody on the bass staff.

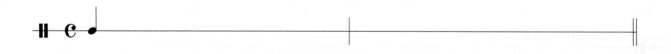

Segment 1   Segment 2

Listen and Write 5.2

A. Hearing scale segments

Listen to short melodies comprised of $\hat{1}$ to $\hat{5}$ of a major scale. Sing what you hear, then write it on the staff provided.

1.

2.

3.

4.

5.

B. Listening to and writing a major melody

Listen to an excerpt from a familiar melody, and complete the following exercises.

1. The excerpt consists of three segments, the first two of which are the same.
- Notate segment 1's five-pitch melody with scale-degree numbers or solfège syllables above the staff provided. The melody begins on $\hat{1}$ (*do*) in F major.
- Use this information to notate segment 1's pitches on the staff with open note heads. Don't worry yet about rhythm.
- Between pitches, write W beneath whole steps and H beneath half steps.
- Play your solution on a keyboard and compare with the recorded performance; correct any errors you hear.

Segment 1: $\hat{1}$ (*do*) _____   _____   _____   _____

2. Now notate segment 3's melody with scale-degree numbers or solfège syllables above the staff provided.
   - The melody begins on $\hat{1}$ (*do*).
   - Then notate segment 3's pitches on the staff with open note heads.
   - Between pitches, write W beneath whole steps and H beneath half steps.
   - Check your solution at a keyboard and correct any errors.

Segment 3: $\hat{1}$ (*do*) ____   ____   ____   ____   ____   ____   ____   ____   ____

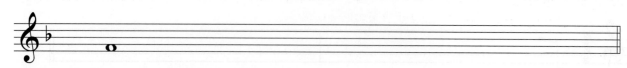

3. On the following rhythm staff, write the rhythm of the entire melody (segments 1, 2, and 3). Use correct notation, beaming, and bar lines. Then, write pitches and rhythm of the entire melody.

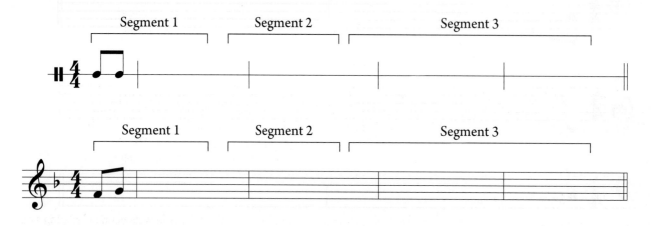

C. Listening to and writing an English folk round

Listen to this English folk round, and complete the following exercises. The melody is four measures long; each measure is a segment.
- The pitches of the first three segments consist of only scale degrees $\hat{1}$, $\hat{3}$, and $\hat{5}$. The fourth segment is a portion of a scale.
- Begin by focusing on the rhythm. Notate the rhythm for each measure on the rhythm staff provided.
- Then write scale-degree numbers or solfège syllables for the pitches under the rhythm staff. (You may abbreviate solfège: *d* = *do*, *s* = *sol*, etc.)
- Finally, combine this information to write the complete music notation on the staff.

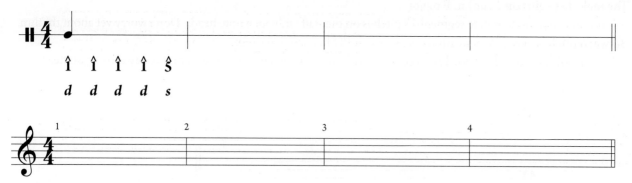

Workbook ASSIGNMENT 5.1

A. Writing ascending major scales

Beginning on the pitch given, build a major scale by adding flats or sharps to the left of the pitches as needed. Be sure to follow the correct pattern of whole and half steps shown.

(1) E♭ major

(2) D major

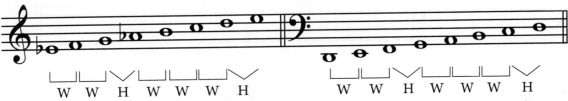

W W H W W W H

W W H W W W H

(3) F major

(4) E major

W W H W W W H

W W H W W W H

B. Writing major scales (ascending and descending)

Beginning on the pitch given, write an ascending and descending major scale. Write accidentals both ascending and descending.

(1) F♯ major

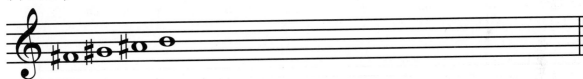

(2) A♭ major

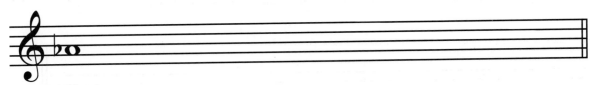

(3) C♯ major

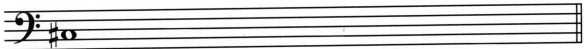

(4) D♭ major

C. Writing melodies from scale degrees

Each of the following sequences of scale degrees and solfège syllables represents a well-known melody. An underlined scale-degree number or solfège syllable indicates a note below the tonic.

- On the top staff, write the major scale specified for the scale degrees and solfège syllables shown.
- Use these labels to write the melody (with accidentals) on the lower staves. (Rhythm is optional.)
- If you know the name of the tune, write it in the blank provided (optional).

(1) A major

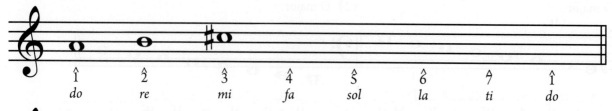

$\hat{1}$ $\hat{2}$ $\hat{3}$ $\hat{4}$ $\hat{5}$ $\hat{6}$ $\hat{7}$ $\hat{1}$

do   re   mi   fa   sol   la   ti   do

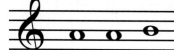

$\hat{1}$ – $\hat{1}$ – $\hat{2}$ – $\underline{\hat{7}}$ – $\hat{1}$ – $\hat{2}$ $\hat{3}$ – $\hat{3}$ – $\hat{4}$ – $\hat{3}$ – $\hat{2}$ – $\hat{1}$ $\hat{2}$ – $\hat{1}$ – $\underline{\hat{7}}$ – $\hat{1}$

do – do – re – <u>ti</u> – do – re   mi – mi – fa – mi – re – do   re – do – <u>ti</u> – do

Name of melody: _____

(2) B♭ major

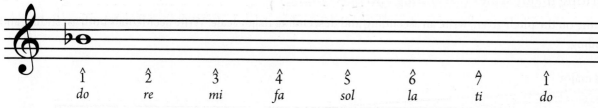

$\hat{1}$ $\hat{2}$ $\hat{3}$ $\hat{4}$ $\hat{5}$ $\hat{6}$ $\hat{7}$ $\hat{1}$

do   re   mi   fa   sol   la   ti   do

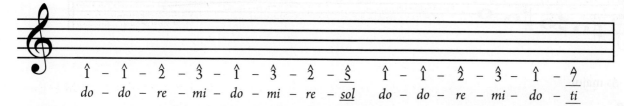

$\hat{1}$ – $\hat{1}$ – $\hat{2}$ – $\hat{3}$ – $\hat{1}$ – $\hat{3}$ – $\hat{2}$ – $\underline{\hat{5}}$ $\hat{1}$ – $\hat{1}$ – $\hat{2}$ – $\hat{3}$ – $\hat{1}$ – $\underline{\hat{7}}$

do – do – re – mi – do – mi – re – <u>sol</u>   do – do – re – mi – do – <u>ti</u>

$\hat{1}$ – $\hat{1}$ – $\hat{2}$ – $\hat{3}$ – $\hat{4}$ – $\hat{3}$ – $\hat{2}$ – $\hat{1}$ – $\underline{\hat{7}}$ – $\underline{\hat{5}}$ – $\underline{\hat{6}}$ – $\underline{\hat{7}}$ – $\hat{1}$ – $\hat{1}$

do – do – re – mi – fa – mi – re – do – <u>ti</u> – <u>sol</u> – <u>la</u> – <u>ti</u> – do – do

Name of melody: _____

Workbook ASSIGNMENT 5.2

A. Key signature warm-up

On the following staves, copy the seven sharps and seven flats in order in each clef. As you write each sharp or flat, say the name of the major key that goes with the number of sharps or flats that you've written so far.

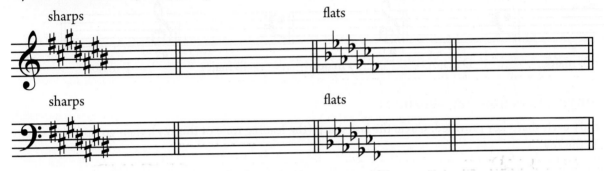

B. Writing key signatures

(1) Write the key signature for each sharp key indicated. Remember: Think one diatonic half step down from the name of the key; this note will be the last sharp.

(2) Write the key signature for each flat key indicated. Remember: Write one flat beyond the name of the key.

(3) Write the key signature for each major key indicated. Remember that the sharps and flats must appear in the correct order and octave.

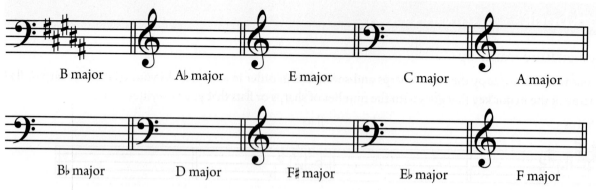

B major   A♭ major   E major   C major   A major

B♭ major   D major   F♯ major   E♭ major   F major

C. Identifying keys from key signatures

(1) Identify each sharp key provided. Circle the last sharp (the leading tone of the key), then go up a half step to name the key.

D _____   _____   _____   _____

_____   _____   _____   _____

(2) Identify each flat key provided. Circle the next-to-last flat to get the name of the key (_or_ go down four scale steps from the last flat).

E♭ _____   _____   _____   _____

_____   _____   _____   _____

(3) Identify the major key associated with each key signature provided.

B♭ _____   _____   _____   _____   _____   _____   _____

_____   _____   _____   _____   _____   _____   _____

Workbook ASSIGNMENT 5.3

A. Writing major scales from scale degrees

Given the scale degree notated on the left, write the appropriate ascending major scale. Begin by writing whole notes on each line and space above the scale degrees shown, then fill in the necessary accidentals.

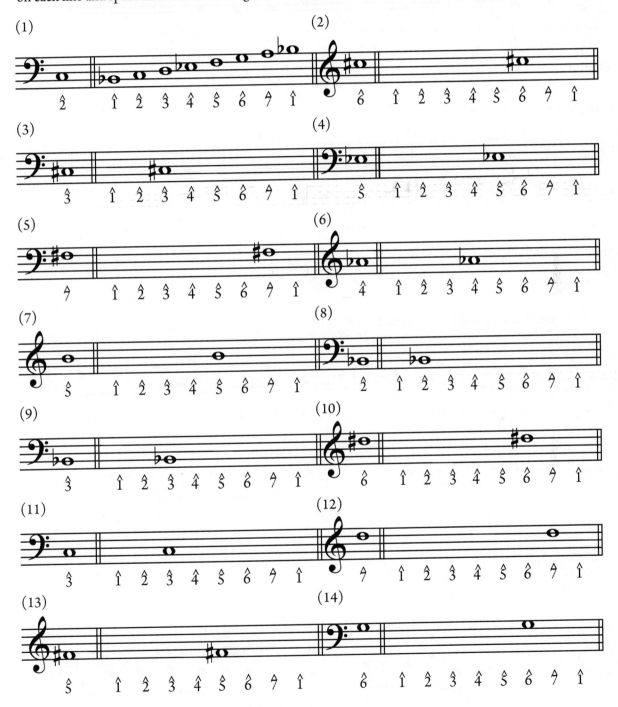

B. Identifying the key from a melody

Look at the key signature and melodic cues from the beginning and end of each song excerpt provided to determine the key. Write the name of the major key or "not major" in the blank. If major, label the scale degrees of the notes to confirm that they fit well in the key you have chosen.

(1) Elvis Presley, "Love Me Tender," mm. 5–8

Key: **G major**

(2) "Shalom, Chaverim," mm. 5–8

Translation: Peace until we meet again

Key: _____

(3) Walk the Moon, "Shut Up and Dance," mm. 10–14

Key: _____

(4) Billie Joe Armstrong and Green Day, "Boulevard of Broken Dreams," mm. 5–6

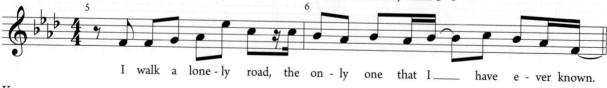

Key: _____

Workbook ASSIGNMENT 5.4

A. Writing major scales

Write the ascending or descending scales indicated, beginning with the specified pitch.

(1) D4 ascending

(2) F♯4 ascending

(3) A♭3 descending

(4) E♭3 ascending

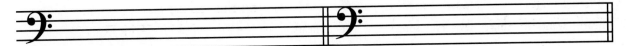

(5) B3 ascending

(6) F3 descending

(7) G5 descending

(8) E4 ascending

(9) D♭3 ascending

(10) B♭3 descending

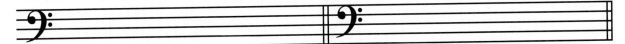

(11) C♯4 ascending

(12) C♭4 ascending

B. Identifying scale degrees in melodies.

Write the appropriate scale-degree numbers or solfège syllables above each note of the melody. Write the name of the key in the blank.

(1) Richard Rodgers and Oscar Hammerstein, "The Sound of Music," mm. 9–15

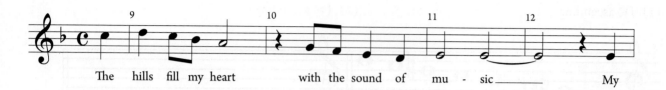

The hills fill my heart with the sound of mu - sic_____ My

heart wants to sing ev - 'ry song it hears.

Key: _____

(2) Don McLean, "American Pie," mm. 1–3. Hint: This melody begins and ends on $\hat{5}$ (*sol*).

A long, long time a-go I can still re-mem-ber how that mu-sic used to make me smile.

Key: _____

C. Scale-degree identification

Complete the table by writing the requested major key, scale degree, or pitch name.

Major Key	Scale Degree	Pitch
(1) E	$\hat{7}$	
(2)	supertonic	C♯
(3) F♯		C♯
(4) E♭	$\hat{3}$	
(5)	$\hat{4}$	G♭
(6)	leading tone	A

Major Key	Scale Degree	Pitch
(7) F	subdominant	
(8) D	leading tone	
(9)	$\hat{4}$	F♯
(10) B	$\hat{5}$	
(11) C	mediant	
(12)	$\hat{6}$	F

Compound Meters

6

KNOW IT? **Take the quiz to focus your studies.**

TOPICS

- Compound meters
- Meter signatures
- Subdivisions
- Duplets and syncopation
- Other compound meters
- Explore further: asymmetrical meters and changing meter

MUSIC

- "Agincourt Song"
- Béla Bartók, "Bulgarian Rhythm"
- Dave Brubeck, "Blue Rondo à la Turk"
- Christopher Cerf and Norman Stiles, "Dance Myself to Sleep"
- Stephen Foster, "Beautiful Dreamer"
- Patrick S. Gilmore, "When Johnny Comes Marching Home"
- "Home on the Range"
- Elisabeth-Claude Jacquet de la Guerre, Gigue, from Suite No. 3 in A Minor
- Gustav Holst, Second Suite in F for Military Band, "Song of the Blacksmith"
- Elton John, Bernie Taupin, and Davey Johnstone, "I Guess That's Why They Call It the Blues"
- Mozart, "Lacrymosa," from *Requiem*
- Smokey Robinson, "You've Really Got a Hold on Me"
- Lalo Schifrin, Theme from *Mission: Impossible*

Compound Meters

Listen to "When Johnny Comes Marching Home," while following Example 6.1. Tap the primary beat with your foot. The beat groups in twos; therefore the meter is duple. Now listen for the beat division and tap it with your hands; the beat divides into threes.

EXAMPLE 6.1   Meter in "When Johnny Comes Marching Home"

Counts	1			2			1			2			1			2			1	
Beats	tap			tap			tap			tap			tap			tap			tap	
Divisions	tap	tap	tap	tap	tap	tap	tap	tap	tap	tap	tap	tap	tap	tap	tap	tap	tap	tap	tap	etc.
Lyrics	When	John- ny	comes mar-			ching	home		a-		gain,	Hur-	rah! _____					Hur _____		rah!

Unlike triplets in simple meter—which occur only occasionally—the three-part division of the beat sounds all the way through the song. The meter is **compound duple**.

> **KEY CONCEPT** In **compound meters**, each beat divides into three parts. As in simple meters, the beats may group into twos (duple), threes (triple), or fours (quadruple); the conducting patterns for duple, triple, and quadruple compound meters are the same as for simple meters.

When counting beat divisions in compound meters, use the same syllables as for triplets: 1 la li 2 la li, and so on. Listen to "When Johnny Comes Marching Home" again, this time following Example 6.2. Sing along using counting syllables. This passage features three of the most common rhythmic patterns in compound meter: ♪♪♪ (counted 1 la li), ♩♪ (1 li) and ♩. (the beat unit). In compound meters, the beat unit is always a dotted note (since, for example, ♪♪♪ = ♩.).

EXAMPLE 6.2   Gilmore, "When Johnny Comes Marching Home," mm. 1–4

> **KEY CONCEPT** In compound meters with a ♩. beat unit, the beat divides into ♪♪♪ and subdivides into ♫♫♫.

Example 6.3 shows all the note values for compound meters with a dotted-quarter beat unit. The dotted-quarter note is the most common beat unit in compound meters.

EXAMPLE 6.3   Note values and rests in compound meters with a dotted-quarter (♩.) beat unit

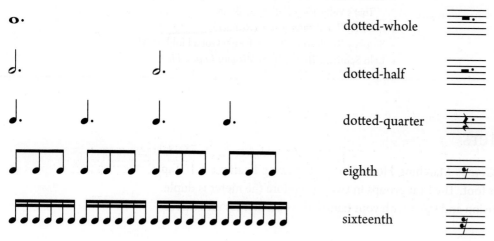

The chart in Example 6.4 gives typical rhythmic patterns in compound meters with a dotted-quarter beat unit. Patterns 1 to 3 only have divisions of the beat, while 4 and 5 include sixteenth-note subdivisions, and 6 is the dotted-quarter note, the beat unit itself. (Patterns 5 and 6 performed together may bring to mind the carol "Silent Night.")

Meter Signatures

In Example 6.2, "When Johnny Comes Marching Home," you may have noticed a new type of meter signature: $\frac{6}{8}$. While simple-meter signatures are straightforward—the top number indicates the number of beats in the measure, and the bottom one is the beat unit—compound-meter signatures require extra steps to interpret. A signature like $\frac{6}{8}$ would seem to indicate six beats per measure, with an eighth note getting the beat, but we have already seen and heard that the dotted-quarter note is the beat unit. In $\frac{6}{8}$, compound duple, there are only two beats per measure, and the numbers in the meter signature represent the beat division.

> **KEY CONCEPT** In compound-meter signatures:
>
> - The top number is 6, 9, or 12, representing duple, triple, or quadruple meter, respectively. Divide this number by three to get the number of beats per measure (two, three, or four). For example, in $\frac{6}{8}$ divide the number 6 by three to get two beats per measure.
> - The bottom number is usually 8, but may be 4 or 16. This number shows the note value of the beat *division*. Add together three of these note values to get the beat unit, which will always be a dotted note (♩., ♩., or ♪.). For example, in $\frac{6}{8}$ add together three eighth notes to get a dotted-quarter beat unit.

Example 6.5 shows an excerpt of a piece in $\frac{9}{8}$, Stephen Foster's "Beautiful Dreamer." To determine the number of beats per measure, divide the number 9 by three: there are three beats per measure. Therefore the meter is **compound triple**. To determine the beat unit, combine three eighth notes (bottom number) to get a dotted-quarter note.

EXAMPLE 6.5   Foster, "Beautiful Dreamer," mm. 5–8

Example 6.6, from Mozart's *Requiem*, is in $\frac{12}{8}$. This is **compound quadruple** meter, again with a dotted-quarter beat unit. As with simple meters, write counts in parentheses for rests or tied notes, as shown in the examples.

EXAMPLE 6.6   Mozart, "Lacrymosa," from *Requiem* (soprano part), mm. 3–4

La - - cry - mo - sa   di - - - es il - la.
1   (2) la li 3   4   1   (2) la li 3   4

The beat divisions in compound meters are performed strong-weak-weak: the beats are stressed and the divisions are not. This pattern gives compound meters their characteristic lilting sound. At the measure level, the metrical accents are the same as for simple meters: duple meters receive a stronger accent on beat 1 and a weaker one on beat 2; triple is strong-weak-weak, and quadruple is strongest-weak-strong-weak.

As in simple meters, a melody may begin with an anacrusis that precedes the first downbeat (see Example 6.2), and the final measure will then be incomplete to balance the anacrusis.

TRY IT #1

Look at the meter signature to determine how many beats are in each measure, then write the counting syllables beneath the melody.

(a)

1   li   2   li   (3) la li

(b)

(c) Cerf and Stiles, "Dance Myself to Sleep," mm. 9–13

Be - cause   I   get   up off my pil - low and   I flip   on the light___   I   get

down   and   get   hip___   in   the   still   of   the night _____

SHOW IT! Assignment 6.1

Subdivisions

In compound meters, each beat division further subdivides into two parts, just as in simple meters. Example 6.7 lists common subdivision patterns for $\frac{6}{8}$, $\frac{9}{8}$, and $\frac{12}{8}$, along with one system of counting syllables.

EXAMPLE 6.7   Common beat subdivisions in $\frac{6}{8}$

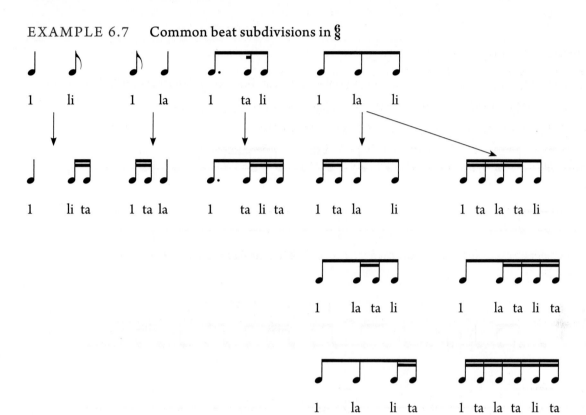

To read rhythms easily in compound meters, memorize these patterns with their syllables, and always beam them to reflect the beat, as shown in Example 6.7. Other patterns can be made by replacing eighth notes with sixteenths, by adding ties or dots, or by substituting equivalent rests.

> **KEY CONCEPT** Always notate rhythmic patterns with beaming that reflects the meter's beat groupings: $\frac{6}{8}$ ♪♪♪♪♪♪, not ♪♪♪♪♪♪.

Example 6.8a shows the melody of "Home on the Range" written with correct beaming. Compare this with the notation in Example 6.8b, which makes the beat unit unclear and the rhythm more difficult to read.

EXAMPLE 6.8   "Home on the Range" with correct and incorrect beaming

(a) Correct beaming

(b) Incorrect beaming

Oh, give me a home, where the buff - a - lo roam, Where the deer and the an - te - lope play —

TRY IT #2

Rewrite the following rhythms with correct beaming to reflect the beat. Practice the rhythms on "ta" or counting syllables and be prepared to perform them in class.

(a)

(b)

SHOW IT! Assignment 6.2

    Rests in compound meters should also be notated to reflect the beat and its division. Observe how the rests are written in the bracketed beats of Example 6.9: two eighth rests at the beginning of measure 7 reflect the beat division, and a dotted-quarter rest in measure 9 represents a full beat of silence. The rests in measure 11 are the most interesting; the two eighth rests finish out the second beat, while the quarter rest that follows makes clear that it belongs to beat 3. Although the notation of measures 7 (beat 1) and 11 (beat 3) differs, both are correct because the rests do not extend into the next beat.

EXAMPLE 6.9   Robinson, "You've Really Got a Hold on Me," mm. 6–11

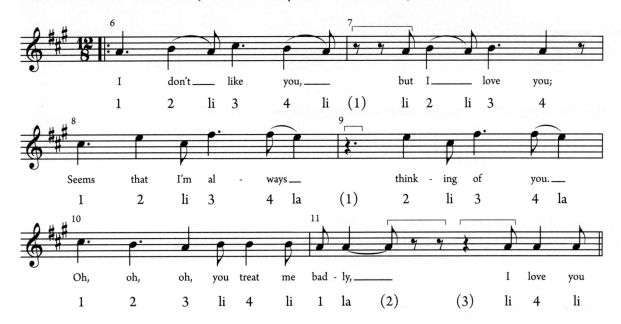

Duplets and Syncopation

While in simple meters you sometimes encounter triplets, which divide the beat into three parts instead of the usual two, the reverse is true in compound meters: you occasionally see a beat divide into two parts instead of the usual three. This two-part division is called a **duplet**. Look at Example 6.10 from "You've Really Got a Hold on Me." The melody is in $\frac{12}{8}$, with an overall triple division of the beat, but in measure 13, a duplet ("on me"), marked with a 2 above the beam, appears on the second beat. This beat is counted 2 &, just as two eighths would be in simple meter with a quarter-note beat. Here, the second half of the duplet is tied over to create a syncopation.

EXAMPLE 6.10   Robinson, "You've Really Got a Hold on Me," mm. 12–13

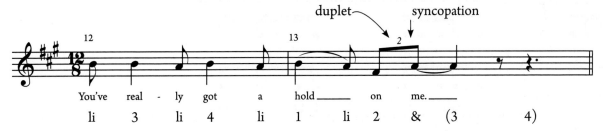

Syncopations in compound meters create offbeat accents in similar ways as in simple meters—with ties, accents, and rests. Three methods for writing syncopations in compound meters are shown in Example 6.11.

EXAMPLE 6.11   Types of syncopation in compound meters

(a) Ties from a weak part of a beat across a stronger part

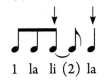

(b) An accent mark on a weak beat or the weak part of a beat

1 **la** li 2 la **li**

(c) A rest on the strong part of a beat that causes a weaker part to sound accented

(1) la

Example 6.12 shows syncopations in "I Guess That's Why They Call It the Blues." After the third beat of measures 22 and 23, a note that begins on the offbeat is tied over the fourth beat and is followed by another offbeat note. These syncopations sound like two-beat triplets, with three quarter notes dividing the two dotted-quarter beats evenly into three parts.

EXAMPLE 6.12 John, Taupin, and Johnstone, "I Guess That's Why They Call It the Blues," mm. 22–24

Typical syncopations created by ties within the beat are shown in Example 6.13, where the dotted-quarter note is the beat unit. Ties are often renotated, as shown in the example, so that an eighth note substitutes for two sixteenths tied together.

EXAMPLE 6.13   Typical syncopations within the beat in compound meters

1 ta   ta li   1 la ta   ta   1 ta   ta   ta

SHOW IT! Assignment 6.3

Other Compound Meters

The compound meters we have considered—$\frac{6}{8}$, $\frac{9}{8}$, and $\frac{12}{8}$—are by far the most common, but others are also possible. Listen to Example 6.14, a melody from fifteenth-century England, while following the notation. Here the lilting ♩♪ of $\frac{6}{8}$ is replaced with ♩♩ of $\frac{6}{4}$ in a meter whose beat unit is a dotted-half note (♩.). Example 6.15 lists various compound meters and shows typical patterns for each beat unit. The dotted-half and dotted-eighth beat units were more prevalent in music written before the nineteenth century than they are today.

EXAMPLE 6.14   "Agincourt Song" (England, c. 1415), mm. 1–4

EXAMPLE 6.15   Compound-meter signatures and typical patterns

Example 6.16 shows how "Home on the Range" would look if notated with three different beat units. The first version (a) is the familiar one, in ⁶⁄₈; the other two versions (b and c) feature dotted-eighth and dotted-half beat units. All three are counted the same, and if performed at the same tempo they would sound the same, though they look quite different.

EXAMPLE 6.16   "Home on the Range" with dotted-quarter, dotted-eighth, and dotted-half beat units

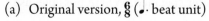

(a) Original version, ⁶⁄₈ (♩. beat unit)

(b) Written in $\frac{6}{16}$ ($\flat$. beat unit)

li   1   la   li   2   li ta   1   ta li   2   li ta   1   li ta   2   ta li   1   (2)

(c) Written in $\frac{6}{4}$ ($\sideset{}{}\downarrow$. beat unit)

li   1   la   li   2   li ta   1   ta li   2   li ta   1   li ta   2   ta li   1   (2)

Example 6.17 shows the opening of a keyboard piece by Elisabeth-Claude Jacquet de la Guerre. This $\frac{6}{4}$ movement has a dotted-half note beat unit and quarter-note beat division. Counts for the melody appear between the staves. (The symbols above and below some of the notes indicate ornaments, or embellishments, heard on the recording.)

EXAMPLE 6.17   Jacquet de la Guerre, Gigue, from Suite No. 3 in A Minor, mm. 1–6

1   li   2   la   li   1   li   2   ta   li   1   li   2   ta   li

1   li   2   1   2   1

TRY IT #3

For each rhythm, provide the missing bar lines that correspond with the meter specified. Where possible, use beaming to help you decide.

(a)

SHOW IT! Assignment 6.4

EXPLORE FURTHER
Asymmetrical Meters and Changing Meter

All the simple and compound meters we have studied so far are considered **symmetrical**, with the primary beats in each measure equally spaced. Listen to Bartók's "Bulgarian Rhythm," with its $\frac{5}{8}$ meter. Here the five eighth notes are divided into two uneven beats of a dotted-quarter note plus a quarter (as shown in the left hand in Example 6.18), creating an **asymmetrical meter**.

EXAMPLE 6.18   Bartók, "Bulgarian Rhythm," mm. 1–2

Now listen to Schifrin's Theme from *Mission: Impossible*, shown in Example 6.19. Its $\frac{5}{4}$ meter signature implies five quarter-note beats per measure, but the beaming and accent marks in the left hand indicate asymmetrical groupings of eighths as 3 + 3 + 2 + 2. Rather than counting this passage as five quarter-note beats, we hear four unequal beats (♩. ♩. ♩ ♩) in a driving, accented rhythm.

EXAMPLE 6.19   Schifrin, Theme from *Mission: Impossible*, mm. 1–2

Other asymmetrical meter signatures you might encounter are $\frac{5}{8}$, $\frac{5}{16}$, $\frac{7}{8}$, and $\frac{7}{16}$; meters with 5 as the top number are usually conducted in two uneven beats, those with 7 on top are generally conducted in three.

Even symmetrical meters may be divided asymmetrically. For example, $\frac{9}{8}$ may be divided into 2 + 2 + 2 + 3 eighth notes, as in Example 6.20. This example has four beats per measure, with the fourth slightly longer than the others. Unlike triplets in simple meters, the duration of the beat division in asymmetrical meters remains consistent. In Brubeck's melody, for example, every eighth note lasts the same amount of time. As a result, the fourth beat lasts longer than the others, as shown.

EXAMPLE 6.20   Brubeck, "Blue Rondo à la Turk," mm. 1–4

Finally, you might find more than one meter in a single piece. Look at Example 6.21, a band piece by Gustav Holst, where each measure has a different meter signature, as marked by arrows. This technique is called **changing meter**.

EXAMPLE 6.21   Holst, Second Suite in F for Military Band, "Song of the Blacksmith," mm. 7–10

Write the appropriate counts for each rhythm. Use "1 &" for a simple beat division and "1 la li" for compound. Practice performing each rhythm, keeping the beat division a consistent duration.

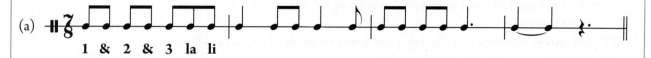

(a)   1 & 2 & 3 la li

(b)

(c)

(d)

Did You Know?

William "Smokey" Robinson (Examples 6.9 and 6.10) was inducted into the Rock and Roll Hall of Fame in 1987, in honor of his extended career as singer-songwriter with the Miracles and his role as talent scout and record producer. During his long association with Detroit-based Motown Records—once the largest black-owned company in the United States—and its founder, Berry Gordy, Robinson worked as songwriter and producer with the Miracles, the Temptations, and Marvin Gaye. Gordy took Robinson under his wing when the young artist was still a teenager, and he released the Miracles' first single when Robinson was eighteen. The group became a hit during the 1960s and early 70s, with such songs as "You've Really Got a Hold on Me," "I Second That Emotion," and "The Tears of a Clown." With Ronnie White of the Miracles, Robinson wrote "My Girl," which became a #1 hit for the Temptations. After splitting from the Miracles in 1972, Robinson enjoyed a strong solo career. In 1999, he received a Grammy Lifetime Achievement Award.

Terms You Should Know

compound meter   duplet
   compound duple
   compound triple
   compound quadruple

Questions for Review

1. Explain the difference between simple meter and compound meter.
2. How do you decide if a piece is in simple or compound meter?
3. How do you know whether a compound meter is duple, triple, or quadruple?
4. What do the upper and lower numbers of a meter signature represent in compound meters?
5. Which numbers may appear in the upper and lower positions of compound-meter signatures?
6. What are the most common compound-meter signatures?
7. In $\frac{6}{8}$ meter, how many beats does a dotted-half note last? A dotted-quarter?
8. If the beat unit is a dotted-quarter note, what note values represent the beat division and subdivision? If the beat unit is a dotted-half note?
9. What guidelines do you follow to decide which notes to beam together in compound meter?
10. Write four common rhythmic patterns that fill one dotted-quarter beat in compound meter.

Reading Review

Match the term on the left with the best answer on the right.

_____ (1) 1 ta li

_____ (2) $\frac{9}{16}$

_____ (3) beat subdivision in $\frac{6}{8}$

_____ (4) duplet

_____ (5) $\frac{6}{4}$

_____ (6) 1 la li

_____ (7) compound meter

_____ (8) $\frac{12}{8}$

_____ (9) 1 ta la ta li

_____ (10) dotted note

(a) type of note that gets one beat in compound meters

(b) type of meter where each beat divides into threes

(c) counting syllables for ♪ ♪ ♪ in $\frac{6}{8}$

(d) counting syllables for ♪. ♪ ♪ in $\frac{6}{8}$

(e) compound meter with four dotted-quarter beats per measure

(f) compound meter with three dotted-eighth beats per measure

(g) division of the beat in two parts in compound meter

(h) ♬♬♬

(i) compound meter with two dotted-half beats per measure

(j) counting syllables for ♬♬♪ in $\frac{6}{8}$

Apply It

A. Identify simple and compound meters

Listen to the following examples to determine whether they are in simple or compound meter, then circle your choice. Tap the beats with your foot and the beat divisions with your hand. Remember that simple-meter beats divide into twos and fours, while compound-meter beats divide into threes.

1. simple   compound

2. simple   compound

3. simple   compound

4. simple   compound

5. simple   compound

B. Read rhythms

Perform these common compound-meter patterns by tapping on the beat or conducting and chanting the rhythm on "ta" or with counting syllables, as directed.

Warm-up

Perform the following rhythms on "ta" or rhythm syllables, as directed. Keep a steady beat by tapping the pulse or conducting, and follow the dynamic markings.

Rhythm 1

Rhythm 2

Rhythm 3

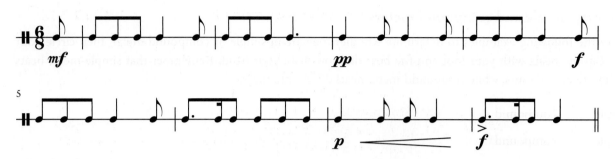

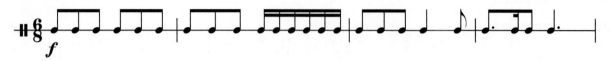

Rhythm 4

Rhythm 5

Rhythm 6

Rhythm 7

Rhythm 8

Perform with a partner. To help you practice, each voice is recorded individually.

C. Sing at sight

Prior to singing a melody, perform the warm-up in its key. Scale-degree numbers and solfège syllables are shown for the first few measures of each melody; continue singing using one of these systems.

Warm-up (Perform up and down.)

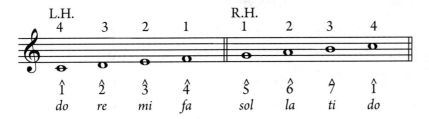

Melody 1 Harold Arlen and E. Y. Harburg, "We're Off to See the Wizard," from *The Wizard of Oz*, mm. 1–8

Melody 2 Traditional, "The Spinning Wheel"

$\hat{3}$ $\hat{2}$ $\hat{1}$ $\hat{1}$ $\hat{1}$ $\hat{7}$ $\hat{6}$ $\hat{5}$ $\hat{4}$ $\hat{3}$ $\hat{2}$ $\hat{1}$ $\hat{7}$ $\hat{1}$
mi re do   do do ti la   sol fa mi   re do ti   do

Melody 3 Traditional, "Whoopee Ti-Yi-Yo"

$\hat{1}$ $\hat{3}$ $\hat{1}$ $\hat{4}$ $\hat{2}$ $\hat{5}$ $\hat{3}$ $\hat{1}$
do   mi do   fa re   sol   mi do

Warm-up (Perform up and down.)

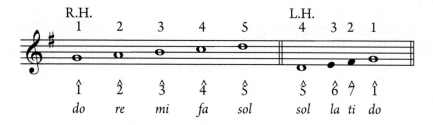

$\hat{1}$ $\hat{2}$ $\hat{3}$ $\hat{4}$ $\hat{5}$ $\hat{5}$ $\hat{6}$ $\hat{7}$ $\hat{1}$
do   re   mi   fa   sol   sol   la ti   do

Melody 4 Louise Reichardt, "Spring Flowers" ("*Frühlingsblumen*"), mm. 1–8 (adapted)

$\hat{3}$ $\hat{3}$ $\hat{4}$ $\hat{3}$ $\hat{4}$ $\hat{5}$ $\hat{3}$
mi   mi fa mi fa sol   mi

Melody 5 Philip P. Bliss, "Wonderful Words of Life," mm. 1–8

Moderato

mi   mi mi fa mi   mi   re   re

Melody 6 Jean-Paul-Égide Martini, "The Pleasure of Love" ("*Plaisir d'amour*"), mm. 1–8. The song "Can't Help Falling in Love" (p. 88) is based on this song.

sol   do   re   mi

Warm-up

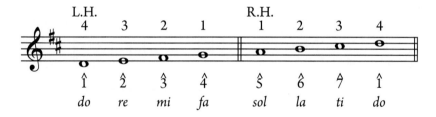

do re mi fa   sol la ti do

Melody 7 Ludwig van Beethoven, Sonatina, WoO, mm. 1–8 (adapted)

mi fa sol do do redo re mi do

Melody 8 Traditional, "Another Jig Will Do," mm. 1–4

$\hat{5}$ $\hat{6}$ $\hat{5}$ $\hat{5}$ $\hat{4}$ $\hat{3}$ $\hat{4}$ $\hat{5}$
sol la sol sol fa mi fa sol

Warm-up (Perform up and down.)

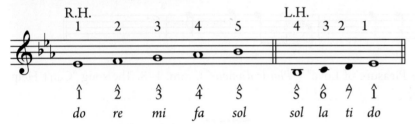

$\hat{1}$ $\hat{2}$ $\hat{3}$ $\hat{4}$ $\hat{5}$ $\hat{5}$ $\hat{6}$ $\hat{7}$ $\hat{1}$
do re mi fa sol   sol la ti do

Melody 9 Traditional, "Red Is the Rose"

$\hat{1}$ $\hat{1}$ $\hat{2}$ $\hat{3}$ $\hat{2}$ $\hat{1}$ $\hat{2}$ $\hat{3}$ $\hat{2}$ $\hat{1}$ $\hat{6}$
do   do   re mi   re do re   mi re   do la

Melody 10 Traditional, "Fanny Power"

Lively

$\hat{5}$ $\hat{1}$ $\hat{5}$ $\hat{1}$ $\hat{2}$ $\hat{3}$ $\hat{4}$ $\hat{3}$ $\hat{2}$
sol do sol do re mi fa mi re

Listen and Write 6.1

A. Writing rhythms in compound meter

Listen to rhythms made up of two patterns from those numbered 1–6. Sing or tap what you hear, then write it on the staff provided.

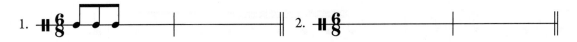

B. Hearing and writing melodies in compound meter

Listen to melodies made from the rhythm patterns combined with pitches in the octave extending from C to C (C–D–E–F–G–A–B–C). Sing what you hear, then write it on the staff provided.

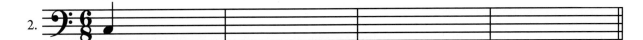

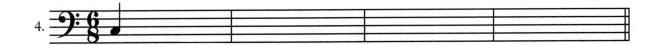

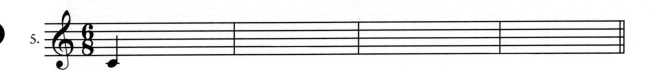

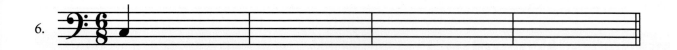

6.

7.

C. Listening to and writing folk songs

1. Listen to a melody and notate only its rhythm, using these patterns and ties.

Hints: Segments 1 and 3 have the same rhythm; 2 and 4 have different rhythms.

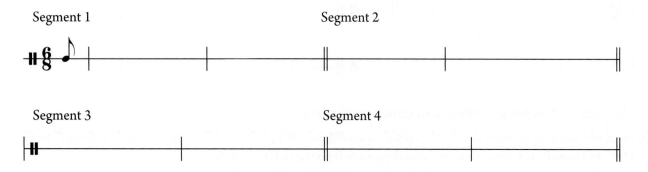

Segment 1   Segment 2

Segment 3   Segment 4

Of the six rhythmic patterns, which is the only one *not* part of the melody? _____

2. Listen to a melody and notate its pitches and rhythms on the staff, using the same patterns as in number 1. Use ties as needed. The beginning is given.

Hints: Segments 1–3 have the same rhythm; the rhythm for segment 4 is different. Writing scale-degree numbers or solfège syllables might help you recall the pitches. Each segment begins with an anacrusis.

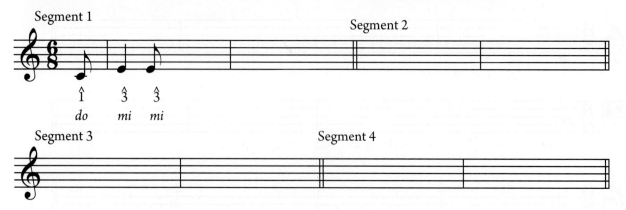

Segment 1   Segment 2

Segment 3   Segment 4

Workbook   ASSIGNMENT 6.1

A. Simple and compound meters

For each meter in the following chart, provide the meter type (e.g., simple triple), the beat unit, and the number of beats per measure.

Meter	Meter type	Beat unit	Beats per measure
$\frac{9}{8}$	**compound triple**	♩.	**3**
¢	_____	_____	_____
$\frac{12}{8}$	_____	_____	_____
$\frac{3}{4}$	_____	_____	_____
$\frac{2}{4}$	_____	_____	_____
$\frac{6}{8}$	_____	_____	_____

B. Understanding beats and divisions

For each rhythm or melody provided, write the counts below the staff.

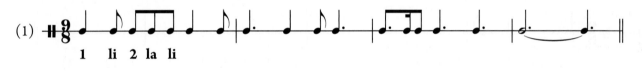

(1)

1   li   2   la   li

(2)

(3)

(4) Leigh Harline and Ned Washington, "Hi-Diddle-Dee-Dee," from *Pinocchio*, mm. 17–20

Hi - did - dle - dee - dee ____ An act - or's life for me ____

(5) Jerry Herman, "Before the Parade Passes By," from *Hello, Dolly!*, mm. 9–15

Go   and   taste   Sat-ur-day's high   life; ____ Be-fore the pa - rade ____ pas - ses by,

At each position marked by an arrow, add one note value to complete the measure in the meter indicated.

(6)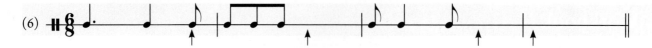

(7)

(8)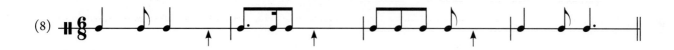

(9)

Notate the rhythm for each set of counts. Perform each rhythm after you've notated it.

(10)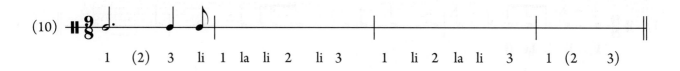

1 (2) 3 li 1 la li 2 li 3   1 li 2 la li 3   1 (2) 3)

(11)

1 la li 2 la   1 li 2 li 1 ta li 2   1 (2)

(12)

1 la li 2 ta li 3   4 li 1 li 2 li 3   (4) 1 la 2 li 3 (4)

(13)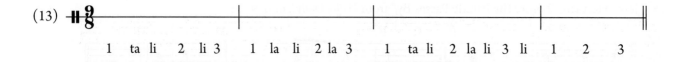

1 ta li 2 li 3   1 la li 2 la 3   1 ta li 2 la li 3 li 1 2 3

Workbook ASSIGNMENT 6.2

A. Divisions and subdivisions in compound meter

Write the counts beneath the staff, then perform each rhythm.

(1)

1 2 3 la ta li

(2)

(3)

For each melody, provide the missing bar lines that correspond with the meter signature given.

(4) Traditional, "The Butterfly"

(5) Fanny Mendelssohn Hensel, "Schwanenlied" (adapted)

(6) Ludwig van Beethoven, String Quartet in F Major, Op. 18, No. 1, second movement (cello part, adapted)

B. Understanding rests

Write the counts for the following melodies in the meter given. If the beginning of a beat coincides with a rest, write the count in parentheses.

(1) Wolfang Amadeus Mozart, "Sull'aria," from *The Marriage of Figaro*, mm. 2–6

Translation: On the breeze, what a gentle zephyr [will whisper].

(2) Handel, "Rejoice Greatly," from *Messiah* (alternate version), mm. 9–14

At each position marked with an arrow, add one rest to complete the measure in the meter indicated. Then add counts beneath the rhythms, and practice counting aloud. If a beat begins with a rest, write the count in parentheses.

(3)

(4)

(5)

(6)

Workbook ASSIGNMENT 6.3

A. Syncopation in compound meters

Indicate each syncopated rhythm with an arrow.

(1) Marc Shaiman and Scott Wittman, "It Takes Two," from *Hairspray*, mm. 6–7

They say it's a man's world. Well, that can - not ___ be de - nied. ___

(2) Andrew Lloyd Webber, "Memory," from *Cats*, mm. 17–20

Some - one mut - ters ___ and a street lamp gut - ters ___ and soon it will be morn - ing.

(3) Elton John, Bernie Taupin, and Davey Johnstone, "I Guess That's Why They Call It the Blues," mm. 12–15

And while I'm ___ a - way, ___ dust out ___ the de - mons in - side ___

B. Writing syncopations

Compose a syncopated compound-meter rhythmic round for performance with classmates. Begin by performing the following three-part round as an example. Divide into three groups; each new group begins when the previous group reaches ②. In your composition:

- Make the three lines distinctive, including rhythms that emphasize different beats or offbeats for contrast.
- Add a text and contrasting dynamics and accents in each line to create an interesting and musical effect in performance.
- Circle each beat in which syncopation occurs.

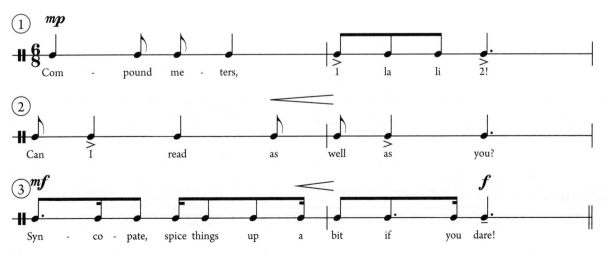

Com - pound me - ters, 1 la li 2!

Can I read as well as you?

Syn - co - pate, spice things up a bit if you dare!

Your composition:

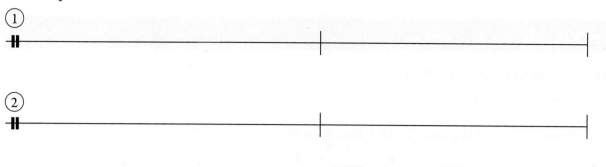

C. Beaming to reflect the meter

Rewrite the following rhythms with correct beaming to reflect the beat. Practice the rhythms on "ta" or counting syllables, and be prepared to perform them in class.

(4) George Frideric Handel, "How Beautiful Are the Feet of Them," from *Messiah*, mm. 5–6

How beau-ti-ful are the feet __ ofthem that   preach the gos-pel of peace,   How

Workbook ASSIGNMENT 6.4

A. Reading rhythms with ♩. and ♪. beat units

Each rhythm has a ♩. beat unit. Rewrite the rhythm on the blank staff with a ♪. beat unit (for example, convert $\frac{6}{4}$ to $\frac{6}{8}$).

(1)

(2)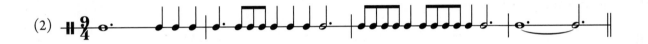

(3)

Jacquet de la Guerre, Gigue, from Suite No. 3 in A Minor, mm. 22–25

(4)

The following rhythm has a ♪. beat unit. Rewrite it with a ♩. beat unit.

(5)

B. Writing a rhythmic duet

Compose a rhythmic duet for two performers, using only these rhythmic patterns.

- Write eight measures in $\frac{6}{8}$ meter.
- Don't include ties. Use eighth, quarter, and dotted-quarter rests only.
- Vary the complexity: Both voices should sound together at times. At other times, when one voice is rhythmically active, the other voice may have rests or longer notes.
- Include dynamic markings to add musical interest.
- If you would like, write a text to be recited with your rhythm, or use "yes" and "no" as in Chapter 3.
- Be prepared to perform your composition with a partner.

Minor Scales and Keys

KNOW IT? **Take the quiz to focus your studies.**

TOPICS

- Parallel keys
- Natural minor
- Harmonic minor
- Melodic minor
- Comparing scale types
- Relative keys
- Minor key signatures and the circle of fifths
- Identifying the key from a score
- Explore further: major and minor pentatonic scales

MUSIC

- Johann Sebastian Bach, Invention in D Minor
- Arcangelo Corelli, Allemanda, from Trio Sonata in A Minor, Op. 4, No. 5
- Jim Croce, "Time in a Bottle"
- Patrick S. Gilmore, "When Johnny Comes Marching Home"
- Wolfgang Amadeus Mozart, *Variations on "Ah, vous dirai-je Maman"*
- John Newton, "Amazing Grace"
- Franz Schubert, Waltz in B Minor, Op. 18, No. 6
- Robert Schumann "Wild Rider"
- "Wayfaring Stranger"

Parallel Keys

Listen to the beginning of "Ah, vous dirai-je Maman" (otherwise known as "Twinkle, Twinkle, Little Star") and a variation on the melody by W. A. Mozart, and compare the right-hand parts shown in Examples 7.1 and 7.2. The beginning of Example 7.2 immediately signals a shift to the **minor mode** by its first three notes: C–D–E♭. The first five notes of the scale in each example—C–D–E–F–G in Example 7.1b and C–D–E♭–F–G in Example 7.2b—differ by only one note: $\hat{3}$ is lowered from E to E♭. (We write the third scale degree in minor as ♭$\hat{3}$ to show that it has been lowered when compared with major, even if the note itself does not have a flat.) These scale segments differ in their arrangement of whole and half steps: W–W–H–W in major becomes W–H–W–W in minor, as marked. Major and minor scales with the same tonic always share their first five notes, except that $\hat{3}$ becomes ♭$\hat{3}$. In the Mozart example, $\hat{6}$ also becomes ♭$\hat{6}$. This is usually the case in minor keys, but it may vary between scales, as we will see shortly.

EXAMPLE 7.1 Mozart, *Variations on "Ah, vous dirai-je Maman,"* mm. 1–8, melody only

(a) Melody

(b) Pitches of the melody

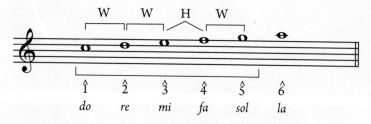

EXAMPLE 7.2 Mozart, *Variations,* Var. VIII, mm. 193–200, right-hand part only

(a) Melody

(b) Pitches of the melody

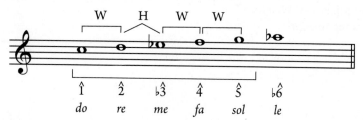

> **KEY CONCEPT** These melodies are written in **parallel keys**: C major and C minor. **Parallel major** and **minor** keys share the same tonic but have different key signatures and a different arrangement of whole and half steps.

The shared tonic between parallel keys is a powerful relationship. It is easy to move between these keys by changing the accidentals or key signature, as in the Mozart example. This shift is known as a **change of mode**.

Now look at the first five solfège syllables provided in Examples 7.1b and 7.2b. Sing $\hat{1}$, $\hat{2}$, $\hat{4}$, and $\hat{5}$ with the same syllables: *do, re, fa,* and *sol*; because the third scale degree differs, shift the syllable from *mi* in major to *me* in minor. (This system, called *do*-based minor, is only one of several for singing in minor keys. Your teacher may specify another.)

Natural Minor

One way to spell a **minor scale** is by taking the parallel major scale (Example 7.3a) and lowering $\hat{3}$, $\hat{6}$, and $\hat{7}$ one chromatic half step, to $\flat\hat{3}$, $\flat\hat{6}$, and $\flat\hat{7}$ (Example 7.3b). The result is known as the **natural minor** scale, with a W–H–W–W–H–W–W pattern. We refer to $\hat{3}$, $\hat{6}$, and $\hat{7}$ (with filled note heads in the example) as the **modal scale degrees** because they help distinguish between major and minor modes. Their solfège syllables reflect the change: *mi* becomes *me*, *la* becomes *le*, and *ti* becomes *te*.

EXAMPLE 7.3   Major scale and parallel natural minor

(a) C major

(b) C natural minor

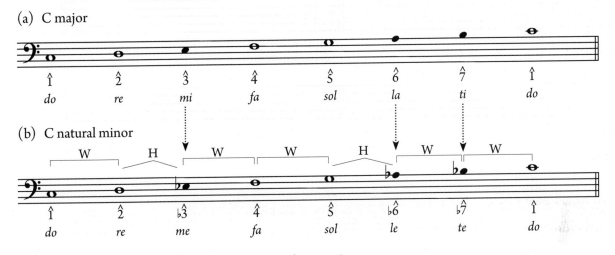

In major keys, there is a special "pull" from $\hat{7}$ up to $\hat{1}$, as the half-step tension of the leading tone wants to move up to the tonic (*ti* to *do*). In natural minor, there is no half-step pull between $\flat\hat{7}$ and $\hat{1}$ (*te* to *do*): these scale degrees are a whole step apart, a defining characteristic of the natural minor sound. Listen to Example 7.4a, in E minor, to hear the whole step D to E in measures 15–16. The E natural minor scale is written as in Example 7.4b. Here, $\flat\hat{7}$ (D) sounds relatively stable, and has none of the pull that a leading tone (D♯) would have to E.

EXAMPLE 7.4   Gilmore, "When Johnny Comes Marching Home"

(a) Measures 13–16

And we'll all feel gay When John-ny comes march-ing home. _____

(b) E natural minor scale

Write the specified major scale on the left-hand side in whole notes. Then rewrite the scale on the right-hand side, lowering $\hat{3}$, $\hat{6}$, and $\hat{7}$ to make a natural minor scale. Use accidentals instead of a key signature.

(a) F major   F natural minor

(b) B major   B natural minor

(c) A major   A natural minor

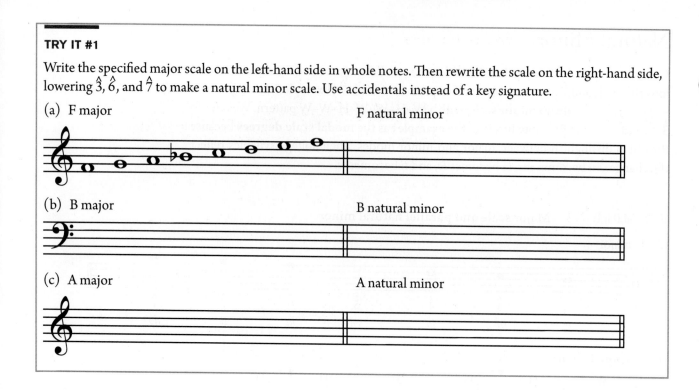

SHOW IT! Assignment 7.1

Harmonic Minor

Now listen to the first eight measures of a minor-key waltz by Franz Schubert, shown in Example 7.5. In measure 1, the upper voice outlines $\hat{1}$, $\flat\hat{3}$, and $\hat{5}$ of the minor scale beginning on B. Every A in Schubert's waltz (left hand, mm. 2, 4, 6, and 7), however, has a sharp, which converts $\flat\hat{7}$ to $\hat{7}$, the leading tone to B. Here, there is the upward pull of leading tone to tonic, just as in major keys.

EXAMPLE 7.5   Schubert, Waltz in B Minor, mm. 1–8

Example 7.6 shows the scale that corresponds with the waltz. This scale, known as **harmonic minor**, features the half-step relationship between $\hat{7}$ and $\hat{1}$ that was missing in natural minor. Because $\hat{7}$ now functions as a leading tone, we sing it on *ti* as in major (not *te*).

EXAMPLE 7.6   B harmonic minor scale

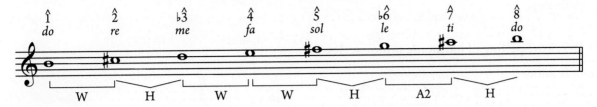

In this scale, the interval between ♭6̂ and 7̂ (*le* and *ti*)—G to A♯ in Example 7.6—is larger than a whole step. It is an **augmented second (A2)**, equivalent to a step and a half. Because of the unusual sound of the A2, harmonic minor is not typically heard in pieces *as a scale*. Instead, the leading tone will generally appear as part of the harmony (the underlying chords, see Chapter 9), as in the Schubert waltz—hence the name, harmonic minor.

Listen to the opening of Bach's Invention in D Minor (Example 7.7a), where ♭6̂ and the leading tone appear melodically. Here Bach places 7̂ (C♯) below ♭6̂ (B♭), in measures 1–2 and 5–6, to avoid the melodic A2. Example 7.7b shows how these scale degrees are typically handled: write 7̂ (*ti*) so that it moves up to 1̂ (*do*); write ♭6̂ (*le*) so that it moves down to 5̂ (*sol*).

EXAMPLE 7.7   Bach, Invention in D Minor, mm. 1–7 (right hand)

(a) Bach's melody

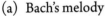

(b) Melodic separation of 7̂ from ♭6̂ (*ti* from *le*)

> **KEY CONCEPT** To write a harmonic minor scale, begin with natural minor and raise ♭7̂ a chromatic half step to make the leading tone (*ti*). If you begin with a major scale, lower 3̂ to ♭3̂ and 6̂ to ♭6̂, but leave 7̂ unaltered.

These alterations sometimes result in odd-looking combinations of accidentals, as in Example 7.8. Example 7.8a shows a scale with flats and a sharp, the result of raising ♭7̂ (F) to create a leading tone. The harmonic minor scale in Example 7.8b begins on a sharped note; such scales typically need a double sharp (×) for the leading tone.

Recall that a double sharp (×) raises a note one whole step; a double flat (♭♭) lowers a note one whole step.

EXAMPLE 7.8   Spelling of harmonic minor scales

(a) G harmonic minor

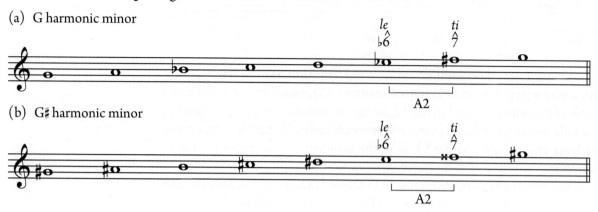

(b) G♯ harmonic minor

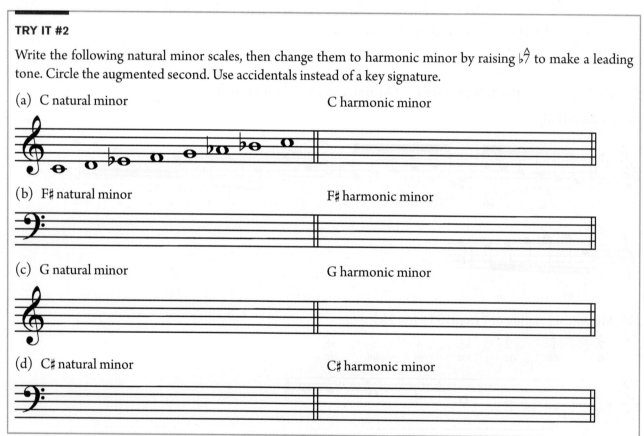

TRY IT #2

Write the following natural minor scales, then change them to harmonic minor by raising ♭$\hat{7}$ to make a leading tone. Circle the augmented second. Use accidentals instead of a key signature.

(a) C natural minor   C harmonic minor

(b) F♯ natural minor   F♯ harmonic minor

(c) G natural minor   G harmonic minor

(d) C♯ natural minor   C♯ harmonic minor

Melodic Minor

Yet another variant of the minor scale is **melodic minor**, which differs in its ascending and descending forms.

KEY CONCEPT Melodic minor is written with $\hat{6}$ and $\hat{7}$ when the scale ascends, reaching upward toward the tonic. In its descending form, it's written with ♭$\hat{7}$ and ♭$\hat{6}$ (like natural minor), pulling downward toward $\hat{5}$.

The left-hand part of the Mozart variation shown in Example 7.9, in C minor, illustrates how this scale is applied in music. In measure 197, Mozart raises $\flat\hat{7}$ to the leading tone (B♭ to B♮), but he also raises $\flat\hat{6}$ to $\hat{6}$ (A♭ to A♮) to avoid the potential augmented second (A♭ to B♮). In measure 198, $\flat\hat{6}$ (A♭) returns because the overall direction of the line here is downward.

EXAMPLE 7.9   Mozart, *Variations on "Ah, vous dirai-je Maman,"* Var. VIII, mm. 197–200

Example 7.10 shows the C melodic minor scale in its ascending and descending forms. Variability in the sixth and seventh scale degrees is typical in minor-key pieces. In C minor, the sixth may appear as A♭ or A♮, while the seventh may appear as B♭ or B♮ depending upon the context and the direction of the melodic line. Solfège syllables for the ascending form of melodic minor match those for major (*la–ti–do*), while syllables for the descending form match those for natural minor (*do–te–le*).

EXAMPLE 7.10   C melodic minor scale

Follow the bass line of Example 7.11, a song in D minor, to see the variability of the sixth and seventh scale degrees in a different musical context. The bass descends chromatically from the tonic D in measure 9 to $\flat\hat{6}$ (B♭) in measure 13. In measures 15–16, the line ascends back to D through the ascending melodic minor ($\hat{5}$–$\hat{6}$–$\hat{7}$, A–B♮–C♯).

EXAMPLE 7.11   Croce, "Time in a Bottle," mm. 9–16

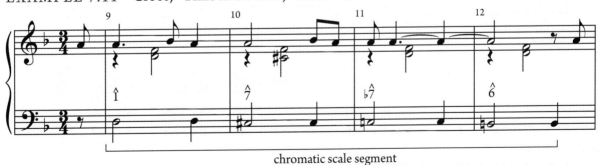

chromatic scale segment

melodic minor segment ($\flat\hat{6}$ descending, $\hat{6}$ and $\hat{7}$ ascending)

Comparing Scale Types

In Example 7.12, C major is aligned with all three forms of the C minor scale. Play each scale. To tell them apart by ear, listen first for the quality of the third ($\hat{3}$ or $\flat\hat{3}$; *mi* or *me*). Then listen for the leading tone: there is no leading tone in natural minor (but $\flat\hat{7}$ instead). In harmonic minor, there *is* a leading tone, and you will hear it approached by the A2 ($\flat\hat{6}$–$\hat{7}$, or *le–ti*). Finally, you hear $\hat{6}$ (*la*) only in major or ascending melodic minor.

EXAMPLE 7.12   Four scales beginning on C

(a) Major

(b) Natural minor

(c) Harmonic minor

(d) Melodic minor

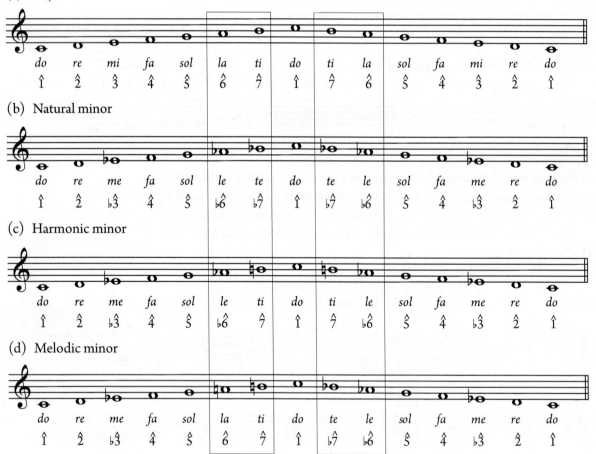

Scale-degree names in minor are identical to those in major (tonic, subdominant, etc.) with only a couple of exceptions. Scale-degree $\flat\hat{7}$ in natural minor is called the **subtonic** because of its placement a whole step below the tonic, and $\hat{6}$ in melodic minor is simply known as the **raised submediant**.

- To write a natural minor scale, write a major scale, then add accidentals to lower $\hat{3}$, $\hat{6}$, and $\hat{7}$ a chromatic half step; or write whole and half steps above the tonic in the pattern W–H–W–W–H–W–W (use each letter name once).
- To write a harmonic minor scale, begin with a natural minor scale and then raise $\flat\hat{7}$ to $\hat{7}$, ascending and descending.
- To write a melodic minor scale, begin with a natural minor scale and then raise $\flat\hat{6}$ and $\flat\hat{7}$ to $\hat{6}$ and $\hat{7}$ ascending only. The ascending form is like major, with $\flat\hat{3}$. The descending form is identical to natural minor.

TRY IT #3

Write the following melodic minor scales, ascending and descending. Use accidentals instead of a key signature.

(a) B melodic minor

(b) F melodic minor

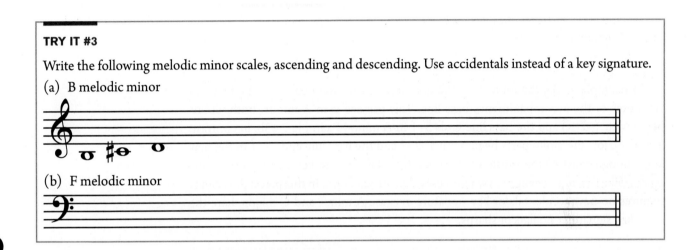

SHOW IT! Assignment 7.2

Relative Keys

Example 7.13 shows two phrases from a sonata by Corelli. Listen to the excerpts to determine the key of each passage. Also listen for $\hat{3}$ or $\flat\hat{3}$ to hear whether the key is major or minor.

EXAMPLE 7.13   Corelli, Allemanda, from Trio Sonata, Op. 4, No. 5

(a) mm. 1–3

(b) mm. 13–15

C major: $\hat{1}$ $\hat{5}$ $\hat{1}$

In Example 7.13a, the tonic is A, the first note of the violin part and the first and last notes of the accompaniment's bass line. This passage is in A minor: both violins begin with $\hat{1}$–$\hat{2}$–$\flat\hat{3}$ and the bass line ends $\hat{5}$–$\hat{1}$ in A minor. Example 7.13b, in contrast, is in C major: the violin parts begin with $\hat{1}$–$\hat{2}$–$\hat{3}$ and the bass line ends $\hat{5}$–$\hat{1}$ in the new key. Though most of the music we have studied stays in one key throughout, many pieces (like this one) change keys, a process called modulation. In this piece, the change requires no new accidentals or key signature because A minor and C major share the same key signature: no flats or sharps.

> **KEY CONCEPT** Keys that share the same key signature (but different tonics) are called **relative keys**.

Example 7.14 aligns the scales of the relative keys E♭ major and C natural minor to show how they are related: they share all the same notes but begin on different pitches.

EXAMPLE 7.14   E♭ major and C natural minor scales

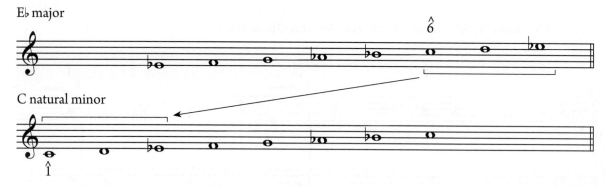

Every major scale has its **relative minor** scale, and every minor scale has its **relative major**. To find the relative minor of any major scale or key, identify $\hat{6}$ of the major scale: that pitch is the tonic of the relative minor. As Example 7.15 shows, the relative minor scale of G major is E minor.

EXAMPLE 7.15 Finding the relative (natural) minor

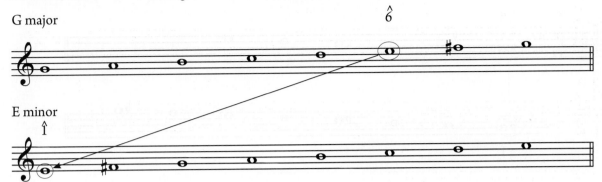

G major

$\hat{6}$

E minor

$\hat{1}$

ANOTHER WAY A shortcut for finding the relative minor key is to count *down* three half steps from the major-key tonic. Be sure to choose the correct spelling: it should conform to the key signature of the major key and span three different letter names. To find the relative minor of A major:

(1) Count down three letter names: A–G–F.
(2) Count down three half steps: A to A♭, A♭ to G, G to G♭.
(3) Change the spelling if it disagrees with step 1. We must respell G♭ as F♯, giving F♯ minor.

TRY IT #4

Given the major key or key signature, supply the name of the relative minor.

Major key	Relative minor	Major key	Relative minor
(a) E major	**C♯ minor**	(g) B♭ major	_____
(b)	_____	(h) C major	_____
(c) D major	_____	(i)	_____
(d) E♭ major	_____	(j) F♯ major	_____
(e)	_____	(k)	_____
(f)	_____	(l)	_____

To find the relative major of any minor scale or key, identify ♭$\hat{3}$ of the minor scale: that note is the tonic of the relative major. As Example 7.16 shows, the relative major of G minor is B♭ major.

EXAMPLE 7.16   Finding the relative major

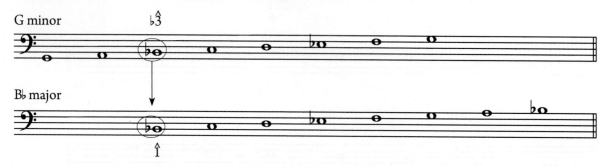

> **ANOTHER WAY** You can also find the relative major by counting *up* three half steps from the minor-key tonic. Again, choose a spelling three letter names away from the tonic. To find the relative major of F minor:
>
> (1) Count up three letter names: F–G–A.
> (2) Count up three half steps: F to F♯, F♯ to G, G to G♯.
> (3) Change the spelling if it disagrees with step 1. We must respell G♯ as A♭, giving A♭ major.

SUMMARY

- Parallel keys share the same tonic, but have different key signatures.
- Relative keys share the same pitches and key signature, but have different tonics.

Minor Key Signatures and the Circle of Fifths

Another way to write a natural minor scale is to think of the relative major and its key signature:

(1) Write the pitches from $\hat{1}$ to $\hat{1}$ of the minor scale without accidentals.
(2) Find its relative major.
(3) Write the key signature of the relative major next to the clef.

For harmonic or melodic minor, add the appropriate accidentals (e.g., a ♯ or ♮ for the leading tone).

For speed and facility in sight-reading and analysis, memorize the minor key signatures just as you have the major ones. The circle of fifths in Example 7.17 shows the key signatures shared by relative major and minor keys. It may help you memorize the minor key signatures. It may also help to remember that key signatures for parallel keys differ by three accidentals. For example, A major has 3 sharps, A minor has 0; B major has 5 sharps, B minor has 2; D major has 2 sharps, D minor has 1 flat.

EXAMPLE 7.17 Circle of fifths with major and minor keys and key signatures

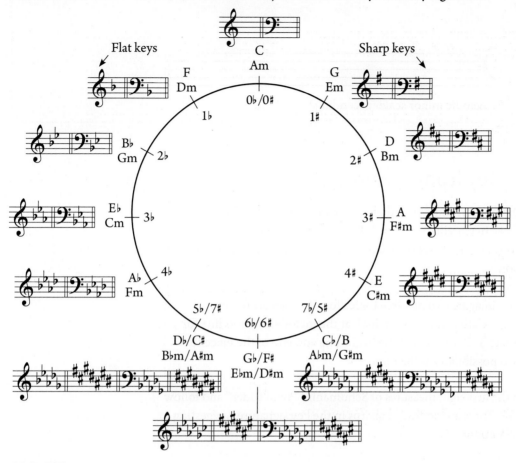

TRY IT #5

For each minor scale requested, first name the relative major key and write its key signature in the left-hand staff. Then, to the right, write the minor scale using that key signature plus accidentals to raise $\flat\hat{6}$ and $\flat\hat{7}$ as needed.

(a) F♯ harmonic minor

Relative major: **A**   F♯ harmonic minor scale

(b) E harmonic minor

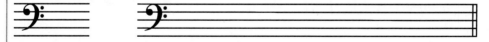

Relative major: ___   E harmonic minor scale

(c) B melodic minor

Relative major: ___   B melodic minor scale (ascending)

(d) B♭ melodic minor

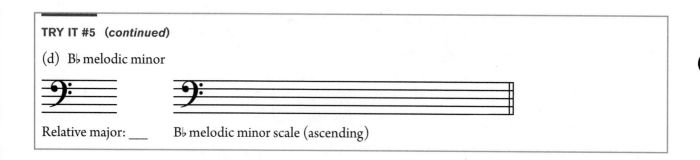

Relative major: ___   B♭ melodic minor scale (ascending)

Identifying the Key from a Score

Finally, since a key signature can indicate either major or minor, how do you know which is the key of a piece? In Corelli's Allemanda (Example 7.13), we interpreted the scale degrees of the melody and the bass line to determine which phrase was in A minor and which was in C major.

> **KEY CONCEPT** Always imagine two possible tonics for a key signature: one for major and one for its relative minor. Then look at the melody and bass line for scale-degree patterns like $\hat{3}$–$\hat{2}$–$\hat{1}$ or $\hat{5}$–$\hat{1}$ at the beginning and end of the piece to signal which of the two possibilities is the tonic.

To practice, listen to the first eight measures of Schumann's "Wild Rider," and follow the score in Example 7.18. There are no flats or sharps in the key signature, suggesting a key of either C major or A minor.

EXAMPLE 7.18   R. Schumann, "Wild Rider," mm. 1–8

Listen first for the lowest notes in the piano part (lower part of the grand staff): the first two measures feature a repeated A3 (the left hand is notated in treble clef) for two measures; it ends in measure 8 with A–E–A ($\hat{1}$–$\hat{5}$–$\hat{1}$ in A minor). The melody begins with E–A ($\hat{5}$–$\hat{1}$), then moves up to C ($\hat{1}$), and it ends with G♯–A ($\hat{7}$–$\hat{1}$ in A harmonic minor). This added accidental G♯, which appears throughout this excerpt as the leading tone to A, is a strong signal of a minor key. These features together confirm that the piece is in A minor rather than C major.

SUMMARY

To determine the key of a piece:

1. Look at the key signature and identify both the major-key and relative-minor-key tonics.
2. Look at the beginning and end of the melody and bass line for motion to or from one of these possible tonic pitches.
3. Look for an accidental that raises $♭\hat{7}$ to $\hat{7}$ to create a leading tone. This signals a minor key.

SHOW IT! Assignment 7.3, 7.4

EXPLORE FURTHER Major and Minor Pentatonic Scales

In addition to major and minor scales, folk, jazz, and popular musicians typically employ pentatonic scales. For an example, look at the melody for "Amazing Grace," shown in Example 7.19. In this melody, there are only five scale degrees, $\hat{1}$, $\hat{2}$, $\hat{3}$, $\hat{5}$, and $\hat{6}$ in G major. This is a major pentatonic scale; pentatonic means *five tones*. Since $\hat{4}$ and $\hat{7}$ are missing, there is no $\hat{7}–\hat{1}$ or $\hat{4}–\hat{3}$ half-step motion. Melodies based on the major pentatonic scale typically are accompanied by chords from the major scale.

EXAMPLE 7.19   Newton, "Amazing Grace," mm. 1–16

(a) Score

(b) G major pentatonic scale

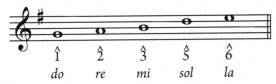

Listen to Example 7.20, "Wayfaring Stranger," another pentatonic melody. From the key signature, the sound of the melody, and the beginning and ending notes, you might guess that the tune is in D minor, but the melody includes only five notes of the D natural minor scale: $\hat{1}$, $\flat\hat{3}$, $\hat{4}$, $\hat{5}$, and $\flat\hat{7}$. This scale is known as **minor pentatonic**. Melodies based on the minor pentatonic scale are often harmonized with chords from the natural minor scale. These are not the only possible pentatonic scales; other pentatonic scales are heard in non-Western and popular music.

EXAMPLE 7.20 "Wayfaring Stranger"

(a) Score

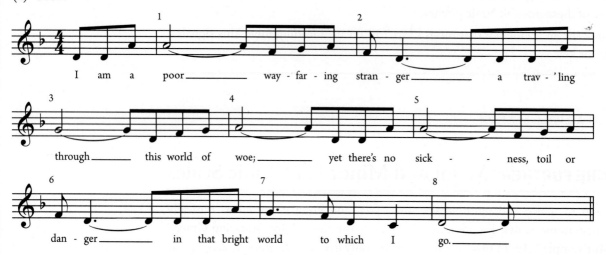

(b) D minor pentatonic scale

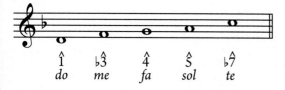

Example 7.21 compares the major and minor pentatonic scales beginning on C: both share C and G ($\hat{1}$ and $\hat{5}$), and each has the quality of the third associated with its name, major or minor.

EXAMPLE 7.21 C pentatonic scales

(a) Major pentatonic

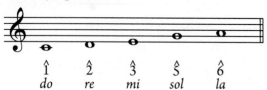

(b) Minor pentatonic

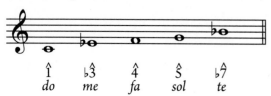

Like relative major and minor keys, there are major and minor pentatonic scales that share the same pitches, but have different tonic notes, as shown in Example 7.22.

> **KEY CONCEPT** One easy way to remember the pattern of the pentatonic scales is to think of the black keys on a piano. Play the black keys from F♯ to F♯ (or G♭ to G♭) as shown in Example 7.22 to make a major pentatonic scale with F♯ as tonic. Then play the same collection of black keys from D♯ to D♯ (or E♭ to E♭) to make a minor pentatonic scale with D♯ as tonic.

EXAMPLE 7.22   Black-key notes as major and minor pentatonic scales

(a) Major pentatonic scale starting on F♯

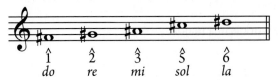

(b) Minor pentatonic scale starting on D♯

Did You Know?

Wolfgang Amadeus Mozart's father, Leopold, a well-known violinist and teacher, took Wolfgang and his older sister "Nannerl" on performance tours throughout Europe before Wolfgang was even ten years old. Mozart also began improvising and composing music while still a child (he wrote his first opera when he was eleven). He went on to write a number of well-loved operas, including *The Marriage of Figaro* and *The Magic Flute,* symphonies, string quartets, and many piano works, including several sets of variations. In a time long before recordings were possible, variations on well-known tunes (Examples 7.1 and 7.2) were popular. Composers and touring performers like Mozart sometimes would improvise variations as court entertainment. Listeners could then recognize the melody as it was embellished in different variations.

Terms You Should Know

augmented second (A2)	modal scale degree	scale-degree names in minor
change of mode	parallel keys	raised submediant
minor mode	parallel major	subtonic
minor scale	parallel minor	
natural minor	relative keys	
harmonic minor	relative major	
melodic minor	relative minor	

Questions for Review

1. Describe the relationship between parallel major and minor keys. Which scale degrees are different?
2. What are the differences between natural minor, melodic minor, and harmonic minor? Describe the steps to change a major scale to each form of minor.
3. Why is the harmonic minor scale rarely found in a melody?
4. How do you know whether to use the raised form of $\hat{6}$ and $\hat{7}$ in melodic minor?
5. What changes in solfège syllables and scale-degree numbers do you make for each form of minor?
6. What do relative keys share? How can this relationship help you to spell minor scales quickly?
7. Given a major key, how do you determine its relative minor? Given a minor key, how do you determine its relative major?
8. When looking at a musical score, how can you tell whether the work is in a major or minor key?

Reading Review

Match the term on the left with the best answer on the right.

_____ (1) $\hat{3}$, $\hat{6}$, and $\hat{7}$	(a) distance from $\hat{2}$ to $\flat\hat{3}$ in natural minor
_____ (2) half step	(b) differs from major by three modal scale degrees
_____ (3) natural minor scale	(c) D major and B minor
_____ (4) whole step	(d) D major and D minor
_____ (5) relative keys	(e) $\flat\hat{7}$ in a natural minor scale
_____ (6) raised submediant	(f) differs from natural minor by the raised leading tone
_____ (7) harmonic minor scale	(g) modal scale degrees
_____ (8) subtonic	(h) $\hat{6}$ in an ascending melodic minor scale
_____ (9) parallel keys	(i) pitches are the same as in natural minor
_____ (10) descending melodic minor	(j) distance from $\flat\hat{7}$ to $\hat{1}$ in natural minor

Apply It

A. Identify scale types

Listen to each melody and write its scale type in the blank. Choose from the following: major, natural minor, harmonic minor, or melodic minor.

1. _____
2. _____
3. _____
4. _____
5. _____
6. _____
7. _____
8. _____
9. _____
10. _____

Listen to the beginning of each excerpt to determine whether it is in a major or minor key. Write your answer in the blank.

11. Franz Schubert, Allegretto, D. 915   _____

12. Fanny Mendelssohn Hensel, "Waldeinsam"   _____

13. Franz Schubert, *Wanderer* Fantasy, Op. 15, Adagio   _____

14. Ludwig van Beethoven, Sonata for Violin and Piano, Op. 30, No. 2, first movement   _____

15. Joseph Haydn, Piano Sonata No. 9, Scherzo   _____

B. Sing and play

Five-finger patterns

1. Play each of these patterns in both hands (separately, then together). Sing on scale-degree numbers or solfège syllables as you play. Sing $\hat{3}$ (*mi*) in major and $\flat\hat{3}$ (*me*) in minor. Then play the same pattern beginning on five other pitches of your choice (or as your teacher directs). Be sure that the arrangement of whole and half steps remains the same.

Three types of minor scales

2. Play each of the following C minor scales while singing on scale-degree numbers or solfège syllables. Listen for the changes in sound (always in the right hand) as you move from natural to harmonic to melodic minor. Then play the same scales beginning on five other pitches of your choice (or as your teacher directs). Be sure that the arrangement of whole and half steps remains the same.

(a) Natural minor

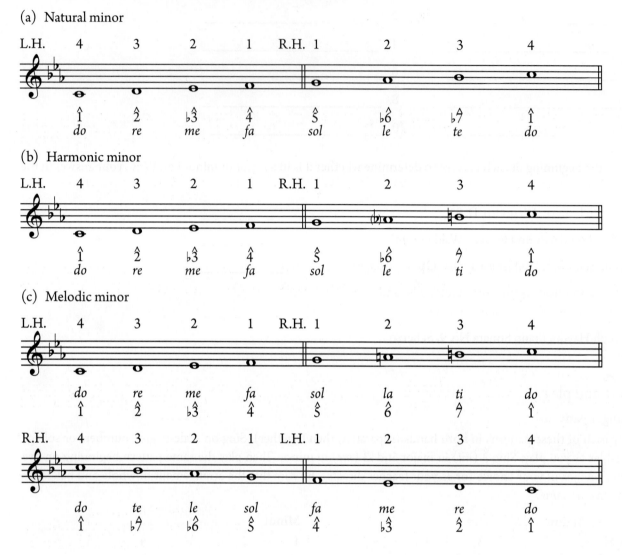

(b) Harmonic minor

(c) Melodic minor

C. Sing at sight

Before performing a minor-key melody, sing and play the warm-up, transposing it if necessary to the key of the melody. For a quick warm-up, perform measures 1–2.

- Natural minor: Perform as written and ignore the accidentals, scale-degree numbers, and solfège syllables in parentheses.
- Melodic minor: Perform with all the parenthetical accidentals, scale-degree numbers, and solfège syllables.
- Harmonic minor: Perform the parentheticals only on $\hat{7}$ (*ti*).

Warm-up

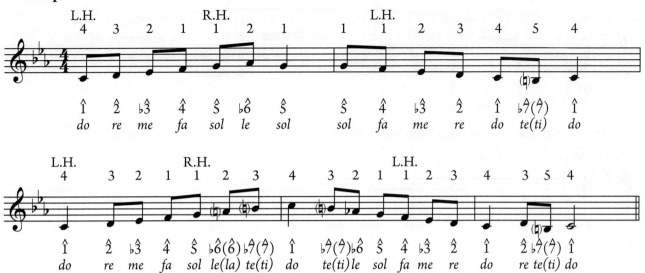

Melody 1 Ronald Blackwell, "Lil' Red Riding Hood," mm. 1–7

Melody 2

Melody 3 Traditional, "Once More My Soul," mm. 1–16

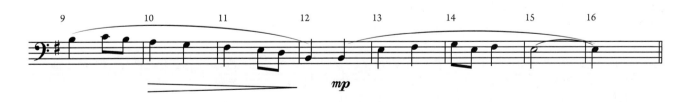

Melody 4 Scott Joplin, "Ragtime Dance," mm. 22–23

mp $\hat{5}$ $\hat{1}$ $\flat\hat{3}$ $\hat{5}$
sol do me sol

Melody 5 Traditional, "My Paddle's Keen and Bright" (Sing by yourself or as a two-part round.)

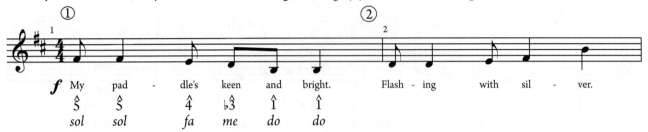

f My pad - dle's keen and bright. Flash - ing with sil - ver.
$\hat{5}$ $\hat{5}$ $\hat{4}$ $\flat\hat{3}$ $\hat{1}$ $\hat{1}$
sol sol fa me do do

Fol - low the wild goose flight, Dip, dip, and swing.

Melody 6 Richard Wagner, Minstrel Theme from *Tannhäuser* (adapted)

mp $\hat{5}$ $\hat{1}$ $\hat{2}$ $\flat\hat{3}$ $\hat{4}$ $\hat{5}$ $\hat{5}$
sol do re me fa sol sol

Melody 7 Traditional, "The Halting March," mm. 1–8

mf $\hat{1}$ $\hat{2}$ $\flat\hat{3}$ $\hat{4}$ $\hat{5}$ $\hat{5}$
do re me fa sol sol

f

Melody 8

mf $\hat{1}$ $\hat{2}$ $\flat\hat{3}$ $\hat{4}$ $\hat{5}$ $\flat\hat{6}$ $\hat{5}$ $\hat{5}$ $\hat{4}$ $\flat\hat{3}$ $\hat{2}$ $\hat{1}$ $\hat{7}$ $\hat{1}$
do re me fa sol le sol sol fa me re do ti do

Melody 9 Charles Gounod, "Funeral March of a Marionette," mm. 1–9 (adapted)

Melody 10 Shaun Welgemoed (aka Shaun Morgan), "Broken," mm. 1–4

D. Read rhythms in simple and compound meters

Perform the following rhythms on "ta" or counting syllables, as directed. Keep a steady beat by tapping the pulse or conducting.

Rhythm 1

Rhythm 2

Rhythm 3

Rhythm 4

Hint: Remember to conduct in two, as indicated by the "cut time" signature.

March

Rhythm 5

Read measures 1–4 (first ending, marked with a "1."); then repeat, this time skipping from measure 3 to the second ending in measure 4 (marked with a "2.") and continue to the end.

Allegro

NAME _____

Listen and Write 7.1

A. Hearing meter and scale type

Listen to the beginning of each excerpt to determine whether it is simple or compound and major or minor, then circle your choices.

1. Bach, Chaconne, from Violin Partita No. 2   simple compound   major minor

2. Schumann, "Trällerliedchen"   simple compound   major minor

3. Chopin, Nocturne, Op. 9, No. 2   simple compound   major minor

4. Bach, Minuet II from Cello Suite No. 1   simple compound   major minor

5. Brahms, Intermezzo, Op. 118, No. 2   simple compound   major minor

6. Holst, Second Suite for Military Band, mvt. 4   simple compound   major minor

7. Purcell, "Music for a While"   simple compound   major minor

B. Hearing and writing melodies in compound meter

- For each of the following melodies, focus first on the rhythm. Tap the beat or conduct (two beats per measure). On the rhythm staff, notate the rhythm.
- Now focus on the pitches. Below each rhythmic value you have notated, write the letter name, scale-degree number, or solfège syllable (your choice) for each pitch of the melody.
- Finally, notate both the rhythm and pitches in the key of C minor.

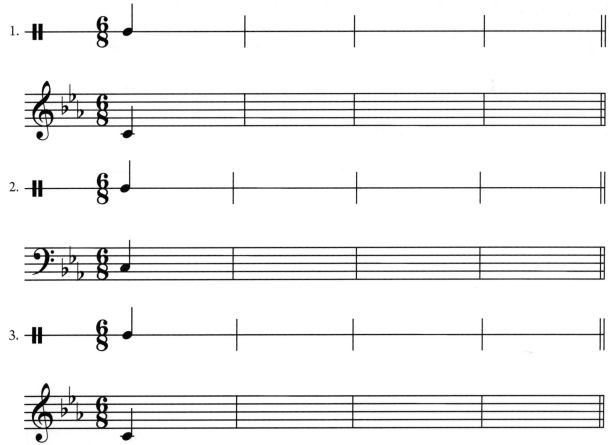

C. Identifying scales

Listen to a scale that begins with the first pitch given. Circle the scale type, then write appropriate accidentals before any pitches that require them.

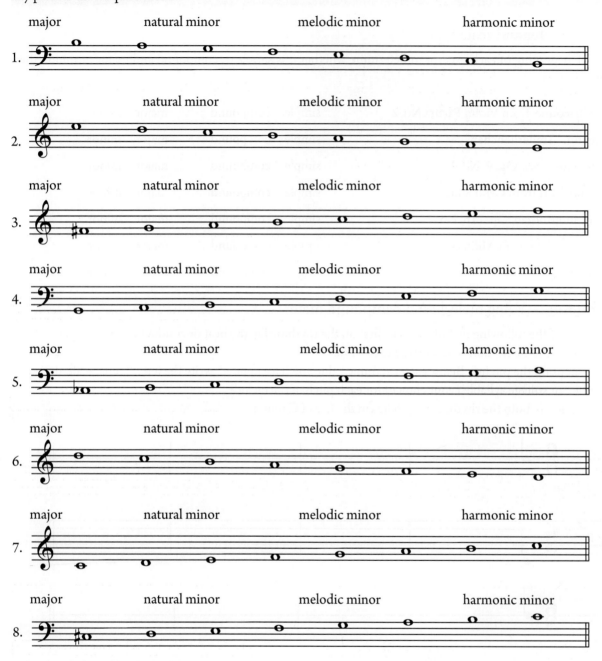

Listen and Write 7.2

A. Hearing and writing melodies in simple meter

Each melody begins on $\hat{1}$ (*do*) with the first two pitches and rhythms provided.

- Listen to determine whether the melody is in a major or minor key. On the treble or bass staff, notate the key signature for the major or minor key, based on the tonic note given.
- Notate the complete rhythm on the rhythm staff.
- Now focus on the pitches. Below each rhythmic value you have notated, write the letter name, scale-degree number, or solfège syllable (your choice) for each pitch of the melody.
- Finally, write the complete melody on the treble or bass staff.

1.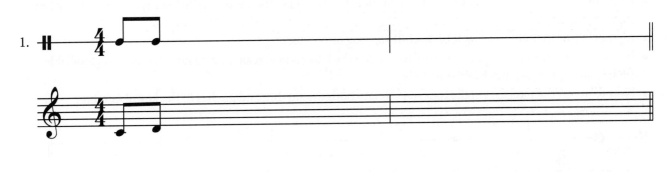

2.

3.

4.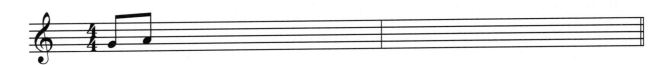

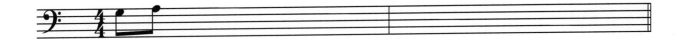

5.

B. Hearing and writing a folk song

Listen to the melody of a traditional American work song, and focus on both its rhythm and its pitches.

- Focus first on the rhythm. Tap the beat or conduct (two beats per measure). Write the rhythm on the rhythm staff.
- Memorize the melody and sing it back while tapping or conducting.
- Below each rhythmic value you have notated, write the letter name, scale-degree number, or solfège syllable (your choice) for each pitch of the melody.
- Now focus on the pitches. On the bass staff, notate both the rhythm and pitches in the key of G minor.

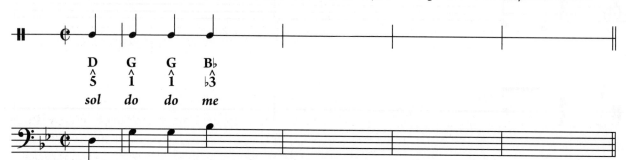

Now listen to the pitches of the bass line, the lowest part in the piano.

Which of the following patterns of scale-degree numbers or solfège syllables correctly represents the pitches of the bass line? Circle the correct answer.

a. $\hat{1}$–$\hat{7}$–$\flat\hat{6}$–$\hat{5}$; do–ti–le–sol

b. $\hat{1}$–$\flat\hat{7}$–$\flat\hat{6}$–$\hat{5}$; do–te–le–sol

c. $\hat{1}$–$\hat{7}$–$\hat{6}$–$\hat{5}$; do–ti–la–sol

Beginning on $\hat{1}$ (do), write the first four pitches of the bass line in the blanks with letters, scale-degree numbers, and solfège syllables. Then write the first four pitches in half notes in the key of G minor on the staff provided.

Workbook ASSIGNMENT 7.1

A. Parallel major and natural minor

The first five notes of a major or minor scale are given. In the blank provided, identify the scale as "major" or "minor."

(1)

_____**minor**_____

(2)

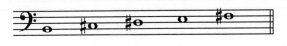

_____

(3)

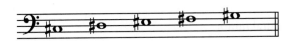

_____

(4)

_____

(5)

_____

(6)

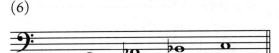

_____

Write each specified major scale, using accidentals rather than a key signature. Next to each major scale, write its parallel natural minor scale (change $\hat{3}$, $\hat{6}$, and $\hat{7}$ to $\flat\hat{3}$, $\flat\hat{6}$, and $\flat\hat{7}$); use accidentals as needed to reflect differences between major and natural minor. Write either scale-degree numbers or solfège syllables beneath the minor scale.

(7) D major   D natural minor

(8) C♯ major   C♯ natural minor

(9) E major   E natural minor

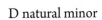

(10) F♯ major

(11) B♭ major   B♭ natural minor

B. Writing natural minor scales

Insert the appropriate accidentals to make a natural minor scale.

(1) C natural minor

W H W W H W W

(2) B natural minor

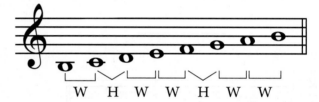

W H W W H W W

(3) G natural minor

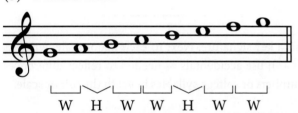

W H W W H W W

(4) D natural minor

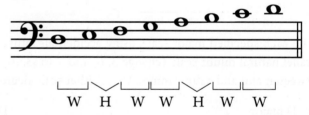

W H W W H W W

(5) C♯ natural minor

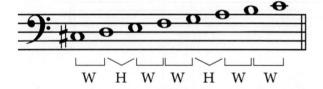

W H W W H W W

(6) F natural minor

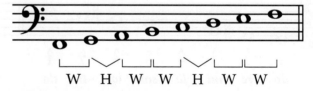

W H W W H W W

(7) E♭ natural minor

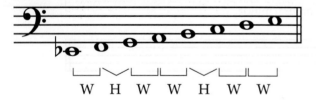

W H W W H W W

(8) G♯ natural minor

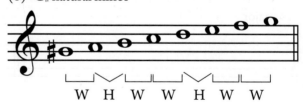

W H W W H W W

Workbook ASSIGNMENT 7.2

A. Writing harmonic minor

Write the natural minor scales specified to the left, using accidentals instead of key signatures. To the right, write a harmonic minor scale beginning on the same note. Circle the augmented second.

(1) D natural minor

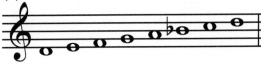

D harmonic minor

(2) F natural minor

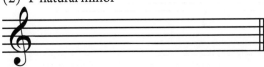

F harmonic minor

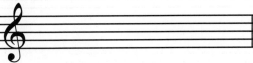

(3) E natural minor

E harmonic minor

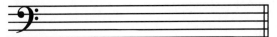

(4) B natural minor

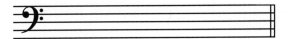

B harmonic minor

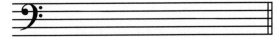

B. Notating melodies from scale degrees and solfège syllables

Notate the melodies given with scale-degree numbers and solfège syllables (no rhythm required). If you know the name of the tune, write it in the blank. (Arrows indicate ascending or descending contour.)

(1) Write this melody in B minor.

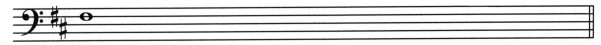

Name of melody (optional): _____

(2) Write this melody in D minor.

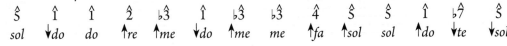

Name of melody (optional): _____

C. Writing melodic minor

Write each natural minor scale specified using accidentals instead of a key signature. Then below it, rewrite as an ascending and descending melodic minor scale, adding accidentals as necessary. Finally, label each pitch of the melodic minor scale with the appropriate scale-degree number or solfège syllable.

(1) A natural minor (ascending)

A melodic minor (ascending and descending)

(2) F♯ natural minor (ascending)

F♯ melodic minor (ascending and descending)

(3) G natural minor (ascending)

G melodic minor (ascending and descending)

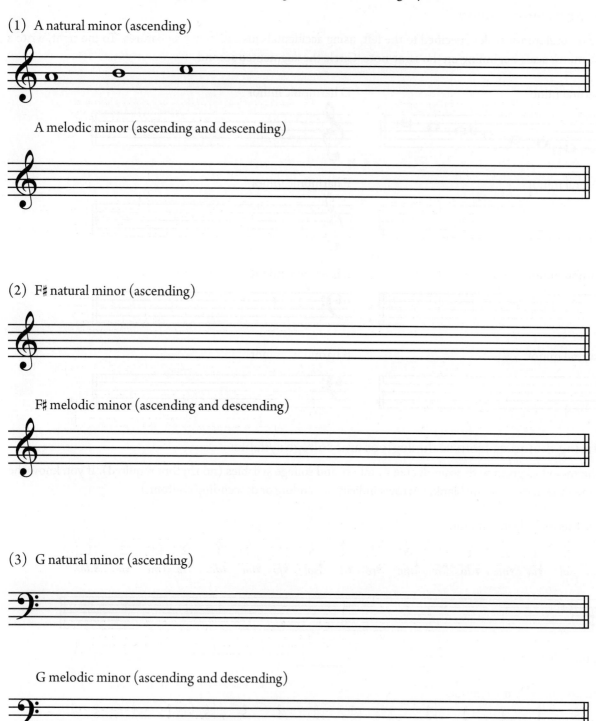

Workbook ASSIGNMENT 7.3

A. Writing relative major and minor scales

In each exercise, write the specified major scale. Then, beneath it, write the three types of relative minor scales (beginning on $\hat{6}$ of the major scale), using accidentals rather than key signatures.

(1) (a) F major

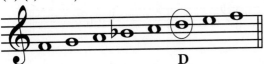

D

(b) Natural minor relative to F major

(c) Harmonic minor relative to F major

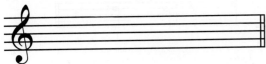

(d) Melodic minor ascending, relative to F major

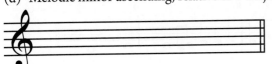

(2) (a) A♭ major

(b) Natural minor relative to A♭ major

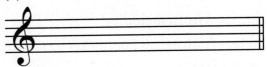

(c) Harmonic relative to A♭ major

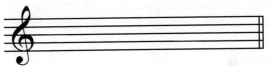

(d) Melodic minor ascending, relative to A♭ major

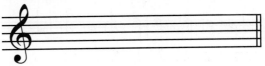

(3) (a) G major

(b) Natural minor relative to G major

(c) Harmonic minor relative to G major

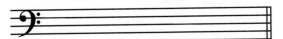

(d) Melodic minor ascending, relative to G major

(4) (a) B major

(b) Natural minor relative to B major

(c) Harmonic minor relative to B major

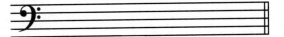

(d) Melodic minor ascending, relative to B major

B. Reading and writing minor key signatures

Write the names of the two keys represented by each signature. Write the major key (uppercase letter) in the top row, and the minor key (lowercase letter) in the bottom row.

Major: __Bb__ ___ ___ ___ ___ ___ ___

Minor: __g__ ___ ___ ___ ___ ___ ___

Major: ___ ___ ___ ___ ___ ___ ___

Minor: ___ ___ ___ ___ ___ ___ ___

C. Analyzing keys from melodies

Determine the key of each melody from the key signature and scale degrees. Write the name of the key in the blank.

(1) Clarke, *Trumpet Voluntary*, mm. 5–8

Key: _____

(2) Tomás Luis de Victoria, "O magnum mysterium," mm. 5–9

et ad - mi - ra - bi - le sa - cra - men - - - - tum,

Key: _____

Translation: [O great mystery] and wondrous sacrament

(3) Bach, Chorale Prelude on "Wachet auf," mm. 1–4

Key: _____

(4) Henry Purcell, "Ah, Belinda, I am prest," from *Dido and Aeneas*, mm. 68–72

Peace __ and I are stran - gers, __ stran - gers __ grown.

Key: _____

Circle the relationship between the keys for each pair of melodies.

(5) Clarke and Victoria are in   parallel keys   relative keys

(6) Bach and Purcell are in   parallel keys   relative keys

Workbook ASSIGNMENT 7.4

A. Writing minor-key melodies

(1) Follow these instructions to compose two minor-key melodies.
- Write one melody in the treble clef and one in the bass clef. Each should be eight measures long.
- For one melody, choose a simple-meter signature; for the other, a compound-meter signature. Include beat patterns from those given.
- Prepare to sing your melody with scale-degree numbers or solfège syllables, or play it on a keyboard.

Simple-meter beat patterns

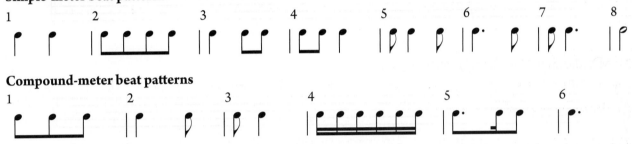

Compound-meter beat patterns

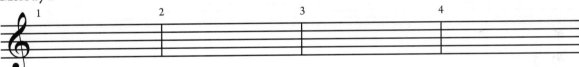

- For each melody, choose a tonic pitch in a key that you can sing comfortably. Begin and end each melody on the tonic pitch.
- Write the minor key signature that goes with the tonic pitch.
- Create an interesting contour.
- End measure 4 on $\hat{2}$, $\hat{5}$, or $\hat{7}$; end measure 8 conclusively on $\hat{1}$.
- When ascending from $\hat{5}$, choose pitches from the ascending melodic minor scale.
- When descending from $\hat{1}$, choose pitches from the natural (descending melodic) minor scale.

Melody 1

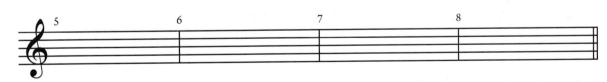

Melody 2

B. Major and minor scales (review)

Spell the specified scales that begin on the pitches given. Write the appropriate key signature, and add any necessary accidentals.

(1) Natural minor, beginning on G:

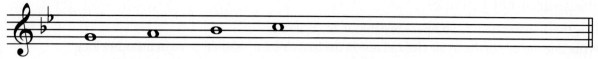

(2) Major, beginning on B♭:

(3) Melodic minor (ascending), beginning on D:

(4) Major, beginning on E:

(5) Harmonic minor, beginning on F:

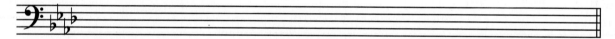

(6) Melodic minor (ascending), beginning on A:

(7) Major, beginning on A♭:

(8) Harmonic minor, beginning on B:

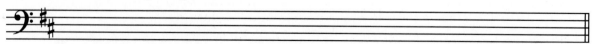

Intervals

KNOW IT? Take the quiz to focus your studies.

TOPICS

- Intervals
- Interval quality
- Spelling intervals method 1: using the white keys
- Inverting intervals
- Spelling intervals method 2: scale and key-signature method
- Augmented and diminished intervals
- Compound intervals
- Consonance and dissonance
- Explore further: doubly augmented and doubly diminished intervals

MUSIC

- "The Ash Grove"
- Johann Sebastian Bach, Invention in D Minor
- Joseph Brackett, "Simple Gifts"
- "Greensleeves"

Intervals

Listen to the first two measures of "Simple Gifts" shown in Example 8.1. This melody, drawn from the A♭ major scale, is mostly made of whole and half steps, with a few skips. Four intervals are circled and labeled in the example.

EXAMPLE 8.1   Brackett, "Simple Gifts," mm. 1–2

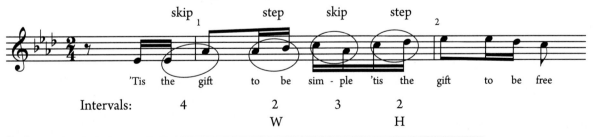

> **KEY CONCEPT** An **interval** measures the distance between two pitches. Intervals are identified by their size (typically a number between 1 and 8) and quality (such as **major**, **minor**, or **perfect**).

The first step in naming an interval is to identify its size, either by counting the letter names from one note to the next or by counting the number of staff lines and spaces spanned. The half and whole steps circled in the example are both seconds, since they span two adjacent letter names (A♭–B♭ and C–D♭). Only two intervals in the melody are not seconds—the E♭4 to A♭4 at the beginning ("'Tis the gift"), and the C5 to A♭4 skip on "simple 'tis." The first of these, spanning four letter names (E♭–F–G–A♭), or four lines and spaces, is a fourth. The second interval is a third, spanning three letter names (C–B♭–A♭). When identifying an interval, always count each letter name, including the first and last notes. Intervals like these, measured between successive pitches, are called **melodic intervals**.

Now listen to a two-part setting of "Greensleeves" (Example 8.2), while paying attention to the intervals formed between the bass-clef pitches and the melody.

EXAMPLE 8.2   "Greensleeves," mm. 1–4

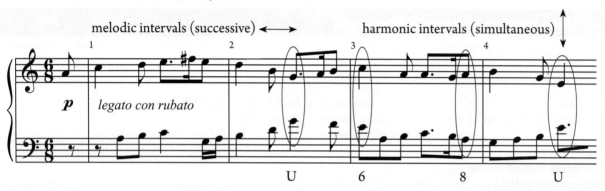

Intervals between pitches heard at the same time are **harmonic intervals**. Name them the same way as melodic intervals—by counting the letter names or lines and spaces encompassed by the interval. In Example 8.2, the harmonic interval circled in the beginning of measure 3, between E4 and C5, is a sixth (E–F♯–G–A–B–C); the interval circled at the end of measure 3 (A3 to A4) is an **octave**. Octaves are abbreviated "8ve" or "8va" (for the Italian, "ottava"). If you see 8va above or below a group of notes, play the notes transposed up or down an octave.

If two parts play the exact same pitch, as at the end of Example 8.2, this "interval," which spans no actual space, is called a **unison** and abbreviated U. When all women or all men sing a melody together, they sing "in unison." (When women and men sing the same melody, they typically sing in octaves.) "Greensleeves" has unisons circled in measures 2 and 4. Example 8.3 illustrates melodic and harmonic interval sizes up to an octave.

EXAMPLE 8.3   Interval sizes

(a) Melodic intervals

(b) Harmonic intervals

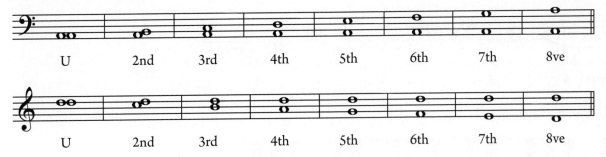

| U | 2nd | 3rd | 4th | 5th | 6th | 7th | 8ve |

| U | 2nd | 3rd | 4th | 5th | 6th | 7th | 8ve |

> **KEY CONCEPT** Learn these landmarks on the staff to identify interval size quickly:
>
> - Thirds, fifths, and sevenths are always written with both pitches on lines or both on spaces.
>   - For thirds, the lines or spaces are adjacent.
>   - For fifths, skip one line or space.
>   - For sevenths, skip two lines or spaces.
> - Seconds, fourths, sixths, and octaves always have one pitch on a line and one on a space.

TRY IT #1

As quickly as possible, write the correct interval size beneath each example. Identify intervals 3, 5, 7 by their line–line or space–space placement, and intervals 2, 4, 6, 8 by their line–space or space–line placement.

(a) **3**　　(b) ___　　(c) ___　　(d) ___　　(e) ___　　(f) ___

Interval Quality

Listen to "The Ash Grove" while following the melody line in Example 8.4. Five thirds are circled. If you play these thirds on a keyboard and count the half steps that they span (remember to check the key signature!), you'll find that some span four half steps (the thirds from E♭ to G, and from D to B♭), and others span three half steps (from G to B♭ and F to A♭), as Examples 8.4b and c show.

EXAMPLE 8.4　"The Ash Grove"

(a) mm. 1–4

M3　　m3　　　　M3　　　　　m3　　　　　　M3

(b) Thirds from measures 1–4

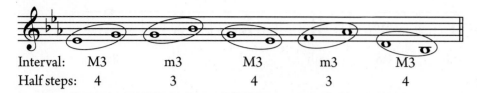

Interval:	M3	m3	M3	m3	M3
Half steps:	4	3	4	3	4

(c) Thirds on the keyboard

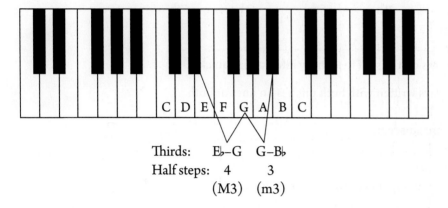

Thirds:	E♭–G	G–B♭
Half steps:	4	3
	(M3)	(m3)

The intervals that span three half steps are called minor thirds (abbreviated m3); those that span four half steps are called major thirds (M3). Both intervals are thirds, but their quality (major versus minor) differs. Similarly, a second can be minor (m2, a diatonic half step) or major (M2, a whole step). All four intervals are shown in Example 8.5.

EXAMPLE 8.5 Interval qualities of seconds and thirds

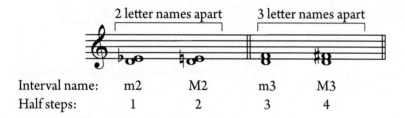

Interval name:	m2	M2	m3	M3
Half steps:	1	2	3	4

> **KEY CONCEPT** When two intervals of the same size (e.g., a third) span a different number of half steps, the difference in their sound is called the **interval quality**.

Interval qualities are associated with particular interval sizes. We have seen minor and major seconds and thirds (Example 8.5); the same distinction holds for sixths and sevenths (m6, M6, m7, and M7). The remaining intervals—unison, fourth, fifth, octave—are called **perfect** (abbreviated P). These intervals are considered the purest acoustically, hence the name "perfect" (PU, P4, P5, P8).

SUMMARY

Interval size	Quality
2, 3, 6, 7	major or minor (not perfect)
U, 4, 5, 8	perfect (not major or minor)

Spelling Intervals Method 1: Using the White Keys

In this chapter, you will learn two ways to identify and spell intervals: (1) by interval types in the C major scale (the white-key method), and (2) by scales and key signatures (the key-signature method). Find the method that allows you to spell intervals most quickly and accurately, then use the second method to check your work. You will also learn a shortcut for spelling larger intervals.

Some musicians find it quick and easy to memorize the intervals found in the C major scale by visualizing them on the keyboard (the white-key notes), on another instrument, or on the lines and spaces of a staff with no accidentals. This method works well for both ascending and descending intervals. Example 8.6 shows seconds, marked on the keyboard from C4 to C5 (a) and arranged on the staff (b). All seconds within the C major scale are M2, except for E–F and B–C, which are m2. As Example 8.6c shows, the interval quality is unchanged if you add the same accidental to both notes.

> **KEY CONCEPT** A major or minor interval retains its quality when matching accidentals are added to both notes. For example, G–A, G♯–A♯, and G♭–A♭ are all M2.

EXAMPLE 8.6   Seconds within the C major scale

(a) On the keyboard

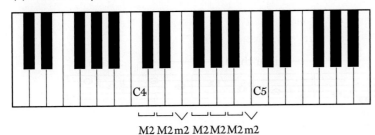

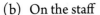

(b) On the staff

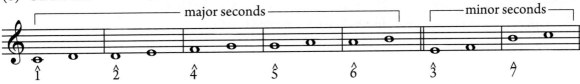

(c) On the staff with matching accidentals added

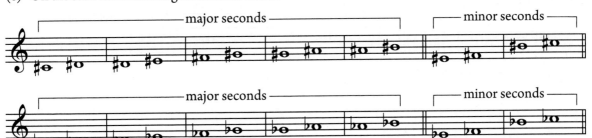

Writing seconds as harmonic intervals on a staff is challenging because the notes are so close together. Example 8.7 shows the correct notation for seconds. Generally, the lower note is written to the left, unless each note has a separate stem. Harmonic unisons are usually shown with two stems.

EXAMPLE 8.7   Notation of unisons and seconds with stems

U   U   2nd   2nd   2nd   2nd   2nd   2nd

Example 8.8 illustrates major and minor thirds. Memorize the qualities of white-key thirds, and play them on a keyboard. Like seconds, if a third has matching accidentals, it retains the size and quality of the white-key interval. For instance, G–B, G♯–B♯, and G♭–B♭ are all major thirds; B–D, B♯–D♯, B♭–D♭ are all minor thirds.

EXAMPLE 8.8   Thirds within the C major scale

(a) On the keyboard

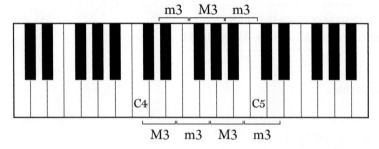

(b) On the staff

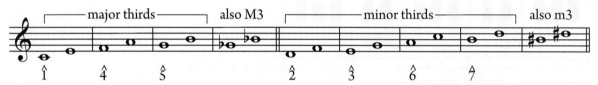

All white-key fourths are perfect except F–B (Example 8.9). Fourths with matching accidentals retain the size and quality of the white-key interval: G–C, G♯–C♯, and G♭–C♭ are all perfect fourths, while F♯–B♯ and F♭–B♭, like F–B, are augmented fourths.

EXAMPLE 8.9   Fourths

(a) Within the C major scale

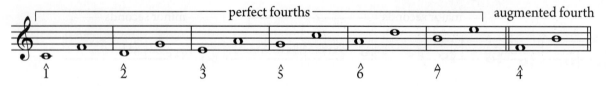

(b) With accidentals

P4   P4   P4

Identify each harmonic or melodic interval given. Intervals with matching accidentals on both notes will have the same quality as their white-key counterparts.

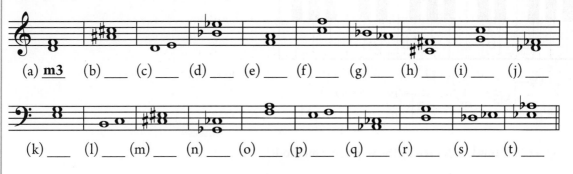

(a) __m3__ (b) ___ (c) ___ (d) ___ (e) ___ (f) ___ (g) ___ (h) ___ (i) ___ (j) ___

(k) ___ (l) ___ (m) ___ (n) ___ (o) ___ (p) ___ (q) ___ (r) ___ (s) ___ (t) ___

The white-key approach works well if the interval you wish to write can be spelled with matching accidentals. If you want an interval with a different quality from the white-key interval with the same letter names, then you will need to adjust one of the notes by adding an accidental.

> **KEY CONCEPT** Minor intervals are a chromatic half step smaller than major, as Example 8.10 shows.
>
> - You can alter a major-quality interval to minor by moving one pitch *toward* the other (Example 8.10a):
>   - lower the top note (F–A becomes F–A♭), or
>   - raise the bottom note (F–A becomes F♯–A).
> - You can alter a minor-quality interval to major by moving one pitch *away from* the other (Example 8.10b)
>   - raise the top note (B–D becomes B–D♯), or
>   - lower the bottom note (B–D becomes B♭–D).

EXAMPLE 8.10   Altering interval qualities

(a) Major to minor

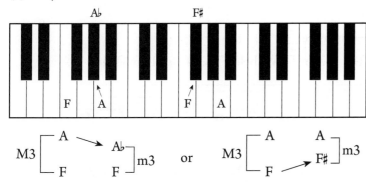

(b) Minor to major

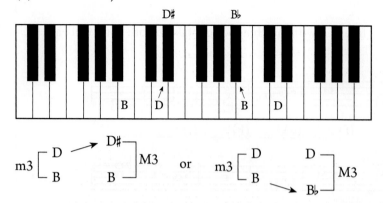

To write any second, third, or fourth by the white-key method:

a. If the given note is a white key, write the white-key interval first, and identify its quality (based on the pattern in C major). Then, if needed, adjust its size by adding a flat or sharp to the *other* note (Example 8.11a).

b. If the given note has an accidental, write the second note head of the interval on the correct line or space for the interval size and add a matching accidental, then follow the same procedure (Example 8.11b).

> **KEY CONCEPT** If you are asked to write an interval up or down from a given note, do not change the given note; make any adjustments for quality to the note you write.

EXAMPLE 8.11   Spelling intervals by C major patterns

(a) Start with a white-key interval and alter the second note.

1. Spell a m3 above C.   2. Spell a M3 above D.   3. Spell a M3 below D.   4. Spell a m3 below B.

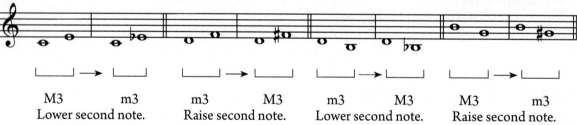

(b) Start with matching accidentals and alter the second note.

1. Spell a m3 above C♯.   2. Spell a M3 above D♭.   3. Spell a M3 below D♭.   4. Spell a m3 below E♯.

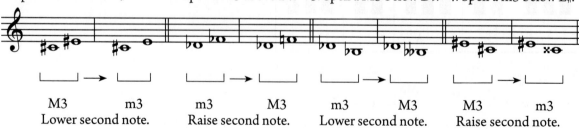

SHOW IT! Assignment 8.1

Inverting Intervals

The white-key intervals for fifths and fourths are shown in Example 8.12. Each perfect fifth pairs with a perfect fourth that has the same letter names (shown by arrows). These intervals are related by inversion. The one white-key diminished fifth, B–F, inverts to the augmented fourth F–B.

EXAMPLE 8.12   Perfect and diminished fifths inverted to fourths

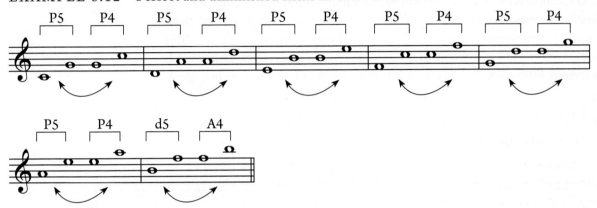

KEY CONCEPT   Intervals related by **inversion** share the same notes but with either (1) the lower pitch raised by an octave, or (2) the upper pitch lowered by an octave. Intervals related by inversion are the unison and octave, second and seventh, third and sixth, and fourth and fifth. In each case, the sum of the two intervals is 9.

Example 8.13a shows a perfect fourth, F4 up to B♭4, followed by the same B♭4 up to F5. The second interval is a perfect fifth. Examples 8.13b and c show a major third and a minor sixth, as well as a major second and a minor seventh. The intervals in each interval pair in the example are inversionally related.

EXAMPLE 8.13   Inversionally related intervals

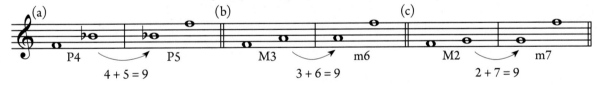

As Example 8.13 shows, a perfect interval inverts to another perfect interval. A major interval inverts to a minor interval (and vice versa): for example, a M3 inverts to a m6 (Example 8.13b) and a M2 inverts to a m7 (Example 8.13c).

SUMMARY

When inverting an interval:

1. Keep one pitch stable. Move the lower note up one octave, or move the upper note down one octave.
   - Perfect intervals remain perfect.
   - Major intervals invert to minor.
   - Minor intervals invert to major.

2. The two interval sizes always sum to 9.
- 1 inverts to 8
- 8 inverts to 1
- 2 inverts to 7
- 7 inverts to 2
- 3 inverts to 6
- 6 inverts to 3
- 4 inverts to 5
- 5 inverts to 4

Inversions provide a quick shortcut for spelling wide intervals, such as fifths, sixths, and sevenths. As Example 8.14a shows, you can spell the minor seventh above D by thinking of its inversion, the major second below D. If you are asked to spell a large interval, think of its inversion: a major second below D is C, therefore a minor seventh above D is C. This process works with or without accidentals: since D♯ up to E is a minor second, D♯ down to E is a major seventh. Example 8.14b and c show how to spell fifths and sixths using inversions.

EXAMPLE 8.14   Spelling large intervals from their inversions

(a) Spelling sevenths using seconds

1. Spell a m7 above D.   2. Spell a M7 below D♯.

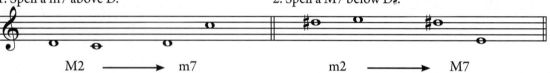

(b) Spelling fifths using fourths

1. Spell a P5 above A.   2. Spell a P5 below A♭.

(c) Spelling sixths using thirds

1. Spell a M6 above A.   2. Spell a m6 below D♭.

TRY IT #3

(a) For each given pair of pitches, name the interval. Then write the inversion, and name the new interval.

(1)   (2)   (3)

<u>m3</u>   <u>M6</u>   ___   ___   ___   ___

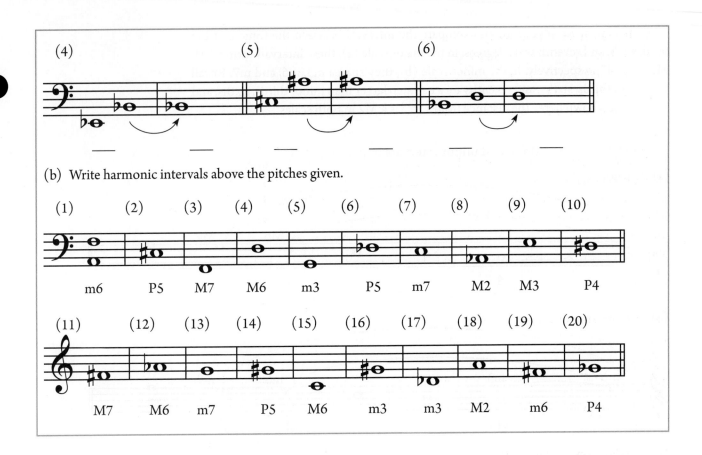

(b) Write harmonic intervals above the pitches given.

(1) (2) (3) (4) (5) (6) (7) (8) (9) (10)

m6   P5   M7   M6   m3   P5   m7   M2   M3   P4

(11) (12) (13) (14) (15) (16) (17) (18) (19) (20)

M7   M6   m7   P5   M6   m3   m3   M2   m6   P4

Spelling Intervals Method 2: Scale and Key-Signature Method

Another way to spell most intervals is by relating them to scales, thinking of the interval's lower note as the tonic ($\hat{1}$). Compare $\hat{1}$, $\hat{4}$, $\hat{5}$, and $\hat{8}$ between the major and minor scales shown in Example 8.15: the pitches are exactly the same. In either kind of scale, the intervals from the tonic to the fourth, fifth, and octave above it are perfect.

EXAMPLE 8.15   Perfect intervals in major and minor scales

(a) F major

(b) F minor

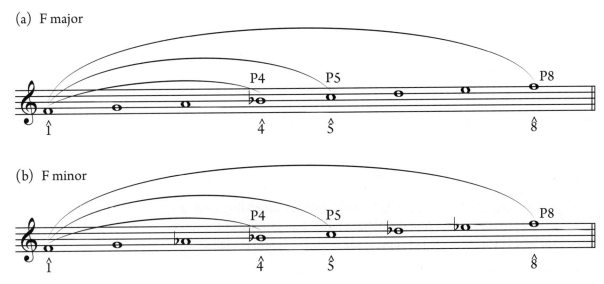

Now look at Example 8.16 and compare the intervals between the tonic and the third, sixth, and seventh scale degrees. In the major scale (a), these intervals form a M3, M6, and M7, respectively. In the minor scale (b), they span a m3, m6, and m7. Recall that major thirds, sixths, and sevenths are a half step larger than minor thirds, sixths, and sevenths, as shown here. The distance from $\hat{1}$ to $\hat{2}$ is a M2 in both scales.

EXAMPLE 8.16   Major and minor intervals in parallel keys

(a) F major

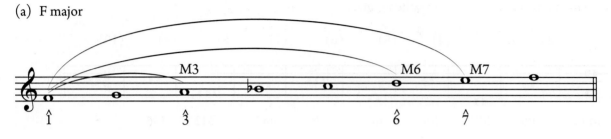

(b) F natural minor

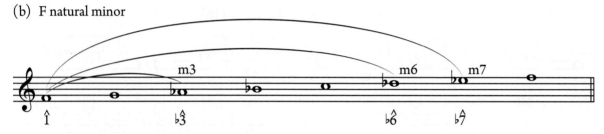

In the descending major scale, the intervals beneath the tonic are all minor or perfect (Example 8.17a). In the descending natural minor scale, intervals are major or perfect, except from $\hat{1}$ down to $\hat{2}$, which is a m7 (Example 8.17b).

EXAMPLE 8.17   Major, minor, and perfect intervals in descending scales

(a) F major

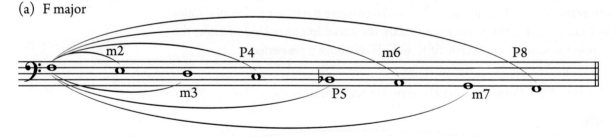

(b) F natural minor

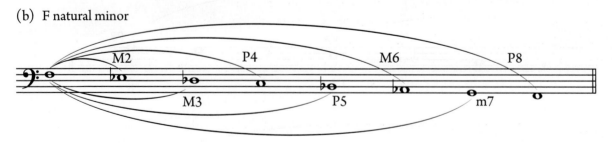

Using the scale and key-signature method, which works well for ascending intervals (with the bottom note given), you imagine the bottom note of an interval as the tonic of a major or minor key. The upper note lies somewhere in the scale and is spelled with accidentals belonging to that key. See Example 8.18 to follow these steps (shown in order vertically).

1. Write the note heads of the interval on the lines or spaces.
2. Think of the key signature of the bottom note. For major intervals, think of the major key signature; for minor intervals, think of the minor key signature. For perfect intervals, either the major or minor key signature works.
3. Add accidentals if necessary.
   - If perfect (U, 4, 5, 8) or major (2, 3, 6, 7), add an accidental to the upper note if needed to match the major key signature of the bottom note (Example 8.18a and c).
   - If minor (3, 6, 7), add an accidental to the upper note if needed to match the minor key signature of the bottom note (Example 8.18b and d).
   - If you want a m2, follow step 1, then add an accidental to the upper note to make a diatonic half step.

EXAMPLE 8.18   Spelling intervals from major and minor scales

(a) Write a M3 above E.   (b) Write a m6 above C.   (c) Write a P5 above F♯.   (d) Write a m3 above E.

Step 1: Write the interval.

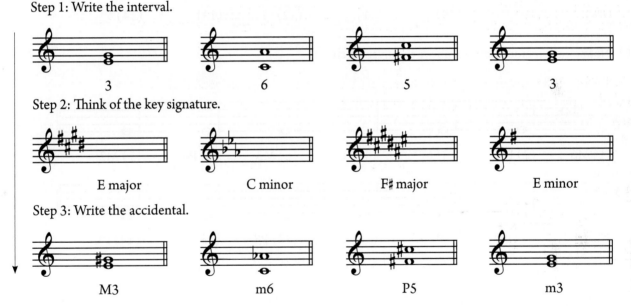

Since a minor interval is a half step smaller than a major interval, you can also use a major key signature (if you know it better) to spell a minor interval, as shown in Example 8.19:

1. Think of the major key signature for the bottom note of the interval.
2. Write the corresponding major interval based on the key signature.
3. Lower the top note by a chromatic half step (don't change the letter name).

EXAMPLE 8.19   Spelling minor intervals from major key signatures

(a) Spelling a m7 above D

1. Write the major   2. Spell a M7.   3. Lower the top note.
   key signature.

(b) Spelling a m3 above G

1. Write the major key signature.
2. Spell a M3.
3. Lower the top note.

TRY IT #4

(a) Identify the size and quality of each melodic interval in the following keys.

A♭ major

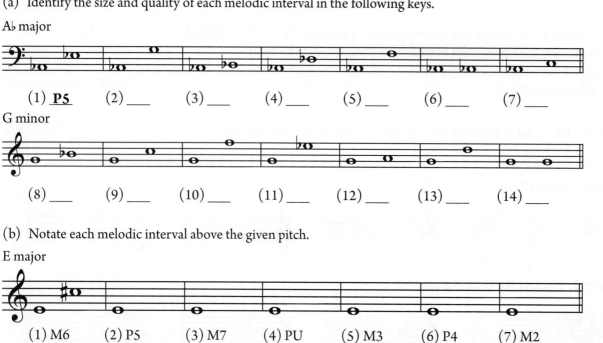

(1) **P5**   (2) ___   (3) ___   (4) ___   (5) ___   (6) ___   (7) ___

G minor

(8) ___   (9) ___   (10) ___   (11) ___   (12) ___   (13) ___   (14) ___

(b) Notate each melodic interval above the given pitch.

E major

(1) M6   (2) P5   (3) M7   (4) PU   (5) M3   (6) P4   (7) M2

F minor

(8) P4   (9) m3   (10) m7   (11) P5   (12) P8   (13) m6   (14) PU

SHOW IT! Assignment 8.2

Finally, you can check the quality of any interval by counting its half steps. The following table summarizes the information you need to know. Write the note heads for the interval's size (spanning the correct number of letter names) first, before counting half steps. Otherwise, you may confuse enharmonic intervals like the A4 and d5 (tritones), which we consider next.

Interval name	Abbreviation	Interval type	Number of half steps
unison	U	1	0
minor second	m2	2	1
major second	M2	2	2
minor third	m3	3	3
major third	M3	3	4
perfect fourth	P4	4	5
tritone	A4 or d5	4 or 5	6
perfect fifth	P5	5	7
minor sixth	m6	6	8
major sixth	M6	6	9
minor seventh	m7	7	10
major seventh	M7	7	11
octave	P8	8	12

Augmented and Diminished Intervals

We have already seen one augmented interval—the augmented second (A2)—as a part of a harmonic minor scale. Bach's Invention in D Minor (Example 8.20) provides examples of other **augmented** and **diminished** intervals. Listen to the beginning, and focus on the bracketed intervals—the right-hand dramatic leap from B♭4 down to C♯4 and back up in measures 1–2 (echoed in the left hand in mm. 3–4), and the right-hand G4 to C♯5 in measure 4.

EXAMPLE 8.20   Bach, Invention in D Minor, mm. 1–5

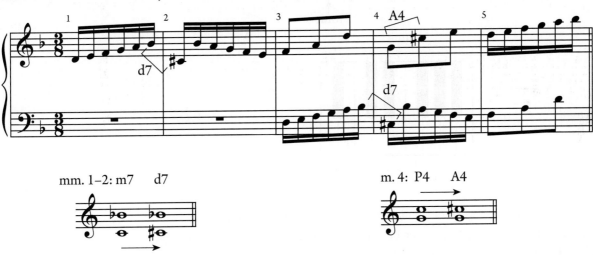

If the B♭4 in measure 1 leaped down to a C4 instead of C♯4, as shown below the example, the interval would be a m7. The interval here is a half step smaller than a m7 (shown by the arrow): a diminished seventh (d7). Now look at measure 4. If this interval were the white-key notes G4–C5, it would be a perfect fourth (P4); G4–C♯4 is a half step larger (shown by the arrow), yielding an augmented fourth (A4). These diminished and augmented intervals are produced by the variants of $\hat{6}$ and $\hat{7}$ that are available in harmonic and melodic minor scales. The A4 occurs in major keys as well, as $\hat{4}$ to $\hat{7}$ (in D major, G–C♯).

> **KEY CONCEPT** When a major or perfect interval is made a chromatic half step larger, call it augmented (C up to A♯ is an A6). When a minor or perfect interval is made a chromatic half step smaller, call it diminished (C up to G♭ is a d5).

As previously mentioned, all the fifths and fourths made between pairs of white-key notes are perfect except one: the interval between F and B (see Example 8.21). This interval may be labeled a diminished fifth (d5) or an augmented fourth (A4), depending on where it is positioned within the major scale (Example 8.22). When $\hat{4}$ is lower than $\hat{7}$, it is an augmented fourth (F–B in C major); $\hat{7}$ lower than $\hat{4}$ makes a diminished fifth (B–F). Since the interval spans exactly three whole steps, it is also called a **tritone** ("tri" means "three"). The A4 and d5 are the only inversionally related intervals that are exactly the same size: they each encompass six semitones.

EXAMPLE 8.21   Fourths made with white-key notes

EXAMPLE 8.22   The A4 and d5 in a C major scale

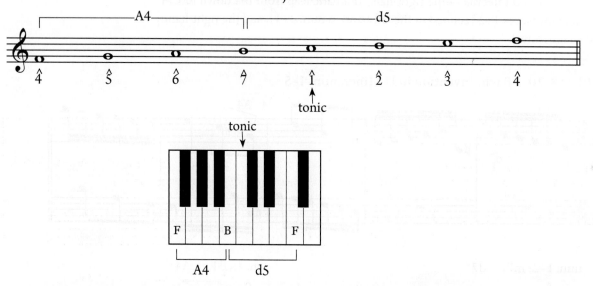

The A4 and d5 are the only diminished and augmented intervals that fall within the major and natural minor scales. Others can be made by raising or lowering diatonic scale degrees by a half step. Only a few—including the A2, A6, and d7—are often found in pieces of music. To spell an augmented or diminished interval, first spell a major, perfect, or minor interval, then use accidentals to adjust its size, as shown in Example 8.23. Don't change the letter name of either pitch. Augmented and diminished intervals are more likely than major, minor, and perfect intervals to require a double sharp (𝄪) or a double flat (♭♭), which raise or lower the pitch by a whole step.

EXAMPLE 8.23   Spelling augmented and diminished intervals

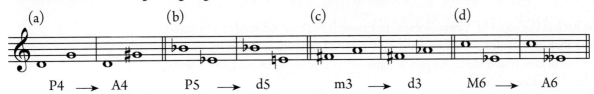

(a)   (b)   (c)   (d)

P4 → A4   P5 → d5   m3 → d3   M6 → A6

The following charts show the interval size produced when you make an interval one chromatic half step smaller (left arrow) or larger (right arrow):

d3 ← m3 → M3   d4 ← P4 → A4   d6 ← m6 → M6   d7 ← m7 → M7
m3 ← M3 → A3   d5 ← P5 → A5   m6 ← M6 → A6   m7 ← M7 → A7

For a	start with	add an accidental to move one pitch
diminished 3, 6, 7	minor 3, 6, 7	inward a half step
diminished 4, 5, 8	perfect 4, 5, 8	inward a half step
augmented 2, 3, 6	major 2, 3, 6	outward a half step
augmented 4, 5, 8	perfect 4, 5, 8	outward a half step

KEY CONCEPT Diminished and augmented intervals can usually be respelled as major or minor intervals. These spellings are **enharmonically equivalent**: for example, A2 and m3 (C–D♯ and C–E♭), d4 and M3 (C–F♭ and C–E), A5 and m6 (C–G♯ and C–A♭), and so on.

TRY IT #5

Spell the following augmented and diminished intervals above the given note. First spell a major, minor, or perfect interval as specified, then alter its quality. Don't change the given note by adding an accidental.

(a) P5   d5   (b) m7   d7   (c) P4   A4   (d) m3   d3

(e) M2   A2   (f) P4   A4   (g) P5   d5   (h) m7   d7

(i) M2   A2   (j) M6   A6   (k) m3   d3   (l) m6   d6

Compound Intervals

If you look back at the score of "Greensleeves" in Example 8.2 (reproduced in Try It #6), you will see that in measure 1 the first harmonic interval actually spans more than an octave: it is an octave plus a third, A3 to C5. This interval is sometimes called a tenth, since it spans ten letter names.

> **KEY CONCEPT** Intervals larger than an octave are **compound intervals**. **Simple intervals** are an octave or smaller in size.

In musical contexts, the most frequent compound intervals you are likely to encounter are ninths, tenths, elevenths, and twelfths—which correspond to an octave plus a second, third, fourth, and fifth (Example 8.24)—although larger compound intervals are possible. To name a compound interval, add 7 to the simple interval. (Add 7 rather than 8 because we began numbering the unison with 1 rather than 0.) For example, a second plus an octave equals a ninth, and a fourth plus an octave equals an eleventh.

EXAMPLE 8.24 Compound intervals

(a) Calculation

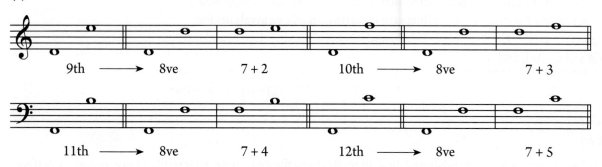

(b) Conversion chart

9th = 2nd	12th = 5th
10th = 3rd	13th = 6th
11th = 4th	14th = 7th

There are times when you need to label the span of an interval as a ninth, tenth, eleventh, or twelfth because the exact musical space spanned by an interval is important to the way it sounds. However, you can usually label compound intervals as simple ones, without regard for the "extra" octaves between pitches, writing 4 instead of 11, or 5 instead of 12. Guidelines for determining the quality of compound intervals are the same as for simple ones.

Listen to "Greensleeves," and identify the harmonic intervals circles in measures 1–4. Identify the size and quality of each interval. For compound intervals, indicate the size and quality of the corresponding simple interval as well.

"Greensleeves," mm. 1–5

Interval:	**m10**	___	___	___	___	___	___
Simple equivalent:	**m3**	___	___	___	___	___	___

Consonance and Dissonance

Over the course of music history, intervals have been characterized as **consonant** if they sound pleasing to the ear or tonally stable, and **dissonant** if they sound jarring or clashing, or as if they need to move somewhere else to find a resting point. Consonance and dissonance are relative terms based on acoustics and compositional practice.

As a rule of thumb, consider perfect unisons, fifths, and octaves and major and minor thirds and sixths to be consonant. Consider seconds and sevenths to be dissonant, as well as any augmented or diminished intervals such as A4 and d5. The fourth as a melodic interval is consonant, but as a harmonic interval it may be treated as a dissonance.

Adding octaves doesn't change consonance or dissonance: tenths are consonances, as are thirds; ninths are dissonances, as are seconds. The concepts of consonance and dissonance will be useful when you write music of your own, since dissonant intervals tend to move toward consonant ones. This motion toward consonance is called **resolution**: dissonant intervals create the "need" to resolve, typically to the closest consonant interval, as illustrated in Example 8.25.

EXAMPLE 8.25   Resolutions of dissonances to consonances

Common harmonic dissonances have standard resolutions: for example, the upper note of a minor seventh tends to resolve down. Resolutions of A4 and d5 are shown in Example 8.25. As inversionally related intervals, they resolve in complementary ways: the A4 resolves out (to a sixth) and the d5 resolves in (to a third). For either, the underlying motion is the same, if viewed in relation to the scale: $\hat{7}$ resolves up to $\hat{1}$, while $\hat{4}$ resolves down to $\hat{3}$.

SUMMARY

- Consonant intervals: PU, P5, P8, m3, M3, m6, M6, melodic P4
- Dissonant intervals: m2, M2, m7, M7, any augmented or diminished interval, harmonic P4

SHOW IT! Assignment 8.3, 8.4

EXPLORE FURTHER Doubly Augmented and Doubly Diminished Intervals

It is possible to make doubly augmented (AA) or doubly diminished (dd) intervals, though they are rare. They are sometimes spelled with double sharps or double flats (Example 8.26) or with one note sharped and the other flatted. To write them, follow the directions discussed previously (without changing any letter names), but move one pitch inward or outward a *whole* step, rather than a half.

EXAMPLE 8.26   Doubly augmented (AA) and diminished (dd) intervals

(a) Fourths

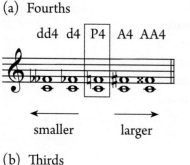

or

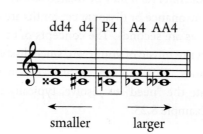

(b) Thirds

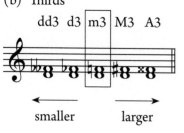

or

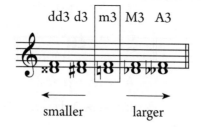

Did You Know?

"Simple Gifts" (Example 8.1) is a Shaker song composed in 1848 by Joseph Brackett. The Shakers were a religious sect active in New England between the mid-eighteenth and early twentieth centuries, known today for music, furniture design, well-run farms, and a belief in equality of the sexes, which became a part of their teaching in the 1780s. "Simple Gifts," which was sung as a part of Shaker religious dance ceremonies, was little known until 1944, when Aaron Copland set it in his ballet *Appalachian Spring* for Martha Graham's modern dance company.

Terms You Should Know

consonant
dissonant
interval
   compound
   enharmonically equivalent
   harmonic
   melodic
   simple

interval inversion
interval quality
   augmented
   diminished
   major
   minor
   perfect

octave
resolution
tritone
unison

Questions for Review

1. What is meant by interval size? By interval quality?
2. Which interval sizes may be major or minor? Perfect? Diminished or augmented?
3. Describe at least three methods for spelling intervals.
4. How do you invert intervals?
5. Describe how to label (or spell) larger intervals by inverting them.
6. How do you identify the name of compound intervals?
7. Which intervals are considered consonant? Dissonant?
8. What should you alter to turn a P4 into a d5? A M6 into an A6? A m3 into an A3?
9. What interval is enharmonically equivalent to a d3? An A4? A m7?
10. Respell D–A♭ enharmonically, then provide the interval name for each spelling.

Reading Review

Match the term on the left with the best answer on the right.

_____ (1) enharmonic intervals

   (a) the distance between pitches measured by counting letter names only

_____ (2) unison

   (b) sound the same but are spelled differently

_____ (3) sum to 9

   (c) only white-key fourth that is not perfect

_____ (4) compound interval

   (d) inversionally related intervals

_____ (5) F–B

   (e) the distance between notes eight letter names apart

_____ (6) interval quality

   (f) "distance" between a note and itself

_____ (7) interval size

   (g) major, minor, perfect, augmented, diminished

_____ (8) octave

   (h) spans more than an octave

Apply It

A. Sing and play in major

1. Warm-up: Perform the C major scale with the fingering shown. In a comfortable octave, sing up and down with letter names, scale-degree numbers, or solfège syllables.

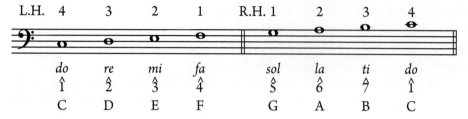

2. For (a) and (b) below:
   - Play and sing as shown—on your own or with your class—and continue the pattern until you sing "perfect octave."
   - Refer to the interval summaries in (c) and (d) for help.
   - When you have mastered C major, transpose these patterns to other keys.

(a) Ascending intervals above tonic

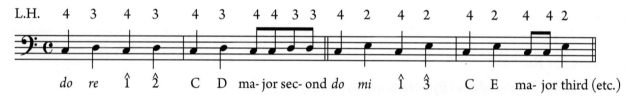

(b) Descending intervals below tonic

(c) Major and perfect intervals above tonic

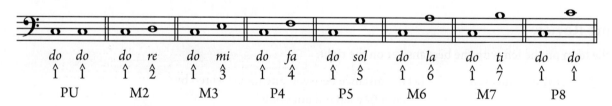

(d) Minor and perfect intervals below tonic

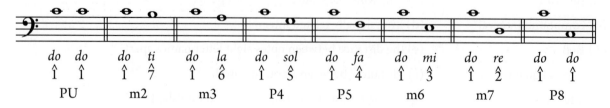

3. You, your instructor, or a partner in your class will choose (1) a starting pitch and (2) a major or perfect interval to spell.
   - Play an ascending major scale from the given starting pitch (using the fingering from A.1) or sing the pattern from A.2 on letter names to discover the interval's correct spelling.
   - Take turns with your partner or other members of the class, beginning on different starting pitches and spell different intervals from major scales.
   - Repeat the exercise, now with descending intervals from the major scale.

B. Sing and play in minor

1. Warm-up: Alter the natural minor scale by lowering $\hat{2}$ to $\flat\hat{2}$ so that all intervals above $\hat{1}$ are minor or perfect. Play and sing—on your own or with your class—the altered scale with letter names, scale-degree numbers, or solfège syllables.

L.H.				R.H.			
4	3	2	1	1	2	3	4
do	ra	me	fa	sol	le	te	do
$\hat{1}$	$\flat\hat{2}$	$\flat\hat{3}$	$\hat{4}$	$\hat{5}$	$\flat\hat{6}$	$\flat\hat{7}$	$\hat{1}$
C	D♭	E♭	F	G	A♭	B♭	C

2. Play and sing intervals above the tonic (a) and below the tonic (b) in a minor scale with $\flat\hat{2}$. Begin as shown, and continue the pattern until you sing "perfect octave."
   - Refer to the interval summaries in c and d for help.
   - When you have mastered C minor, transpose these patterns to other keys.

(a) Ascending intervals above tonic

do ra $\hat{1}$ $\flat\hat{2}$ C D♭ mi-nor sec-ond do me $\hat{1}$ $\flat\hat{3}$ C E♭ mi-nor third (etc.)

(b) Descending intervals below tonic

do te $\hat{1}$ $\flat\hat{7}$ C B♭ ma-jor sec-ond do le $\hat{1}$ $\flat\hat{6}$ C A♭ ma-jor third (etc.)

(c) Minor and perfect intervals above tonic

do	do	do	ra	do	me	do	fa	do	sol	do	le	do	te	do	do
$\hat{1}$	$\hat{1}$	$\hat{1}$	$\flat\hat{2}$	$\hat{1}$	$\flat\hat{3}$	$\hat{1}$	$\hat{4}$	$\hat{1}$	$\hat{5}$	$\hat{1}$	$\flat\hat{6}$	$\hat{1}$	$\flat\hat{7}$	$\hat{1}$	$\hat{1}$
PU		m2		m3		P4		P5		m6		m7		P8	

(d) Major and perfect intervals below tonic

do	do	do	te	do	le	do	sol	do	fa	do	me	do	ra	do	do
$\hat{1}$	$\hat{1}$	$\hat{1}$	$\flat\hat{7}$	$\hat{1}$	$\flat\hat{6}$	$\hat{1}$	$\hat{5}$	$\hat{1}$	$\hat{4}$	$\hat{1}$	$\flat\hat{3}$	$\hat{1}$	$\flat\hat{2}$	$\hat{1}$	$\hat{1}$
PU		M2		M3		P4		P5		M6		M7		P8	

3. You, your instructor, or a partner in your class will choose (1) a starting pitch and (2) a minor or perfect interval to spell.

- Play an ascending altered minor scale from the given starting pitch (using the fingering from B.1) or sing the pattern from B.2 on letter names to discover the interval's correct spelling.
- Take turns with your partner or other members of the class, beginning on different starting pitches and spell different intervals from major scales.
- Repeat the exercise, now with descending intervals from the altered minor scale.

C. Identify intervals

Listen to the following intervals, organized in sets of ten. In the blanks provided, write the interval's quality and size (M3, m6, P5, etc.):

- On the first hearing, sing the interval back, then write the size only (6, 3, 2, 5, etc.). You may sing up or down the scale to count scale degrees.
- On the second hearing, sing the interval back, and add the interval quality (M6, m3, m2, P5, etc.).
- Before the third hearing, your teacher will announce the beginning pitch of each interval. On your own staff paper, notate this pitch and then write the second pitch on the staff, including any necessary accidental. Don't alter the given pitch.
- Finally, check your answer with the class.

Ascending major and perfect intervals

1. __P5__ 2. _____ 3. _____ 4. _____ 5. _____

6. _____ 7. _____ 8. _____ 9. _____ 10. _____

Descending minor and perfect intervals

11. __m2__ 12. _____ 13. _____ 14. _____ 15. _____

16. _____ 17. _____ 18. _____ 19. _____ 20. _____

Ascending minor and perfect intervals

21. __m3__ 22. _____ 23. _____ 24. _____ 25. _____

26. _____ 27. _____ 28. _____ 29. _____ 30. _____

Descending major and perfect intervals

31. __M2__ 32. _____ 33. _____ 34. _____ 35. _____

36. _____ 37. _____ 38. _____ 39. _____ 40. _____

41. __m6__ 42. _____ 43. _____ 44. _____ 45. _____

46. _____ 47. _____ 48. _____ 49. _____ 50. _____

D. Sing at sight

These melodies are ordered by type of interval featured. Before working on the melody, determine the key and play and sing that major scale on a keyboard. Identify examples of the interval in the melody. Play and sing the interval; find its position in the scale you just played. Then practice rhythm and pitches separately before combining them.

Melodies featuring seconds and thirds

Melody 1 "Banana Boat Song," mm. 1–10

Melody 2 "Shenandoah"

Melodies featuring fourths and fifths

Melody 3 Wolfgang Amadeus Mozart, "Alleluia," mm. 1–4

This melody may be sung as a round. You can practice singing the round with the recording; when it reaches 2, sing from the beginning.

Melody 4 Robert Lowry, "How Can I Keep from Singing," mm. 1–8

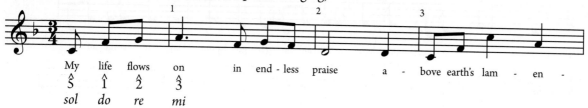

Melody 5 Schubert, "Am Flusse" (On the River), mm. 1–7

Melodies featuring sixths and sevenths

Melody 6 George F. Root, "There's Music in the Air," mm. 1–8

Melody 7 "Music Alone Shall Live"
This melody may be performed as a round.

All things shall per - ish from un - der the sky. Mu - sic a - lone shall live,

$\hat{3}$ $\hat{3}$ $\hat{3}$ $\hat{2}$
mi mi mi re

mu - sic a - lone shall live, mu - sic a - lone shall live, ne - ver to die.

Melody 8 Joseph Kosma, "Autumn Leaves," mm. 9–16

mf $\hat{1}$ $\hat{2}$ $\flat\hat{3}$ $\flat\hat{6}$
do re me le

E. Read rhythms

These rhythms provide a review of duplets and triplets (Chapter 6). Perform using "ta" or counting syllables while tapping a steady beat or conducting. Remember to perform all dynamic indications and accents (>).

Rhythm 1

Rhythm 2

Rhythm 3

Listen and Write 8.1

A. Identifying intervals from familiar music

Sometimes the easiest way to remember the sound of an interval is to associate it with a familiar melody. Play each of the following intervals, then write the name of a piece that begins with or features the interval, either ascending or descending. Provide a melody for at least eight of the twelve intervals. Be prepared to sing your examples in class.

m2 _____

M2 _____

m3 _____

M3 _____

P4 _____

Tritone _____

P5 _____

m6 _____

M6 _____

m7 _____

M7 _____

P8 _____

B. Hearing and writing intervals

Listen to the following intervals, recorded in sets of ten. Each interval begins with the given pitch. In the blank beneath the staff, write the interval's quality and size (M3, m6, P5, etc.), as well as an arrow up or down to show its direction. Then write the second pitch on the staff, including any necessary accidental. Don't alter the given pitch.

Perfect fourths, perfect fifths, and tritones (d5, A4)

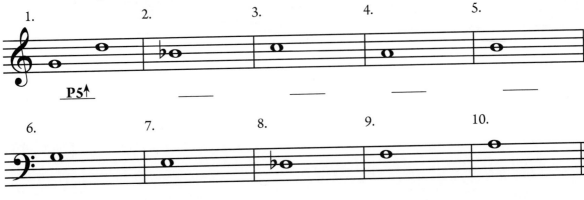

Listen and Write 8.2

A. Hearing and writing a melody

Listen to a carol and focus on both its rhythm and its pitches.

1. Focus your attention on the right-hand melody. Which is the first harmonic interval in the right hand? (Hint: This harmonic interval is heard repeatedly.)

   a. third   b. fourth   c. fifth   d. sixth

2. Writing the melody:
   - Listen to the rhythm. Tap the beat or conduct (two beats per measure). On the rhythm staff, notate the rhythm of the melody.
   - Now focus on the pitches. Below each note on the rhythm staff, write the melody with scale-degree numbers or solfège syllables.
   - Finally, notate both the rhythm and pitches in the key of C major.

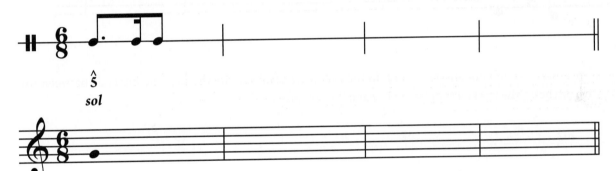

3. Hearing the accompaniment:
   - Now focus on the lower voices in the piano accompaniment. Which of the following repeated rhythms is heard in the accompaniment?

4. The accompaniment begins with what harmonic interval?

   a. m3   b. M3   c. P4   d. P5

B. Hearing and writing a jazz melody

Listen to eight measures of a jazz standard and complete the following exercises.

1. Notate from the beginning of the melody to the downbeat of measure 6.
   - Focus first on the rhythm. Tap the beat or conduct in two. On the rhythm staff, finish notating the rhythm (up to measure 6).
   - Now focus on the pitches. Below each note on the rhythm staff, write scale-degree numbers or solfège syllables (up to measure 6).
   - Finally, on the treble staff finish notating the rhythm and pitches for the melody.

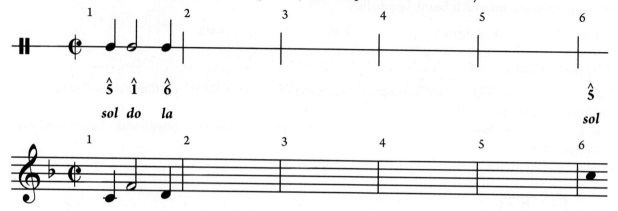

2. Look at measures 1–5 of your answer to (1). In the following blanks, write the melodic intervals between the successive pitches. (The interval for pitches 1–2 and 2–3 are provided.)

   1 __P4__ __m3__ 2 ___ ___ 3 ___ ___ 4 ___ ___ 5 ___ ___

3. Which is a correct notation of the end of the melody (measures 7–8)? Circle your answer.

   a.

   b.

   c.

   d.

4. Listen to bass pitches 1–4. Circle the answer that correctly represents the notes.

   a. $\hat{1}$–$\hat{7}$–$\hat{2}$–$\hat{1}$; *do–ti–re–do*

   b. $\hat{1}$–$\hat{6}$–$\hat{2}$–$\hat{5}$; *do–la–re–sol*

   c. $\hat{1}$–$\hat{2}$–$\hat{7}$–$\hat{1}$; *do–re–ti–do*

   d. $\hat{1}$–$\hat{3}$–$\hat{7}$–$\hat{4}$; *do–mi–ti–fa*

Workbook ASSIGNMENT 8.1

A. Writing melodic intervals

Write a whole note on the correct line or space to make each interval specified. Don't add sharps or flats. Check your answers by counting the letter names from the given note to the one you have written. Remember to include the given note.

Write the specified melodic interval above the given note.

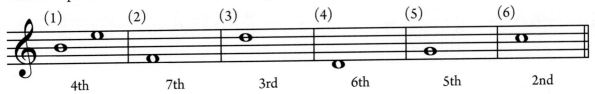

4th   7th   3rd   6th   5th   2nd

Write the specified melodic interval below the given note.

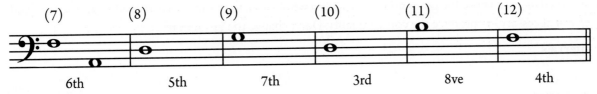

6th   5th   7th   3rd   8ve   4th

B. Identifying interval size in context

For each circled interval, write the correct interval size in the blank provided.

(1) Mozart, Piano Sonata in C Major, K. 545, first movement, mm. 1–4

(2) Bach, "Aus meines Herzens Grunde," mm. 1–4

Aus   mei - nes   Her - zens   Grun - de

C. Identifying intervals

Label each interval with its quality and size (e.g., m6).

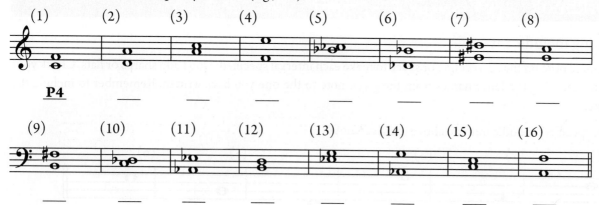

D. Writing major and perfect intervals

Write the specified interval above the given note. First write a whole note to create the correct interval size, then add an accidental (if necessary) to produce the correct quality. Don't change the given note.

Melodic intervals

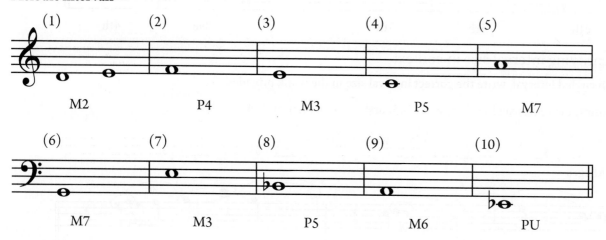

Harmonic intervals

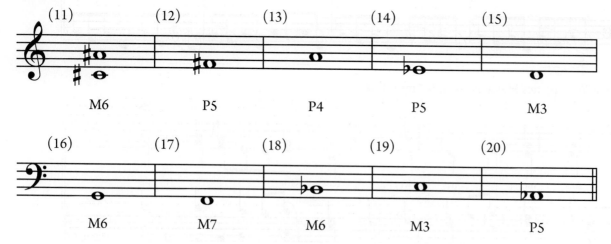

Workbook ASSIGNMENT 8.2

A. Writing intervals

Write each specified harmonic interval above the given note. Don't change the given note.

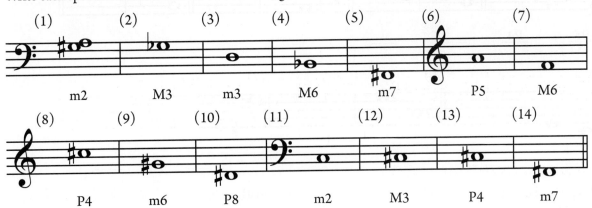

Write each specified harmonic interval below the given note.

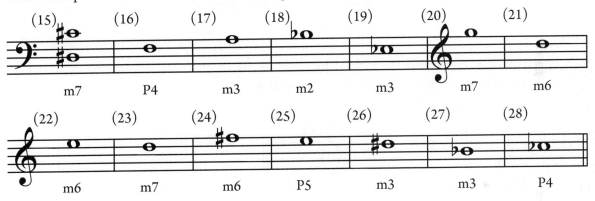

Write the specified melodic interval below the given note.

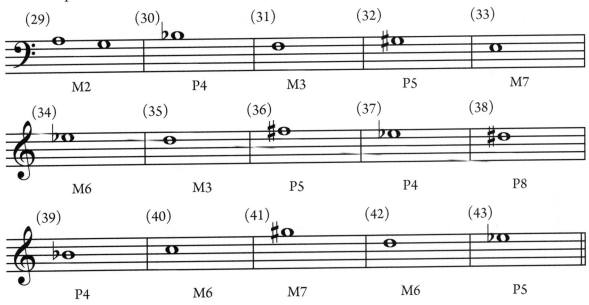

B. Inverting intervals

Identify each interval shown, then invert the interval by rewriting the second note followed by the first note transposed up an octave. Identify the new interval you have written.

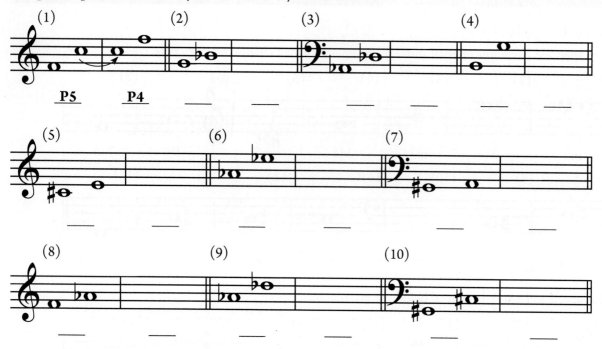

Identify each interval shown, then invert the interval by rewriting the second note followed by the first note transposed down an octave. Identify the new interval you have written.

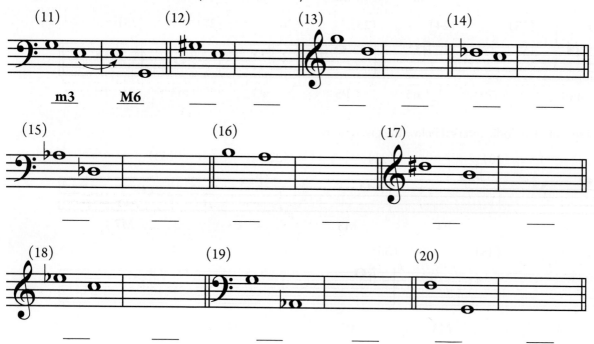

Workbook ASSIGNMENT 8.3

A. Identifying diminished and augmented intervals

Write the name (e.g., A4) under each interval.

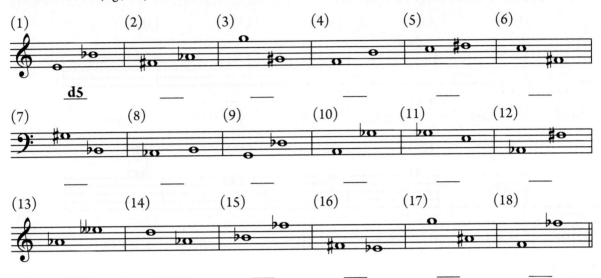

d5

B. Writing diminished and augmented intervals

Write each specified melodic interval below the given note.

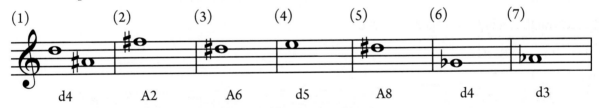

d4   A2   A6   d5   A8   d4   d3

Write each specified melodic interval above the given note.

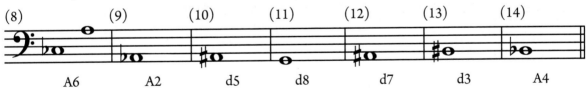

A6   A2   d5   d8   d7   d3   A4

C. Writing melodic compound intervals

Write the specified melodic compound interval above or below the given note. (Hint: Subtract 7 to find the simple-interval equivalent.)

Write the compound interval above the given note.

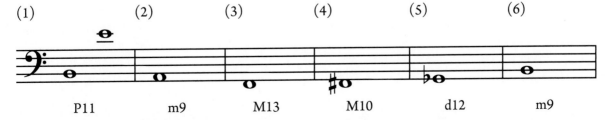

P11   m9   M13   M10   d12   m9

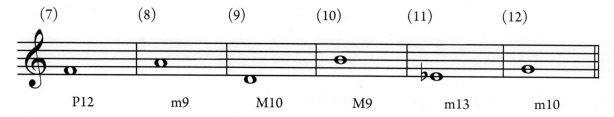

(7) P12 (8) m9 (9) M10 (10) M9 (11) m13 (12) m10

Write the compound interval below the given note.

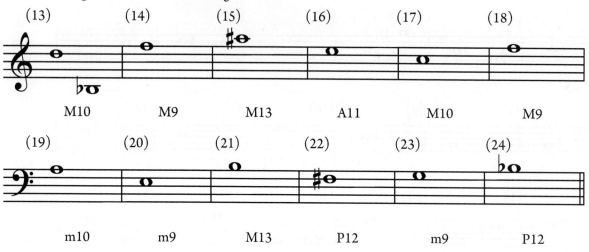

(13) M10 (14) M9 (15) M13 (16) A11 (17) M10 (18) M9

(19) m10 (20) m9 (21) M13 (22) P12 (23) m9 (24) P12

D. Intervals in context

Listen to this excerpt before analyzing it. Write the names of the two circled pitches in the blank above the staff, incorporating accidentals from the key signature, then label the intervals with both quality and size (e.g., M7) in the blank below the staff.

Foster, "Jeanie with the Light Brown Hair," mm. 1–6

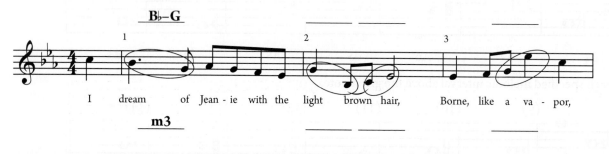

I dream of Jean-ie with the light brown hair, Borne, like a va-por,

on the sum-mer's air; I see her trip-ping where the bright streams play,

Workbook ASSIGNMENT 8.4

A. Identifying intervals

Label each interval with its quality and size (e.g., m6).

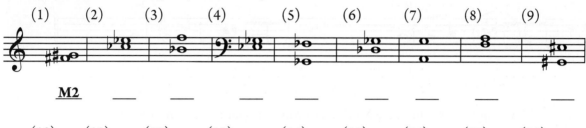

B. Writing melodic intervals

Write a whole note on the correct line or space to make each interval specified. Don't change the given note.

Write the specified melodic interval above the given note.

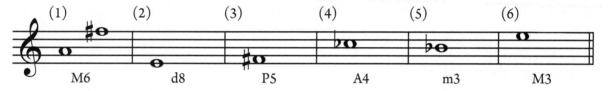

Write the specified melodic interval below the given note.

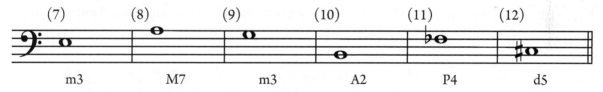

Write the specified melodic interval above and below the given note.

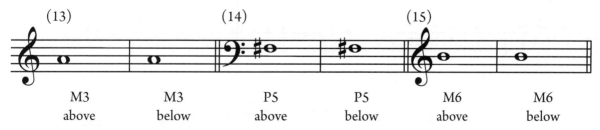

C. Melodic intervals in context

Listen to these excerpts. Write the names of the circled pitches in the blank above the staff, incorporating accidentals from the key signature, then label the intervals with both quality and size (e.g., M7) in the blank below the staff.

(1) Phillips, "Blues for Norton," mm. 17–20

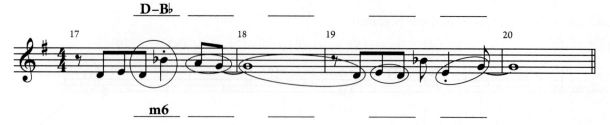

(2) Anonymous, Minuet in D Minor, from the *Notebook for Anna Magdalena Bach*, mm. 9–16

D. Harmonic intervals in context

Listen to measures 1–24 (the theme). Between the staves, write the number of the interval between the highest and lowest notes on each beat (ignore the small thirty-second notes in mm. 15 and 23, as well as the sixteenth notes in mm. 7, 15, and 23). Write the simple-interval number of any compound interval a twelfth or larger (e.g., 5 instead of 12).

Mozart, *Variations on "Ah, vous dirai-je Maman,"* mm. 1–24

Triads and Seventh Chords

9

KNOW IT? **Take the quiz to focus your studies.**

TOPICS

- Triads
- Triad qualities in major keys
- Triad qualities in minor keys
- Spelling triads
- Triad inversion
- The dominant seventh chord
- Spelling the dominant seventh chord
- Seventh chord inversion
- Explore further: other seventh chords

MUSIC

- Johann Sebastian Bach, "Wachet auf" (Chorale No. 179)
- "Come, Ye Thankful People, Come"
- "My Country, 'Tis of Thee"

Triads

In most musical settings, melodic and harmonic intervals sound together; the horizontal and vertical components join to form a musical fabric, called a musical **texture**. For example, a hymn-style texture has four parts—two sung by women (labeled S for soprano and A for alto) and two sung by men (labeled T for tenor and B for bass), as Example 9.1 shows.

EXAMPLE 9.1   "My Country, 'Tis of Thee," mm. 1–6

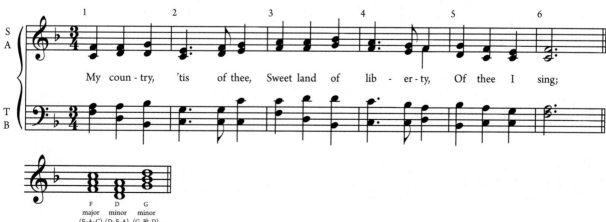

233

In hymn (or SATB) style, the top part—the soprano line—normally sings the melody, the lowest part—the bass line—provides a foundation, and the alto and tenor parts fill in between them. When all voices in a musical texture move together with nearly identical rhythm, as in hymn style, the texture is **homophonic,** and intervals made by the voices singing together form **chords.**

Listen again to "My Country, 'Tis of Thee" (Example 9.1) to hear several different types of chords. As with scales, you can examine chord types by collecting the pitches used (leaving out repeated notes) and writing them on the staff in order within an octave or by writing the pitch letter names arranged in thirds (don't forget to check the key signature). The pitches in each chord of the first measure of the example are shown below the staff; each of these chords is a triad.

> **KEY CONCEPT** **Triads** are three-note chords; in their most basic position, they are built from stacking two thirds, one on top of the other, as shown in Example 9.2.

EXAMPLE 9.2   Intervals in major and minor triads

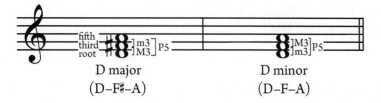

The lowest note in this position is the **root** of the chord. The middle note (a third above the root) is the **third**, and the top note (a fifth above the root) is the **fifth**. The **major triad** has a M3 between its root and third and a m3 between its third and fifth; the **minor triad** has the opposite—a m3 between root and third and a M3 on the top. The difference between triad types is known as the triad's **quality**. Triads are named by the letter name of their root combined with their quality (e.g., G major or B minor). The first chord in "My Country" is an F major triad, the second is a D minor triad, and the third is a G minor triad, as shown. To make a four-note chord like those in Example 9.1, one of the members of the triad (usually the root) will be **doubled**— that is, the same chord member will appear in two places, one or more octaves apart. Sometimes doubling occurs in two voices in the same octave, as in Example 9.1 on the last beat of "liberty," where the sopranos and altos both sing F4 (shown with stems up and down).

Triad Qualities in Major Keys

Example 9.3 gives the quality for each triad built on scale degrees of the F major scale.

EXAMPLE 9.3   Triads built above the F major scale and their qualities

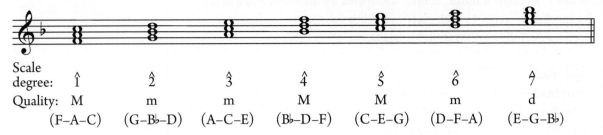

Scale
degree: $\hat{1}$ $\hat{2}$ $\hat{3}$ $\hat{4}$ $\hat{5}$ $\hat{6}$ $\hat{7}$
Quality: M   m   m   M   M   m   d
          (F–A–C) (G–B♭–D) (A–C–E) (B♭–D–F) (C–E–G) (D–F–A) (E–G–B♭)

In major keys, the triads built on $\hat{1}$, $\hat{4}$, and $\hat{5}$ are major, and the triads built on $\hat{2}$, $\hat{3}$, and $\hat{6}$ are minor. The triad built on $\hat{7}$, with a diminished fifth between its root and fifth and with both of its thirds minor, is called a **diminished triad.**

SUMMARY

You can identify triads by considering their intervals. Major, minor, and diminished triads built above F are shown here for comparison.

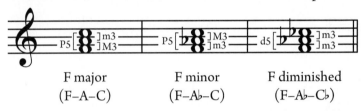

F major   F minor   F diminished
(F–A–C)   (F–A♭–C)   (F–A♭–C♭)

There are several ways to label chords. You can refer to triads in a key by the scale degree on which they are built (for example, "a triad on $\hat{2}$") or by the scale-degree name. Tonic, subdominant, dominant, and so on refer both to the scale degrees and to the triads built on them. Musicians often label chords with Roman numerals, as shown in Example 9.4.

> **KEY CONCEPT   Roman numerals** are a convenient way of labeling both a chord's scale-degree position (I to vii°) and also its quality: a capital numeral indicates a major triad (I, IV, V), and a lowercase numeral a minor triad (ii, iii, vi). For diminished triads, add a small raised (superscript) circle to the lowercase numeral (vii°). When using Roman numerals, always indicate the key (as in Example 9.4, on the left).

EXAMPLE 9.4   Triad labels in F major

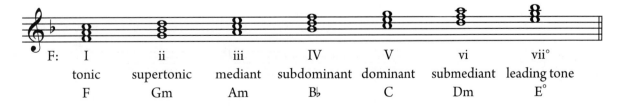

F: I   ii   iii   IV   V   vi   vii°
      tonic   supertonic   mediant subdominant dominant submediant leading tone
       F   Gm   Am   B♭   C   Dm   E°

KEY CONCEPT In popular music, chords are labeled by their root and quality, without a specific reference to their place in the key (without a Roman numeral). This book uses the following symbols for triads:

G major triad	G
G minor triad	Gm or Gmin
G diminished triad	G° or Gdim
G augmented triad	G⁺ (see p. 237)

Your teacher may prefer another system, such as an uppercase letter for major and a lowercase letter for minor. There are many variants of these labels.

Example 9.5 illustrates how to label chords from "Come, Ye Thankful People, Come." The key of the piece, F, is given to the left, before the Roman numerals.

EXAMPLE 9.5   "Come, Ye Thankful People, Come," mm. 5–6

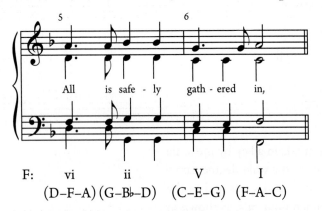

F: vi   ii   V   I
(D–F–A) (G–B♭–D) (C–E–G) (F–A–C)

Triad Qualities in Minor Keys

Example 9.6a shows the triads that can be built above the scale degrees of a natural minor scale. The triads on $\hat{1}$, $\hat{4}$, and $\hat{5}$ are minor; those on $\hat{3}$, $\hat{6}$, and $\hat{7}$ are major; and the triad on $\hat{2}$ is diminished.

EXAMPLE 9.6   Triads built above the G minor scale

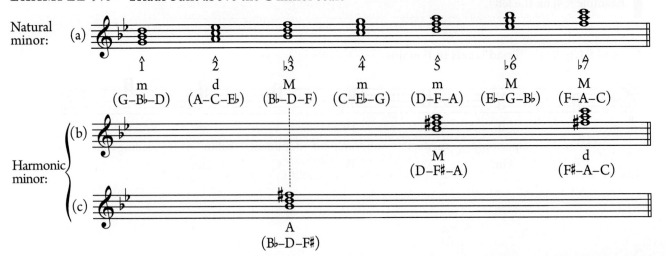

As we learned earlier, ♭$\hat{7}$ in minor is often raised to make a leading tone. In that case, the triads on $\hat{5}$ and $\hat{7}$ become major and diminished, respectively (Example 9.6b). Example 9.6c illustrates what happens to the triad on ♭$\hat{3}$ (B♭–D–F♯) with the raised leading tone: there are now major thirds between both root and third, and third and fifth. Since the interval between the root and fifth is an augmented fifth, this type of chord is called an **augmented triad** (labeled A or Aug). Unlike the other triads in the example, this one is not usually found in minor-key pieces.

The Roman numerals for each triad in G minor are shown in Example 9.7, along with the scale-degree names and chord symbols. To label an augmented chord (Example 9.7c), add a superscript plus sign to an uppercase Roman numeral (III⁺).

EXAMPLE 9.7   Triad labels in G minor

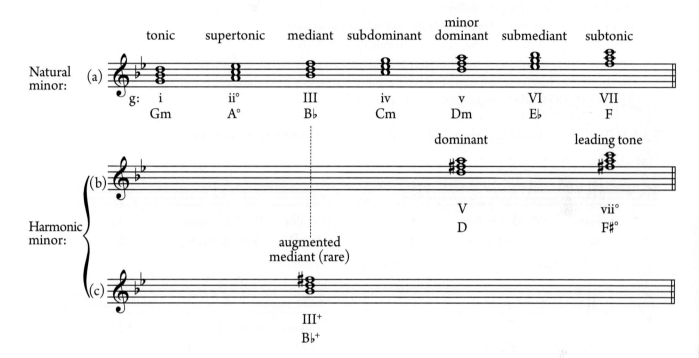

KEY CONCEPT Triads that appear often in minor keys are i, ii°, iv, V, VI, and vii°. The major triad on $\hat{5}$ (V) and the diminished triad on the leading tone (vii°) are more typical than v and VII, because of their strong motion from the leading tone to the tonic. When you write V and vii° in minor keys, remember to raise ♭$\hat{7}$ to $\hat{7}$ to make the leading tone.

Spelling Triads

Triads are essential building blocks for music in many styles. Here are three ways to identify and spell triads: (1) by key signatures, (2) by triads in the C major scale, and (3) by intervals. Find the method that allows you to spell triads most quickly and accurately, then use a second one to check your work.

Method 1 This method draws on your knowledge of key signatures and scales, and works well for constructing major and minor triads. Example 9.8 illustrates the procedure.

1. Begin by writing the note heads stacked in thirds above the root, without accidentals: either line-line-line or space-space-space.
2. Imagine that the root of the triad is $\hat{1}$ of a key, with triad notes $\hat{3}$ and $\hat{5}$ above it.
3. *If you are constructing a major triad*, imagine that the root of the triad is $\hat{1}$ of a major key, and think of the major key signature. Add accidentals to the third and fifth, from the key signature of the root.
   - For example, for an A major triad (Example 9.8a): the key signature requires F♯, C♯, and G♯. For the pitches shown, C needs to be sharped: A–C♯–E.
4. *If you are constructing a minor triad*, imagine that the root of the triad is $\hat{1}$ of a minor key, and think of the minor key signature. Add accidentals to the third and fifth, from the key signature of the root.
   - For example, for an F minor triad (Example 9.8c): the key signature requires B♭, E♭, A♭, and D♭. For the pitches shown, A needs to be flatted: F–A♭–C.
5. Another way to construct a minor triad is to begin with a major triad, and lower the third by a chromatic half step (F–A–C becomes F–A♭–C). If you lower the fifth as well, the triad becomes diminished (F–A♭–C♭).

EXAMPLE 9.8   Building major and minor triads from their key signatures

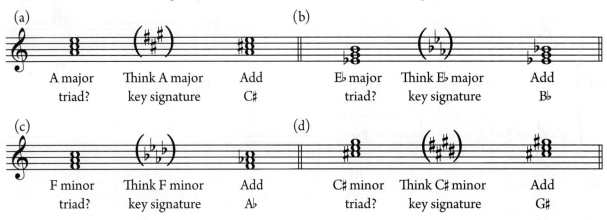

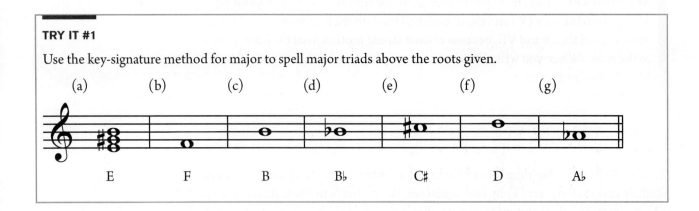

TRY IT #1

Use the key-signature method for major to spell major triads above the roots given.

Use the key-signature method for minor to spell minor triads above the roots given.

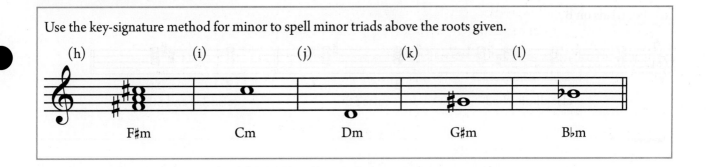

(h)   (i)   (j)   (k)   (l)

F♯m   Cm   Dm   G♯m   B♭m

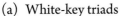

SHOW IT! Assignment 9.1

Method 2 If you like to visualize triads on the keyboard or staff, first learn the qualities of each scale-degree triad in C major (Example 9.9a) from the piano white keys or note heads on the staff.

- Triads on C, F, and G remain major if all the accidentals match (Example 9.9b). To make a minor triad, lower the third a half step. To make an augmented triad, raise the fifth a half step.
- Triads on D, E, and A remain minor if all the accidentals match (Example 9.9c). To make a major triad, raise the third a half step. To make a diminished triad, lower the fifth a half step.
- Triads on B remain diminished if all the accidentals match (Example 9.9d). To make a minor triad, raise the fifth a half step. To make a major triad, raise both the third and fifth a half step.

EXAMPLE 9.9   Spelling triads from C major

(a) White-key triads

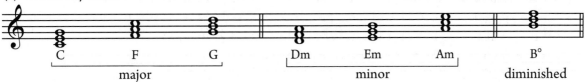

C   F   G   Dm   Em   Am   B°

major   minor   diminished

(b) For triads on C, F, and G

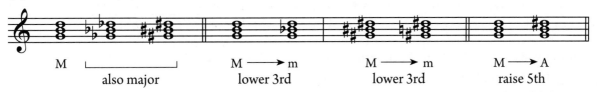

M   M ⟶ m   M ⟶ m   M ⟶ A

also major   lower 3rd   lower 3rd   raise 5th

(c) For triads on D, E, and A

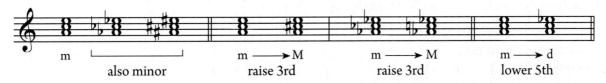

m   m ⟶ M   m ⟶ M   m ⟶ d

also minor   raise 3rd   raise 3rd   lower 5th

(d) For triads on B

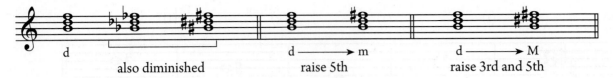

d

also diminished

d ——→ m
raise 5th

d ——→ M
raise 3rd and 5th

TRY IT #2

Write the following major and minor triads, then alter each major triad to make it augmented and each minor triad to make it diminished.

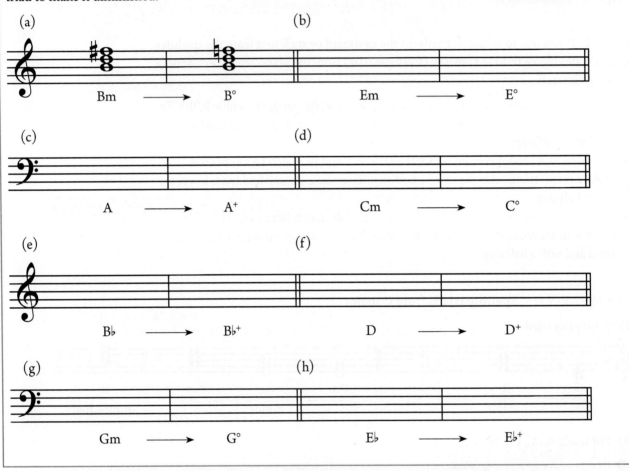

(a)

Bm ——→ B°

(b)

Em ——→ E°

(c)

A ——→ A⁺

(d)

Cm ——→ C°

(e)

B♭ ——→ B♭⁺

(f)

D ——→ D⁺

(g)

Gm ——→ G°

(h)

E♭ ——→ E♭⁺

Method 3 Finally, you can spell triads by dividing them into their component intervals, following these steps (Example 9.10).

1. Write the root of the triad.
2. Add the fifth:
   - For a major or minor triad, write a P5 above the root.
   - For an augmented triad, make it an A5.
   - For a diminished triad, make it a d5.
3. Add the third:
   - For a major or augmented triad, add a M3 above the root.
   - For a minor or diminished triad, add a m3 above the root.

EXAMPLE 9.10   Spelling triads by intervals

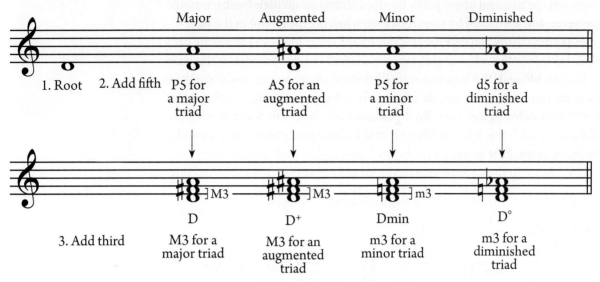

You can also spell root-position triads by stacking thirds (Example 9.11).

EXAMPLE 9.11   Spelling triads in stacked thirds

Triad Inversion

Sometimes you will see triads arranged so that they are not stacked in thirds above their root. For an example, look at the third chord of "My Country" in Example 9.12. It is a G–B♭–D triad, but the third of the chord (B♭) is in the bass and also is doubled.

EXAMPLE 9.12   "My Country, 'Tis of Thee," m. 1

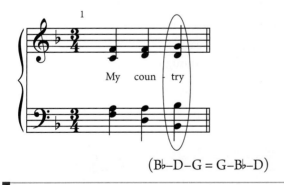

(B♭–D–G = G–B♭–D)

> **KEY CONCEPT** When the root of the chord is in the bass (lowest voice), the chord is in **root position**. If a chord member other than the root is in the bass, the chord is said to be **inverted**:
>
> • when the third is in the bass, the chord is in **first inversion**;
> • when the fifth is in the bass, the chord is in **second inversion**.

Inverted triads sound different from root-position triads because there are different intervals between the bass and upper parts. Inverted chords retain their basic harmonic identity, however, and are named by their root even when the root is not in the bass.

With root-position triads, you hear the intervals P5 and either M3 or m3 above the bass, but inversions bring out other intervals that can be made with the chord's tones, as shown in Example 9.13a: m6, M6, and P4. It is customary to label a triad and its inversions with numbers that represent their intervals, which are called **figures** from their use in an eighteenth-century compositional style called figured bass. Root-position triads have a fifth and third above the bass, for a figure of $\frac{5}{3}$; this figure is often omitted because root position is assumed if there is no figure given. First inversion is labeled $\frac{6}{3}$, or simply ^{6}, and second inversion is labeled $\frac{6}{4}$. Example 9.13b shows these chords voiced in four parts with typical doubling.

EXAMPLE 9.13   C major triad and its inversions

(a) Inversion labels

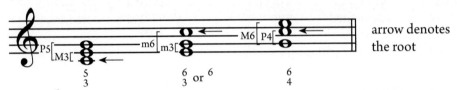

(b) Typical doubling

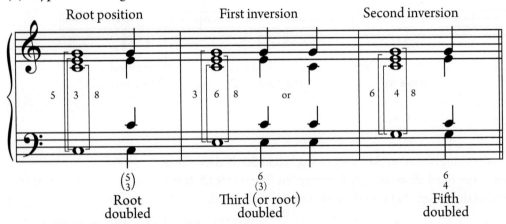

You can also show the inversion of a chord by adding its figure after the Roman numeral (V^6, ii^6) to show a chord's scale degree, quality, and inversion in one space-saving label. In Example 9.14, the Roman numerals show how all three inversions of the F major chord sound in turn. In this passage, the harmony changes every two measures. Measure 7 expresses F major throughout; beat 2 is a I^6 and beat 3 is a I^6_4 even though F is temporarily absent on these beats.

EXAMPLE 9.14   "My Country, 'Tis of Thee," mm. 7–10

Example 9.15 shows each triad position in **keyboard style**, with three notes in the right hand and one in the left. In this style, the three notes in the right hand must fit within a single octave, so that they are easy to play with one hand on a keyboard. The note in the left hand—the bass note—determines whether the triad is in root position, first inversion, or second inversion.

EXAMPLE 9.15   Triad positions in keyboard style

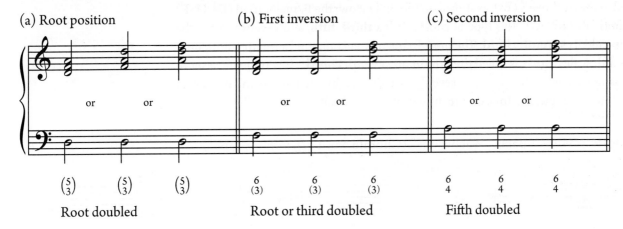

(a) Root position

(b) First inversion

(c) Second inversion

Root doubled

Root or third doubled

Fifth doubled

KEY CONCEPT When you add a fourth voice, you must double one of the three notes of the triad (Example 9.15). While there is some flexibility in choosing a doubling, it is customary to double:

- the root of root-position triads,
- any member of first-inversion triads except the leading tone,
- the third of first-inversion diminished triads,
- the fifth of second-inversion triads.

TRY IT #3

Write each triad in the inversion specified in keyboard style. Be sure that the arrangement of chord tones in the right hand fits within one octave and results in a correct doubling when the left hand is added.

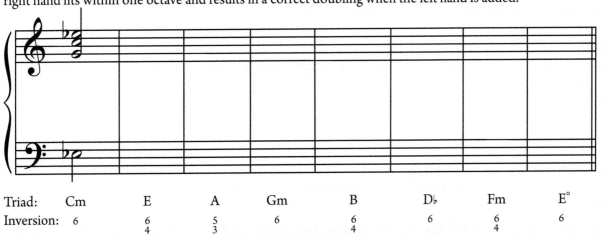

Triad:	Cm	E	A	Gm	B	D♭	Fm	E°
Inversion:	6	6/4	5/3	6	6/4	6	6/4	6

SHOW IT! Assignment 9.2, 9.3

The Dominant Seventh Chord

Example 9.16 shows an SATB chorale, "Wachet Auf," with each half measure reduced to its underlying chord. Ignore the circled notes for now. Most of these chords are triads; however, measure 35 has two four-note chords made of four *different* pitches (with no doubling). We will focus on the second of these (Bb–D–F–Ab), and return to the other in "Explore Further" (p. 246). The chord on the second half of measure 35 has four notes stacked in thirds above $\hat{5}$ (Bb), as shown on the staff below: the Bb major triad (Bb–D–F) plus another third (Ab). This type of chord, with a **third, fifth**, and **seventh** above the **root**, is called a **seventh chord**. The most frequently encountered seventh chord, built on the fifth scale degree, is called the **dominant seventh chord**. The dominant seventh chord is normally written V[7] ("five-seven") or indicated by the letter name of its root plus a 7 (for example, Bb7 for a dominant seventh chord built on the root Bb).

EXAMPLE 9.16   Bach, "Wachet auf" (Chorale No. 179), mm. 33–36

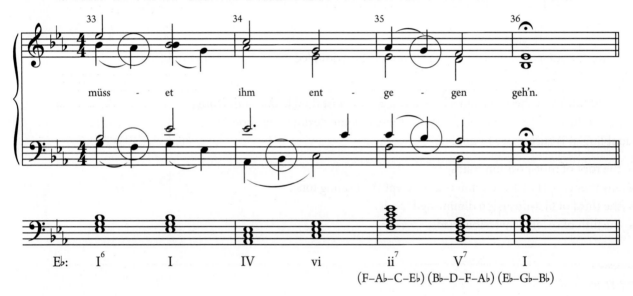

Spelling the Dominant Seventh Chord

To spell a dominant seventh chord, use one of the following methods.

Method 1 First write a major triad, then add a minor third above the triad's fifth, as shown in Example 9.17a. Check that the interval between the root and seventh is a minor seventh.

Method 2 Write the note head for the seventh chord's root, then stack three thirds above it (line-line-line-line or space-space-space-space).

- Ask yourself: In which key is this chord's root $\hat{5}$?
- Complete the spelling of the seventh chord using accidentals from that key signature.

In Example 9.17b, the Bb root is $\hat{5}$ in the key of Eb major. The key signature of three flats (Bb, Eb, Ab) requires that we spell the chord with Ab. Check the intervals above the bass using method 1.

EXAMPLE 9.17   Spelling a dominant seventh chord

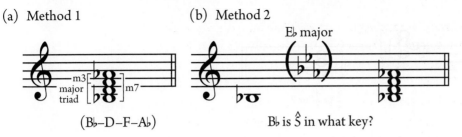

(a) Method 1

(b) Method 2

(Bb–D–F–Ab)

Bb is $\hat{5}$ in what key?

TRY IT #4

Spell a dominant seventh chord above each of the roots provided.

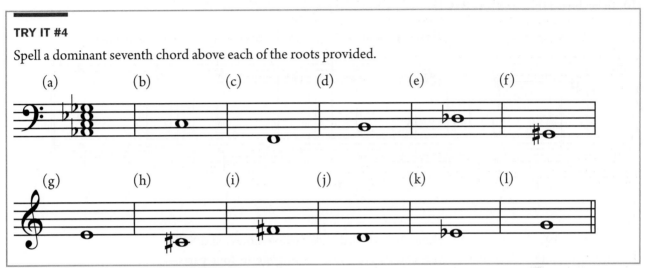

(a)   (b)   (c)   (d)   (e)   (f)

(g)   (h)   (i)   (j)   (k)   (l)

Seventh Chord Inversion

Seventh chords may also be inverted, as shown in measure 9 of Example 9.18. (The circled notes are not part of the chord.) The chord here is a dominant seventh (in the key of F), C–E–G–Bb, appearing successively with the root, third, and fifth in the bass.

EXAMPLE 9.18   "My Country, 'Tis of Thee," mm. 7–10

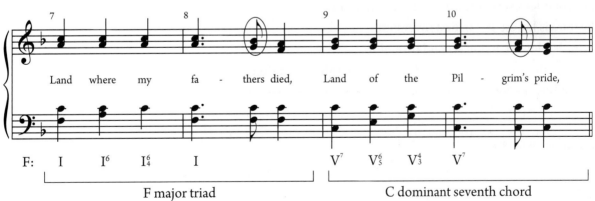

Land   where   my   fa - thers died,   Land   of   the   Pil - grim's pride,

F: I   I⁶   I⁶₄   I   V⁷   V⁶₅   V⁴₃   V⁷

F major triad   C dominant seventh chord

Since they include four chord members, seventh chords have three inversions in addition to root position. Example 9.19a shows a G dominant seventh chord (in the key of C) in root position, then first, second, and third inversion. The first set of numbers beneath each indicates all the intervals formed above the bottom note—for example, the root position has 7, 5, and 3 above the bass, while the first inversion has 6, 5, and 3. These figures are usually simplified: 7 for root position, $^6_5$ for first inversion, $^4_3$ for second inversion, and $^4_2$ or ^{2} for third inversion.

EXAMPLE 9.19   G dominant seventh chord and its inversions

(a) On a treble staff

$$\begin{array}{ccc} \begin{smallmatrix}7\\5\\3\end{smallmatrix} \text{ or } 7 & \begin{smallmatrix}6\\5\\3\end{smallmatrix} \text{ or } \begin{smallmatrix}6\\5\end{smallmatrix} & \begin{smallmatrix}6\\4\\3\end{smallmatrix} \text{ or } \begin{smallmatrix}4\\3\end{smallmatrix} & \begin{smallmatrix}6\\4\\2\end{smallmatrix} \text{ or } \begin{smallmatrix}4\\2\end{smallmatrix} \text{ or } 2 \end{array}$$

(b) In keyboard style and SATB style

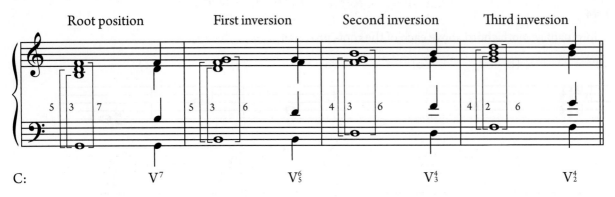

Root position   First inversion   Second inversion   Third inversion

C: V^7 V^6_5 V^4_3 V^4_2

Example 9.19b shows the same chord in keyboard style (whole notes) and SATB style (quarter notes). Inverted seventh chords are usually complete in four parts—nothing is doubled or omitted—but you may encounter the root-position dominant seventh chord with two roots ($\hat{5}$), a third ($\hat{7}$), and a seventh ($\hat{4}$), but no fifth ($\hat{2}$).

SUMMARY

The inversion of a triad or seventh chord is determined by the bass, the lowest-sounding pitch.

- If the root is lowest (in the bass), it is **root position**.
- If the third is lowest, it is in **first inversion**.
- If the fifth is lowest, it is in **second inversion**.
- If the seventh of a seventh chord is lowest, it is in **third inversion**.

SHOW IT! Assignment 9.4

EXPLORE FURTHER   Other Seventh Chords

Seventh chords may be built on every degree of the scale (not just $\hat{5}$), resulting in many different types of sonorities.

> **KEY CONCEPT** A seventh chord is named for the quality of its triad plus the quality of its seventh.

Example 9.20 illustrates the five most-common seventh-chord types, with an example of each built above middle C. A major-major seventh chord (MM7) is a major triad plus a M7; a minor-minor seventh chord (mm7) is a minor triad plus a m7. A MM7 is often called a major seventh chord (or major seventh), a mm7 is a minor seventh chord, and a major-minor seventh chord (Mm7) is a dominant seventh. A seventh chord built from a diminished triad and minor seventh (dm7) is typically called a half-diminished seventh chord, abbreviated $^{\varnothing}$7, and a chord built from a diminished triad and a diminished seventh (dd7) is a fully diminished seventh (or just a diminished seventh chord), abbreviated $^{\circ}$7.

To label seventh chords with Roman numerals, use the Roman numeral for that triad in the key, and add ^{7} for MM, Mm, and mm chords, $^{\varnothing}$7 for the half-diminished seventh chord, and $^{\circ}$7 for the fully diminished seventh chord. For information regarding seventh chord qualities in major and minor keys, see Appendix 6.

EXAMPLE 9.20   Seventh chords built above middle C

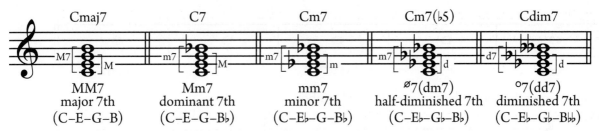

MM7	Mm7	mm7	$^{\varnothing}$7(dm7)	$^{\circ}$7(dd7)
major 7th	dominant 7th	minor 7th	half-diminished 7th	diminished 7th
(C–E–G–B)	(C–E–G–B♭)	(C–E♭–G–B♭)	(C–E♭–G♭–B♭)	(C–E♭–G♭–B♭♭)

Popular-music chord symbols are shown above the staff, as in Example 9.20. Although seventh chords appear frequently in popular music, the labels used to designate them are not completely standardized. Alternate labels for seventh chords built above C are listed in Example 9.21.

EXAMPLE 9.21   Seventh-chord symbols

Seventh-chord type	Abbreviation	Chord symbol
Major	MM7	Cmaj7, CM7, Cma7, CΔ7
Dominant	Mm7	C7
Minor	mm7	Cmin7, Cmi7, Cm7, C–7
Half-diminished	$^{\varnothing}$7 or dm7	C$^{\varnothing}$7, Cmin7(♭5)
Diminished	$^{\circ}$7 or dd7	C$^{\circ}$7, Cdim7, Cd7

To spell a specific seventh chord above a given root, first spell the correct quality triad, then add the correct quality seventh. Example 9.22 illustrates the steps for writing a minor seventh chord above F:

(1) Spell a minor triad, F–A♭–C.
(2) Add the seventh, E (a third above the fifth of the triad).
(3) Check the seventh's quality; if it is not correct, add an accidental. Since F to E is a major seventh, lower the E to E♭.
(4) Use this shortcut to check the quality of the seventh: invert the seventh to make a second. If the second is minor, the seventh is major; if the second is major, the seventh is minor.

EXAMPLE 9.22   Steps to spell a minor seventh chord

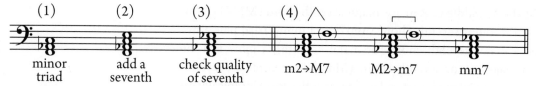

(1)   (2)   (3)   (4) ∧

minor   add a   check quality   m2→M7   M2→m7   mm7
triad   seventh   of seventh

TRY IT #5

(a) Write the specified seventh chord above the given root.

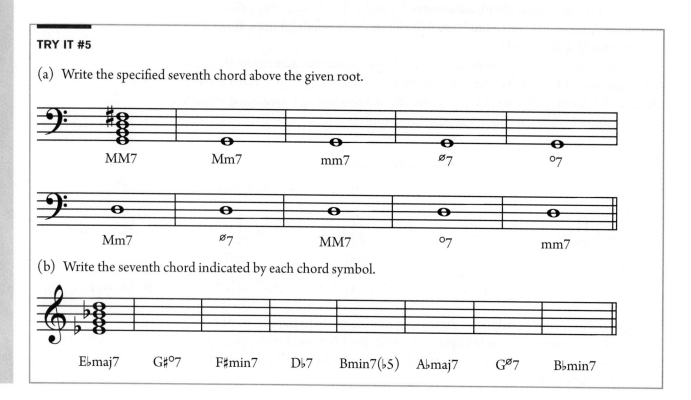

MM7   Mm7   mm7   ⌀7   °7

Mm7   ⌀7   MM7   °7   mm7

(b) Write the seventh chord indicated by each chord symbol.

E♭maj7   G♯°7   F♯min7   D♭7   Bmin7(♭5)   A♭maj7   G⌀7   B♭min7

Did You Know?

The melody that we know as "My Country, 'Tis of Thee," (Example 9.1) or "America" is even more well-known in England as "God Save the King" (or "God Save the Queen," depending on the current monarch). The origin of the melody remains a mystery. It was first published in England in 1744, and became popular after a version with words by Thomas Arne was performed in London's Drury Lane and Covent Garden theaters in September 1745. Arne's lyrics rallied support for King George II and decried the Scots, led by "Bonnie Prince Charlie," his Stuart rival for the throne. Later, both Beethoven and Haydn incorporated this melody into their own compositions.

In the 1790s, the melody became the Danish national anthem, and, with the "God Save the King" text, it has also remained a national song for former British colonies including Canada and Australia. The text beginning "My country, 'tis of thee," written by Samuel Francis Smith, was first performed on July 4, 1831. Over a century later, on August 28, 1963, Martin Luther King quoted Smith's lyrics in his "I have a dream" speech from the steps of the Lincoln Memorial, as he called on the nation to "let freedom ring."

Terms You Should Know

chord

chord members
  root
  third
  fifth
  seventh
dominant seventh chord
doubling
figures
homophony
inverted chords
keyboard style

Roman numerals
seventh chord
texture
triad
triad names
  tonic
  supertonic
  mediant
  subdominant
  dominant
  submediant
  leading tone

triad qualities
  augmented
  diminished
  major
  minor
triad and seventh-
  chord positions
  root position
  first inversion
  second inversion
  third inversion

Questions for Review

1. What is the difference between a major and minor triad? A minor and diminished triad? A major and augmented triad?
2. What are the intervals in a major triad? In a minor triad?
3. What are several methods for spelling triads?
4. On which scale degrees are major triads found in major keys? In minor keys?
5. On which scale degrees are minor triads found in major keys? In minor keys?
6. On which scale degrees are diminished and augmented triads found in major keys? In minor keys?
7. What information does a Roman numeral provide?
8. Which Arabic numerals are used to show each triad position (root position, first inversion, second inversion)?
9. What are two methods for spelling a dominant seventh chord?

Reading Review

Match the term on the left with the best answer on the right.

_____ (1) Roman numerals	(a) chord position with the seventh in the bass
_____ (2) D–F♯–A♯	(b) the seventh chord built on $\hat{5}$
_____ (3) first inversion	(c) figure for a first-inversion triad
_____ (4) $^6_4$	(d) diminished triad
_____ (5) third inversion	(e) chord position with the third in the bass
_____ (6) $^4_3$	(f) figure for a first-inversion seventh chord
_____ (7) dominant seventh chord	(g) used to represent the scale degree of the root and the quality of triads and seventh chords
_____ (8) ^{6}	(h) chord position with the fifth in the bass
_____ (9) D–F–A♭	(i) figure for a second-inversion triad
_____ (10) second inversion	(j) figure for a third-inversion seventh chord
_____ (11) $^4_2$	(k) augmented triad
_____ (12) $^6_5$	(l) figure for a second-inversion seventh chord

Apply It

A. Play and sing triads

Major and minor triads

1. Play and sing $\hat{1}$ to $\hat{5}$ of a major scale: think of the key signature or the pattern of whole and half steps (W–W–H–W). Now perform a major triad: $\hat{1}$, $\hat{3}$, and $\hat{5}$ of the scale segment you just played. Sing with letter names, scale-degree numbers, or solfège syllables. (In class, one student may play while others sing.)

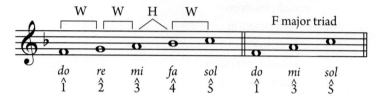

2. Repeat the process with $\hat{1}$ to $\hat{5}$ of a minor scale.

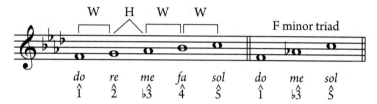

3. You, your instructor, or a partner in your class will choose a starting pitch to be the triad root. Play only the root and then sing the major and minor triads from this root on scale-degree numbers or solfège syllables. Pay careful attention to singing the correct third, major or minor. When moving from major to minor, lower $\hat{3}$ to $\flat\hat{3}$ (*mi* to *me*).

Augmented and diminished triads

- You, your instructor, or a partner in your class will choose a starting pitch to be the triad root.
- First perform a major triad, then raise the fifth a half step to create an augmented triad. While you play, sing the pitches with letter names. Each time you alter the fifth, keep the same letter, but change its accidental (for example, A becomes A♯, not B♭).
- From each of the given roots, perform a minor triad, then lower the fifth a half step to create a diminished triad.

B. Identify triad qualities

Listen to the triads, organized in sets of ten. In the blanks provided, write each triad's quality (M, m, A, or d). As a class activity, you may divide triad identification into stages, which may be completed on different days if desired:

- On the first hearing, sing the triad back.
- On the second hearing, listen for the quality of its thirds and fifth; then write the triad's quality in the blank (M, m, A, or d).
- Before the third hearing, your teacher will announce the beginning pitch of each triad. On your own staff paper, notate this pitch and then write the remaining pitches on the staff, including any necessary accidentals. Don't alter the given pitch.
- Finally, check your answer with the class.

Major and minor triads (played as a melody)

1. _____   2. _____   3. _____   4. _____   5. _____
6. _____   7. _____   8. _____   9. _____   10. _____

Major and minor triads (played as a chord)

11. _____   12. _____   13. _____   14. _____   15. _____
16. _____   17. _____   18. _____   19. _____   20. _____

Diminished and augmented triads (played as a melody)

21. _____   22. _____   23. _____   24. _____   25. _____
26. _____   27. _____   28. _____   29. _____   30. _____

C. Sing at sight

First determine the key of the melody. Most of these melodies feature the tonic triad; play and sing a warm-up on $\hat{1}-\hat{3}-\hat{5}-\hat{3}-\hat{1}-\hat{7}-\hat{1}$ for major or $\hat{1}-\flat\hat{3}-\hat{5}-\flat\hat{3}-\hat{1}-\hat{7}-\hat{1}$ for minor. Sing with scale-degree numbers or solfège syllables; the first few are given. Check yourself on a keyboard or listen to the recording *after* you sing the melody.

Melody 1 Jimmy Driftwood, "The Battle of New Orleans," mm. 9–12

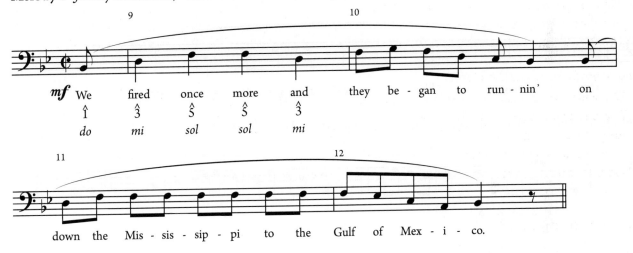

Melody 2 Traditional, "I Had a Little Nut Tree," mm. 1–4

Melody 3 Joseph Haydn, Seven German Dances, No. 6, mm. 1–8

mf

$\hat{1}$	$\hat{3}$	$\hat{5}$	$\hat{4}$	$\hat{3}$	$\hat{2}$
do	mi	sol	fa	mi	re

Melody 4 Neil Diamond, "Song Sung Blue," mm. 1–7

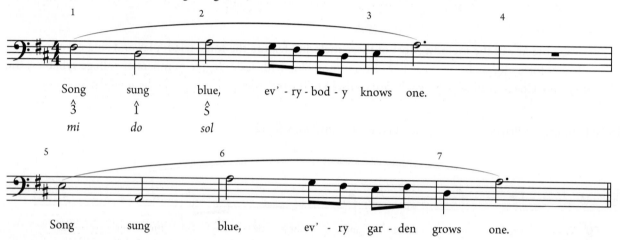

Song sung blue, ev'-ry-bod-y knows one.

$\hat{3}$	$\hat{1}$	$\hat{5}$
mi	do	sol

Song sung blue, ev' - ry gar-den grows one.

Melody 5 Pyotr Ilyich Tchaikovsky, French Folk Song (adapted) mm. 1–8

$\hat{5}$	$\hat{1}$	$\hat{2}$	$\flat\hat{3}$	$\hat{4}$	$\hat{5}$
sol	do	re	me	fa	sol

Melody 6 George Gershwin, "They Can't Take That Away from Me," mm. 8–15

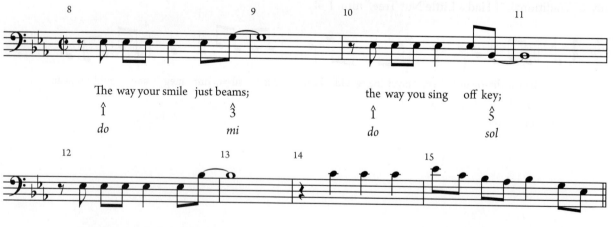

The way your smile just beams;   the way you sing off key;

$\hat{1}$	$\hat{3}$	$\hat{1}$	$\hat{5}$
do	mi	do	sol

the way you haunt my dreams;   no, no, they can't take that a-way from me.

Melody 7 Traditional, "The Minstrel Boy," mm. 1–4

The min-strel boy to the war is gone, in the ranks of death you will find him.

$\hat5$ $\hat1$ $\hat2$ $\hat4$ $\hat3$ $\hat2$ $\hat1$ $\hat3$ $\hat5$ $\hat1$

sol do re fa mi re do mi sol do

Melody 8 Leopold Mozart, Burleske, mm. 1–8

Melody 9 Dmitry Kabalevsky, Toccatina, mm. 1–13

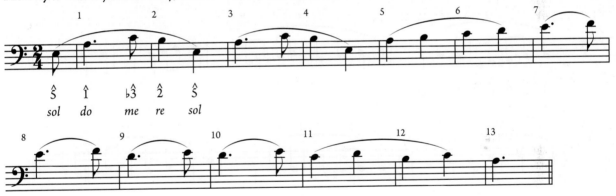

$\hat5$ $\hat1$ $\flat\hat3$ $\hat2$ $\hat5$

sol do me re sol

Melody 10 Traditional, "The Kerry Cow," mm. 1–16

$\hat{5}$ $\hat{6}$ $\hat{5}$ $\hat{4}$ $\hat{3}$ $\hat{5}$ $\hat{1}$
sol la sol fa mi sol do

Melody 11 Traditional, "Arfon" (French and Welsh melody), mm. 1–12

$\hat{5}$ $\hat{1}$ $\hat{1}$ $\hat{7}$ $\hat{6}$ $\hat{5}$ $\hat{1}$ $\hat{2}$ $\flat\hat{3}$
sol do do ti la sol do re me

Melody 12 Traditional, "St. James Infirmary"

What is the quality of the triad outlined in this melody?

D. Read rhythms

Rhythm 1

When you reach the *D.C. al Coda* instruction, return to the beginning and perform until the θ (coda sign), then skip to the θ on the last line.

Rhythm 2

Rhythm 3

When you reach the *D.C. al Fine* instruction, return to the beginning of the rhythm and perform the first two lines again. Stop when you reach the *Fine*.

Rhythm 4

Listen and Write 9.1

A. Identifying triad types

Listen to a series of triads. In the blanks, write their qualities (M, m, A, or d).

1. _____ 2. _____ 3. _____ 4. _____ 5. _____

6. _____ 7. _____ 8. _____ 9. _____ 10. _____

11. _____ 12. _____ 13. _____ 14. _____ 15. _____

B. Hearing and writing triadic melodies

Listen to one-measure melodies composed with $\hat{1}$ to $\hat{5}$ of major and minor scales. For each, sing back what you hear. Above the staff, write the scale-degree numbers or solfège syllables for the melodies (write $\hat{3}$ or *mi* for major keys, and $\flat\hat{3}$ or *me* for minor). You may sketch in the rhythm as well. Finally, write the pitch and rhythmic notation on the staff.

1.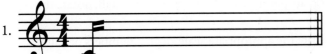

2.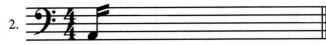

3.

4.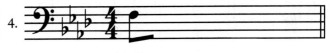

5.

6.

7.

8.

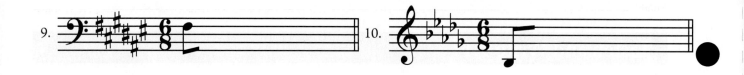

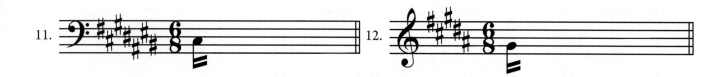

C. Hearing and writing a melody in compound meter

Listen to the beginning of a piano work by Franz Schubert and complete the following exercises.

1. Throughout the excerpt, the melody is doubled at which interval?

   (a) m3   (b) P5   (c) M6   (d) P8

2. Writing the melody:
   - Listen to the rhythm. Tap the beat or conduct (two beats per measure). On the rhythm staff, notate the rhythm of the melody.
   - Now focus on the pitches. Below the rhythm staff, write the appropriate scale-degree numbers or solfège syllables.
   - Finally, notate both the rhythm and pitches in the key of C minor.

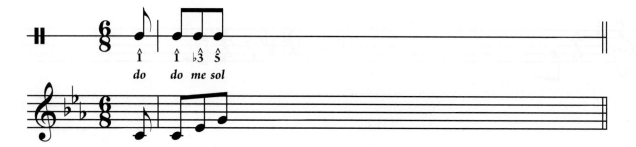

3. Rewrite the melody in the key of D minor. For help, recall the solfège syllables or scale-degree numbers you have written.

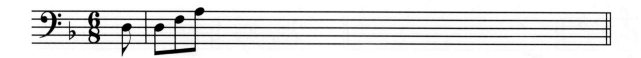

Workbook ASSIGNMENT 9.1

A. Building triads above major scales

Write the requested ascending major scale in whole notes. Above each scale degree, write the third and fifth to create a triad, adding accidentals as needed for that key. Triad qualities and Roman numerals are provided below the staff. Check that the chord you have written matches the specified quality.

(1)

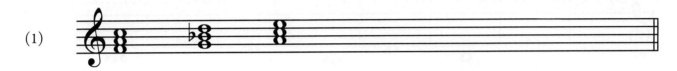

Triad quality:	M	m	m	M	M	m	d
Roman numeral:	F: I	ii	iii	IV	V	vi	vii°

(2)

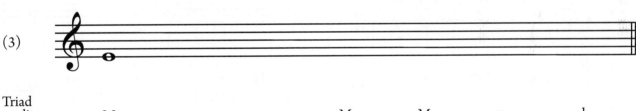

Triad quality:	M	m	m	M	M	m	d
Roman numeral:	A: I	ii	iii	IV	V	vi	vii°

(3)

Triad quality:	M	m	m	M	M	m	d
Roman numeral:	E: I	ii	iii	IV	V	vi	vii°

(4)

Triad quality:	M	m	m	M	M	m	d
Roman numeral:	D♭: I	ii	iii	IV	V	vi	vii°

B. Writing triads

Write a triad of the specified quality above each root given.

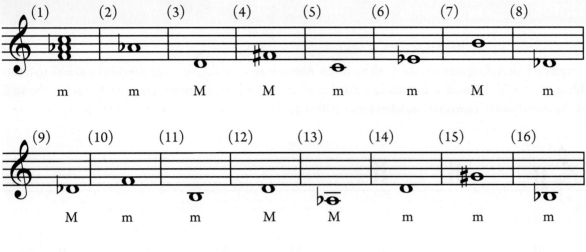

C. Identifying major and minor triads in musical contexts

In the following excerpt, identify each chord by writing the triad as letters (root, third, fifth) below the staff. Then in the blanks for the triad quality, write M (for major) or m (minor) to indicate the chord quality. Remember to apply accidentals from the key signature. Finally, write a Roman numeral for each chord in the key specified.

"Old Hundredth," mm. 1–6

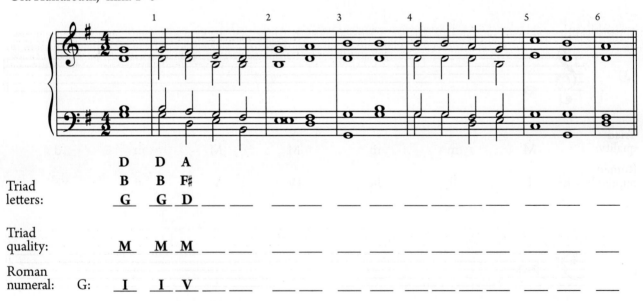

Workbook ASSIGNMENT 9.2

A. Building triads above minor scales

Write the requested ascending harmonic minor scale in whole notes. Above each scale degree, write the third and fifth to create a triad, adding accidentals as needed for that key. Use the leading tone (raised) for triads built on $\hat{5}$ and $\hat{7}$. Triad qualities and Roman numerals are provided below the staff. Check that the chord you have written matches the specified quality.

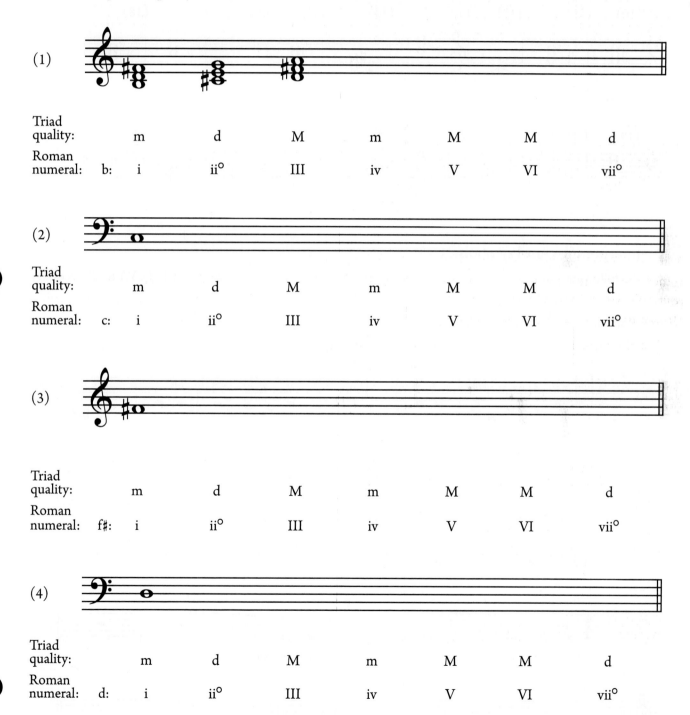

(1)

Triad quality:		m	d	M	m	M	M	d
Roman numeral:	b:	i	ii°	III	iv	V	VI	vii°

(2)

Triad quality:		m	d	M	m	M	M	d
Roman numeral:	c:	i	ii°	III	iv	V	VI	vii°

(3)

Triad quality:		m	d	M	m	M	M	d
Roman numeral:	f♯:	i	ii°	III	iv	V	VI	vii°

(4)

Triad quality:		m	d	M	m	M	M	d
Roman numeral:	d:	i	ii°	III	iv	V	VI	vii°

B. Identifying major and minor triads

Identify the root and quality of each of the following triads (e.g., B♭m).

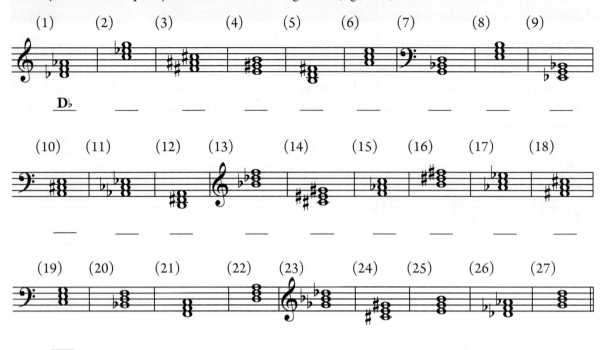

C. Interpreting chord symbols

On the following staves, write each chord specified by the chord symbols above the melody. Write all necessary accidentals, including those in the key signature.

(1) Bono and U2, "All Because of You," mm. 5–8

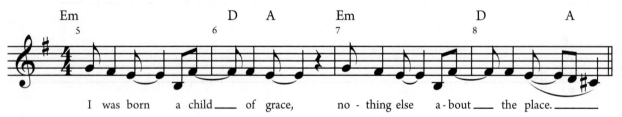

(2) Bono and U2, "One Step Closer," mm. 25–28

Workbook ASSIGNMENT 9.3

A. Writing major triads

Write the major key signature requested, then write the tonic triad (built from scale degrees $\hat{1}$, $\hat{3}$, and $\hat{5}$), using accidentals from the key signature.

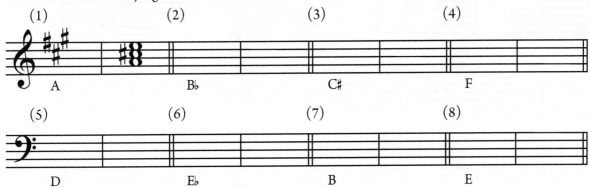

Write major triads above each given note. First draw the note heads (line-line-line or space-space-space), then think of the major key signature of the bottom note to help you spell the chord.

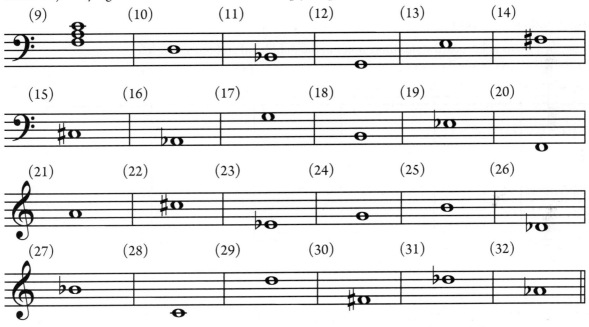

B. Writing minor triads

Rewrite each major triad, and lower its third to make a minor triad.

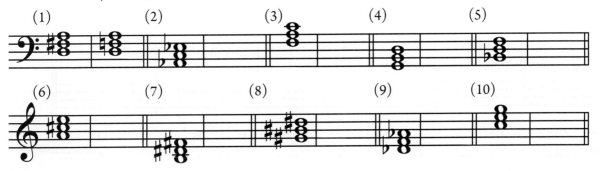

Consider each pitch as the root of a minor triad, then complete the triad.

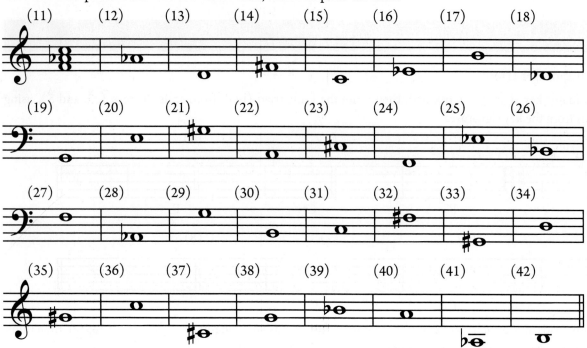

C. Writing triads in inversion

Write the specified triads in keyboard style (three notes in the right hand and one in the left).

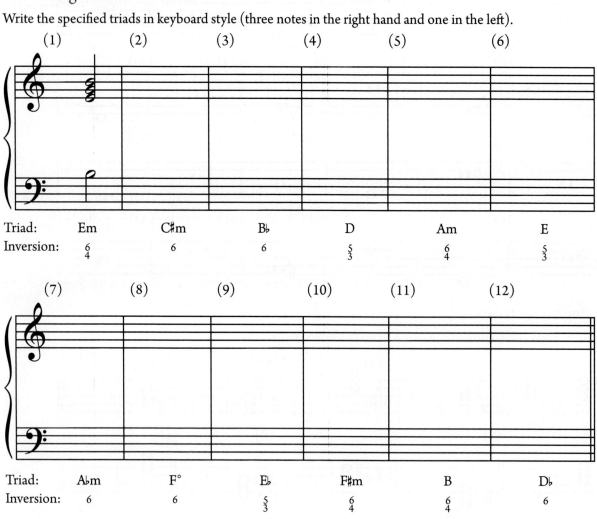

Triad:	Em	C♯m	B♭	D	Am	E
Inversion:	6/4	6	6	5/3	6/4	5/3

Triad:	A♭m	F°	E♭	F♯m	B	D♭
Inversion:	6	6	5/3	6/4	6/4	6

Workbook ASSIGNMENT 9.4

A. Writing major and minor triads

Write each triad specified.

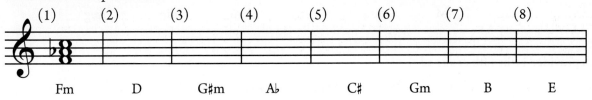

(1)	(2)	(3)	(4)	(5)	(6)	(7)	(8)
Fm	D	G♯m	A♭	C♯	Gm	B	E

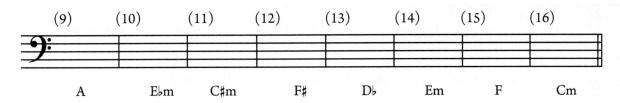

(9)	(10)	(11)	(12)	(13)	(14)	(15)	(16)
A	E♭m	C♯m	F♯	D♭	Em	F	Cm

B. Writing dominant seventh chords

Write a dominant seventh chord above each given root, following one of the methods described in the chapter. Don't change the given pitch.

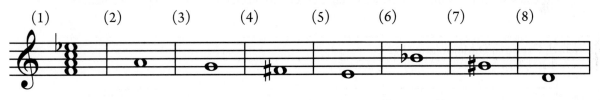

C. Writing triads

Write the requested triads, following one of the methods described in the chapter. Don't change the given pitch. An example is shown for each set of triads, with the starting note indicated by an arrow.

Each pitch provided is the root of a triad.

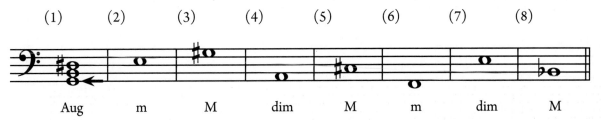

(1)	(2)	(3)	(4)	(5)	(6)	(7)	(8)
Aug	m	M	dim	M	m	dim	M

Each pitch provided is the third of a triad.

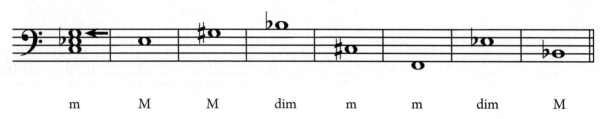

	(9)	(10)	(11)	(12)	(13)	(14)	(15)	(16)
	m	Aug	M	dim	m	m	dim	Aug

Each pitch provided is the fifth of a triad.

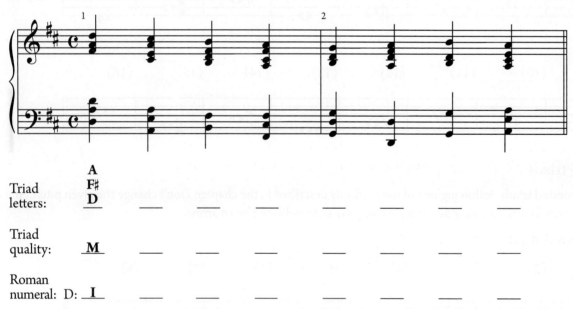

	(17)	(18)	(19)	(20)	(21)	(22)	(23)	(24)
	m	M	M	dim	m	m	dim	M

D. Identifying major and minor triads in musical contexts

In the following excerpt, identify each chord by writing the triad as letters (root, third, fifth) below the staff. Then in the blanks underneath, write M (for major) or m (minor) to indicate the chord quality. Remember to apply accidentals from the key signature. Finally, write a Roman numeral for each chord in the key specified.

Johann Pachelbel, Canon in D Major, mm. 1–2

Triad
letters: **A**
          F#
          D   ___   ___   ___   ___   ___   ___   ___

Triad
quality: **M**   ___   ___   ___   ___   ___   ___   ___

Roman
numeral: D: **I**   ___   ___   ___   ___   ___   ___   ___

Melody Harmonization and Cadences 10

KNOW IT? Take the quiz to focus your studies.

TOPICS

- Triads on $\hat{1}$, $\hat{4}$, and $\hat{5}$ and the seventh chord on $\hat{5}$
- Melody, motive, and phrase
- Harmonizing major melodies with the basic phrase model
- Cadence types
- The subdominant in the basic phrase
- Melodic embellishments and melody harmonization
- Harmonizing minor-key melodies
- Writing chord progressions
- Explore further: keyboard accompaniment

MUSIC

- Johann Sebastian Bach, "Wachet auf" (Chorale No. 179)
- "Chartres"
- "For He's a Jolly Good Fellow"
- Stephen Foster, "Oh! Susanna"
- "Go Down, Moses"
- "Home on the Range"
- "Merrily We Roll Along"
- "My Country, 'Tis of Thee"
- "Rosa Mystica"
- Franz Schubert, Waltz in B Minor
- "Wayfaring Stranger"

Triads on $\hat{1}$, $\hat{4}$, and $\hat{5}$ and the Seventh Chord on $\hat{5}$

The chords most often encountered in major- and minor-key pieces are those built on $\hat{1}$, $\hat{4}$, and $\hat{5}$—the tonic, subdominant, and dominant triads—and the dominant seventh chord on $\hat{5}$. Listen to the end of "My Country, 'Tis of Thee" in Example 10.1 to hear them. The excerpt begins with the pitches of the tonic triad in the key of F major: F–A–C ($\hat{1}$–$\hat{3}$–$\hat{5}$).

EXAMPLE 10.1   "My Country, 'Tis of Thee," mm. 11–14

		F–A–C		Bᵇ–D–F	C–E–G–Bᵇ	F–A–C
		($\hat{1}$–$\hat{3}$–$\hat{5}$)		($\hat{4}$–$\hat{6}$–$\hat{1}$)	($\hat{5}$–$\hat{7}$–$\hat{2}$–$\hat{4}$)	($\hat{1}$–$\hat{3}$–$\hat{5}$)
		tonic		subdominant	dominant	tonic
		triad		triad	seventh	triad
F:		I		IV	V⁷	I

Example 10.1 ends with notes from the subdominant triad, Bb–D–F ($\hat{4}$–$\hat{6}$–$\hat{1}$), and the dominant seventh chord, C–E–G–Bb ($\hat{5}$–$\hat{7}$–$\hat{2}$–$\hat{4}$), followed by a return of the tonic.

> **KEY CONCEPT** The tonic (I) and dominant (V or V⁷) harmonies are the most essential in creating a sense of key. The subdominant triad (IV), combined with the tonic and dominant triads, allows harmonization of many types of melodies.

TRY IT #1

On the following staves, write the scale for each major key listed, using accidentals rather than key signatures. Label each pitch with a scale-degree number. Then write the tonic, subdominant, and dominant triads, as well as the dominant seventh chord, for each key, and label them with chord symbols above and Roman numerals below, as shown. The root of each chord is provided.

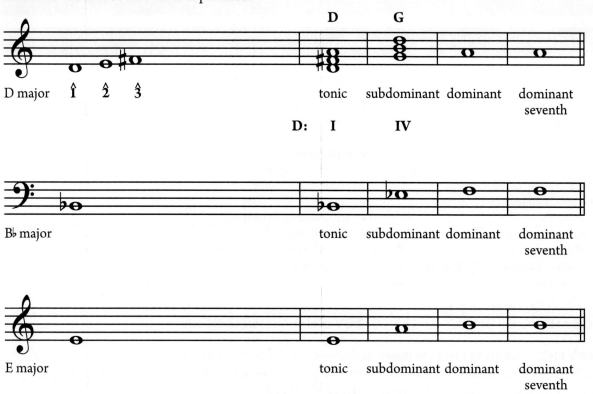

The most common triads in minor-key pieces are also the tonic, subdominant, and dominant. If you spell these triads with the accidentals from a minor key signature, each has a minor quality, and would be indicated with lowercase Roman numerals: i, iv, v. As shown in Example 10.2, composers raise b$\hat{7}$ to make a leading tone, yielding the harmonic minor scale, a major dominant triad (V), and the dominant seventh chord (V⁷).

EXAMPLE 10.2   Triads on $\hat{1}$, $\hat{4}$, and $\hat{5}$ (and V⁷) in B harmonic minor

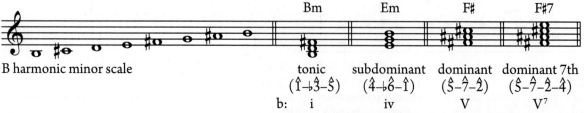

Listen to the opening measures of Schubert's Waltz in B Minor (Example 10.3), consisting of a minor-key melody harmonized by the tonic triad and dominant seventh. Focus first on the melody in the right-hand part (treble clef) of measures 1–2, then compare with the notes of the left hand (bass clef).

EXAMPLE 10.3   Schubert, Waltz in B Minor, mm. 1–8

In measure 1, the scale degrees in both hands are exactly the same—$\hat{1}$, $\flat\hat{3}$, and $\hat{5}$ (*do–me–sol*), the tonic triad in B minor—but in different octaves and arrangements. The melody in this measure outlines the tonic triad (i), and is harmonized with that chord. In measure 2, the melody has $\hat{2}$, $\hat{4}$, and $\hat{5}$—pitches of the V⁷ chord, which are accompanied by $\hat{5}$, $\hat{7}$, and $\hat{4}$. Both hands together make the complete V⁷ (F♯–A♯–C♯–E).

> **KEY CONCEPT** An **accompaniment** is music played by a keyboard, guitar, or other instrument that provides harmonies to support a melody. When writing an accompaniment in a minor key, raise $\flat\hat{7}$ in the dominant harmony to make a leading tone (see Chapter 9), unless the melody features $\flat\hat{7}$ from the natural minor scale.

The arrangement of musical lines in Example 10.3—with melody in one hand and chords in the other—is called **melody and accompaniment**, one of the most common musical textures.

TRY IT #2

Write the scale requested, then the corresponding triads on $\hat{1}$, $\hat{4}$, and $\hat{5}$. Label the triads with chord symbols and Roman numerals as shown. For the harmonic minor scales, make the dominant a major triad (write $\hat{7}$ rather than $\flat\hat{7}$) and follow with a dominant seventh chord.

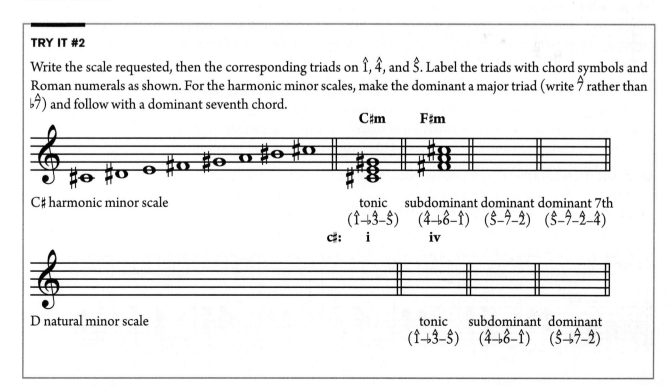

C♯ harmonic minor scale   tonic   subdominant dominant   dominant 7th
                                ($\hat{1}$–$\flat\hat{3}$–$\hat{5}$) ($\hat{4}$–$\flat\hat{6}$–$\hat{1}$) ($\hat{5}$–$\hat{7}$–$\hat{2}$) ($\hat{5}$–$\hat{7}$–$\hat{2}$–$\hat{4}$)

c♯:   i   iv

D natural minor scale   tonic   subdominant dominant
                              ($\hat{1}$–$\flat\hat{3}$–$\hat{5}$) ($\hat{4}$–$\flat\hat{6}$–$\hat{1}$) ($\hat{5}$–$\flat\hat{7}$–$\hat{2}$)

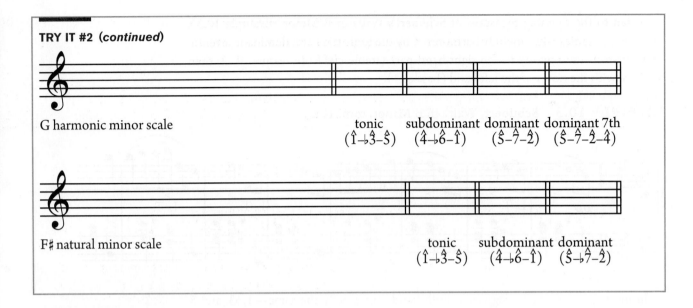

G harmonic minor scale

tonic ($\hat{1}$–♭$\hat{3}$–$\hat{5}$)   subdominant ($\hat{4}$–♭$\hat{6}$–$\hat{1}$)   dominant ($\hat{5}$–$\hat{7}$–$\hat{2}$)   dominant 7th ($\hat{5}$–$\hat{7}$–$\hat{2}$–$\hat{4}$)

F♯ natural minor scale

tonic ($\hat{1}$–♭$\hat{3}$–$\hat{5}$)   subdominant ($\hat{4}$–♭$\hat{6}$–$\hat{1}$)   dominant ($\hat{5}$–♭$\hat{7}$–$\hat{2}$)

SHOW IT! Assignment 10.1

Melody, Motive, and Phrase

Look again at the opening of Schubert's waltz, shown in Example 10.4, focusing this time on the melody. The melody begins with an ascending tonic triad, set with a distinctive dotted rhythm. This rhythm repeats four times in the melody, creating a memorable motive.

> **KEY CONCEPT** A **motive** is the smallest recognizable musical idea. Motives have distinctive rhythms or pitches, and may be repeated exactly or varied.

Now focus on the chords in the left-hand part. The Roman numerals below the staff indicate where Schubert uses tonic and dominant harmonies. The two harmonies alternate, one per measure, until measures 7–8. There, the pace of harmonic change speeds up, with two chords in measure 7 leading to a resting point, called a cadence, in measure 8. This cadence concludes a musical phrase.

> **KEY CONCEPT** A **phrase** is a basic unit of musical thought, similar to a sentence in language. The typical phrase—like most sentences—has a beginning, a middle, and an end. The end is marked by a **cadence**: the harmonic, melodic, and rhythmic features that make the phrase sound like a complete thought. Phrases are typically 4 or 8 measures in length.

EXAMPLE 10.4   Schubert, Waltz in B Minor, mm. 1–8

b: i   V⁷   i   V⁷   i   V⁷   i   V⁷   i

cadence

The rate at which chords change, called the **harmonic rhythm**, is one of the ways you can distinguish one style from another: a harmonic rhythm of one or two chords per measure is typical of waltzes; in hymns, every beat may have a new chord type; and in folk styles, the same chord may last for two or more measures. In all of these styles, the harmonic rhythm tends to speed up at the cadence to articulate the phrase ending.

Harmonizing Major Melodies with the Basic Phrase Model

Chords are typically used in a specific order, called a **harmonic progression** or **chord progression**. A simple folk song may require only two chords: tonic and dominant. The tonic usually comes first to establish the key, followed by a dominant triad or seventh chord, which leads back to the tonic. When we choose chords to accompany a melody, this process is called **harmonizing** a melody.

Listen to "Oh! Susanna" while following the score in your anthology (p. 349). At the second verse, where the guitar accompaniment begins, listen to how the chords change. Example 10.5 shows the second verse harmonized with two chords: D (the tonic) and A7 (the dominant seventh). The notes of the melody tell the accompanist which chords to use. For example, measures 1–3 feature Ds, F♯s, and As, while measure 4 begins with an E that would clash with a D chord but works well with an A7. The circled notes, labeled P and N, are not part of the chord; these will be discussed on page 276.

EXAMPLE 10.5   Foster, "Oh! Susanna" mm. 1–8 (verse 2)

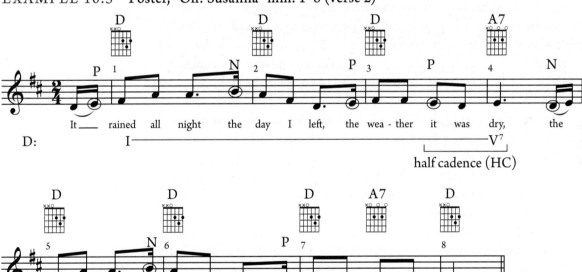

Also shown above the staff as part of the chord symbols are fretboard diagrams, which illustrate the guitar fingerings. The vertical lines represent guitar strings, the horizontal lines show the frets, and the black dots indicate where to place your fingers. (See Appendix 7 for more on guitar chords.)

> **KEY CONCEPT** After the chords progress from tonic to dominant, they almost always return "home" to tonic in a progression that outlines the simplest version of the **basic phrase**: I–V–I. As we add more chords we will show their positions within an expanded basic phrase.

Cadence Types

Every phrase ends with a two-chord pattern called a cadence. Cadences are typically marked by a longer melody note (as in mm. 4 and 8 of Example 10.5) or by rests that break up the flow of the tune. Importantly, they are also marked by specific melodic–harmonic patterns known as the half, authentic, and deceptive cadence types. Of these, the half and authentic types are by far the most common.

Phrases may end on a dominant chord for an inconclusive or incomplete sound, making an **inconclusive cadence**. Listen again to Example 10.5, focusing on the end of the first phrase, at the words "it was dry" (m. 4). This type of ending is called a **half cadence** (abbreviated **HC**). The word "half" signals that the musical idea has not come to an end but must continue to another phrase before it can sound complete. Half cadences end on a dominant harmony accompanying a melody that ends on $\hat{2}$ (or less commonly on $\hat{5}$ or $\hat{7}$).

Often, as in "Oh! Susanna," a phrase ending on a half cadence is paired with another phrase that begins the same way but returns to the tonic. This basic phrase progression sounds more complete, and the music can end here. Measures 5–8 of Example 10.5 follow this pattern. The cadence in measure 8, called an **authentic cadence** (**AC**), is formed when a dominant harmony moves to a tonic harmony to make a **conclusive cadence**. For the strongest type of ending, called a **perfect authentic cadence** (**PAC**), use the progression V or V⁷ to I with both chords in root position (root of the chord in the bass) and the melody ending with $\hat{2}$–$\hat{1}$ or $\hat{7}$–$\hat{1}$. For a somewhat less conclusive authentic cadence—an **imperfect authentic cadence** (**IAC**)—end the melody on $\hat{3}$ or $\hat{5}$ or write the dominant harmony in an inversion.

You may encounter another type of inconclusive cadence: the deceptive cadence. To see a deceptive cadence, look at Example 10.6, a chorale by J. S. Bach. The melody in measures 19 and 20 descends $\hat{3}$–$\hat{2}$–$\hat{1}$ to the tonic (E♭), and the V⁷ seems prepared to resolve to I, but instead it moves to vi—a chord that shares two of its three pitches with I (E♭ and G), but has a minor quality. This bait-and-switch strategy gives the cadence its name: a **deceptive cadence** (**DC**) moves from V or V⁷ to vi, instead of I. In this chorale, Bach places the deceptive cadence here because he is setting two phrases with different texts but with the same melody—after the DC, the repetition of the phrase (mm. 21–24) ends with a PAC.

EXAMPLE 10.6 Bach, "Wachet auf" (Chorale No. 179), mm. 17–24

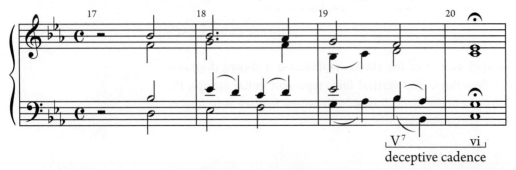

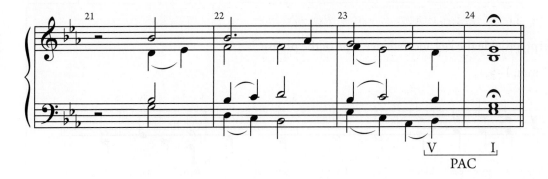

Not all V–vi motion creates a deceptive cadence; you may instead find a deceptive resolution of the dominant harmony in the middle of a phrase that cadences a few beats, or even a few measures, later. For an example, listen to the opening of "My Country, 'Tis of Thee," shown in Example 10.7.

EXAMPLE 10.7   "My Country, 'Tis of Thee," mm. 1–6

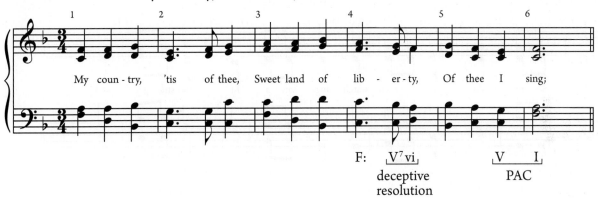

Although phrases are typically organized in four-bar units, this one consists of four bars plus two additional measures that end with a PAC. The first four bars end with a deceptive resolution of V⁷ to vi; here, the deception is not really a cadence, since the music moves on immediately to the PAC. This type of V–vi deceptive resolution is more common than a phrase ending with a true DC.

SUMMARY

Cadence types

- Perfect authentic cadence (PAC), V or V⁷ to I or i in root position: ends with $\hat{1}$ in the soprano; the strongest conclusive cadence.
- Imperfect authentic cadence (IAC), V or V⁷ to I or i: ends with $\hat{3}$ or, less commonly, $\hat{5}$ in the soprano, or places the dominant harmony in inversion; a less conclusive cadence.
- Half cadence (HC): ends on V or V⁷; an inconclusive cadence.
- Deceptive cadence, V or V⁷ to vi or VI: avoids the expected tonic resolution; an inconclusive cadence.

TRY IT #3

For each hymn excerpt, provide the key and cadence type of the phrase.

(a) "Rosa Mystica," mm. 1–5

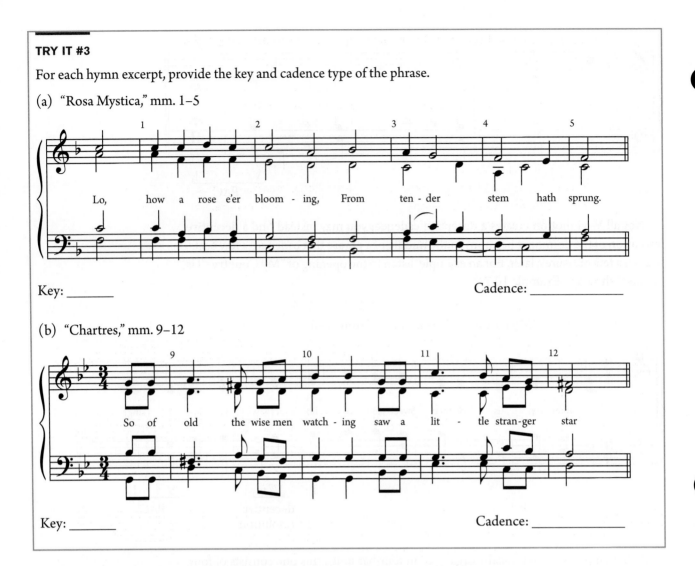

Lo, how a rose e'er bloom-ing, From ten-der stem hath sprung.

Key: _____   Cadence: _____

(b) "Chartres," mm. 9–12

So of old the wise men watch-ing saw a lit - tle stran-ger star

Key: _____   Cadence: _____

SHOW IT! Assignment 10.2

The Subdominant in the Basic Phrase

For slightly more elaborate phrases, you may need a subdominant chord. This triad usually appears in one of two places within the basic phrase. First, because it shares $\hat{1}$ with the tonic triad, it can appear between two tonic triads to extend the tonic sound. We hear this technique in "Home on the Range" (Example 10.8). Scale degrees $\hat{6}$ (E) and $\hat{4}$ (C) in measure 2 indicate that the IV chord would work well there. As in previous examples, circled notes are not part of the harmonies specified by the guitar chords.

EXAMPLE 10.8   "Home on the Range," mm. 1–4 (verse 2)

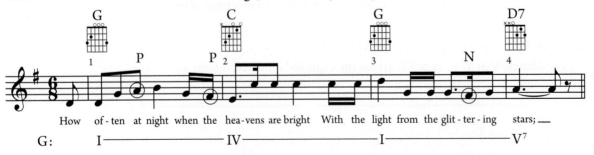

How of-ten at night when the hea-vens are bright With the light from the glit-ter-ing stars; __

G: I————————— IV ————————— I ————————— V⁷

274   **CHAPTER TEN** Melody Harmonization and Cadences

The second place you might see the subdominant triad is immediately prior to the dominant at the cadence.

> **KEY CONCEPT** The subdominant harmony completes the phrase model: I–IV–V–I.

The subdominant provides additional harmonic interest in the phrase, leading away from the tonic harmony and preparing for the arrival of the dominant. Example 10.9 illustrates both contexts for the subdominant triad in "For He's a Jolly Good Fellow." In the second half of the song, the F major triad in measure 5 leads to the subdominant (B♭) to prepare the V⁷–I perfect authentic cadence. In the first half, a IV chord appears in measure 2 between two tonic triads.

EXAMPLE 10.9   "For He's a Jolly Good Fellow," mm. 1–8

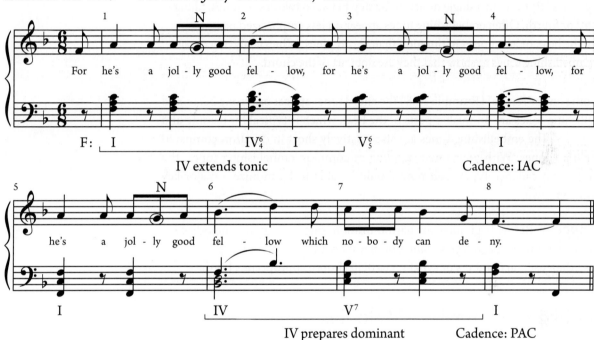

SUMMARY

When harmonizing a melody, think of the melody as scale degrees.

- When $\hat{1}$, $\hat{3}$, and $\hat{5}$ appear near each other, harmonize them with a tonic triad.
- If $\hat{1}$ is repeated for a long time or if $\hat{4}$ and $\hat{6}$ appear, you might insert a subdominant triad, which can move back to the tonic or on to a dominant harmony.
- Though $\hat{5}$ can be harmonized with the tonic, when it appears in close proximity to $\hat{7}$ or $\hat{2}$ or near the end of the phrase, harmonize it with a V or V⁷ chord.
- Keep this basic phrase progression in mind: I–IV–V–I.

SHOW IT! Assignment 10.3

Melodic Embellishments and Melody Harmonization

In the melodies we have examined so far, there are some notes that don't fit into the accompanying chord. These notes are called **embellishing tones**: they embellish, or decorate, the melody by filling in between members of the chord. Look back at "Home on the Range" (Example 10.8). The circled A4 and F♯4 in measure 1 are called **passing tones**: the A4 passes by step between two chord tones (G4 and B4), and the F♯4 passes between G4 (part of the I chord) and E4 (part of the IV chord). The circled F♯4 near the end of measure 3 is a **neighbor tone**—it moves by step away from the chord tone (G4) and comes right back. Passing tones and neighbor tones are the most common types of embellishing tones.

> **KEY CONCEPT** Neighbor tones (N) reverse direction, stepping up (or down) from the chord tone to the neighbor, then stepping back down (or up) to the chord tone. Passing tones (P) move in a single direction by step between two chord tones, filling in a third or fourth. Often embellishing tones appear on less emphasized beats or parts of the beat, or are shorter in duration than chord tones. When analyzing music, circle embellishing tones to show that they are not part of the chord.

In "Home on the Range" (Example 10.8) the chord tones appear on strong beats, and the embellishing tones are on weaker parts of the beat, which is typical for passing and neighbor tones. The embellishing tones are also relatively short in duration compared with the chord tones. With your understanding of common embellishing tones, the basic phrase, and cadence types, you now should be able to harmonize a major-key melody on your own.

> **KEY CONCEPT** Before beginning any harmonization, sing through the melody on scale-degree numbers or solfège syllables or play it on an instrument to hear how it sounds. Then use the numbers or syllables to help choose appropriate chords.

Harmonizing Minor-Key Melodies

You can harmonize minor melodies with triads on $\hat{1}$, $\hat{4}$, and $\hat{5}$ in much the same way as major-key melodies. The only difference is in the treatment of the seventh scale degree—whether to add an accidental to make a leading tone or to use the minor dominant (v). Compare the seventh scale degrees in two melodies, "Go Down, Moses" (Example 10.10) and "Wayfaring Stranger" (Example 10.11), to consider how they should be harmonized.

EXAMPLE 10.10   "Go Down, Moses," mm. 1–8

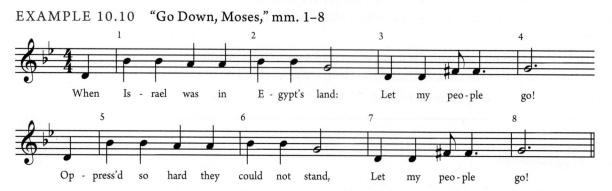

EXAMPLE 10.11   "Wayfaring Stranger," mm. 1–8

I   am   a   poor_____ way - far - ing   stran - ger_____ a   trav - 'ling

through_____ this world of   woe; _____ yet there's   no   sick - - ness, toil or

dan - ger_____ in   that bright world   to   which   I   go. _____

"Go Down, Moses" is based on the G harmonic minor scale, with two flats in the key signature and an F♯ leading tone (making $\hat{7}$–$\hat{1}$). In contrast, "Wayfaring Stranger" shows no leading tone (C♯) and ends ♭$\hat{7}$–$\hat{1}$ (C♮–D); its pitches are drawn from the natural minor scale. Each melody ends with dominant-to-tonic motion, but "Go Down, Moses" calls for a major dominant triad in measure 7, and "Wayfaring Stranger" requires a minor dominant.

In Example 10.12, the beginning of "Go Down, Moses," scale degrees appear beneath the staff and chord symbols appear above. Each chord choice corresponds with the melody, and the progression of chords follows the i–V–i basic phrase model. The dominant seventh at the cadence makes a harmonically strong ending for the authentic cadence. The second phrase (Example 10.13) can be harmonized the same way.

EXAMPLE 10.12   "Go Down, Moses," mm. 1–4

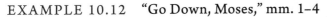

When   Is - rael was   in   E - gypt's land: Let   my   peo - ple   go!

$\hat{5}$ ♭$\hat{3}$ ♭$\hat{3}$ $\hat{2}$ $\hat{2}$ ♭$\hat{3}$ ♭$\hat{3}$ $\hat{1}$ $\hat{5}$ $\hat{5}$ $\hat{7}$ $\hat{7}$ $\hat{1}$

g: i   V   i   i   V^7 i

In Example 10.13, the end of "Wayfaring Stranger," the subdominant (Gm) in measure 7 harmonizes $\hat{4}$ (G) and extends the tonic sound. The circled G in measure 5 is a passing tone, moving between the chord tones F and A. Sing the melody while playing these chords on a guitar or keyboard, and hear how the harmonic rhythm speeds up at the cadence.

EXAMPLE 10.13 "Wayfaring Stranger," mm. 5-8

yet there's no sick - ness, toil or dan - ger _____ in that bright

$\hat{1}$ $\hat{1}$ $\hat{5}$ $\hat{5}$ $\flat\hat{3}$ $\hat{4}$ $\hat{5}$ $\flat\hat{3}$ $\hat{1}$ $\hat{1}$ $\hat{1}$ $\hat{5}$

d: i _____

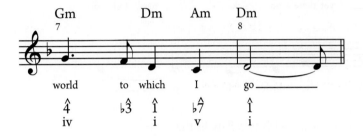

world to which I go _____

$\hat{4}$ $\flat\hat{3}$ $\hat{1}$ $\flat\hat{7}$ $\hat{1}$

iv i v i

SUMMARY

To harmonize a melody with triads on $\hat{1}$, $\hat{4}$, and $\hat{5}$:

- First play or sing it with scale-degree numbers or solfège syllables.
- Let the scale-degree function of the melody notes (tonic, dominant, etc.) help you choose appropriate chords:

If the melody features	use
$\hat{1}$ or $\hat{3}$ ($\flat\hat{3}$ in minor)	tonic harmony (I or i).
$\hat{2}$ or $\hat{7}$	dominant harmony (V or V^7).
$\hat{4}$ or $\hat{6}$ ($\flat\hat{6}$ in minor)	subdominant harmony (IV or iv).
$\flat\hat{7}$ in minor	minor dominant (v).
$\hat{5}$	either tonic or dominant harmony; let your ear be your guide.

- Plan phrase beginnings and endings first, then fill in the remaining chords.
- Listen for the end of each phrase. If the melody ends on $\hat{2}$, $\hat{5}$, or $\hat{7}$, use the dominant harmony. If it ends on $\hat{1}$ or $\hat{3}$, use tonic harmony.
- If a portion of the melody includes several members of a triad, harmonize it with that triad.
- Where possible, follow the I-V-I or I-IV-V-I progression of the basic phrase; you may also use IV between two tonic triads.
- Aim for a fairly uniform harmonic rhythm. In folk or popular styles, the chord may change just once or twice per measure, with quicker changes at the cadence.

SHOW IT! Assignment 10.4

Writing Chord Progressions

Now that you know about the I, IV, and V chords, you can play the chords on a keyboard by arranging the notes to play the chord with one hand, as shown in Example 10.14. Learn these patterns in each hand separately: they are arranged to connect one note smoothly with the next.

> **KEY CONCEPT** When you connect chords:
>
> - Aim primarily for smooth motion by step.
> - If two consecutive chords share tones, keep the common tone in the same part.
> - You may occasionally move by **skip** (a third or fourth).
> - Avoid **leaps** (larger than a fourth), except in the bass.
> - Correctly resolve dissonant intervals and scale degrees with strong tendencies (like $\hat{7}$–$\hat{1}$).

Example 10.14 gives the basic phrase progression in parallel keys—D major and D (harmonic) minor. The fingering pattern is the same for both, but in minor keys lower $\hat{3}$ and $\hat{6}$ by a half step in the tonic and subdominant chords. When accompanying a song, these patterns would likely be played either in the right hand with the chord roots in the left (Example 10.14b), or with the melody in the right hand and the chords in the left (Example 10.14c).

EXAMPLE 10.14 Chord progressions with I, IV, and V

(a) Finger numbering

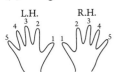

(b) Basic phrase (I–IV–V–I) with right-hand chords

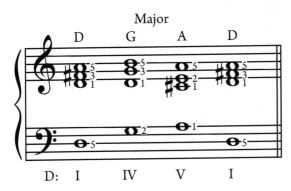
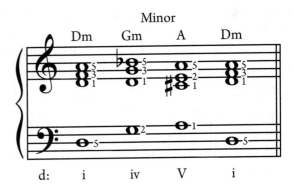

(c) Basic phrase (I–IV–V–I) with left-hand chords (melody in right hand)

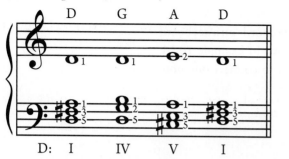

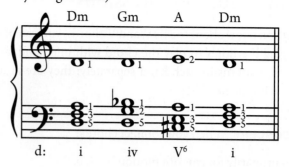

(d) In traditional keyboard settings, avoid jumping between root-position chords (in either hand)

Avoid   Avoid

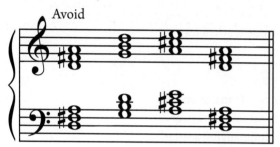

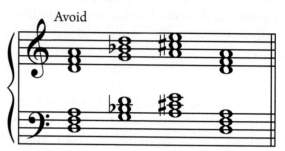

Examples 10.14b and c show the basic phrase progression (I–IV–V–I) with the chords connected correctly. Example 10.14d shows poor **chord connection**, which is avoided in keyboard settings because of its lack of smooth motion. If you wish, you may substitute a V^7 for the V chord; do this by replacing $\hat{2}$ (E, the fifth of the chord) with $\hat{4}$ (G, the seventh of the chord).

The opening portion of your melody may provide an opportunity to extend the tonic harmony with a IV chord. Example 10.15 illustrates a common way to connect I and IV.

EXAMPLE 10.15   Extending the tonic harmony with IV

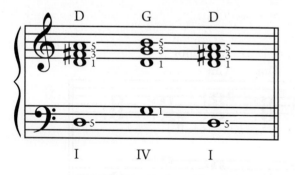

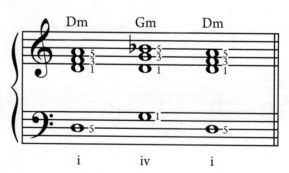

Once you have harmonized a major or minor melody, you are ready for a performance. Folk songs often are performed with two optional sections, one before the song's melody is sung, called an **introduction**, and one afterwards, called a **coda** or ending. In folk traditions, these may be improvised by the accompanist using a phrase or progression from the song. For an example of a composed introduction, look at Wand and Garrett's "Dallas Blues" in your anthology (p. 372).

Write the chord connections specified below the staff (for treble clef, use Example 10.14b as your model; for bass clef, use 10.14c). Include appropriate accidentals for the key.

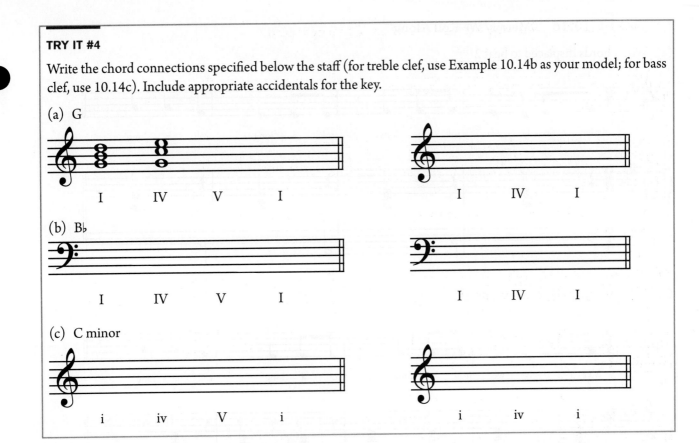

(a) G

   I   IV   V   I   I   IV   I

(b) B♭

   I   IV   V   I   I   IV   I

(c) C minor

   i   iv   V   i   i   iv   i

EXPLORE FURTHER Writing Keyboard Accompaniments

One way to write keyboard accompaniments for songs is to take the basic chord progressions and play them in different keyboard styles. Example 10.16 shows four simple accompaniment patterns for the beginning of the folk song "Merrily We Roll Along," harmonized with only I and V chords. You can use these as templates to write your own accompaniments. Example 10.16a is a chordal pattern with roots in the bass on the downbeat and chords in the right hand delayed to beat 2. Example 10.16b is a more rhythmic version, where the chords come on the & of each beat (the offbeat) and $\hat{5}$ is played in the bass on beat 2, similar to a march. For a chordal accompaniment of a triple-meter melody, you might use a waltz bass—one bass note on the downbeat and chords on beats 2 and 3 (see Schubert's Waltz in B Minor, anthology, p. 369).

EXAMPLE 10.16 "Merrily We Roll Along"

(a) With chords displaced to beat 2

(b) With march-style accompaniment

(c) With eighth-note arpeggiated accompaniment

Example 10.16c shows an arpeggiated accompaniment, which is often used in lyrical settings. An **arpeggio** is the "spreading out" of chord tones by playing them one pitch at a time rather than together. In 10.16c the chord is arpeggiated as even eighth notes. Try each of these accompaniments to see what effects the accompaniment can have on the character of a melody.

TRY IT #5

Write a four-measure accompaniment in $\frac{2}{4}$ meter for the progression I–I–V⁷–I in A major. Use Examples 10.14 and 10.16 as your models.

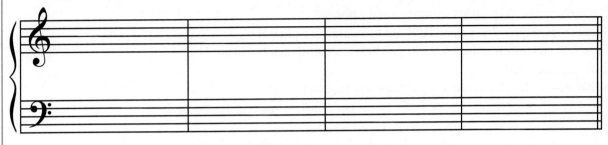

As we near the end of this text, we challenge you to continue exploring music—by listening, playing, singing, and writing. Use the instructions in the following pages to write a folk, blues, or popular song of your own. Be curious, take more courses, and above all, experience music of many styles, periods, and regions. In the twenty-first century, the whole world of music is open to you. Explore and enjoy!

Did You Know?

Schubert's Waltz in B Minor (Example 10.3) is one of thousands of waltzes written by composers during the nineteenth century—a time when making music in the home was commonplace and music recording and replay devices had not yet been invented. Most families who could afford one owned a piano, and children were expected to learn to play. Musical gatherings of family and friends in the evening might include anything from solo piano works, to piano reductions of symphonic movements, to accompanied songs or accompanied solo instruments. Waltzes for keyboard could be played simply for enjoyment, or they could accompany the group in dancing. The waltz was a popular triple-meter dance in which couples whirled around in a circle, with their steps tracing ever-larger circles across the room until they returned again to their starting point.

Terms You Should Know

accompaniment
basic phrase
cadence
  authentic (AC)
  conclusive
  deceptive (DC)
  imperfect authentic
    (IAC)
  perfect authentic (PAC)
  half (HC)
  inconclusive

chord (harmonic)
  progression
coda
embellishing tone
  neighbor tone
  passing tone
harmonic rhythm
harmonize
introduction
leap

melody and
  accompaniment
motive
phrase
skip
triad
  dominant
  subdominant
  tonic

Questions for Review

1. Which scale degrees make up the dominant seventh chord?
2. How do you know when a phrase ends?
3. What are the chords in a basic phrase progression?
4. For each cadence type, what harmonies end a phrase?
5. What are two typical ways for a IV chord to be used in a phrase?
6. How do you know whether a note in a melody is a chord member or an embellishing tone?
7. What are the steps in harmonizing a major-key melody?
8. What quality (major or minor) are the chords built on $\hat{1}$, $\hat{4}$, and $\hat{5}$ of a major scale? Of a natural minor scale? Of a harmonic minor scale?
9. Which scale degree is typically raised in minor? In which chords is it usually raised?
10. How is harmonizing a minor-key melody different from harmonizing a major-key melody?

Reading Review

Match the term on the left with the best answer on the right.

_____ (1) tonic triad

_____ (2) harmonic rhythm

_____ (3) perfect authentic cadence

_____ (4) dominant triad

_____ (5) chord progression

_____ (6) deceptive cadence

_____ (7) subdominant triad

_____ (8) cadence

_____ (9) phrase

_____ (10) chord connection

_____ (11) embellishing tones

_____ (12) passing tone

_____ (13) neighbor tone

_____ (14) half cadence

(a) an embellishing tone approached and left by step in the same direction

(b) phrase ending on the dominant (V or V⁷)

(c) triad built on $\hat{5}$

(d) the rate at which chords change

(e) triad built on $\hat{1}$

(f) the harmonic, melodic, and rhythmic features that end a musical phrase

(g) notes move primarily by step or common tone

(h) an embellishing tone that moves by step away from a chord tone, then returns

(i) the order of chords harmonizing a melody

(j) a basic unit of musical thought, similar to a sentence in language

(k) dominant-to-tonic phrase ending, with $\hat{1}$ in the melody and $\hat{5}$–$\hat{1}$ in the bass.

(l) notes in a melody that are not a part of the harmony

(m) triad built on $\hat{4}$

(n) substitutes vi for I at the phrase ending

Apply It

A. Play and sing

1. Begin by playing the following D major scale (using any fingering).
   - Sing along with letter names, scale-degree numbers, or solfège syllables.
   - Then play major triads built on $\hat{1}$, $\hat{4}$, and $\hat{5}$ and the dominant seventh chord (on $\hat{5}$).
   - Next, you, your instructor, or a partner in your class will choose a new tonic starting pitch. Play the major scale and chords in the new key.
   - Repeat this process several times with different tonic pitches.

Example: D major

2. Repeat the activity of A.1, but now with the natural and harmonic minor scales. As before, play the scale and chords in several keys, beginning on pitches chosen by you, your instructor, or your partner.

Example: D minor

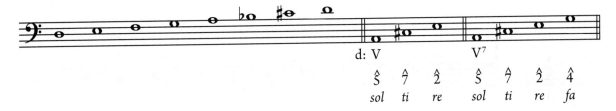

B. Sing at sight

Practice each melody on scale-degree numbers, or solfège syllables, or the lyrics shown, using skills developed in previous chapters. Then sing as a round (a new group enters at each circled number) to hear the chords formed by the combined voices.

Melody 1 Traditional, "Ah, Poor Bird"

Round in three parts

Ah, poor bird, take your flight far a-bove the sor-rows of this dark___ night.

Melody 2 Traditional, "Music Alone Shall Live"

All things shall per - ish from un - der the sky;

mus - ic a - lone shall live, mus - ic a - lone shall live,

mus - ic a - lone shall live, ne - ver to die.

Melody 3 Philip Hayes, "By the Waters of Babylon"

By _____ the wa - ters, the wa - ters of Ba - by - lon,

We lay down and wept ___ and wept ___ for thee Zi - on,

We re - mem - ber thee, re - mem - ber thee, re - mem - ber thee Zi - on.

Melody 4 Traditional, "Dona Nobis Pacem"

Do - na no - bis pa - cem, pa - cem, Do - na___

no - bis, pa - - - cem. Do - na no - bis pa - cem,

Do - na no - bis pa - - - cem. Do - na

no - bis - pa - cem, Do - na no - bis, pa - - - cem.

C. Improvise a melody

Listen to the recording of the following harmonic progression. Then improvise melodies (vocally or on an instrument) that fit the chords of the progression.

- For the pitches of your melody, choose chord members (G, B, or D in m. 1), but also experiment with passing tones or neighbor tones between chord members (for example, you might use G–A–B in m. 1).
- Choose simple rhythms like those shown in the example, repeating rhythmic motives.
- In class, take turns singing along with the recording or create a class combo with your instructor on the piano, plus guitar, bass, and drum set, if available.
- The music, in G major, is organized in four, two-measure units that may be repeated as many times as you like, with different class members supplying an improvised melody each time. Each unit consists of three major triads: I, IV, and V. The final measure, a tonic triad, is to be added at the conclusion of the performance.

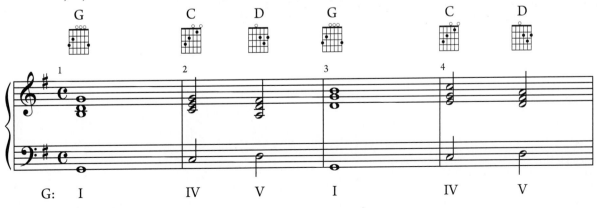

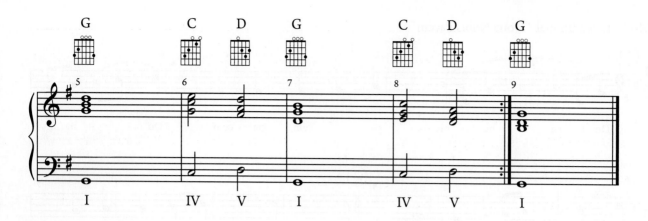

D. Read rhythms

Rhythms 1–2 feature swing rhythms. Swung eighths are written "straight" but are performed unevenly as long-short:

Rhythm 1

Swing

Rhythm 2

Swing

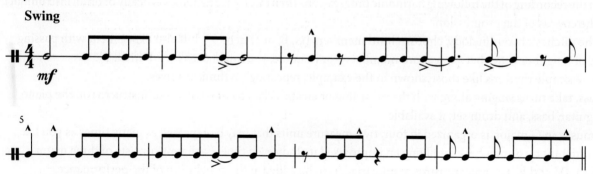

Listen and Write 10.1

A. Hearing and writing melodies

Listen to the recorded melodies. Sing what you hear, then write it on the staves provided. (Optional: You may write the rhythm on the rhythm staves before combining with the pitches of the melodies.)

1.

2.

3.

4.

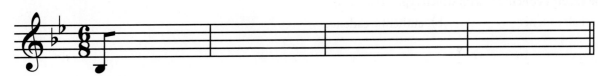

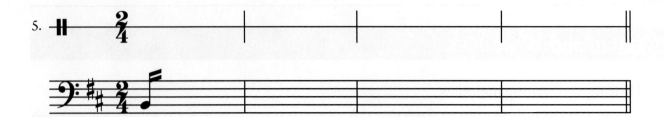

5.

B. Hearing and writing a melody in cut time

Listen to the beginning of a piano work by Muzio Clementi and complete the following exercises.

1. On which scale type is the excerpt based?

    (a) major   (b) natural minor   (c) harmonic minor

2. Writing the melody:
    - Listen to the rhythm. Tap the beat or conduct (two beats per measure). On the rhythm staff, notate the rhythm of the melody.
    - Now focus on the pitches. Below the staff, write the appropriate scale-degree numbers or solfège syllables.
    - Finally, notate both the rhythm and pitches in the key of C major.

3. The largest skip in the melody is which interval?

    (a) m3   (b) P4   (c) P5   (d) P8

4. The cadence at measure 4, beat 1, is of which type?

    (a) half cadence   (b) authentic cadence

5. The excerpt concludes with which type of cadence?

    (a) half cadence   (b) authentic cadence

Listen and Write 10.2

A. Review: Intervals

Listen to the recorded intervals. The first note of each is notated on the staff; don't change the given pitch. In the blank write the interval size and quality and an arrow to show its direction (↑ or ↓). Then notate the second pitch played.

M3↑

B. Review: Triad types

Listen to the recorded root-position triads. The root of each is notated on the staff; don't change the given pitch. In the blank, write the triad's quality (M, m, A, or d). Then notate the triad, including any necessary accidentals. Pay attention to the clef that is indicated.

For example, if you hear a minor triad whose root is B♭, write "m" in the blank, then notate the third and fifth.

m   **m**

Major, minor, diminished, and augmented triads (played as a melody)

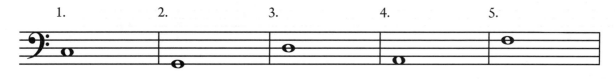

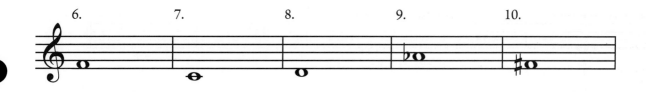

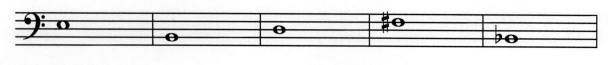

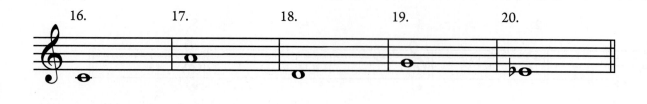

Major, minor, diminished, and augmented triads (played as a chord)

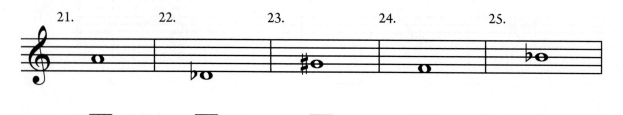

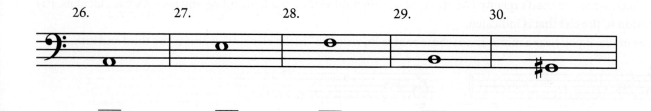

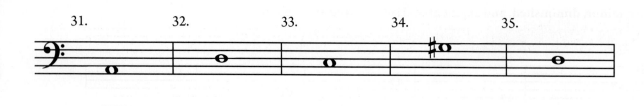

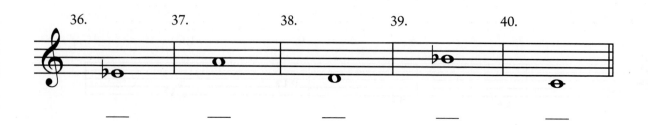

Workbook ASSIGNMENT 10.1

A. Writing triads on 1̂, 4̂, and 5̂ in major keys

Write the following major scales using accidentals rather than key signatures, then write the specified triads in that key.

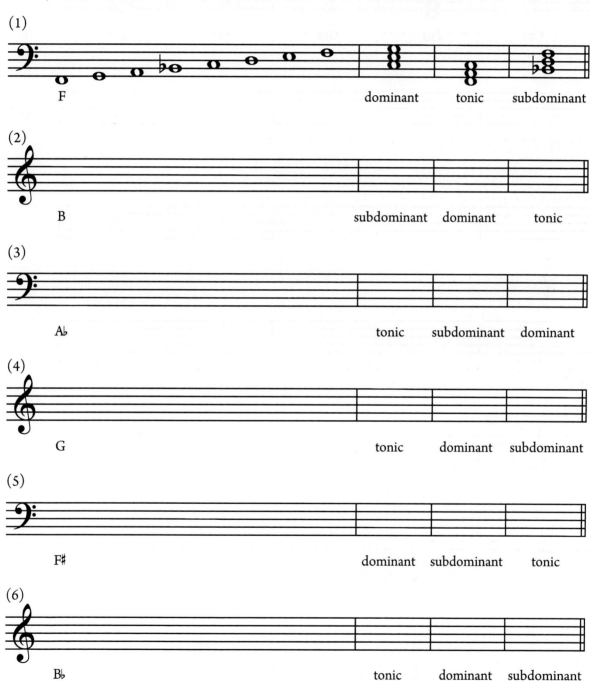

(1)

F   dominant   tonic   subdominant

(2)

B   subdominant dominant   tonic

(3)

A♭   tonic   subdominant   dominant

(4)

G   tonic   dominant   subdominant

(5)

F♯   dominant subdominant   tonic

(6)

B♭   tonic   dominant   subdominant

B. Writing triads on $\hat{1}$, $\hat{4}$, and $\hat{5}$ in minor keys

For each minor key given, write the key signature and the requested triads in that key, then label them with the letter name and quality (for example, Am, D7).

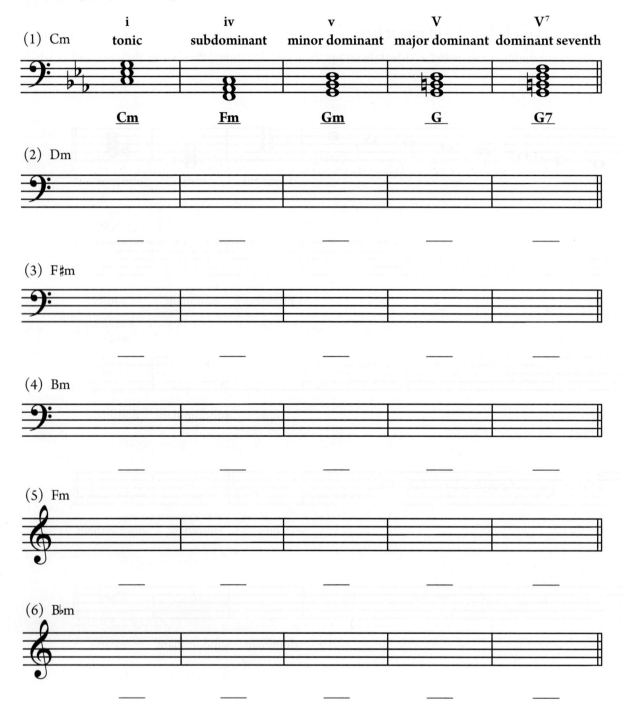

NAME _____

Workbook ASSIGNMENT 10.2

A. Cadence types

Identify the key of each excerpt. Then label the cadence at the end as a half cadence (HC), authentic cadence (AC), or deceptive cadence (DC). Refer to the chord symbols to identify the chords at the cadence.

(1) Robert Lowry, "How Can I Keep from Singing?," mm. 5–8

Key: __F__   Cadence: __HC__

(2) Ashman and Menken, "Beauty and the Beast," mm. 50–52

Key: _____   Cadence: _____

(3) Rodgers and Hammerstein, "Edelweiss," from *The Sound of Music*, mm. 5–12

Key: _____   Cadence: _____

(4) Charnin and Strouse, "Tomorrow," mm. 26–30

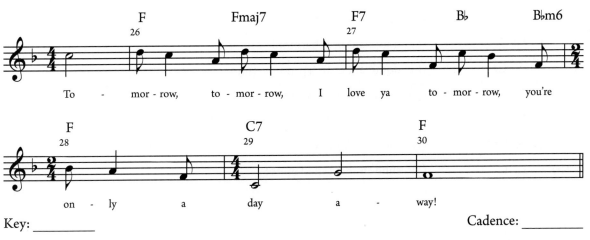

Key: _____   Cadence: _____

(5) If the chord symbol for measure 30 of "Tomorrow" were Dm, the cadence would be a(n) _____

B. Identifying major and minor triads in musical contexts

- Identify each chord by writing the letter names of the notes in that triad (stacked in thirds).
- Then write M (for major) or m (minor) to indicate the chord quality. Remember to apply accidentals from the key signature.
- Next, write a Roman numeral for each chord in the key specified. (Ignore circled notes.) Two chords are in first inversion; for these add the figure ⁶ to the Roman numeral.
- Finally, label the cadence type.

"Nun danket," mm. 1–4

Letter names:

Bb	Bb	Bb
G	G	G
Eb	Eb	Eb

Triad quality: **M** **M** **M**

Roman numeral: Eb: **I**   **I**   **I⁶**

Cadence: _____

C. Matching

Match the pitches in the first column with the harmonies in the second.

_____	(1) E–G♯–B	(a) tonic in Bb minor
_____	(2) B–D–F♯	(b) subdominant in C minor
_____	(3) A–C–E	(c) tonic in F♯ minor
_____	(4) G–Bb–D	(d) subdominant in E minor
_____	(5) F–Ab–C	(e) dominant in A harmonic minor
_____	(6) C♯–E–G♯	(f) dominant in Bb harmonic minor
_____	(7) Bb–Db–F	(g) subdominant in G minor
_____	(8) F–A–C	(h) dominant in E natural minor
_____	(9) F♯–A–C♯	(i) tonic in C♯ minor
_____	(10) C–Eb–G	(j) subdominant in D minor

Workbook ASSIGNMENT 10.3

A. Analysis

The first eight measures of "Wild Rider" use chord progressions and types of chord connections discussed in Chapter 10 in the left-hand part, with a melody in the right-hand part that arpeggiates the chords. Start by examining the melody and identifying the key and mode. Then identify the chords by writing Roman numerals in the blanks (no need to indicate inversions) and label the cadences in the blanks.

Schumann, "Wild Rider," mm. 1–8

Key: _____   **i**   _____   **i**   _____   _____   _____   _____   _____

Cadence type: _____

_____   _____   _____   _____   _____   _____   _____

Cadence type: _____

Look at the remainder of the piece in your anthology (p. 371). Then answer the following questions.

(1) Measures 9–16 are in a new key. What is that key?

(2) How does the texture of measures 9–16 differ from the opening?

(3) How does the final portion of the work (m. 17 to the end) relate to earlier sections?

Now listen to Schumann's "Wild Rider" while looking at the complete score in the anthology. What do you notice about the last part of the piece? (Hint: It should seem familiar!)

B. Analysis

The progression in this familiar passage is based on chords studied in this chapter. Skips between chord tones and embellishments add interest to the melody. Listen to this excerpt, then look at the bass-clef part to identify the chord for each measure. Write the chords (for example, A♭) and Roman numerals in the blanks below the staff, and circle and label any passing or neighbor tones in the treble-clef melody.

Sousa, "The Stars and Stripes Forever," mm. 37–52

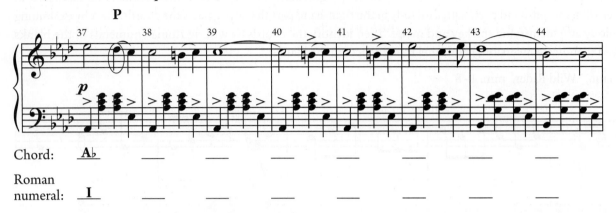

Chord: __A♭__ ___ ___ ___ ___ ___ ___ ___

Roman
numeral: __I__ ___ ___ ___ ___ ___ ___ ___

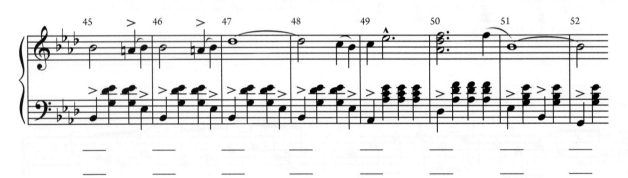

C. Analysis

Identify each chord by writing the letter names of the notes of the triad or seventh chord stacked in thirds. Write the chord symbols for the chords you have notated and label the cadence type. Finally, label the circled pitches in the melody as passing (P) or neighbor (N) tones.

Mozart, Piano Sonata in C Major, K. 545, first movement, mm. 1–4

Letter
names: __C–E–G__ __G–B–D–F__ ___ ___ ___ ___ ___

Chord
symbols: __C__ __G7__ ___ ___ ___ ___ ___

Cadence type: _____

Workbook ASSIGNMENT 10.4

A. Harmonizing melodies

For each folk tune, play or sing the melody to determine the key and whether it is major or minor. Next, write in the scale-degree numbers, and select the chords. Write the appropriate chord symbols in the blanks above the staff to represent the tonic, subdominant, and dominant seventh harmonies and the Roman numerals below. Write one or two chords per measure. Circle and identify the embellishing tones as P (passing) or N (neighbor). Label the cadences (HC, IAC, or PAC). After you finish, sing the melody while playing the chords on a keyboard.

(1) "Wade in the Water," mm. 1–8
(This natural minor tune is altered at the cadence with a leading tone. Choose an appropriate harmony there.)

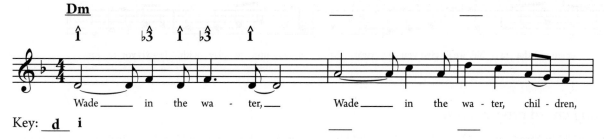

Key: __d__ **i**

(2) "Yankee Doodle," mm. 1–8

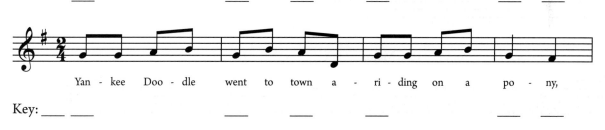

Key: ___ ___

Cadence: _____

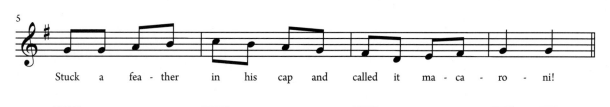

Cadence: _____

(3) "Hanukkah Song," mm. 1–8

Choose different harmonies for $\hat{4}$ on the rhyming words "menorah" and "horah," with an authentic cadence on "horah."

O Ha-nuk-kah, O Ha-nuk-kah, come light the me-no-rah! Let's have a par-ty, we'll all dance the ho-rah.

Key: ___

Gath - er round the ta - ble, we'll give you a   treat, Se - vi - vo - nim to play with, le - vi - vot to eat.

B. Writing chord progressions

Write the chord progressions on the staff. Include the key signature, and write each chord in whole notes. Connect the chords smoothly, using inversions as needed for stepwise chord connections. Commas and periods in the chord progressions indicate the end of a phrase; label the cadence at the end of each phrase (AC or HC).

(1) A♭: A♭–A♭–E♭–E♭, A♭–A♭–E♭7–A♭.

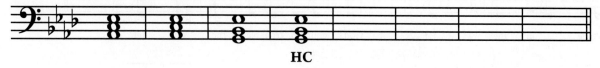

HC

(2) F: F–C7–F–C7–C7, F–B♭–F–C7–F.

(3) Transpose the progression from (2) to E Major.

MAKE MUSIC

Write a Folk Song

TOPICS

- Quaternary song form
- Writing folk melodies

MUSIC

- "The Ash Grove"
- Stephen Foster, "Oh! Susanna"
- "Greensleeves"

Quaternary Song Form

Listen to the folk song "Greensleeves," arranged for piano, and consider the patterns of musical repetition and contrast formed by its phrases. When you consider a piece's division into sections, its patterns of repetition and contrast, and its harmonic structure (including changes of key), you are considering its **form**. This melody has four phrases, making a **quaternary** (four-phrase) **song form**. Example A.1 shows the first two phrases of the song.

EXAMPLE A.1   "Greensleeves," mm. 1–8

301

The melody's first two phrases start the same but end differently: the first phrase ends with an inconclusive HC and the second with a conclusive PAC.

> **KEY CONCEPT** When two phrases are paired so that the first ends with an inconclusive cadence and the second with a conclusive cadence, they are called a **period**. The first cadence in a period is typically a HC, but may also be an IAC. The phrases themselves are called the **antecedent** (comes first and ends inconclusively) and the **consequent** (finishes the period by ending conclusively).

Musical periods are shaped not only by their cadence structure, but also by melodic repetition or contrast. When the melody of two phrases begins identically, or when the second phrase is quite similar to the first, they make a **parallel period**. Phrases are often labeled with lowercase letters to represent their design. "Greensleeves" begins with a parallel period, **a a′**. When the melodic lines of phrases in a period start quite differently from each other, they form a **contrasting period (a b)**. Example A.2 shows the patterns of cadences and phrase designs associated with parallel and contrasting periods.

EXAMPLE A.2   Designs for parallel and contrasting periods

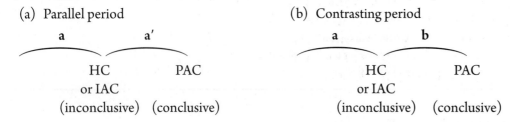

(a) Parallel period

a   a′

HC   PAC
or IAC
(inconclusive) (conclusive)

(b) Contrasting period

a   b

HC   PAC
or IAC
(inconclusive) (conclusive)

Example A.3 shows the second half of the piece, phrases 3 and 4. Phrase 3 is a contrasting phrase, in a higher register with a **dotted-quarter-note** high point that descends toward the cadence. Phrase 4 begins the same way as phrase 3, differing only in its last two measures and forming a parallel period. If you give each phrase a letter, the form of "Greensleeves" is **a a′ b b′**.

EXAMPLE A.3   "Greensleeves," mm. 9–16

Each of the folk songs considered here has four measures in each phrase, resulting in a 16-bar melody. In many songs, the phrases are twice as long: the melody spans 32 measures. This length is so typical that quaternary form is often called **32-bar song form**. These song forms may be written with various phrase designs, most commonly **a a′ b a′**, **a a′ b a″**, **a a′ b c**, or **a a′ b b′** (all beginning with a parallel period), or **a b a′ b′**, **a b c b**, **a b a c**, or **a b c a** (all beginning with a contrasting period).

For an example of 32-bar song form, listen to the traditional folk song "The Ash Grove" while following the score in your anthology (p. 340). As you listen, think about how the song divides into four parts. The first part is the eight-measure phrase shown in Example A.4. The second unit of this song has the same melody as the first, but with a different text.

EXAMPLE A.4   "The Ash Grove," mm. 1–8

Now look at the second half of the song in your anthology. These measures begin with a contrasting phrase that features a two-measure melodic idea that is repeated twice, each time transposed down a step. This phrase ends with a half cadence. The opening melody returns after this cadence, identical to the first and second parts of the song. We can now diagram the entire form of "The Ash Grove" as **a a b a**, as shown in Example A.5. Listen again, while following the diagram for its phrase and cadence types.

EXAMPLE A.5   32-bar song form in "The Ash Grove"

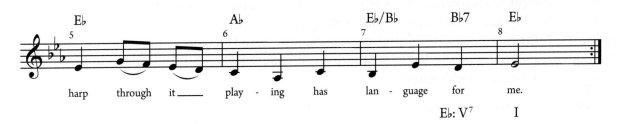

Writing Folk Melodies

Because there are so many types of melodies, no list of instructions can cover all the possibilities. Before beginning, you should have a style of melody in mind and should immerse yourself in examples of that style. We will focus on writing quaternary song forms in a folk style similar to "Greensleeves" and "The Ash Grove."

Most melodies move primarily by step (**conjunct motion**), with just a few well-placed larger intervals (**disjunct motion**). In their disjunct portions, melodies might move through the notes of a triad, with small skips of a third or fourth; wider jumps with larger intervals, called leaps, are less common. As you begin to write your own tunes, build melodic shapes that are fairly simple, with stepwise motion and small skips, and with clear harmonic goals at each cadence. As a very general principle, melodies often begin in a low or middle register, ascend to a high point, then descend to the tonic, making an arch shape. The end of each phrase is marked by one or more notes of longer duration. When phrases are paired, the first phrase will often take an arch shape but descend only to $\hat{2}$ for a HC; the second phrase will then continue to the tonic to produce an authentic cadence, forming a two-phrase period.

All these principles are at work in "Oh! Susanna" (Example A.6). The melody begins with an antecedent–consequent pair: the first phrase comes to rest on $\hat{2}$ over a half cadence (m. 4), and the second concludes with $\hat{2}$–$\hat{1}$ over a PAC (m. 8). Though their endings are different, the two phrases begin identically and form a parallel period (**a a'**). The tune also illustrates several other melody-writing principles. It features a memorable ♫ ♩. ♫ **rhythmic motive** (circled) that recurs throughout, and it outlines the underlying harmonic progression I–V–I (shown with chord symbols) with chord tones decorated by passing and neighbor tones.

EXAMPLE A.6   Foster, "Oh! Susanna," mm. 1–8

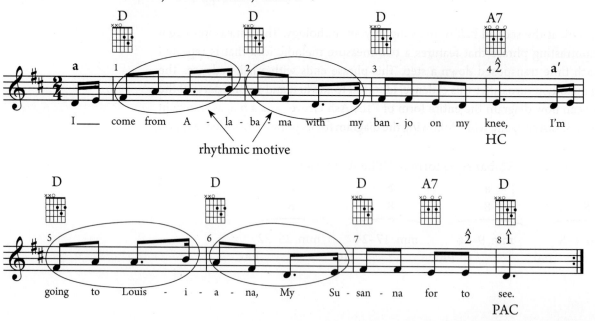

Example A.7 shows the **b** phrase and return of the opening **a** material to complete the form. The **b** phrase contrasts with the rest of the song with its subdominant harmony and longer-duration quarter notes, and the absence of an anacrusis and the ♪♪ ♪.♪ motive. The highest pitch in the melody, B4, heard briefly in the **a** phrases as a neighbor tone, sounds for a full measure (m. 10); in its new rhythmic and harmonic context in the **b** phrase, this B4 is the high point or **climax** of the song.

Look at the score to "Oh! Susanna" in your anthology (p. 349). Below the notation, you will see sets of alternate lyrics, called **verses**, to be sung to the same music each time the singer repeats the melody. (Occasionally, the words of the verses will require slight alterations to the rhythm of the melody, but the pitches stay the same.) In addition, some folk songs have a phrase or two that make up the **chorus**, where both the words and the music repeat exactly each time the melody is sung. The chorus of "Oh! Susanna" extends from measure 9 to 16.

EXAMPLE A.7   Foster, "Oh! Susanna," mm. 9–16

Terms You Should Know

32-bar song form

antecedent phrase

bridge

chorus

climax

conjunct motion

consequent phrase

disjunct motion

form

period

 contrasting

 parallel

quaternary song form

rhythmic motive

verse

A. Sing at sight

Sing each of these folk songs on scale-degree numbers or solfège syllables, then sing again with each verse of the lyrics. Identify the length of each phrase, label each with letters **a**, **b**, **c**, and so on, and notate the scale degrees with which each melodic phrase ends. Optional: Choose chords at each phrase ending for a cadence (PAC, IAC, or HC).

Melody 1 "Sweet Betsy from Pike"

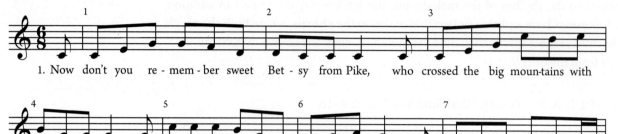

2. One evenin' quite early they camped on the Platte
   Down by the road on a green shady flat,
   Where Betsy got tired and lay down to repose,
   And Ike he just gazed on his Pike County rose.

3. They soon reached the desert where Betsy gave out;
   Down in the sand she lay rollin' about
   While Ike in great tears looked on in surprise.
   He said, "Betsy get up, you'll get sand in your eyes."

Melody 2 "On Top of Old Smokey"

2. Though courting's a pleasure and parting is grief
   A false-hearted lover is worse than a thief.

3. For a thief will just rob you and take what you have
   But a false-hearted lover will lead you to the grave.

Melody 3 "Down in the Valley"

1. Down in the val - ley, the val - ley so low,_____ Hang your head o - ver, hear the wind blow._____ Hear the wind blow, dear, hear the wind blow,_____ Hang your head o - ver, hear the wind blow._____

2. Roses love sunshine, violets love dew,
   Angels in heaven know I love you;
   Know I love you, dear, know I love you,
   Angels in heaven know I love you.

3. Writing this letter, containing three lines,
   Answer my question, "Will you be mine?"
   "Will you be mine, dear, will you be mine,"
   Answer my question, "Will you be mine?"

Melody 4 "Land of the Silver Birch"

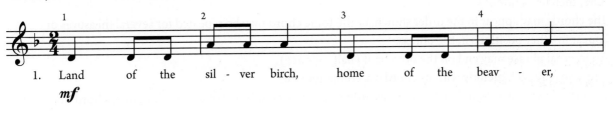

1. Land of the sil - ver birch, home of the beav - er,

mf

where still the might - y moose wan - ders at will.

Chorus

Blue lake and rock - y shore I will re - turn once more.

Boom did - dy boom boom boom did - dy boom boom boom did - dy boom boom boom!

p   *cresc.*   *f*

2. High on a rocky ledge
   I'll build my dwelling,
   close to the water's edge
   silent and still.

3. My heart grows sick for thee
   here in the low lands
   I will return to thee
   hills of the north.

B. Harmonize a melody

1. Play the basic phrase progression in D major and D minor on a keyboard, using the fingerings shown.

   - As you play, sing along with the highest voice on scale-degree numbers or solfège syllables; then sing the lowest voice in the same way.
   - Play it again in C major and F major. (If necessary, write it in the new key first, and then play it.)

D major basic phrase:

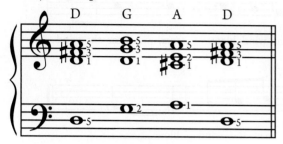

D minor basic phrase:

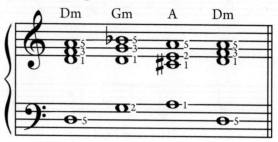

2. Return to the melodies in Part A.

   - For each melody, play the basic phrase progression in the key of the melody.
   - Then sing the melody while finding the appropriate harmony from this group of chords to harmonize each measure or half measure.
   - For the minor-key melody, use a major-quality V chord unless scale degree ♭7̂ (the subtonic) appears in the tune; then use a minor v.
   - The chords may appear in the order shown, or the tonic chord may be repeated for several measures or appear in other positions in the phrase.
   - An internal phrase may end on the dominant (half cadence).
   - Sing and play each melody with its chordal accompaniment.
   - If you wish, you may complete this exercise using guitar instead (see Appendix 7 for guitar chord fingerings).

Workbook ASSIGNMENT A.1

Harmonizing a melody

- For each folk tune given, play or sing the melody to determine the key and mode (major or minor). Write in the scale-degree numbers for each pitch.
- Then select chords, with one or two chords per measure. Write the chord symbols in the blanks above the staff to represent the tonic, subdominant, and dominant seventh harmonies and the Roman numerals below. Label the cadences.
- Circle and identify the embellishing tones as P (passing) or N (neighbor).
- Label the form with phrase letters in the blank at the end of each melody. After you finish, sing the melody while playing the chords on a keyboard or guitar.

(1) "Yankee Doodle"

(2) Gilmore, "When Johnny Comes Marching Home"

When John-ny comes march-ing home a-gain, Hur-rah!_____ Hur-rah!_____ We'll

Key: ___ ___ ___ ___ ___ ___ ___ ___

Cadence: ___

give him a heart-y wel-come then, Hur-rah!_____ Hur-rah!_____ The

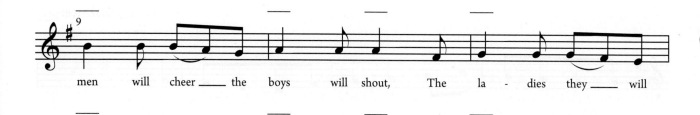

men will cheer_____ the boys will shout, The la - dies they_____ will

all turn out, And we'll all feel gay When John-ny comes march-ing home._____

Cadence: ___

Form: _____

Project A: Write a Folk Song

Compose a quaternary-form song in folk style with lyrics. Use these examples as models:

"Oh! Susanna"	**a a′ b a′**	(anthology, p. 349)
"Greensleeves"	**a a′ b b′**	(anthology, p. 351)

Assignment A.1 provides two additional sixteen-measure examples. "The Ash Grove" (**a a b a**) is thirty-two measures, but also is a good model. On your own staff paper, notate the vocal melody, lyrics, and chord symbols. If you want to create a simple keyboard accompaniment (or as your teacher directs), see step 6. Otherwise you can perform your song with simple chords (for guitar or another instrument) from the score with melody, lyrics, and chord symbols. Practice your song and solo for performance in class, or get a friend to help you perform it.

Step-by-step instructions:

Your composition should model folk style. The style is conveyed through:

- a smooth melodic line with lots of stepwise motion, a few skips, and not many leaps (if any);
- simple rhythmic patterns that conform to a standard simple or compound meter with a quarter-note or dotted-quarter-note beat unit (and few, if any, sixteenth notes), and that fit well with the spoken rhythms of the text;
- one or two melodic and rhythmic motives that provide continuity through the song;
- a contrasting third phrase (**b**);
- and a text that tells a story or sets a scene.

(1) Prepare your score on staff paper. You will need 16 measures for the quaternary song form, plus four measures for the introduction and four measures for the ending or coda (if you choose to add them or if your teacher directs). Your song will have these parts:

- optional introduction (4 measures)
- vocal melody (16 measures, four 4-measure phrases), with two sets of lyrics
- optional ending or coda (4 measures)

After you draft the portions of your song, you can write them into your score. You may write melody first (follow steps 2, 3, 4 in order) or you may write your lyrics first (follow steps 4, 2, 3).

(2) Begin the melody with a musical period: this will be the first two phrases of your quaternary song.

- Map out eight blank measures on staff paper—four on the top staff and four aligned beneath them on the second staff.
- Choose a key, mode (major or minor), and meter.
- Sketch the end of each melodic phrase first: the first phrase should end on $\hat{3}$–$\hat{2}$ (HC) in measure 4; the second phrase should end on $\hat{2}$–$\hat{1}$ or $\hat{7}$–$\hat{1}$ (PAC) in measure 8. Write the chords for the cadences.
- Begin the melody on a member of the tonic triad ($\hat{1}$, $\hat{3}$, or $\hat{5}$). If you want to include an anacrusis, write one that suggests dominant harmony (using $\hat{5}$ or $\hat{7}$), moving to $\hat{1}$ on the downbeat of measure 1. Include notes from the tonic triad in the first measure to imply a tonic chord, and embellish them with passing or neighbor tones if you wish.
- Think about a logical progression of chords for measures 2, 3, and 4. Since measure 4 ends the first phrase with a half cadence, you might want to use I–I–IV–V or I–IV–I–V or I–I–I–V for the first four measures. For the second phrase, choose from I–I–V–I or I–IV–V–I, with one harmony per measure, or have two chords (such as I–V or IV–V) in the third measure of the phrase to speed up the harmonic rhythm. Write Roman numerals under each measure or chord symbols above each measure to represent the chords you have chosen.

- Select pitches from the harmonies you have chosen to sketch a melodic outline for the first phrase (measures 1–4). Melodies are often shaped like a large arch—beginning relatively low at the start, moving up to a high point in the middle, then descending to the tonic at the end.
- Compose at least two memorable melodic and rhythmic ideas or motives that you use more than once. You may create these by filling in between chord tones with passing and neighbor tones. Connect the beginning and middle of your melody to the half cadence you have already written in measure 4.
- Check your melodic line by singing or playing it. It should have rhythmic and melodic interest, and one high point.
- When you have written measures 1–2, copy them into measures 5–6 to make a parallel period, then write a continuation of phrase 2 that connects to the PAC you have written. This forms the **a a′** of the quaternary form.

(3) Now compose the second half of the quaternary form.

- Map out eight more blank measures on staff paper. Decide on the form you wish for the entire song, then follow the instructions below for the design you have chosen.
- For an **a a′ b a′** design (like "Oh! Susanna"), copy measures 5–8 to make the last phrase (measures 13–16). Phrase 4 may be identical to phrase 2, or you may embellish or vary it to produce the last phrase **a″**. Now create phrase 3, the contrasting **b** phrase. Allow this phrase to rise to the highest register of the song to form the musical climax. Create a different rhythmic pattern, such as one using longer durations, to contrast with rhythmic motives of the **a** phrase. End the third phrase with a harmonically inconclusive cadence (on V) to prepare for the return of **a**.
- For an **a b a′ b′** design (like "Clementine"), you can repeat the first two phrases to make the second half of the **quaternary** form, but vary the melody lines a little and/or have a change of text.
- For an **a a′ b b′** design (like "Greensleeves"), follow the parallel period of phrases 1 and 2 with a second parallel period (phrases 3 and 4) that differs in melodic contour and/or rhythmic motives from the first two phrases.

(4) For lyrics, you may write your own, or use a preexisting poem.

- One type of four-phrase song is the ballad, which tells a story. Let the **a** phrases narrate the story, and the bridge (**b**) encapsulate its emotional impact. Your lyrics, or the poem you select, may have parallel ideas in the **a** and **a′** phrases (phrases 1 and 2), to correspond to the patterning in the music.
- Your poem or lyrics should have two stanzas, which will be sung to the same melodic line and with the same accompaniment.
- Place rhymes at the end of phrases, and within phrases, if you like, or select a poem with rhymes that may appear at the end of phrases.
- Read the text aloud and mark the syllables that you consider strong or accented. You will need to align strong beats (or parts of beats) in the melody with accented syllables of your text.
- Compose rhythms for your melody that approximate those of the spoken lyrics. You can do this by setting the lyrics to the melody you have written, or writing the lyrics first, and setting them with the melody.
- The text may have a general sentiment or mood that you wish to evoke through music.

(5) To create an introduction, you may use the chords from the first four measures (keyboard or guitar only). For an ending, you may repeat the last four measures, slowing down.

(6) If you wish, or as your teacher directs, prepare a simple keyboard accompaniment or perform your song from the melody and chord symbols, playing chords based on the keyboard arrangements of progressions from Chapter 10 or using the guitar chords in Appendix 7.

(7) In your performance, play the introduction (optional), then sing through the melody twice, once with the first stanza of lyrics and once with the second stanza, then play the ending (optional).

Write a Blues Song

TOPICS

- The blues scale
- 12-bar blues

MUSIC

- Count Basie, "Splanky"
- Joel Phillips, "Blues for Norton"
- Hart A. Wand and Lloyd Garrett, "Dallas Blues"

The Blues Scale

The blues, which grew out of African American musical practice, has become one of the most important influences on popular music in the world today. Listen to "Blues for Norton" (anthology, p. 365). It is scored for jazz or blues **combo**, a small instrumental ensemble usually consisting of (at least) a solo instrument, keyboard, bass, and drum set (snare drum, bass drum, and cymbals). The solo instruments in "Blues for Norton" are clarinet and alto saxophone. Usually, as here, the drummer's rhythms are improvised and not notated in the score.

Listen to the last few measures while following the score in Example B.1a. The key signature and prominence of F in the clarinet line (mm. 20, 22) and at the cadence suggest that the work is in F major, but the melody features a repeated and prominent $\flat\hat{3}$ (A♭). The piano part includes both A♭ and A♮, and sometimes plays $\hat{3}$ (A♮) while the solo instrument plays $\flat\hat{3}$ (A♭), as in measures 23–24. In addition, the piano has both $\hat{7}$ and $\flat\hat{7}$ (E♮ and E♭). The lowered third and seventh scale degrees are two of the possible **blue notes** in this style, which help to give the blues its distinctive sound. Both pitches come from the **blues scale**, shown in Example B.1b

EXAMPLE B.1 Phillips, "Blues for Norton," mm. 20–24

(a) Score

(b) Blues scale

> **KEY CONCEPT** The blues scale shares most of its pitches with the natural minor scale, omitting $\hat{2}$ and $\flat\hat{6}$ and with an added $\sharp\hat{4}/\flat\hat{5}$. A performance of a blues melody with a major-key accompaniment blurs the distinction between major and minor by including both $\hat{3}$ and $\flat\hat{3}$ and both $\hat{7}$ and $\flat\hat{7}$.

Example B.2 shows the blues scale beginning on C; sing the scale to become familiar with its sound. The raised fourth or flatted fifth (here, F♯ or G♭) changes spelling with the direction of the melody: the blues player's tuning on this note may be slightly higher when ascending (F♯) and slightly lower when descending (G♭). The accidentals in the scale ($\flat\hat{3}$, $\sharp\hat{4}/\flat\hat{5}$, and $\flat\hat{7}$) are the blue notes. When writing blues, use the major key signature of the tonic pitch and add accidentals as needed, as in "Blues for Norton."

EXAMPLE B.2 Blues scale on C

The anthology includes two scores for "Blues for Norton": one is a full score that shows what each instrumentalist plays on the recording (p. 366); more often, blues performers play from a **lead sheet** (p. 365), which gives the primary melody plus chord symbols. Instrumentalists improvise their parts from these musical cues. Follow the lead sheet as you listen to the recording. The piano part, not included in the lead sheet, is created spontaneously by the pianist, who follows the chord symbols. Likewise, the bass player not only supplies the roots of the chords, but also adds considerable melodic and rhythmic interest to the performance with improvised stepwise motion and some arpeggiations of harmonies.

Example B.3 is the lead sheet for the first twelve bars of Count Basie's "Splanky." Listen while following along. (The performance also includes a long piano introduction not shown here.) This melody is made of short melodic patterns referred to as **riffs**, labeled in Example B.3. The treatment of the riff features a **call-and-response** structure, where the original riff is the "call" and the descending riff the "response." An extension of the riff concludes the 4-bar unit. Compare the pitches of Example B.3 with the blues scale shown in Example B.2.

EXAMPLE B.3   Count Basie, "Splanky," mm. 1–12

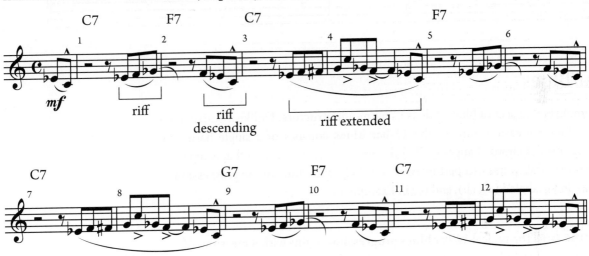

> **KEY CONCEPT** Although the blues scale sounds minor, with $\flat\hat{3}$ and $\flat\hat{7}$, it is typically harmonized by chords from a major key. This juxtaposition of major-key harmonies with the minor-sounding scale in the solo parts accounts for much of the distinctive character of blues compositions.

In "Splanky," the key signature provided is for C major, but the melody is based on the C blues scale, necessitating many accidentals. Basie's melody draws on the full blues scale on C except for B♭ (which, however, is present in the C7 chord, C–E–G–B♭). The F♯ (♯$\hat{4}$) in the ascending melody in measure 3 becomes a G♭ (♭$\hat{5}$) in measure $\hat{4}$ when the melody descends. The notes E♮ and E♭ ($\hat{3}$ and ♭$\hat{3}$) are heard simultaneously, as is typical: the melody in measure 1 features the blue note E♭, while the C7 chord harmonizing it has E♮.

Write blues scales that begin on the pitches given, ascending and descending, and label the scale-degree numbers. Supply the appropriate major key signature, and add accidentals. Remember to use ♯4̂ ascending and ♭5̂ descending.

(a) B♭:   (ascending)   (descending)

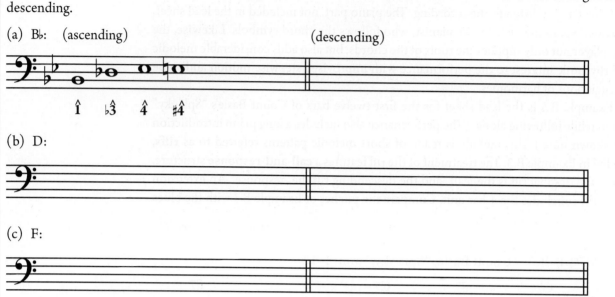

1̂   ♭3̂   4̂   ♯4̂

(b) D:

(c) F:

12-Bar Blues

Another important aspect of blues style is its harmonic structure. Unlike a 32-bar song form, with four 8-measure phrases, the **12-bar blues** consists of a single harmonic progression or set of chord changes (called **changes** by jazz musicians) that is repeated many times over the course of a performance. It is helpful to think of the progression as three 4-bar units, labeled (a), (b), and (c) in Example B.4.

> **KEY CONCEPT** The typical 12-bar **blues progression** begins with 4 measures of tonic harmony (a), followed by 2 measures of IV and 2 measures of I (b). The last 4 measures (c) feature the chords V–IV–I and end with a final tonic measure. This last measure may serve as an optional **turnaround**, with V or V⁷ instead of (or after) the tonic, leading back to the beginning (a) for another repetition of the progression.

EXAMPLE B.4   12-bar blues progression

(a)   I⁽⁷⁾ | | | |

(b)   IV⁽⁷⁾| | I⁽⁷⁾ | |

(c)   V⁽⁷⁾ | IV⁽⁷⁾ | I⁽⁷⁾ | (V⁽⁷⁾):‖

(optional turnaround)

Each harmony in the 12-bar blues may be played as a triad or dominant seventh chord, as shown. This basic progression may be varied by adding or omitting chords—see "Dallas Blues" (anthology, p. 372), an early blues composition, for a variant.

In popular styles such as jazz and the blues, harmonic progressions and dissonance are treated differently from their counterparts in classical styles. First, the seventh chord is considered as stable as the triad. Seventh chords may appear on any degree of the scale and on nearly every change of chord. Second, while in classical music chordal sevenths are considered a dissonance that must resolve down by stepwise motion, in popular styles sevenths may be left unresolved for their color or dramatic effect. Third, the progression V–IV (or V^7–IV^7) is an integral part of the 12-bar blues (occurring at its final cadence) and is standard practice in rock, but it is rare in classical compositions and folk songs.

Example B.5 shows the blues progression for "Splanky" in score notation, without the melody. The four slashes in each measure mean that performers should improvise on each chord for four beats—the voicing and rhythm of the chord are up to the performer, in collaboration with the other members of the combo. The chords whose symbols are given in parentheses may be omitted. To play a basic version of these chords, use the fingerings and keyboard arrangements from Chapter 10.

EXAMPLE B.5   Score notation for 12-bar blues

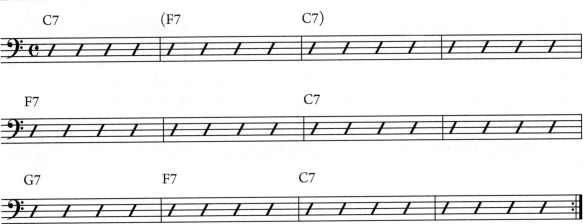

Listen again to "Splanky," following the chord changes; it may help to sing the chord roots along with the recording. Try out its progression on a keyboard (you can simply play the chord once per measure, or repeat it on each beat), then play through Basie's melody or create your own, drawing on the C blues scale from Example B.2. In traditional blues practice, players first perform the initial tune and progression (together called the **head**), then with each successive chorus, various performers improvise over the chord changes. The head usually returns at the end of the performance, and sometimes in the middle as well. The 12-bar blues progression was adopted by rock musicians in the 1950s and appears in songs of many styles after that time.

Terms You Should Know

12-bar blues	call-and-response	lead sheet
blue notes	changes	turnaround
blues progression	combo	
blues scale	head	

Apply It

A. Sing at sight

- Perform the rhythm of the melody alone, while tapping or conducting the beat. Then perform with a swung rhythm.
- Perform the blues scale warm-up for each melody on scale-degree numbers or solfège syllables.
- Sing the pitches of the melody, then combine the pitches with the rhythm.

Melodies 1 and 2 are blues melodies, but they do not follow the "standard" twelve-bar blues harmonic progression. Melodies 3 and 4 are blues melodies with chord progressions that can serve as models for your own writing projects. You may sing Melodies 3 and 4 along with the recording provided for Part B.

Warm-up

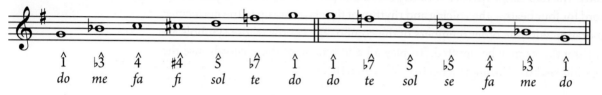

Melody 1 Duke Ellington and Irving Mills, "It Don't Mean a Thing," mm. 9–16

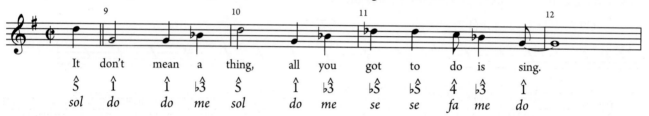

Warm-up

Melody 2 Traditional, "Wade in the Water"

wade____ in the wa - ter,__ God's goin' to trou-ble the wa - ter.__

See that band all dressed_ in white, God's goin' to trou-ble the wa - ter.__ The

lead - er looks like the Is - rael - ite,__ God's goin' to trou-ble the wa - ter.__

Warm-up

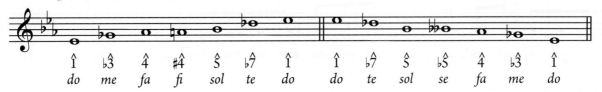

$\hat{1}$ $\flat\hat{3}$ $\hat{4}$ $\#\hat{4}$ $\hat{5}$ $\flat\hat{7}$ $\hat{1}$ $\hat{1}$ $\flat\hat{7}$ $\hat{5}$ $\flat\hat{5}$ $\hat{4}$ $\flat\hat{3}$ $\hat{1}$
do me fa fi sol te do   do te sol se fa me do

Melody 3 Joel Phillips, "Tired of Work-in' Blues"

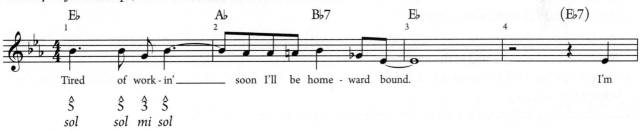

Tired of work - in'_____ soon I'll be home - ward bound. I'm

$\hat{5}$ $\hat{5}$ $\hat{3}$ $\hat{5}$
sol   sol mi sol

tired of work - in'_____ can't wait to lay me down.__ I

hear my Sav - ior call - in'_____ there is no sweet - er sound.__

Warm-up

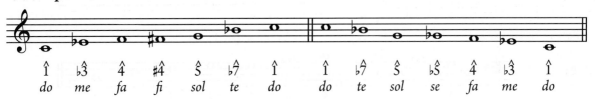

$\hat{1}$ $\flat\hat{3}$ $\hat{4}$ $\#\hat{4}$ $\hat{5}$ $\flat\hat{7}$ $\hat{1}$ $\hat{1}$ $\flat\hat{7}$ $\hat{5}$ $\flat\hat{5}$ $\hat{4}$ $\flat\hat{3}$ $\hat{1}$
do me fa fi sol te do   do te sol se fa me do

Melody 4 Joel Phillips, "Rock around the Corner"

Gon-na rock a-round the corn-er to-night____ with you.   The boys and girls are gon-na come and rock a-round too. The

ŝ ŝ î î 3 3 ŝ ŝ
sol sol do do mi mi sol sol

mom-mas and the pa-pas gon-na rock a-long.   Danc — ing and a-sing-ing this rock - in' lit-tle song.

Ba - by won't you join me? ____   Ain't gon - na rock you too long. ____

B. Improvise blues riffs

A blues progression is provided in C. Follow these instructions to improvise blues riffs. Sing them on solfège syllables or on "ba," and perform with swung rhythms.

- Begin by tapping or conducting along with the recorded progression, to count out the measures of the 12-bar blues and become oriented to the harmonies.
- Improvise a 2-bar riff in measures 1–2. Repeat it in measures 5–6 and 9–10 using pitches of the blues scale and the appropriate harmony.
- Alternatively, improvise a variant of the opening riff in measures 5–6 and 9–10.
- Prepare your improvisation for performance in class; take turns exchanging parts until each person has had the opportunity to improvise.

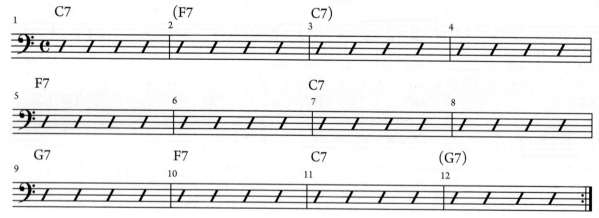

C blues scale

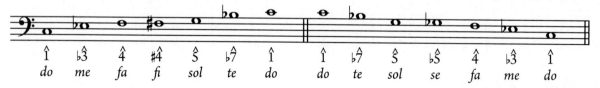

î ♭3 4 #4 ŝ ♭7 î î ♭7 ŝ ♭ŝ 4 ♭3 î
do me fa fi sol te do do te sol se fa me do

Workbook   ASSIGNMENT B.1

A. Blues scales

Spell the blues scales that begin on the pitches given. Write the appropriate key signature and accidentals (both ascending and descending). Remember to use ♯$\hat{4}$ ascending and ♭$\hat{5}$ descending.

(1) Beginning on G:

(2) Beginning on B♭:

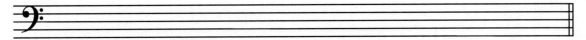

(3) Beginning on D:

(4) Beginning on E:

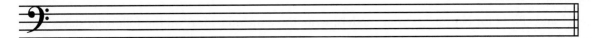

B. Writing blues progessions

Write the changes for the 12-bar blues. Write one chord symbol above each measure.

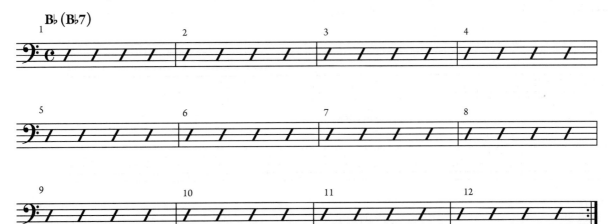

C. Analyzing a blues melody

(1) The melody of "Blues for Norton," shown here, is based on only a few short melodic ideas that are repeated and expanded. The initial melodic idea consists of two motives: a C–D–C neighbor plus a leap to A♭, and a scale segment A♭–G–F. This basic melodic idea is repeated exactly in measures 2–3, then the rhythm of the scale segment is varied in measure 4. Draw a circle around all of the C–D–C–A♭ statements and a box around all of the A♭–G–F statements. The circles and boxes may overlap.

(2) In measures 6–9, how is the melodic motive varied? In measures 10–11?

D. Writing a blues melody

Using "Splanky" and "Blues for Norton" as your models, write three melodic ideas on the following staves using a blues scale in the key of your choice (each melodic idea in a different key). Next to each melodic idea, write one variant (for example, change the melodic direction or add, replace, or remove a note). Then select your best ideas (with their variants) and use them to compose a 12-bar blues melody. Copy the melody on staff paper and be prepared to perform it in class, or use it for your song in Project B.

Melodic idea 1:   Variant:

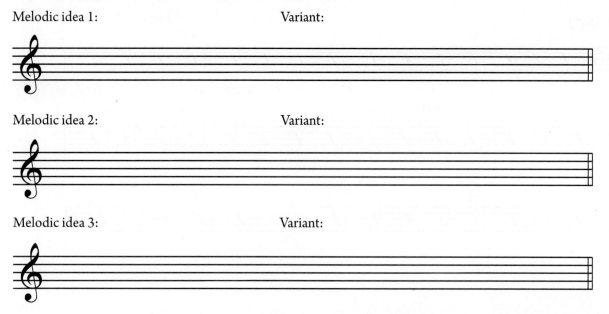

Melodic idea 2:   Variant:

Melodic idea 3:   Variant:

Project B: Writing a Song in Blues Style

Compose a song in blues style with lyrics, in the form described here. Use examples from Apply It and in your anthology as models: "Dallas Blues," "Splanky," and "Blues for Norton." Notate the song on a score or lead sheet (as your teacher directs), showing the vocal melody and lyrics, the instrumental melody, and chord symbols.

This type of composition is intended for performance by a jazz or blues combo, which may include keyboard, a melodic instrument (trumpet, saxophone, flute, or trombone are typical, but don't consider that a limitation), or voice, and a bass (who reads from the lead sheet) and drum set (whose part is usually improvised). Practice your song and solo for performance in class, or get a friend to help you perform it.

Step-by-step instructions:

Your composition should model blues style. The style is conveyed through:

- the conflict between the major-key chords in the accompaniment and the minor-inflected melody
- characteristic rhythmic patterns including swung rhythms (notated as straight eighth notes, but played swung)
- short, memorable melodic motives
- lyrics in the format of call, response, and conclusion.

Closely observe the compositions you are modeling to create your own composition in that style.

(1) Prepare your score or lead sheet (see p. 365 and "Blues for Norton" in the anthology for examples). You will need 24 measures (enough to perform the 12-bar blues progression twice—once with a vocal part and once with an instrumental part) plus 4–12 measures for an optional introduction and 4 measures for the ending or coda. Use the common time ($\mathbf{c}$) meter signature. Your song will have these parts:

- introduction (4–12 measures)
- vocal melody (12 measures) with your lyrics
- instrumental melody (12 measures)
- ending (4 measures).

(2) For the vocal melody, create lyrics.

- Most blues songs are about love gone awry or about some other life problem (such as losing a job, someone moving away, etc.). Though blues lyrics tend to be about something that has gone wrong, blues songs are not necessarily sad overall . . . singing the blues helps put a better perspective on the problem, perhaps.
- Keep the language direct or even simple and conversational. Slang is typical (for example, "You ain't nothin' but a hound dog," "My mama done tol' me," etc.).
- Blues lyrics often have double meanings or implied subtexts—for example, the "hound dog" in Big Mama Thornton's "Hound Dog" is two-legged (a man).
- Each blues progression consists of three segments, each four measures long:
  o segment 1 (measures 1–4) states the idea or "problem" (call),
  o segment 2 (measures 5–8) restates the idea either exactly or in a varied form (response),
  o segment 3 (measures 9–12) reveals a consequence or outcome of the problem (conclusion).

The lyrics to W. C. Handy's "St. Louis Blues" are a good example:

I hate to see that evening sun go down,	call
I hate to see that evening sun go down,	response
'Cause, my baby, he's gone left this town.	conclusion
Feelin' tomorrow like I feel today,	call
If I'm feelin' tomorrow like I feel today,	response
I'll pack my truck and make my get away.	conclusion

In your performance, either the sung melody or the instrumental melody can be played first, followed by the other setting.

(3) Transpose the harmonic progression shown to another key of your choice (not C major), using a major key signature with one to three flats or sharps. Chords in parentheses are optional; the chord prior to them can continue through those measures. All seventh chords are major-minor (dominant) seventh qualities; alternatively you may use triads (no seventh) for I and IV (C and F in C major). Use this progression as accompaniment for both the vocal and instrumental parts. You may also use the entire progression or the first four measures (keyboard only) as an introduction, and you may repeat the last four measures as an ending.

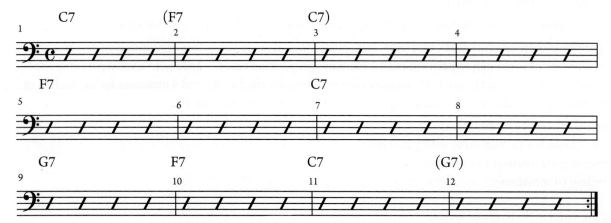

(4) Write the blues scale in the key you have chosen, to serve as a collection of notes from which to improvise melodic ideas. Use the scale given here (in C) as a model, but transpose it to match your harmonic progression.

(5) A suggested way to start composing your melodies is by playing the chords of the progression and improvising above the chords. You may use chord tones, but also connect between chord tones using notes of the blues scale.

- The instrumental solo melodies often feature short riffs, as shown in "Splanky" and "Blues for Norton," that are expanded or elaborated over the course of the instrumental solo. Choose interesting rhythms for the instrumental melody; it is possible to create a stylistic blues melody using mostly rhythmic motives with relatively simple melodic motives.
- Blues vocal melodies often do not align rhythmically with the change of chords at the beginning of each measure: they may begin with an anacrusis prior to the chord change, or enter off the downbeat just after a chord change.
- Write down your best melodic ideas and work with those to create your melodies.

Write a Popular Song

TOPICS

- Form
- Harmonic loops

MUSIC

- John Lennon and Paul McCartney, "Ticket to Ride"
- Katy Perry, Lukasz Gottwald, Max Martin, Bonnie McKee, and Henry Walter, "Roar"

Form

A good way to begin our study of recent popular music is to focus on its musical **form**: the organization of the song into sections. Most contemporary popular songs feature repeated verses and choruses that are independent small sections.

> **KEY CONCEPT** The term **verse** designates a musical section that appears in a song multiple times with the same music but different text, while **chorus** refers to a section of music that is repeated with the same (or similar) text. A **bridge** features music that has its own lyrics, and contrasts with the verse and chorus in melody or rhythm. It typically appears once, prior to the final return of the verse and/or chorus, preparing the final return of sections repeated throughout the song.

Listen to the beginning of The Beatles' "Ticket to Ride"; the form is shown in Example C.1. It may help to conduct along with the song to count the measures.

EXAMPLE C.1 Form in Lennon and McCartney, "Ticket to Ride"

Intro		4 measures
⌈ Verse	"I think I'm . . ."	8 measures
⌊ Chorus	"She's got a . . ."	8 measures
⌈ Verse	"She said . . ."	8 measures
⌊ Chorus	"She's got a . . ."	8 measures
Bridge	"I don't know . . ."	9 measures
⌈ Verse	"I think I'm . . ."	8 measures
⌊ Chorus	"She's got a . . ."	8 measures
Outro		2 measures

After a brief instrumental introduction (an **intro**), the song begins with the verse followed by the chorus. The music for the verse then repeats, with different text, followed by the chorus. Before the final verse and chorus, there is a bridge, a term that for post-1950s popular music denotes a musical section, contrasting with the verse and chorus, that appears in the second half of the song to prepare for the last statement of the verse and chorus. The verse and chorus return after the bridge. Finally, the song ends with a concluding **outro**—instrumental music to end the song. An outro may consist of a simple "repeat and fade" or other concluding music.

In many songs, the sections are distinguished from each other not only by the type of lyrics employed, but also by the character of the melody and rhythms. Consider the start of the verse and the beginning of the chorus of "Ticket to Ride." The melody of the verse is divided into short segments that enter before the downbeat of the measure ("I think," "the girl"), repeats some pitches and rhythms ("think it's today" and "going away"), may not completely fit within the chord progression ("the girl that's driving me mad"), and includes syncopation (on "today" and "away," for example). In contrast, the melody of the chorus enters strongly on the downbeat with lyrical phrases and note values of longer durations. This contrast is called a loose verse, tight chorus structure.

This song also illustrates the use of a **hook**—a musical setting of a few words or a phrase, which usually includes the title, that is repeated and becomes the most "catchy" or memorable part of the song. For this song, the hook ("a ticket to ride") occurs in the chorus, as is typical, though a hook may appear elsewhere, including in a line of text appended to the end of a verse, chorus, or other section, called a **refrain**.

Many recent songs also include short sections before and after the chorus: a section after a verse that prepares for the entrance of the chorus is called a **prechorus**, and in very recent songs, some songwriters include a **postchorus** after a chorus to prepare for the return of the verse.

Katy Perry's chart-topping song from 2013, "Roar," provides an example of most of these formal elements—intro, verse, chorus, prechorus, postchorus, and bridge (see Example C.2). Here, the repeated text plays a role in distinguishing the sections: the prechorus has the same text each time it returns, which differentiates it from the verse; and the postchorus also features the same text each time, with the repeated syllable "Oh" distinguishing it from the chorus.

EXAMPLE C.2   Form in "Roar"

Intro		2 measures (4 measures in video version)
Verse 1:	"I used to bite my tongue . . ."	4 measures
Verse 2:	"I guess that I forgot . . ."	4 measures
Prechorus:	"You held me down . . ."	4 + 4, for 8 measures*
Chorus:	"I got the eye . . ." [refrain]	8 measures*
Postchorus:	"Oh oh oh . . ." [refrain]	5 measures*
Verse 3:	"Now I'm floating . . ."	4 measures
Prechorus:	"You held me down . . ."	4 + 4, for 8 measures*
Chorus:	"I got the eye . . ." [refrain]	8 measures*
Postchorus:	"Oh oh oh . . ." [refrain]	5 measures*
Bridge:	(instrumental, then) "Roar-oar . . ."	3 + 4, for 7 measures
Chorus:	"I got the eye . . ." [refrain]	8 measures
Postchorus:	"Oh oh oh . . ." [refrain]	9 measures; extension

*ambiguous phrase boundary

These extra sections in postmillennial songs contribute to a feeling of shifting levels of intensity and energy: in this track, the prechorus between the verse and chorus builds anticipation of the chorus; likewise, though at the same volume as the chorus, the repeated "Oh oh oh" of the postchorus releases some of the intensity. Both the chorus and prechorus end with the refrain line "You're gonna hear me roar!," which includes the hook of the song.

While almost the entire song is set over a repeating four-measure harmonic loop (discussed next), the vocal line sometimes enters after the downbeat (as in the verses) but at other times the vocal lines enters with an anacrusis to the downbeat (as in the prechorus and chorus). The shifting of the entry relative to the strong downbeat of each measure corresponds to the assertiveness of the text, with the longest anacrusis on "I got the eye . . ." (chorus). Since phrase and section lengths in popular songs tend to be regular, any irregularities or ambiguities like these may signal significant sectional divisions in the form.

The bridge, substantially different from the rest of the song, provides a **build** (an increase in intensity in anticipation of the chorus), with the instruments cutting out to signal the **drop** just prior to the return of the drums and full texture in the final chorus.

Harmonic Loops

Many recent songs, like "Roar," are built on a **harmonic loop**—three or, more typically, four chords that are repeated in order over and over underneath the melody. Listen again to "Roar" while following Example C.3, which gives the chords of the harmonic loop. This progression is repeated throughout the song except for the bridge.

EXAMPLE C.3   "Roar" harmonic loop

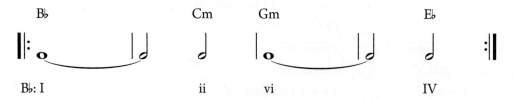

B♭: I   ii   vi   IV

A very common four-chord harmonic loop is shown in Example C.4a, in a keyboard arrangement similar to those in Chapter 10. To create a bass line, play the chord roots (C–G–A–F) in your left hand or on a bass. Many songs use this progression; a few that you might know are "Wrecking Ball" (Miley Cyrus), "Just What I Needed" (The Cars), "The Edge of Glory" (Lady Gaga), "Can You Feel the Love Tonight" (Elton John), and "Demon" (Imagine Dragons). This progression is also useful because it can be rotated to begin with the vi chord, as shown in Example C.4b, which is the foundation for many more songs, including Toto's "Africa," Pitbull's "Give Me Everything," Kelly Clarkson's "Stronger," and Adele's "Hello." For a 1950s doo-wop feeling, the same four chords are used in a slightly different order in Example C.4c—the "Heart and Soul" progression. Example C.4d provides another option, which is also used in recent songs. Since each of these harmonic loops ends on a chord that is not tonic, the harmonic progression can loop back around to the beginning without the chords themselves creating a cadence. To end a phrase or section, the melody will need to create a sense of cadence, or the IV or V at the end of a loop will need to resolve to I. Use one of these progressions to write a popular song that sounds contemporary.

EXAMPLE C.4   Harmonic loops in C major

(d)

Terms You Should Know

bridge	form	outro
build	harmonic loop	postchorus
chorus	hook	prechorus
drop	intro	verse

Apply It

A. Sing at sight

- Perform the rhythm of the melody alone, while tapping or conducting the beat.
- Sing the pitches of the melody, then combine pitches and rhythm.

Melody 1 Taylor Swift and Liz Rose, "Teardrops on My Guitar," mm. 13–16 (verse)

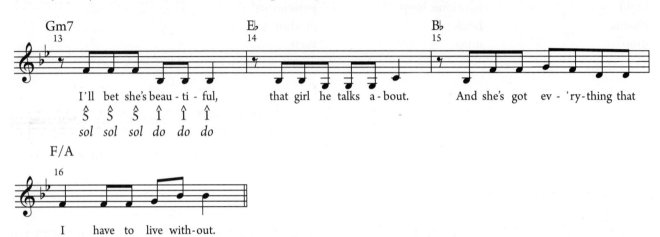

Melody 2 Taylor Swift and Liz Rose, "Teardrops on My Guitar," mm. 31–34 (chorus)

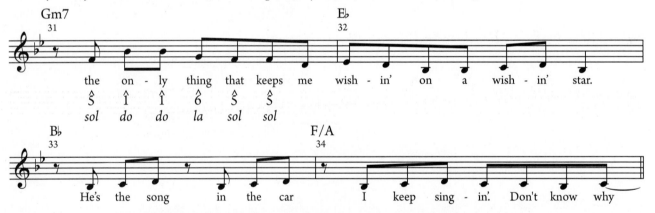

Melody 3 Ed Sheeran and Amy Wadge, "Thinking Out Loud," mm. 1–4 (verse)

Melody 4 Katy Perry, Lukasz Gottwald, Max Martin, Bonnie McKee, and Henry Walter, "Roar," mm. 3–6 (verse)

I used to bite my tongue and hold my breath, scared to rock the boat and make a mess.

1̂ 5̂ 5̂ 5̂ 3̂
do sol sol sol mi

So I sat qui‑et‑ly, a‑greed po‑lite‑ly.

Melody 5 Katy Perry, Lukasz Gottwald, Max Martin, Bonnie McKee, and Henry Walter, "Roar," mm. 11–14 (verse)

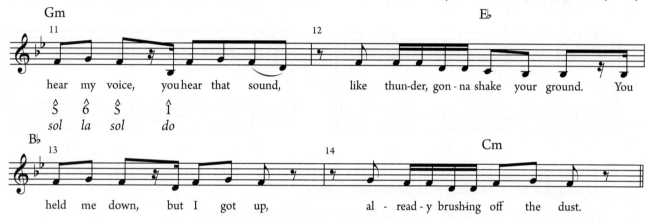

hear my voice, you hear that sound, like thun‑der, gon‑na shake your ground. You

5̂ 6̂ 5̂ 1̂
sol la sol do

held me down, but I got up, al‑read‑y brush‑ing off the dust.

Melody 6 Ed Sheeran and Amy Wadge, "Thinking Out Loud," mm. 28–31

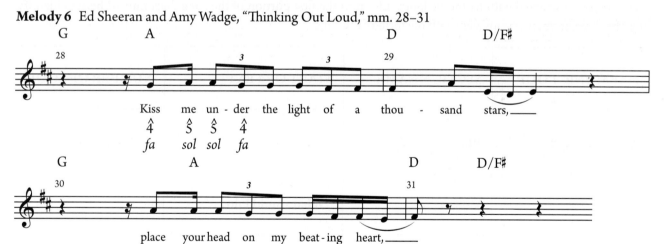

Kiss me un‑der the light of a thou‑sand stars,___

4̂ 5̂ 5̂ 4̂
fa sol sol fa

place your head on my beat‑ing heart,___

B. Improvise melodies

Four two-measure harmonic loops are shown next; recordings are provided to accompany your improvisations. Choose one of these for your improvisation. Follow the instructions to improvise a melody in popular style.

- Begin by tapping or conducting along with the recorded progressions, two beats per chord, to become oriented to the harmonies.
- Improvise a melody on scale-degree numbers or solfège syllables.
- Use the melodies from Part A as models.
- Melodies are typically repetitive and include rests.
- Prepare your improvisation for performance in class.

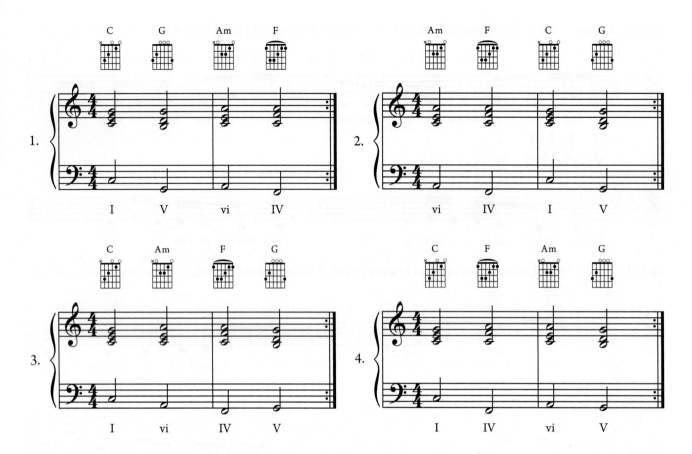

C. Listening for chord changes in harmonic loops

1. Listen to John Stephens and Toby Gad's "All of Me" (as sung by John Legend) online.

This song is constructed with harmonic loops. Listen to the first portion of the song diagrammed here to identify how the three harmonic loops align with the form of the song.

HARMONIC LOOP	SECTION NAME	START OF TEXT	NUMBER OF LOOPS
1	Intro	(no text)	1 (2 in video)
1	Verse 1	"What would I do . . ."	4
2	Prechorus	"My head's under water . . ."	2
3	Chorus	"Cause all of me . . ." "Cause I give you all . . ."	2 2

2. Intro and verse—first harmonic loop

A four-measure harmonic loop underlies the intro and first verse. The beginning of the harmonic loop is shown here, with one chord of the loop per measure. In the song, the harmonic rhythm is one chord per measure—when you hear the chords and bass note change, it signals the start of the next measure. The chords are played with a syncopated rhythm, as shown:

- Beginning on the F given, listen for the bass line and notate it by ear on the bass staff. These pitches are the roots of major chords.
- From the notes you have written, write the chord symbols in the blanks provided and the pitches of the right hand on the treble staff.
- Write these pitches so that they can be played by one hand and follow smoothly from the given chord.
- Finally, write the Roman numerals for these triads in A♭ major below the staff.

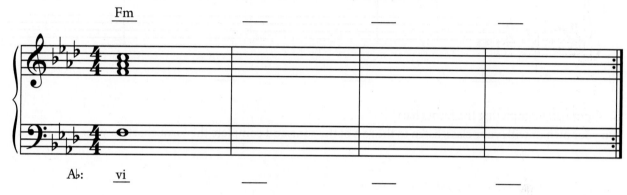

3. Prechorus—second harmonic loop ("My head's under water…")

The entry of a B♭m chord marks the end of the verse and the start of a new loop. This loop is also four measures long, but consists of only three chords (the first one is repeated).

- Beginning on the B♭ given, listen for the bass line and notate it by ear on the bass staff. After the repeated B♭, these pitches are the roots of major chords.
- From the notes you have written, write the chord symbols in the blanks provided above the staff, the pitches of the right hand on the treble staff, and the Roman numerals below the grand staff.

4. Chorus—third harmonic loop ("Cause all of me . . .")

In the chorus, the harmonic rhythm has changed so that each chord lasts two measures, which makes the loop eight measures long. (The bass note on the first and fourth chords sometimes changes octave when the chord is repeated.)

- Listen to the chorus, then fill in the bass line, chord symbols, Roman numerals, and the pitches of the chords as before.
- All triads except the second one of this loop are major (the second is minor).

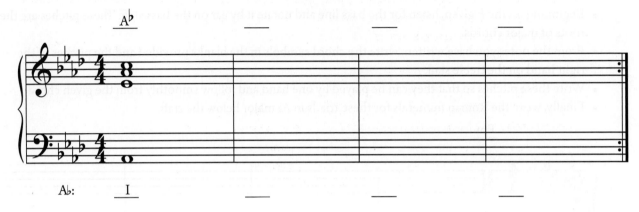

A♭:   I

5. Optional: Completing the form chart.

On your own or with your class, listen to the rest of the song and complete the form chart on your own paper.

Workbook ASSIGNMENT C.1

A. Analysis: Lennon and McCartney, "Eight Days a Week"

Listen to this song and construct a form diagram on your own paper, then answer the following questions. For the start of each first line of text (if any), circle the section name (verse, chorus, bridge, instrumental break, outro) and identify the number of measures in that section. (Conduct in $\frac{4}{4}$ meter and count the measures.) The song begins with an introduction that is four measures long.

(1) "Ooh I need your . . ." is the start of which type of section?

    (a) verse   (b) chorus   (c) bridge   (d) instrumental break   (e) outro

    This first section is _____ measures long.

(2) "Love you . . ." is the start of which type of section?

    (a) verse   (b) chorus   (c) bridge   (d) instrumental break   (e) outro

    The second section is _____ measures long.

(3) "Eight days . . ." is the start of which type of section?

    (a) verse   (b) chorus   (c) bridge   (d) instrumental break   (e) outro

    This section is _____ measures long.

(4) When the words "Ooh I need your . . ." return, it is the start of which type of section?

    (a) verse   (b) chorus   (c) bridge   (d) instrumental break   (e) outro

    This section is _____ measures long.

(5) When the words "Love you . . ." return, it is the start of which type of section?

    (a) verse   (b) chorus   (c) bridge   (d) instrumental break   (e) outro

    This section is _____ measures long.

(6) The song ends with a repeat of the refrain line "Eight days a week" and instrumental music. This last section is called a(n)

    (a) verse   (b) chorus   (c) bridge   (d) instrumental break   (e) outro

B. Green Day "21 Guns"

Listen to this song (either the original Green Day version or the version from the Broadway musical *American Idiot*) and construct a form diagram on your own paper, then answer the following questions. For the start of each first line of text (if any), circle the section name (verse, chorus, bridge, instrumental break, outro) and identify the number of measures in that section. (Conduct in $\frac{4}{4}$ meter and count the measures.) The song begins with an introduction that is four measures long.

(1) The text "Do you know . . ." is the start of which type of section?

    (a) verse   (b) chorus   (c) bridge   (d) instrumental break   (e) outro

    This first section is _____ measures long.

(2) The text "Does the pain . . ." is the start of which type of section?

    (a) verse   (b) chorus   (c) bridge   (d) instrumental break   (e) outro

    The second section is _____ measures long.

(3) The text "One, 21 . . ." is the start of which type of section?

    (a) verse   (b) chorus   (c) bridge   (d) instrumental break   (e) outro

    This section is _____ measures long.

(4) The next two sections are based on music of previous sections, but the words are changed. Which of the following best describes these next sections, beginning with the words "When you're at . . ." and "Your faith walks . . ."?

    (a) repeat of the first and second sections   (b) repeat of the second and third sections

(5) The new section beginning with "Did you try . . ." is best labeled as:

    (a) verse   (b) chorus   (c) bridge   (d) outro

    This section is _____ measures long.

    This section is followed by an instrumental break in the Green Day version of the song.

(6) The text "When it's time . . ." is the start of which type of section?

    (a) verse   (b) chorus   (c) bridge   (d) instrumental break   (e) outro

    This section is _____ measures long.

(7) The song ends with two repetitions of one of the previous sections—which concludes the song?

    (a) verse   (b) chorus   (c) bridge   (d) instrumental break   (e) outro

Project C: Writing a Song in a Recent Popular Style

Compose a song with lyrics in a recent popular style that is based on a harmonic loop. Use examples in your textbook as models, or you may model your song on a recent song you like that fits with these instructions. On your own staff paper, notate the song on a score that shows the vocal melody, lyrics, and chord symbols. If you want to create a simple keyboard accompaniment for the harmonic loops, use Example C.4 for models; otherwise you can perform your song with simple chords (for guitar or another instrument) from the score. Practice your song for performance in class, or get a friend to help you perform it.

Step-by-step instructions:

Your composition should model a recent popular song style with a harmonic loop. The style is conveyed through:

- employment of a harmonic loop as the underlying chord progression for the song;
- $\frac{4}{4}$ meter using primarily the beat unit and divisions of the beat (and few, if any, sixteenth notes) with some rests and syncopation;
- one or two melodic and rhythmic "hooks" (motives) that provide continuity through the song;
- and a text that tells a story or sets a scene or mood.

Closely observe the compositions you are modeling to create your own composition in that style.

(1) Prepare your score. You will need a total of 24 measures: 16 measures for the verse/chorus portion of the song (repeated with different words on the verse and the same words on the chorus), plus four measures for the intro and four measures for the outro. Your song will have these sections:

- intro (4 mm./one time through the loop)
- verse 1 (vocal melody; 8 mm./two times through the loop)
- chorus 1 (vocal melody; 8 mm./two times through the loop)
- verse 2 (same melody as verse 1 but different words, written under the lyrics of the first verse on your score)
- chorus 2 (same as chorus 1)
- outro or coda (4 mm./one time through the loop)

After you map the sections of your song, label their positions on the empty staves of your score. In your performance, plan to play the intro, then sing through the verse and chorus twice, once with the first stanza of lyrics for the verse and once with the second stanza, then play the ending. You may repeat the outro and fade out, if you wish—especially if the loop you choose does not end on the tonic harmony.

(2) Choose one of the harmonic loops, which will form a foundation for your song.

- Map out 16 blank measures on staff paper for your draft—eight for the verse and eight for the chorus.
- Choose a key and mode (major or minor).
- Use $\frac{4}{4}$ meter.
- Write the chords for the four-measure harmonic loop, transposed to the key you have chosen. You may use any key other than C major. You may have one chord per measure, or you may have a chord hold over so the next one enters midmeasure (as in "Roar").

(3) Create the lyrics. You may write your own, or use a preexisting poem.

- The verses generally tell a story, while the chorus encapsulates its emotional impact.
- Your verse lyrics should have two stanzas (verse 1 and verse 2), which will be sung to the same melodic line and with the same accompaniment.

- The chorus typically expresses the overall idea of the song, and usually contains the hook—a melodic and rhythmic idea capturing the main concept of the song.
- Consider employing repeated words or images that might suggest musical motives.
- Compose rhythms for your melody that approximate those of the spoken lyrics. You can do this by setting the lyrics to the melody you have written, or writing the lyrics first, and setting them to the melody.

(4) Compose the vocal melody. Melodic ideas should coordinate with the chords in the harmonic loop.

- Verse melodies in recent songs composed with loops typically feature short melodic ideas, each comprised of only a few pitches. The melodic ideas often enter either before or after the downbeat of the measure (a loose verse design).
- Select pitches from the harmonies you have chosen to sketch a melodic outline for the verse (mm. 1–8). Consider using short, repeated, melodic and rhythmic ideas.
- The verse melody may end on a conclusive melodic cadence or may end inconclusively, depending on the loop you have selected.
- Both verse and chorus melodies should primarily use steps, skips, and repeated notes with very few leaps. The melody should be easy to sing.
- Chorus melodies in recent songs composed with loops typically feature more melodic continuity than verses, with important melody notes on the downbeats of measures, aligning with the change of chords (a tight chorus design).
- For the chorus, choose a pitch from the harmonies in each measure to be the main framework for the chorus melody. That pitch may be sustained or repeated, or embellished by neighbor and passing tones, or by motion to another note of the harmony.
- The chorus melodies often end on a conclusive melodic cadence, which may overlap the start of the next loop (if the start of that loop is I), or the melody may end prior to the end of the loop (if needed to end on I).
- Keep in mind that both verse and chorus melodies are often shaped in a large arch—beginning relatively low at the start, moving up to a high point in the middle, then descending toward the tonic at the end.
- Check your verse or chorus melodic line by singing or playing it. It should have a pleasing shape, rhythmic and melodic interest, and a high point.

(5) For an intro you can use the chords of the harmonic loop. For an outro, you can repeat the harmonic loop, perhaps fading out.

(6) Prepare a performance for class with a simple keyboard accompaniment or perform your song from a lead sheet, playing basic chords based on the keyboard arrangements of harmonic loop progressions in this chapter.

Anthology

"The Ash Grove"   340

Johann Sebastian Bach, Invention in D Minor   342

Bach, "Wachet auf" (Chorale No. 179)   344

Joseph Brackett, "Simple Gifts"   347

"Come, Ye Thankful People, Come" ("St. George's Windsor")   348

Stephen Foster, "Oh! Susanna"   349

Patrick S. Gilmore, "When Johnny Comes Marching Home"   350

"Greensleeves"   351

"Home on the Range"   353

Scott Joplin, "Solace" (excerpt)   354

Wolfgang Amadeus Mozart, String Quartet in D Minor, K. 421, third
    movement   357

Mozart, *Variations on "Ah, vous dirai-je Maman"* (excerpts)   360

"My Country, 'Tis of Thee" ("America")   363

John Newton, "Amazing Grace"   364

Joel Phillips, "Blues for Norton"   365

Franz Schubert, Waltz in B Minor, Op. 18, No. 6   369

Robert Schumann, "Wild Rider"   371

Hart A. Wand and Lloyd Garrett, "Dallas Blues"   372

"The Ash Grove"

"The Ash Grove" is a traditional Welsh folk song that has been sung to various lyrics. The words shown here are by the nineteenth-century English playwright John Oxenford. Two versions are shown: a lead sheet, in which the performer improvises an accompaniment from chord symbols, and an arrangement for piano.

a. Lead sheet

b. With written-out accompaniment

Arranged by Joel Phillips

Johann Sebastian Bach (1685–1750)

Invention in D Minor

Around 1720, Bach composed fifteen two-voice contrapuntal keyboard works, called inventions, for his ten-year-old son, Wilhelm Friedemann. Bach's inventions were intended to teach students how to play two simultaneous lines on the harpsichord and how to develop a musical idea in the course of a piece.

Johann Sebastian Bach
"Wachet auf" (Chorale No. 179)

The chorale melody "Wachet auf" appears in several movements of Bach's Cantata No. 140 (1731) of the same name. The chorale and cantata are frequently performed in the weeks leading up to Christmas.

Wa - chet auf! ruft uns die Stim -
Mit - ter - nacht heisst die - se Stun -

Wa - - - - chet auf! ruft
Mit - - - - ter - nacht heisst

me, Der Wäch - ter sehr hoch
de, Sie ruf - en uns mit

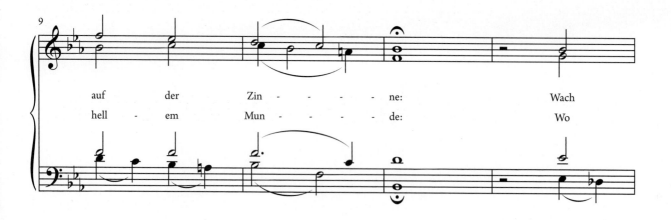

auf der Zin - - - ne: Wach
hell - em Mun - - - de: Wo

euch be - reit zu der Hoch - - - zeit, Ihr

müss - et ihm ent - ge - gen geh'n. _____

TEXT AND TRANSLATION

Wachet auf, ruft uns die Stimme,
Der Wächter sehr hoch auf der Zinne:
Wach auf, du Stadt Jerusalem!

Mitternacht heisst diese Stunde,
Sie rufen uns mit hellem Munde:
Wo seid ihr klugen Jungfrauen?

Wohl auf, der Bräut'gam kommt,
Steht auf, die Lampen nehmt!
Halleluia!

Macht euch bereit
Zu der Hochzeit,
Ihr müsset ihm entgegen geh'n.

Wake up! the voice calls to us,
The watchman high on the wall calls,
Wake up, city of Jerusalem!

Midnight this hour is called,
They call us with bright voices,
Where are you, wise virgins?

Wake up, the bridegroom comes,
Stand up, take up the lamps!
Halleluia!

Make yourselves ready
For the wedding.
You must go out to meet him.

Joseph Brackett (1797–1882)

"Simple Gifts"

The tune "Simple Gifts" was written in 1848 by Brackett, a member of the American Shaker religious order. While often considered a hymn, it was originally intended for dancing, as its lyrics suggest: "to turn, turn will be our delight, 'till by turning, turning we come round right." "Simple Gifts" has been arranged by many artists, including folk singer Judy Collins and composer Aaron Copland. Even more recently, the tune was featured in a work titled "Air and Simple Gifts," composed by John Williams for the 2009 inauguration of President Barack Obama.

'Tis the gift to be sim-ple 'tis the gift to be free 'Tis the

gift to come down where we ought to be And when we find our-selves in the

place just right 'Twill be in the val-ley of love and de-light.

When true sim-pli-ci-ty is gained To bow and to bend we shan't be a-shamed To

turn, turn will be our de-light 'Till by turn-ing, turn-ing we come round right.

"Come, Ye Thankful People, Come" ("St. George's Windsor")

George J. Elvey, who was organist at St. George's Church in Windsor, England, composed this tune in 1858. Though it originally had a different text, in the United States the music is most frequently sung to the text shown here, "Come, Ye Thankful People, Come," and is associated with the Thanksgiving holiday.

1. Come, ye thank - ful peo - ple, come, Raise the song of har - vest home;
2. All the world is God's own field, Fruit un - to his praise to yield;

All is safe - ly gath - ered in, Ere the win - ter storms be - gin.
Wheat and tares to - geth - er sown, Un - to joy or sor - row grown.

God, our Ma - ker, doth pro - vide For our wants to be sup - plied;
First the blade, and then the ear, Then the full corn shall ap - pear;

Come to God's own tem - ple, come, Raise the song of har - vest home.
Grant, O har - vest Lord, that we Whole - some grain and pure may be.

Stephen Foster (1826–1864)

"Oh! Susanna"

This song, published in 1848, exemplifies the style of Stephen Foster, whose parlor and minstrel songs achieved enormous popularity in his day. In fact, many of his songs continue to be so well known that they are assumed to be folk songs rather than nineteenth-century compositions. Although some of Foster's songs seem to glorify the slavery and plantations of the Old South, he was born in Pittsburgh and only visited the South once.

1. I— come from A - la - ba - ma with my ban - jo on my knee, I'm going to Louis - i-

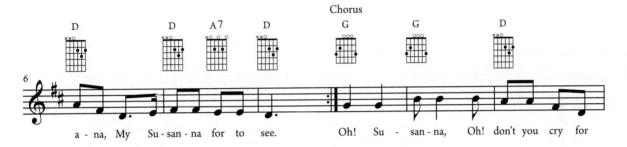

a - na, My Su - san - na for to see. Oh! Su - san - na, Oh! don't you cry for

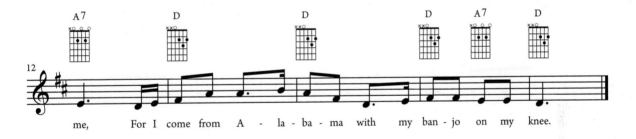

me, For I come from A - la - ba - ma with my ban - jo on my knee.

2. It rained all night the day I left
   The weather was so dry;
   The sun so hot I froze myself,
   Susanna, don't you cry.
   Chorus

3. I had a dream the other night,
   When everything was still.
   I thought I saw Susanna
   A-coming down the hill.
   Chorus

4. The buckwheat cake was in her mouth,
   The tear was in her eye,
   Says I, "I'm coming from the South."
   Susanna, don't you cry.
   Chorus

Patrick S. Gilmore (1829–1892)

"When Johnny Comes Marching Home"

Patrick Gilmore was born in Ireland in 1829 and immigrated to Boston in 1849, where he was a band leader. Gilmore wrote "When Johnny Comes Marching Home" during the Civil War, when his band served the Massachusetts 24th Regiment. Two of Gilmore's lasting contributions to American culture include the founding of the first Promenade Concert in America, the forerunner of the Boston Pops concerts, and the establishment of Gilmore's Concert Garden, which became Madison Square Garden.

1. When John - ny comes march - ing home a - gain, Hur - rah!_____ Hur - rah!_____ We'll
2. Get read - y for the Ju - bi - lee, Hur - rah!_____ Hur - rah!_____ We'll

give him a heart - y wel - come then, Hur - rah!_____ Hur - rah!_____ The
give_____ the he - ro three times three, Hur - rah!_____ Hur - rah!_____ The

men will cheer_____ the boys will shout, The la - dies they_____ will
lau - rel wreath is read - y now To place up - on_____ his

all turn out, And we'll all feel gay When John - ny comes march - ing home.__
loy - al brow, And we'll all feel gay When John - ny comes march - ing home.__

"Greensleeves"

"Greensleeves" is a traditional English folk song; though its date of composition is unknown, it is first mentioned in print in 1580. The music originally accompanied a ballad about a woman, referred to as Lady Greensleeves, who discourteously rejects a suitor. The music has also been sung with numerous other texts, including the well-known Christmas carol, "What Child Is This?" Two arrangements are shown here, the first a simple diatonic setting, and the second a more highly embellished setting with some chromatic harmonies.

a. Simple arrangement

Arranged by Jane Piper Clendinning

b. Embellished arrangement

Arranged by Joel Phillips

Expressive ♩. = 96

"Home on the Range"

This song, from the 1870s, is the official state song of Kansas. Its lyrics have appeared in several forms by different authors; the original ("The Western Home"), by Brewster Higley, was published in 1873, but the most familiar lyrics today are those written by John A. Lomax in 1910. The melody was composed by Daniel E. Kelly, an amateur musician who played violin with a family band. The song has become a folk anthem of the American West and has appeared in many plays and movies, including "Where the Buffalo Roam" (performed by Neil Young in 1980) and "The Messenger" (performed by Willie Nelson in 2009).

2. How often at night when the heavens are bright
   With the lights from the glittering stars;
   Have I stood there amazed and asked as I gazed
   If their glory exceeds that of ours.
   Chorus

3. Oh, give me a land where the bright diamond sand
   Flows leisurely down the stream;
   Where the graceful white swan goes gliding along,
   Like a maid in a heavenly dream.
   Chorus

Scott Joplin (1868–1917)

"Solace" (excerpt)

"Solace," published in 1909, is not a typical rag, though it does make use of the syncopation that characterizes ragtime. It is sometimes listed with the subtitle "A Mexican Serenade," and it bears some resemblance to the tango. Like other Joplin compositions, "Solace" found renewed fame as a result of its inclusion in the 1973 film *The Sting*, starring Paul Newman and Robert Redford.

Joplin, "Solace" (excerpt)   **355**

Wolfgang Amadeus Mozart (1756–1791)
String Quartet in D Minor, K. 421, third movement

This quartet, composed in 1783, is part of a set of six quartets that Mozart published together and dedicated to the composer Joseph Haydn. During Mozart's lifetime, Haydn's quartets were widely admired; in his "Haydn Quartets," Mozart takes inspiration from the older composer in crafting this music.

Menuetto D.C.

Wolfgang Amadeus Mozart
Variations on "Ah, vous dirai-je Maman" (excerpts)

Mozart composed this theme and variations early in the 1780s. The theme is a French folk song, "Ah, vous dirai-je Maman," the same tune as "Twinkle, Twinkle, Little Star." Because the tune is so familiar, this set is an ideal vehicle for studying variation technique.

"My Country, 'Tis of Thee" ("America")

This tune, sung with different texts, has been the national anthem of Great Britain, Germany, Denmark, and Prussia. In 1831, Samuel Francis Smith was given a score of the German version by American hymnist Lowell Mason, who asked for a translation. Instead, Smith was inspired to write new lyrics, which have become beloved as an American patriotic song.

1. My coun - try, 'tis of thee, Sweet land of lib - er - ty,
2. My na - tive coun - try, thee, Land of the no - ble free,

Of thee I sing; Land where my fa - thers died, Land of the
Thy name I love; I love thy rocks and rills, Thy woods and

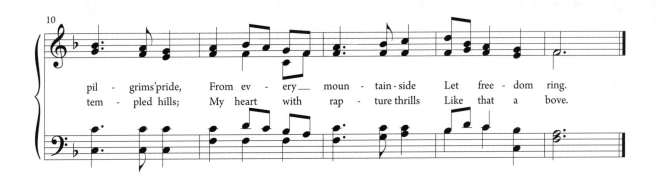

pil - grims'pride, From ev - ery __ moun - tain - side Let free - dom ring.
tem - pled hills; My heart with rap - ture thrills Like that a - bove.

John Newton (1725–1807)

"Amazing Grace"

John Newton, composer of and collaborator on hundreds of Christian hymns, is most famous for his lyrics to "Amazing Grace." Newton's words have been sung to various melodies over the years, but in the early nineteenth century they were joined to the tune shown here. Newton was a minister of the Church of England for the last forty years of his life. He served in London and Olney, where he and collaborator William Cowper published *Olney Hymns* (1779), which includes the text of "Amazing Grace." Newton spent his younger years as the captain of an English slave ship and converted to Christianity during a storm at sea. "Amazing Grace" is thought to be autobiographical; phrases like "a wretch like me" refer to his days as slave trader.

2. Through many dangers, toils, and snares,
   I have already come;
   'Twas grace has brought me safe thus far,
   And grace will lead me home.

3. The Lord has promised good to me.
   His word my hope secures;
   He will my shield and portion be
   As long as life endures.

Joel Phillips (b. 1958)

"Blues for Norton"

Joel Phillips, one of the authors of this text, composed "Blues for Norton" on June 6, 2006—6-6-06. Although Christians often view the number 666 negatively, in Jewish mysticism it is seen as the number of creation and physical perfection of the world (according to Genesis, the world was created in six days). "Norton" has six letters, so Phillips's music is based on a six-note riff stated in each of six phrases. Ideally the work would be performed by a sextet! The smaller notes in measures 13–22 show how a second solo instrument can interact with the first in a call-and-response texture.

a. Lead sheet

b. Full score (all instruments sound as notated)

Franz Schubert (1797–1828)

Waltz in B Minor, Op. 18, No. 6

The waltz is a dance in triple meter that enjoyed great popularity in Germany and Austria in the nineteenth century. This one belongs to a set of dance pieces Schubert composed in 1815. At parties, Schubert frequently improvised short piano waltzes, like this one, for dancing.

Robert Schumann (1810–1856)

"Wild Rider"

Schumann completed his *Album for the Young*, a collection of pedagogical piano pieces, in 1848. Several of the pieces were originally written for Clara and Robert Schumann's daughter Marie. Like the one that appears here, most of the compositions in the album have descriptive titles and are short character pieces that depict the "story" of their titles.

Hart A. Wand and Lloyd Garrett
"Dallas Blues"

Hart A. Wand was a German immigrant whose family first settled in Oklahoma after the 1889 Land Rush. He made his living primarily as a businessman, but was also a bandleader. "Dallas Blues" is one of the earliest published examples of the blues. Wand composed the tune and chord progression for piano and Garrett added the lyrics a few years later.

go - ing back,___ go - ing back to stay there till I die_____ (un - til I die).
Dal - las Blues___ and your lov - in' man is al - most dead_____ (is al-most dead).

I've got the Dal-las Blues and the Main Street heart dis - ease_____ (it's buz - zin'
I'm goin' to put my - self___ on a San - ta Fe and go_____ (I'm goin' to

p-f

'round),_____ I've got the Dal - las Blues___ and the Main Street heart___ dis -
go),_____ I'm goin' to put my - self___ on a San - ta Fe___ and

Appendix 1
Try It Answers

Chapter 1

TRY IT #1

(a) C   (b) E   (c) G   (d) E   (e) D   (f) C   (g) E   (h) D   (i) B   (j) E   (k) A
(l) E   (m) F   (n) B   (o) D

TRY IT #2

(a)
(1) B   (2) C   (3) F   (4) G   (5) D   (6) A   (7) D   (8) F   (9) G   (10) E
(11) C   (12) E

(b)

You_____   You may say_____ I'm a dream-er.   But I'm not the on - ly one.

(1) **E** (2) **G**   (3) **A**   (4) **B** (5) **C**   (6) **B**   (7) **E**

TRY IT #3

(a)
(1) F   (2) G   (3) D   (4) B   (5) F   (6) A   (7) C   (8) G   (9) B   (10) E
(11) A   (12) C

(b)

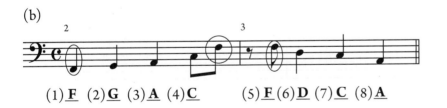

(1) **F** (2) **G** (3) **A** (4) **C**   (5) **F** (6) **D** (7) **C** (8) **A**

TRY IT #4

(a) G3   (b) F3   (c) G1   (d) C2   (e) F1

TRY IT #5

(a) B3   (b) C6   (c) D4   (d) B5   (e) F3   (f) C4   (g) E6   (h) A5   (i) A3   (j) D6
(k) G3   (l) A2   (m) D4   (n) E2   (o) F4   (p) E3   (q) C2   (r) B3   (s) F2   (t) C3

TRY IT #6

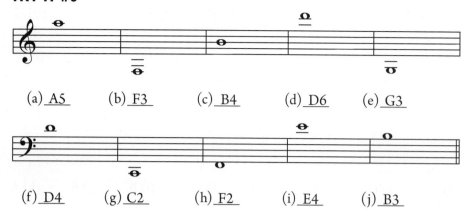

(a) __A5__   (b) __F3__   (c) __B4__   (d) __D6__   (e) __G3__

(f) __D4__   (g) __C2__   (h) __F2__   (i) __E4__   (j) __B3__

TRY IT #7

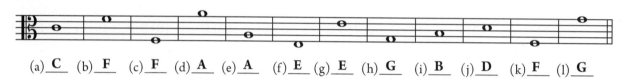

(a) __C__ (b) __F__ (c) __F__ (d) __A__ (e) __A__ (f) __E__ (g) __E__ (h) __G__ (i) __B__ (j) __D__ (k) __F__ (l) __G__

(m) __C__ (n) __A__ (o) __F__ (p) __E__ (q) __B__ (r) __D__ (s) __E__ (t) __F__ (u) __C__ (v) __G__ (w) __D__ (x) __E__

Chapter 2

TRY IT #1

(a) F♯   (b) C   (c) B♭   (d) F   (e) C♯   (f) C♭   (g) G♯   (h) D♯

TRY IT #2

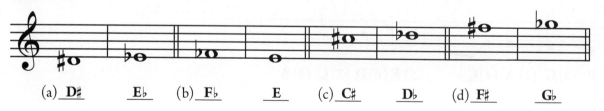

(a) __D♯__   __E♭__   (b) __F♭__   __E__   (c) __C♯__   __D♭__   (d) __F♯__   __G♭__

(e) __D♭__   __C♯__   (f) __G♭__   __F♯__   (g) __A♯__   __B♭__   (h) __D♯__   __E♭__

TRY IT #3

(a)

(1) G♯ or A♭   (2) C♮ or B♯   (3) B♭ or A♯   (4) F or E♯   (5) D♯ or E♭   (6) G♯   (7) B♭   (8) E   (9) D♯   (10) A♭

(b)
(1) H   (2) H   (3) W   (4) W   (5) H   (6) W   (7) N   (8) N   (9) W   (10) H
(11) H   (12) H   (13) W   (14) H

(c) H, W, H, W, H

TRY IT #4

(a) W   (b) N   (c) H   (d) H   (e) N   (f) W   (g) N   (h) N   (i) W   (j) H

TRY IT #5

(a)   (b)   (c)   (d)   (e)

(f)   (g)   (h)   (i)   (j)

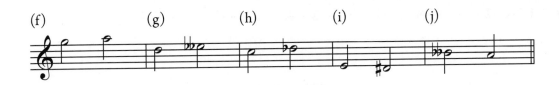

Chapter 3

TRY IT #1

TRY IT #2

(a)

(b)

TRY IT #3

(a)

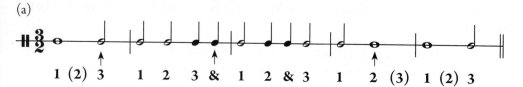

1 (2) 3   1 2 3 & 1 2 & 3 1 2 (3) 1 (2) 3

(b)

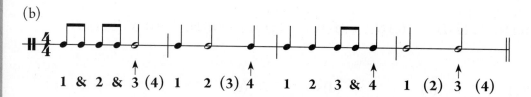

1 & 2 & 3 (4) 1 2 (3) 4 1 2 3 & 4 1 (2) 3 (4)

(c)

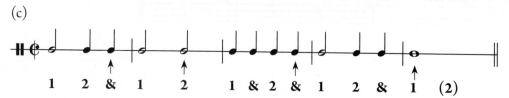

1 2 & 1 2   1 & 2 & 1 2 & 1 (2)

TRY IT #4

(a)

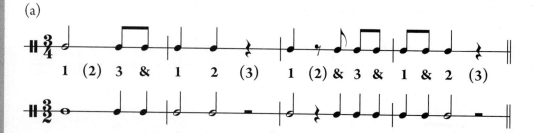

1 (2) 3 & 1 2 (3) 1 (2) & 3 & 1 & 2 (3)

(b)

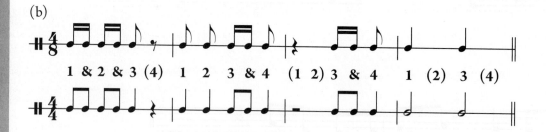

1 & 2 & 3 (4) 1 2 3 & 4 (1 2) 3 & 4 1 (2) 3 (4)

Chapter 4

TRY IT #1

(a)

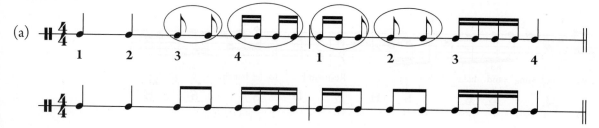

1   2   3   4   1   2   3   4

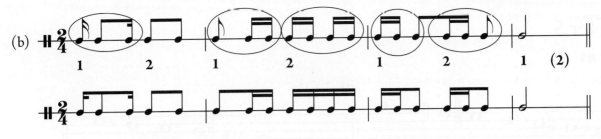

(b) $\frac{2}{4}$

1   2   1   2   1   2   1   (2)

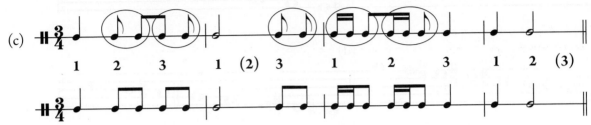

(c) $\frac{3}{4}$

1   2   3   1   (2)   3   1   2   3   1   2   (3)

TRY IT #2

(a) $\frac{3}{4}$

1   (2)   &   3   &   (1)   2   3   a   1   &   (2)   &   3   1   (2   3)

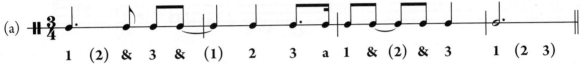

(b) $\frac{2}{4}$

1   e   &   a   (2)   &   1   &   (2) e   &   a   1   a   2   &   (1)   &   2   a   1   (2)

(c) $\frac{4}{4}$

1   (2)   (3)   &   4   &   1   a   (2)   &   3   (4)   1   e & a   2   a   3   &   (4)   &   1   (2   3   4)

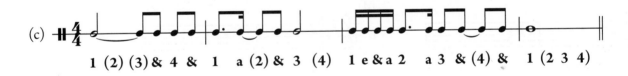

TRY IT #3

(a)

$\frac{2}{4}$

1   e   &   a   (2) e   &   a   (1) e   a   (2)   &   1   e   &   a   (2) e   &   a   (1)   e   a   (2)   &

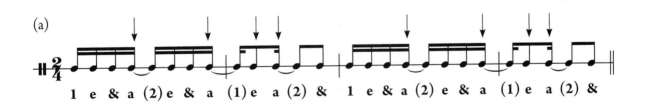

(b)

$\frac{2}{4}$

1   e   a   (2)   &   a   1   e   &   a   2   e   a   (1)   (2) e   &   a   1   (2)

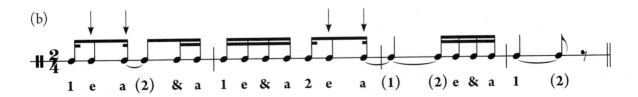

Chapter 5

TRY IT #1

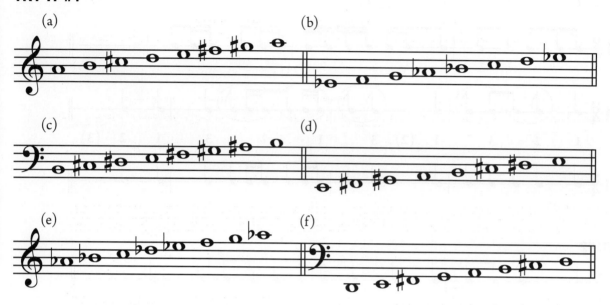

TRY IT #2

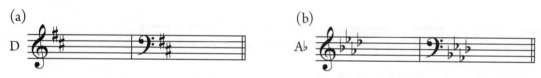

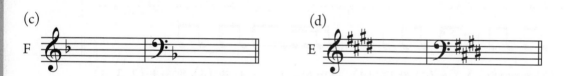

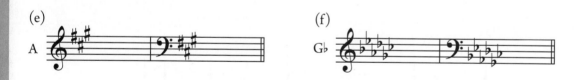

TRY IT #3

(a) B (b) Db (c) Ab (d) D (e) A (f) Bb (g) F# (h) E (i) Gb (j) F

TRY IT #4

- Key signature suggests: Ab major
- Last six scale degrees: $\hat{1}–\hat{1}–\hat{2}–\hat{1}–\hat{7}–\hat{1}$
- First six scale degrees: $\hat{5}–\hat{5}–\hat{1}–\hat{1}–\hat{2}–\hat{3}$
- Key of piece: Ab major

Chapter 6

TRY IT #1

(a)

1 li 2 li (3) la li 1 la 2 la li 3 (1) la li 2 la li 3 1 (2 3)

(b)

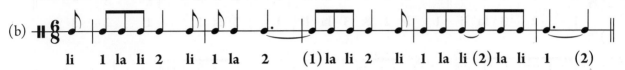

li 1 la li 2 li 1 la 2 (1) la li 2 li 1 la li (2) la li 1 (2)

(c)

(1) 2 3 4 1 li 2 li 3 li 4 li 1 li 2 li 3 4 li

1 li 2 li (3) 4 li 1 li 2 li 3 (4)

TRY IT #2

(a)

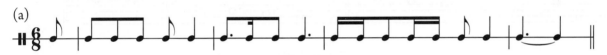

(b)

TRY IT #3

(a)

(b)

(c)

(d)

TRY IT #4

(a)

1 & 2 & 3 la li   1   2 & 3   li   1 & 2 & 3   1 (2   3)

(b)

1   2   3 la li   1   li 2 & 3 la li   1   2 & 3   1   2   3

(c)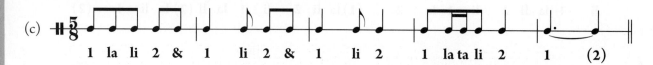

1 la li 2 &   1   li 2 &   1   li 2   1 la ta li 2   1   (2)

(d)

1   2 la li 3 &   1 & 2   li 3 &   1 & 2 la li 3   1 & 2   (3)

Chapter 7

TRY IT #1

(a) F major   F natural minor

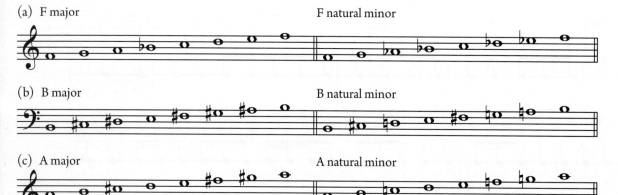

(b) B major   B natural minor

(c) A major   A natural minor

TRY IT #2

(a) C natural minor   C harmonic minor

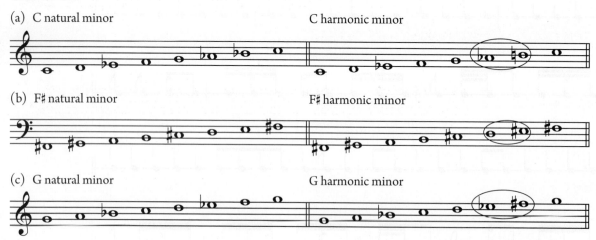

(b) F♯ natural minor   F♯ harmonic minor

(c) G natural minor   G harmonic minor

(d) C♯ natural minor   C♯ harmonic minor

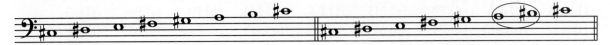

TRY IT #3

(a) B melodic minor

(b) F melodic minor

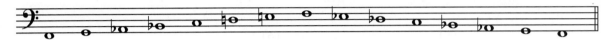

TRY IT #4

(a) C♯ minor   (b) F minor   (c) B minor   (d) C minor   (e) G♯ minor   (f) D minor
(g) G minor   (h) A minor   (i) B♭ minor   (j) D♯ minor   (k) F♯ minor   (l) E minor

TRY IT #5

(a)

Relative major: A   F♯ harmonic minor scale

(b)

Relative major: G   E harmonic minor scale

(c)

Relative major: D   B melodic minor scale (ascending)

(d)

 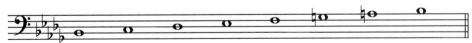

Relative major: D♭   B♭ melodic minor scale (ascending)

Chapter 8

TRY IT #1

(a) 3   (b) 7   (c) 8   (d) 2   (e) 5   (f) 3

TRY IT #2

(a) m3   (b) m3   (c) M2   (d) P4   (e) M3   (f) P4   (g) M2   (h) P4   (i) P4   (j) m3

(k) m3   (l) m2   (m) M3   (n) P4   (o) M3   (p) m2   (q) m3   (r) P4   (s) M2   (t) P4

TRY IT #3

(a)

(1)   (2)   (3)

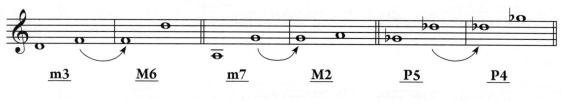

(4)   (5)   (6)

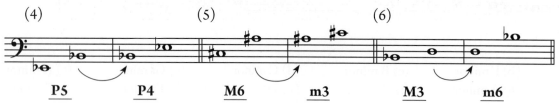

(b)

(1) (2) (3) (4) (5) (6) (7) (8) (9) (10)

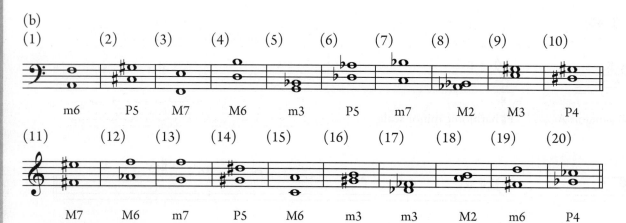

(11) (12) (13) (14) (15) (16) (17) (18) (19) (20)

TRY IT #4

(a)

(1) P5   (2) M7   (3) M2   (4) P4   (5) M6   (6) PU   (7) M3

(8) m3   (9) P4   (10) m7   (11) m6   (12) M2   (13) P5   (14) PU

(b)

(1)   (2)   (3)   (4)   (5)   (6)   (7)

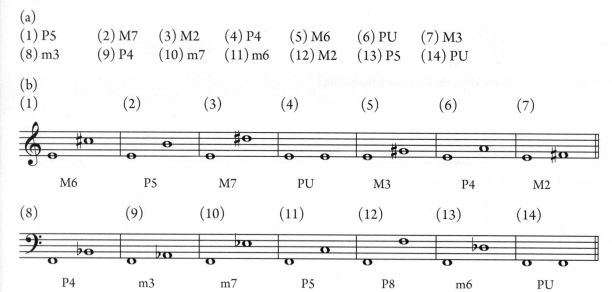

TRY IT #5

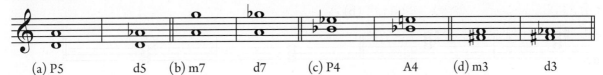

(a) P5   d5   (b) m7   d7   (c) P4   A4   (d) m3   d3

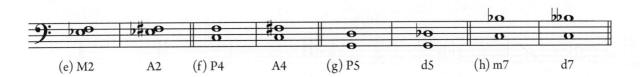

(e) M2   A2   (f) P4   A4   (g) P5   d5   (h) m7   d7

(i) M2   A2   (j) M6   A6   (k) m3   d3   (l) m6   d6

TRY IT #6

p   *legato con rubato*

Interval:	**m10**	**P12**	**M6**	**A4**	**m6**	**m7**	**M9**	**M2**
Simple equivalent:	**m3**	**P5**	___	___	___	___	**M2**	___

Chapter 9

TRY IT #1

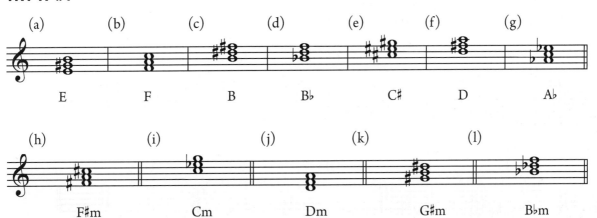

(a)   (b)   (c)   (d)   (e)   (f)   (g)

E   F   B   B♭   C♯   D   A♭

(h)   (i)   (j)   (k)   (l)

F♯m   Cm   Dm   G♯m   B♭m

TRY IT #2

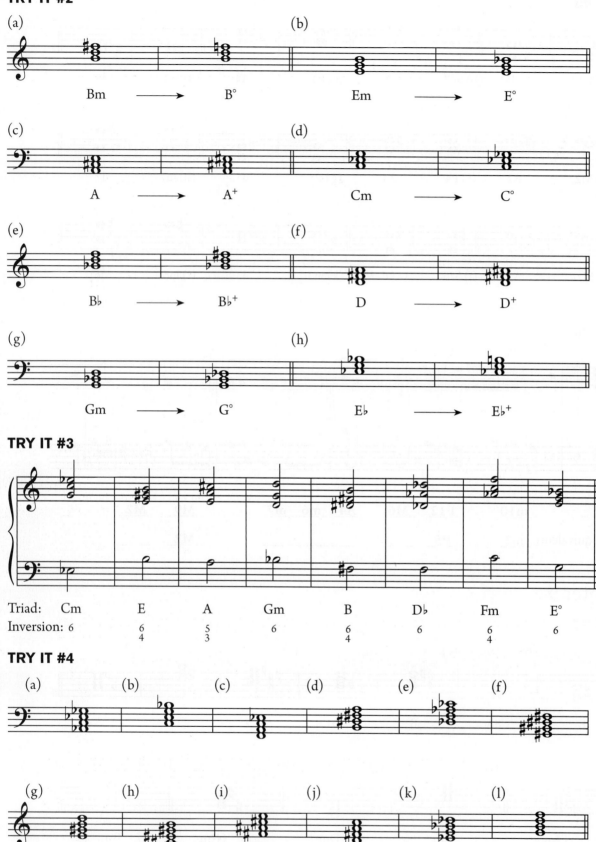

(a)

Bm ⟶ B°

(b)

Em ⟶ E°

(c)

A ⟶ A⁺

(d)

Cm ⟶ C°

(e)

B♭ ⟶ B♭⁺

(f)

D ⟶ D⁺

(g)

Gm ⟶ G°

(h)

E♭ ⟶ E♭⁺

TRY IT #3

Triad:	Cm	E	A	Gm	B	D♭	Fm	E°
Inversion:	6	6/4	5/3	6	6/4	6	6/4	6

TRY IT #4

(a) (b) (c) (d) (e) (f)

(g) (h) (i) (j) (k) (l)

TRY IT #5

(a)

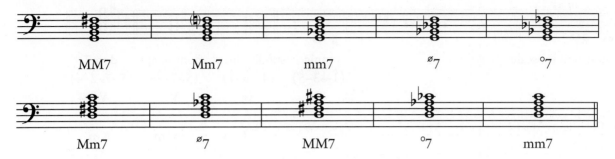

MM7 Mm7 mm7 ⌀7 °7

Mm7 ⌀7 MM7 °7 mm7

(b)

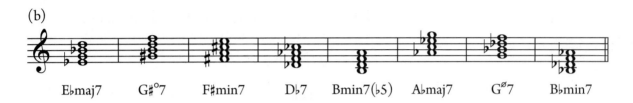

E♭maj7 G♯°7 F♯min7 D♭7 Bmin7(♭5) A♭maj7 G⌀7 B♭min7

Chapter 10

TRY IT #1

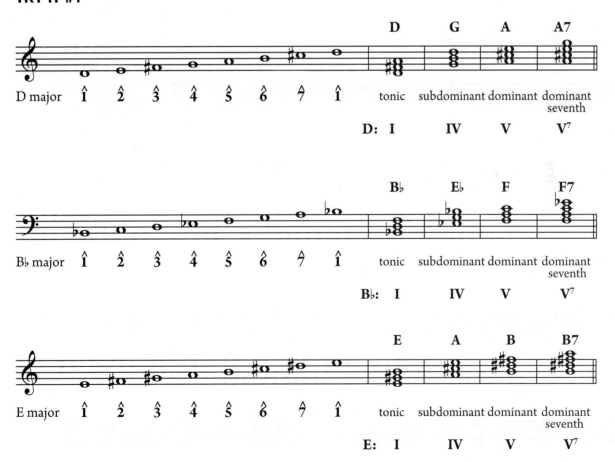

TRY IT #2

C# harmonic minor scale

C#m — tonic (1̂–♭3̂–5̂)
F#m — subdominant (4̂–♭6̂–1̂)
G# — dominant (5̂–7̂–2̂)
G#7 — dom7 (5̂–7̂–2̂–4̂)

c#: i   iv   V   V⁷

D natural minor scale

Dm — tonic (1̂–♭3̂–5̂)
Gm — subdominant (4̂–♭6̂–1̂)
Am — dominant (5̂–♭7̂–2̂)

d: i   iv   v

G harmonic minor scale

Gm — tonic (1̂–♭3̂–5̂)
Cm — subdominant (4̂–♭6̂–1̂)
D — dominant (5̂–7̂–2̂)
D7 — dom7 (5̂–7̂–2̂–4̂)

g: i   iv   V   V⁷

F# natural minor scale

F#m — tonic (1̂–♭3̂–5̂)
Bm — subdominant (4̂–♭6̂–1̂)
C#m — dominant (5̂–♭7̂–2̂)

f#: i   iv   v

TRY IT #3

(a) Key: F, cadence: PAC   (b) Key: g, cadence: HC

TRY IT #4

(a) G

I   IV   V   I   I   IV   I

(b) B♭

I   IV   V   I   I   IV   I

(c) C minor

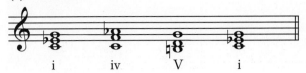 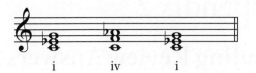

   i   iv   V   i   i   iv   i

TRY IT #5

One possible answer:

Make Music A: Write a Folk Song

TRY IT #1

a a′ b a′

Make Music B: Write a Blues Song

TRY IT #1

(a)

$\hat{1}$ ♭$\hat{3}$ $\hat{4}$ ♯$\hat{4}$ $\hat{5}$ ♭$\hat{7}$ $\hat{1}$ $\hat{1}$ ♭$\hat{7}$ $\hat{5}$ ♭$\hat{5}$ $\hat{4}$ ♭$\hat{3}$ $\hat{1}$

(b)

$\hat{1}$ ♭$\hat{3}$ $\hat{4}$ ♯$\hat{4}$ $\hat{5}$ ♭$\hat{7}$ $\hat{1}$ $\hat{1}$ ♭$\hat{7}$ $\hat{5}$ ♭$\hat{5}$ $\hat{4}$ ♭$\hat{3}$ $\hat{1}$

(c)

$\hat{1}$ ♭$\hat{3}$ $\hat{4}$ ♯$\hat{4}$ $\hat{5}$ ♭$\hat{7}$ $\hat{1}$ $\hat{1}$ ♭$\hat{7}$ $\hat{5}$ ♭$\hat{5}$ $\hat{4}$ ♭$\hat{3}$ $\hat{1}$

Appendix 2

Reading Review Answers

Chapter 1

(1) h   (2) c   (3) i   (4) f   (5) q   (6) g   (7) d   (8) a
(9) o   (10) p   (11) r   (12) j   (13) l   (14) n   (15) e   (16) m
(17) k   (18) b

Chapter 2

(1) e   (2) b   (3) h   (4) c   (5) l   (6) g   (7) f   (8) a
(9) j   (10) i   (11) k   (12) d

Chapter 3

(1) h   (2) c   (3) e   (4) r   (5) i   (6) a   (7) j   (8) p
(9) l   (10) g   (11) m   (12) d   (13) f   (14) q   (15) o   (16) n
(17) b   (18) k

Chapter 4

(1) c   (2) a   (3) b   (4) f   (5) h   (6) e   (7) i   (8) d
(9) g

Chapter 5

(1) c   (2) f   (3) g   (4) d   (5) l   (6) e   (7) k   (8) j
(9) a   (10) h   (11) b   (12) i

Chapter 6

(1) d   (2) f   (3) h   (4) g   (5) i   (6) c   (7) b   (8) e
(9) j   (10) a

Chapter 7

(1) g   (2) a   (3) b   (4) j   (5) c   (6) h   (7) f   (8) e
(9) d   (10) i

Chapter 8

(1) b   (2) f   (3) d   (4) h   (5) c   (6) g   (7) a   (8) e

Chapter 9

(1) g   (2) k   (3) e   (4) i   (5) a   (6) l   (7) b   (8) c
(9) d   (10) h   (11) j   (12) f

Chapter 10

(1) e   (2) d   (3) k   (4) c   (5) i   (6) n   (7) m   (8) f
(9) j   (10) g   (11) l   (12) a   (13) h   (14) b

Appendix 3
Glossary

12-bar blues: See *blues progression*.

32-bar song form: See *quaternary song form*.

A

a a b a: See *quaternary song form*.

accent: Stress given to a note or some other musical element that brings it to the listener's attention. Accents can be created by playing louder or softer, using a different timbre or articulation, speeding up or slowing down, or slightly changing rhythmic durations.

accidental: A symbol that appears before a note to raise or lower its pitch chromatically, without changing its letter name. See also *sharp, flat, natural, double sharp,* and *double flat.*

accompaniment: Music played by keyboard, guitar, or other instruments providing harmonies to support a sung or played melody.

alto: The second-highest voice in four-part (SATB) writing, notated in the treble clef, usually directly below the soprano; usually sung by women with lower voices.

alto clef: A C-clef positioned on a staff so that the middle line indicates middle C (C4).

anacrusis: A note or group of notes that precedes a downbeat, sometimes shown in an incomplete measure. Also called an upbeat or pickup.

antecedent phrase: The first phrase of a period, ending with an inconclusive cadence (usually a half cadence).

arpeggio: A chord played one pitch at a time.

ascending contour: A musical line that generally goes up, from lower pitches to higher ones.

asymmetrical meter: Meter with beat units of unequal duration. These irregular beat lengths are typically (though not always) created by five or seven beat divisions grouped into unequal lengths such as 2 + 3 or 2 + 3 + 2.

augmented interval: An interval one chromatic half step larger than a major or perfect interval.

augmented second: The distance between $\flat\hat{6}$ and $\hat{7}$ in the harmonic minor scale; equivalent to three half steps.

augmented triad: A triad that has a major third between its root and third, and between its third and fifth. The interval between its root and fifth is an augmented fifth.

authentic cadence (AC): A conclusive cadence in which V or V^7 progresses to I.

B

bar: See *measure*.

bar line: A vertical line, extending from the top of the staff to the bottom, that indicates the end of a measure.

basic phrase: A phrase that consists of an opening tonic area, an optional predominant area, a dominant area, and tonic closure.

bass: The lowest voice in four-part (SATB) writing, notated in the bass clef; usually sung by men with lower voices.

bass clef: Clef positioned on a staff to indicate F; its two dots surround the F3 line. (Also known as the F-clef.)

beam: A line that connects two or more note stems within a beat unit to indicate eighth, sixteenth, or thirty-second notes.

beat: The primary pulse in musical meter. Normally represents an even and regular division of musical time.

beat division: The secondary pulse in musical meter; beats may be divided into two parts (simple meter) or three parts (compound meter).

beat subdivision: A further division of the beat division into two parts; for example, a quarter note in simple meter divides into two eighths and subdivides into four sixteenths.

beat unit: The duration assigned to the basic pulse.

blue note: One of three pitches (of the blues scale) that appear in jazz and popular music for expressive effect: $\flat\hat{3}$, $\sharp\hat{4}$ (or $\flat\hat{5}$), and $\flat\hat{7}$.

blues progression: A chord progression (normally twelve bars long) typical of the blues: four measures of I, two measures each of IV and I, one measure each of V, IV, and I, finishing with I (or V for a turnaround). All harmonies may be either triads or seventh chords.

blues scale: A scale that shares most pitches with the natural minor scale, omitting $\hat{2}$ and $\flat\hat{6}$ and adding $\sharp\hat{4}/\flat\hat{5}$. Since the blues scale includes $\flat\hat{3}$ and $\flat\hat{7}$, it blurs the distinction between major and minor when it is used over a major-key blues progression.

bridge: (1) The contrasting **b** section in an **a a b a** 32-bar song form. (2) A section in a popular song that contrasts with the verse and chorus, and enters more than halfway through the song to prepare for their return.

build: In a popular song, an increase in intensity that anticipates the chorus.

C

C-clef: A movable clef that identifies which line on a staff designates middle C (C4) by the point at which its two curved lines join together in the middle. Common C-clefs include the alto and tenor clefs.

cadence: The end of a phrase, where harmonic, melodic, and rhythmic features mark the close of a complete musical thought. See also *authentic cadence, half cadence, deceptive cadence*.

change of mode: Transforming a melody or harmony from major to minor, or the reverse, by altering the quality of the third, sixth, and seventh scale degrees.

changes: Jazz term for harmonic progressions; short for chord changes.

changing meter: Meter that changes from measure to measure.

chord: Pitches sounded at the same time. See also *triad, seventh chord*.

chord connection: Links between chords in a musical composition; should aim for smooth motion by step, keep common tones in the same part, and correctly resolve dissonances.

chord members: The pitches that make up a chord.

chord progression: The specific order in which chords appear.

chorus: Section of music that is repeated with the same text.

chromatic: Pitches from outside a diatonic (major or natural minor) scale. The chromatic collection consists of all twelve pitches within an octave.

chromatic half step: A semitone spelling that uses the same letter name for both pitches (e.g., D and D♯).

chromatic scale: A scale consisting of all twelve pitches within the octave; the distance between each note and the next is a half step.

circle of fifths: A circular diagram representing the relationship between keys; clockwise motion around the circle shifts a key up by a P5 and removes a flat or adds a sharp; counterclockwise motion shifts a key down by a P5 and removes a sharp or adds a flat.

clef: A symbol on the far left of a staff that shows which pitch (and octave) is represented by each line and space. See also *treble clef, bass clef, C-clef, alto clef, tenor clef*.

climax: The musical high point of a melody or piece.

coda: Section at the end of a piece.

combo: A small instrumental ensemble for playing jazz or popular music, usually consisting of (at least) a solo instrument, keyboard, bass, and drum set.

common tones: When connecting two chords, pitches shared between them that are kept in the same voice or part to make a smooth transition between them.

compound duple: Meter with 2 beats in a measure, each beat divided into 3 (e.g., $\frac{6}{8}$ or $\frac{6}{4}$).

compound interval: An interval larger than an octave.

compound meter: Meter where the beat divides into threes and subdivides into sixes. The top number of compound meter signatures is 6, 9, or 12 (e.g., $\frac{9}{4}$ or $\frac{6}{8}$).

compound quadruple: Meter with four beats in a measure, each beat divided into 3 (e.g., $\frac{12}{8}$ or $\frac{12}{4}$).

compound triple: Meter with three beats in a measure, each beat divided into 3 (e.g., $\frac{9}{8}$ or $\frac{9}{4}$).

conclusive cadence: A relatively strong cadence that can end a section or piece.

conducting pattern: A specific pattern, one for each meter, that conductors outline with arm and wrist motions to set the tempo and maintain the beat for the musicians.

conjunct motion: Melodic motion that is primarily by step, making a smooth line.

consequent phrase: The second phrase of a period, ending with a strong harmonic conclusion, usually an authentic cadence.

consonance: A relative term based on acoustic properties of sound and on the norms of compositional practice. A consonant interval—unison, third, fifth, sixth, or octave—is considered pleasing to hear. A fourth is considered a consonance when written melodically but a dissonance when written harmonically.

contour: The shape of a melody; its motion up and down. Common contours include ascending, descending, arch, V-shape, and wave.

contrary motion: Two melodic lines or voices moving in opposite directions.

contrasting period: A period in which the two phrases do not share the same initial melodic material.

crescendo: An indication to increase the dynamic level.

D

deceptive cadence (DC): The cadence V$^{(7)}$–vi in major or V$^{(7)}$–VI in minor.

decrescendo: See *diminuendo*.

descending contour: A melodic line that generally goes down, from higher pitches to lower ones.

diatonic half step: A semitone spelling that uses different letter names for the two pitches (e.g., D and E♭).

diatonic scale: Scales made by rotating the step pattern W–W–H–W–W–W–H; the major and natural minor scales, and the modes (Dorian, Phrygian, Lydian, Mixolydian, and Locrian) are all diatonic scales.

diminished interval: An interval one half step smaller than a minor or perfect interval.

diminished seventh chord: A seventh chord consisting of a diminished triad with a diminished seventh above its root.

diminished triad: A triad that has a minor third between its root and third, and between its third and fifth. The interval between its root and fifth is a diminished fifth.

diminuendo: An indication to decrease the dynamic level; same as *decrescendo*.

disjunct motion: Melodic motion primarily by skip or leap that does not make a smooth line.

dissonance: A relative term based on acoustic properties of sound and on the norms of compositional practice. A dissonant interval—second, tritone, seventh, or any augmented or diminished interval—is considered unpleasant or jarring to hear. A fourth is considered a dissonance when written harmonically but a consonance when written melodically.

division: See *beat division*.

dominant: (1) Scale degree $\hat{5}$; (2) the triad built on $\hat{5}$.

dominant seventh chord: A seventh chord consisting of a major triad with a minor seventh above its root.

dot: Rhythmic notation that adds half of a note's own value to its duration (e.g., the duration of a dotted-half note equals a half note plus a quarter note).

double flat: An accidental (♭♭) that lowers a pitch two half steps without changing its letter name.

double sharp: An accidental (×) that raises a pitch two half steps without changing its letter name.

doubling: (1) Reinforcing a melodic line by adding voices or instruments at the unison or octave. (2) A pitch of a triad or seventh chord that appears in two parts to make four parts in SATB writing.

downbeat: The first beat of a measure, which has the strongest accent or emphasis; named for the downward motion of the conductor's hand.

drop: The return of the drums and full texture in the chorus of a popular song; often preceded by a build and sometimes by a brief pause or silence.

duple meter: Meter with two beats in each measure.

duplet: In compound meter, a division of the beat into two, instead of three, equal parts.

duration: The length of time represented by a note or rest.

dynamic level: The degree of loudness in performance. Extends from ***ppp*** (very soft) to ***fff*** (very loud).

E

eighth note: A stemmed filled note head with one flag or beam (♪); equivalent to two sixteenth notes.

eighth rest: A silence represented by ♪, equal in duration to an eighth note.

embellishing tones: Pitches that decorate tones in a melodic line. See also *neighbor tone, passing tone*.

enharmonic: Different names for the same pitch (e.g., E♭ and D♯).

enharmonic equivalence: The idea that two or more possible names for a single pitch (e.g., C♯, D♭, B𝄪) are musically the same.

enharmonically equivalent intervals: Two intervals that can be respelled with enharmonically equivalent notes (e.g., A2 and m3).

F

fifth: Interval spanning five letter names; within a triad or seventh chord, the pitch located a fifth above the root.

figures: Arabic numerals used to represent chords as intervals above a bass note.

first inversion: A triad or seventh chord with its third in the bass.

fixed *do*: See *solfège, fixed-do*.

flag: A short arc attached to the right side of a note stem, at the opposite end from the note head; each flag divides the duration of a note in half (e.g., a sixteenth note has two flags and is half of an eighth note, which has one flag).

flat: An accidental (♭) that lowers a pitch by one half step without changing its letter name.

form: A pattern of repeated, similar, and contrasting passages in a piece of music.

forte (*f*): A loud dynamic level. A louder dynamic level is *ff* (*fortissimo*); a softer dynamic level is *mf* (*mezzo forte*).

G

grand staff: Two staves, one in treble clef and one in bass clef, connected by a curly brace; typically used in piano music.

H

half cadence (HC): An inconclusive cadence ending on the dominant.

half-diminished seventh chord: A seventh chord consisting of a diminished triad with a minor seventh above its root.

half note: A stemmed hollow notehead; its duration is equivalent to two quarter notes.

half rest: A silence represented by ▬ sitting on top of the third staff line, equal in duration to a half note.

half step: The distance between a pitch and the next closest pitch on the keyboard.

harmonic interval: The span between two pitches played simultaneously.

harmonic loop: In recent popular music, a series of three or, more typically, four chords that are repeated in order over and over underneath a melody.

harmonic minor scale: See *minor scale*.

harmonic progression: *See chord progression*.

harmonic rhythm: The rate at which chords change (e.g., one chord per measure or one chord per beat).

harmonize: To choose chords to accompany a melody.

head: In jazz or blues, the main musical idea played at the beginning of the piece; it recurs, alternating with sections of instrumental or vocal improvisation.

homophony: Texture in which all voices are vertically aligned to move together in the same (or nearly the same) rhythm.

hook: A musical setting of a few words or a phrase, usually including the title, that is repeated and becomes the most memorable part of a song.

I

imperfect authentic cadence (IAC): An authentic cadence weakened (1) by inverting V or (2) by the soprano ending on a scale degree other than 1̂.

inconclusive cadence: Ending that is used for the first phrase of a period or prior to the end of a section; any type of cadence involving V and I other than a perfect authentic cadence.

instrumental break: Section in the middle of a song played only by instruments, often based on the verse.

interval: The distance between two pitches.

interval inversion: Transformation of an interval by transposing the lower note up an octave or the upper note down an octave, which changes the interval size and quality. When perfect intervals are inverted they remain perfect; major intervals become minor (and vise versa); augmented intervals become diminished (and vice versa). The size of an interval and its inversion sum to 9 (e.g., m2 becomes M7, P4 becomes P5, etc.).

interval quality: The property that distinguishes between two intervals of the same generic size (e.g., major third and minor third), accounting for their differing number of half steps. Interval quality can be major, minor, perfect, diminished, or augmented.

intro: Music, usually instrumental, that introduces a popular song.

introduction: Music at the beginning of a piece that prepares for the entry of the main melody.

inversion: See *interval inversion, inverted chord*.

inverted chord: A chord with its third, fifth, or seventh (instead of the root) in the bass.

K

key: (1) Music in a major or minor key employs notes of the major or minor scale so that the first note is the primary scale degree around which all others relate hierarchically. Keys are named by the first scale degree and the type of scale used (e.g., G minor). (2) The levers on an instrument that can be depressed with a finger to make a pitch sound (e.g., piano keys).

key signature: A pattern of sharps or flats (or no sharps or flats) that appears immediately following the clef on a staff, showing which notes, in any octave, are to be sharped or flatted consistently throughout the piece. The key signature helps identify the key of the piece; each signature is used for two keys—one major and one minor.

keyboard style: Texture with three notes of each chord in the right hand and one in the left.

L

lead sheet: Performance score for jazz and popular music consisting of a melody and chord changes.

leading tone: (1) Scale-degree $\hat{7}$, which tends to lead upward toward the tonic; (2) the triad built on $\hat{7}$.

leap: A melodic interval larger than a fourth; less common in melodies than steps or skips.

ledger line: Short line parallel to the lines of a staff to extend the staff for higher or lower notes.

letter name: The name for a particular pitch, employing letters A–G, that corresponds to its place on the staff or a musical instrument.

loose verse/tight chorus: Style in recent popular songs in which the verse has short, disconnected melodic segments that enter before or after the chord change, contrasting with the chorus, where the melody is more continuous and aligned more tightly with the chord changes.

M

major interval: Seconds, thirds, sixths, and sevenths above $\hat{1}$ of a major scale.

major key: Music comprised of notes drawn from the major scale; the key is named by the first scale degree and type of scale (e.g., B major).

major pentachord: The first five notes of a major scale (e.g., C–D–E–F–G in C major).

major pentatonic: A five-note scale consisting of $\hat{1}$, $\hat{2}$, $\hat{3}$, $\hat{5}$, and $\hat{6}$ of a major scale.

major scale: A seven-note scale beginning $\hat{1}$ (*do*)–$\hat{2}$ (*re*)– $\hat{3}$ (*mi*) with the pattern of whole and half steps W–W–H–W–W–W–H; it shares the same key signature as its relative minor.

major seventh chord: A major triad with a major seventh above its root.

major tetrachord: A series of four notes that form an ascending W–W–H pattern; building block of a major scale.

major triad: A triad that has a major third between its root and third, and a minor third between its third and fifth. The interval between its root and fifth is a perfect fifth.

measure: A unit of grouped beats, beginning and ending with bar lines.

mediant: (1) Scale degree $\hat{3}$; (2) the triad built on $\hat{3}$.

melodic interval: The distance between two notes played one after another.

melodic minor scale: See *minor scale*.

melody: (1) A succession of pitches and rhythms in a single line; (2) the main musical idea, or "tune," in a piece of music.

melody and accompaniment: A musical texture featuring a primary melody in one part and accompanying harmonies in the other.

meter: The grouping and division of beats in regular, recurring patterns.

meter signature: A sign that appears at the beginning of a piece, after the clef and key signature, that indicates the meter type (duple, triple, quadruple) and beat division (simple, compound); also called a time signature.

metrical accent: An emphasis on a note resulting from its placement on a strong beat.

mezzo forte (mf), mezzo piano (mp): Medium dynamic levels between *piano* and *forte*; *mp* is louder than *p*, and *mf* is softer than *f*.

middle C: C4; the C located at the center of the piano keyboard.

minor interval: Thirds, sixths, and sevenths above $\hat{1}$ of a minor scale; seconds between $\hat{7}$ and $\hat{1}$ in a major, harmonic minor, or ascending melodic minor scale.

minor key: Music comprised of notes drawn from the minor scale; the key is named by the first scale degree and type of scale (e.g., B minor).

minor mode: Mode incorporating $\flat\hat{3}$, $\flat\hat{6}$, and $\flat\hat{7}$, with a minor tonic triad.

minor pentachord: The first five notes of a minor scale (e.g., C–D–E♭–F–G in C minor).

minor pentatonic: A five-note scale consisting of $\hat{1}$, $\flat\hat{3}$, $\hat{4}$, $\hat{5}$, and $\flat\hat{7}$ of a minor scale.

minor scale: A seven-note scale beginning $\hat{1}$ (*do*)–$\hat{2}$ (*re*)–$\flat\hat{3}$ (*me*) that occurs in three forms: natural, harmonic, and melodic. The natural minor scale is an ordered collection of pitches arranged according to the pattern of whole and half steps W–H–W–W–H–W–W; it shares the same key signature as its relative major. The harmonic minor scale has raised $\hat{7}$. The melodic minor has raised $\hat{6}$ and $\hat{7}$ ascending, but takes the natural minor form descending.

minor seventh chord: A minor triad with a minor seventh above its root.

minor triad: A triad that has a minor third between its root and third, and a major third between its third and fifth. The interval between its root and fifth is a perfect fifth.

modal scale degrees: The third, sixth, and seventh scale degrees, which are one half step lower in minor keys than in major.

motive: The smallest recognizable musical idea. Motives may be characterized by their pitches, contour, and rhythm, but rarely include a cadence. Generally they are repeated (exactly or varied).

musical alphabet: The letters A, B, C, D, E, F, and G, which are used to name musical pitches.

N

natural: An accidental (♮) that cancels a sharp or flat.

natural minor scale: See *minor scale*.

neighbor tone: A melodic embellishment that decorates a pitch by moving a step above or below it, then returning to the original pitch.

note: The representation of a musical sound with a note head on the staff. The position of the note head indicates the pitch; duration is indicated by whether the note head is filled or hollow and the presence of a stem, beam, or flag.

note head: A small oval used to notate a pitch on the staff. Hollow note heads normally represent a longer duration than filled note heads.

O

octave: (1) The distance of eight musical steps; the interval size 8. (2) The particular part of the musical range where a pitch sounds (e.g., C4, or middle C, is a C in a particular octave).

octave equivalence: The concept that pitches eight steps apart (sharing the same name) sound similar.

octave number: An Arabic numeral used with a pitch's letter name to indicate in which register that pitch sounds (e.g., C4 is the C in the fourth octave, or middle C)

offbeat: A weak beat or weak portion of a beat.

outro: In popular music, the concluding musical idea, after the last verse or chorus. May consist of a "repeat and fade" of music that has been heard before.

P

parallel fifths: See *parallel motion*.

parallel keys: Major and minor keys sharing the same letter name, but with different pitches for $\hat{3}$, $\hat{6}$, and $\hat{7}$ (e.g., F major and F minor).

parallel major: The major key that has the same tonic as a given minor key (e.g., F minor's parallel major is F major). The parallel major raises the third, sixth, and seventh scale degree of a minor key.

parallel minor: The minor key that has the same tonic as a given major key (e.g., F major's parallel minor is F minor). The parallel minor lowers the third, sixth, and seventh scale degrees of a major key.

parallel motion: Two melodic lines or voices moving in the same direction by the same interval. Parallel fifths, octaves, and unisons are not generally permitted in SATB writing, while parallel thirds and sixths are common.

parallel octaves: See *parallel motion*.

parallel period: A period in which the two phrases begin with the same melodic material.

parallel unison: See *parallel motion*.

passing tone: A melodic embellishment that fills the space between chord members. Passing tones are approached and left by step in the same direction.

pentatonic scale: A five-note scale. See *major pentatonic* and *minor pentatonic*.

perfect authentic cadence (PAC): A strong conclusive cadence in which (1) root position $V^{(7)}$ progresses to root position I, and (2) the soprano moves from $\hat{2}$ or $\hat{7}$ to $\hat{1}$.

perfect interval: Unisons, fourths, fifths, and octaves above $\hat{1}$ in a major or minor scale.

period: A musical unit consisting of two phrases. The first phrase ends with an inconclusive cadence (usually a HC); the ending of the second answers it with a more conclusive cadence (usually a PAC).

phrase: A basic unit of musical thought, similar to a sentence in language. The typical phrase—like most sentences—has a beginning, a middle, and an end. A phrase must end with a cadence.

piano (p): A soft dynamic level. A softer dynamic level is pp (*pianissimo*); a louder dynamic level is mp (*mezzo piano*).

pickup: See *anacrusis*.

pitch: A musical sound in a particular octave or register.

postchorus: Section that follows the chorus in a popular song and prepares for the return of the verse.

prechorus: Section after the verse of a popular song that prepares for the chorus.

Q

quadruple meter: Meter with four beats in each measure.

quality: See *interval quality, triad quality*.

quarter note: A stemmed filled note head (♩); equivalent to two eighth notes.

quarter rest: A silence represented by 𝄽, equal in duration to a quarter note.

quaternary song form: A song form consisting of four phrases, usually with an **a a b a** or **a b c b** design. Each phrase is generally eight bars long, though some folk songs have four-measure phrases. In **a a b a** form, the first two phrases begin the same (they may be identical or differ at the cadence). They are followed by a contrasting section (the bridge) and then a return to the opening material.

R

raised submediant: Raised $\hat{6}$ in the melodic minor scale.

refrain: The section of a song that recurs with the same music and text.

register: The highness or lowness of a pitch or passage; the particular octave in which a pitch sounds.

relative keys: Major and minor keys that share the same key signature (e.g., C major and A minor).

relative major: The major key that shares the same key signature as a given minor key. The relative major has the same pitches as its relative minor but it begins on $\flat\hat{3}$ of the minor key.

relative minor: The minor key that shares the same key signature as a given major key. The relative minor has the same pitches as its relative major, but it begins on $\hat{6}$ of the major key.

resolution: See *resolve*.

resolve: To move the voices of an interval or triad from dissonance to consonance.

rest: A duration of silence.

rhythm: The durations of pitch and silence (notes and rests) used in music.

rhythm clef: Two short, thick, vertical lines at the beginning of a single-line staff, used to notate unpitched percussion parts.

rhythmic motive: A motive that maintains its rhythm, but changes its contour and intervals.

riff: a repeated instrumental motive in jazz and blues styles.

Roman numeral: A symbol used to represent the scale degree a chord is built on, as well as its quality.

root: The lowest pitch of a triad or seventh chord when the chord is spelled in thirds.

root position: A chord voiced with the root in the bass.

S

SATB: An abbreviation indicating the four voice ranges: soprano, alto, tenor, and bass; also indicates a particular musical style or texture: hymn or chorale style.

scale: An ordered collection of pitches.

scale degree: The position of a note in a scale; identified by scale-degree names or scale-degree numbers (e.g., tonic, $\hat{1}$).

scale-degree names: Names for the position of a note in a scale; these include tonic, supertonic, mediant, subdominant, dominant, submediant, leading tone, and subtonic.

scale-degree numbers: Numbers for the position of a note in a scale, written with a caret over a number (e.g., $\hat{1}$, $\hat{5}$).

score: Notated music.

second inversion: A triad or seventh chord voiced with its fifth in the bass.

semitone: Half step.

seventh: An interval spanning seven letter names; as a dissonance, the seventh above the root of a chord normally resolves down.

seventh chord: A four-note chord with a third, fifth, and seventh above its root; a triad with a third added above its fifth.

sharp: An accidental ($\sharp$) that raises a pitch a half step without changing its letter name.

similar motion: Two melodic lines or voices moving in the same direction, but not by the same interval. This type of motion connects two harmonic intervals that are not the same size.

simple duple: Meter with two beats in a measure, each beat divided into two (e.g., $\frac{2}{4}$).

simple interval: An interval of an octave or smaller.

simple meter: Meter where the beat divides into twos and subdivides into fours. The top number of simple meter signatures is 2, 3, or 4 (e.g., $\frac{3}{4}$ or $\frac{4}{4}$).

simple quadruple: Meter with four beats in a measure, each beat divided into two (e.g., $\frac{4}{4}$).

simple triple: Meter with three beats in a measure, each beat divided into two (e.g., $\frac{3}{4}$ or $\frac{3}{8}$).

sixteenth note: A stemmed filled notehead with two flags or beams (♪); two sixteenth notes equal an eighth note.

sixteenth rest: A silence represented by ♪, equal in duration to a sixteenth note.

skip: A melodic interval of a third or fourth; used to move between notes of a triad.

slur: An arc that connects two (or more) different pitches and affects performance articulation but not duration. In piano music, they tell the performer to play the slurred notes smoothly; in vocal music, the slurred notes are sung on one syllable or in one breath.

solfège, fixed-*do*: A singing system in which a particular syllable is associated with a particular pitch (*do* is always C, *re* is always D, etc.) no matter what the key.

solfège, movable-*do*: A singing system in which a particular syllable is associated with a particular scale step (*do* is always $\hat{1}$, *re* always $\hat{2}$, etc.) no matter what the key.

soprano: The highest voice in four-part (SATB) writing, notated in treble clef; usually sung by women with higher voices.

staff: The five parallel lines on which music is written. (Plural form is *staves*.)

stem: A vertical line attached to a note head; it generally extends upward if the note is written below the middle line of the staff and downward if the note is written on or above the middle line.

step: The distance between adjacent pitches in a scale, may be a half step (one semitone) or a whole step (two semitones).

stepwise motion: Transition from one pitch to the next by half or whole step.

subdivision: See *beat subdivision*.

subdominant: (1) Scale degree $\hat{4}$; (2) the triad built on $\hat{4}$.

submediant: (1) Scale degree $\hat{6}$; (2) the triad built on $\hat{6}$.

subtonic: (1) Scale degree $\flat\hat{7}$ of the natural minor scale, located a whole step below the tonic; (2) the triad build on $\flat\hat{7}$.

supertonic: (1) Scale degree $\hat{2}$; (2) the triad built on $\hat{2}$.

swung eighths: A performance practice where a rhythm notated with even eighth notes is performed unevenly, with more time allotted to the first eighth and less to the second in each pair.

symmetrical meter: Meter with beat units of equal duration.

syncopation: Rhythmic displacement of accents created by dots, ties, rests, dynamic markings, or accent marks.

T

tempo: How fast or slow music is played.

tempo indication: A marking, often in Italian, printed in a score to indicate how fast the music is to be played. Typical markings, from slow to fast, include *adagio, andante, allegro, presto*.

tendency tone: A chord member or scale degree whose relation to the surrounding tones requires a particular resolution (i.e., chordal sevenths must resolve down, and leading tones must resolve up).

tenor: The second-lowest voice in four-part (SATB) writing, sounding between the alto and bass parts; may be notated in the bass clef in SATB voicing in hymn style, or in the treble clef in keyboard-style voicing. In performance scores for choirs, the tenor may be written in treble clef and sung down an octave.

tenor clef: A C-clef positioned on a staff so that the fourth line from the bottom indicates middle C (C4).

tetrachord: A four-note segment of a scale with a particular pattern of whole and half steps.

texture: Describes the number of instruments playing (solo or ensemble), the number of different melodic or harmonic layers sounding at once, and the relationship of these layers or instruments to each other.

third: Interval spanning three letter names; within a triad or seventh chord, the pitch located a third above the root.

third inversion: A seventh chord with its seventh in the bass.

tie: A small arc connecting note heads of two identical pitches to indicate the durations are to be combined together, without rearticulating the pitch. Used to notate durations extending across a bar line and for durations that cannot be represented with dotted notes.

timbre: Describes the quality of a musical sound, such as its instrumentation.

time signature: See *meter signature*.

tonic: (1) Scale degree $\hat{1}$; (2) the triad built on $\hat{1}$.

transpose: To renotate a melody or harmony at a different pitch level or in a different key while maintaining the intervals between its elements.

transcription: (1) A rhythmic pattern rewritten in a different meter, but sounding the same if it is played at the same tempo. (2) A piece written for one instrument or ensemble arranged to be played by another (e.g., an orchestra piece transcribed for band). (3) A score notated from a recorded performance.

treble clef: Clef positioned on a staff to indicate G by means of the end of its curving line; it circles the line that represents G4. (Also known as the G-clef.)

triad: A three-note chord with a third and fifth above its starting point, or root.

triad and seventh chord positions: See *inverted chord*.

triad names: Names for triads based on the scale degrees of their roots; these include tonic, supertonic, mediant, subdominant, dominant, submediant, leading tone, and subtonic.

triad quality: A description of a triad according to the quality of its stacked thirds and outer fifth: major, minor, diminished, or augmented.

triple meter: Meter with three beats in each measure.

triplet: In simple meter, a division of the beat into three, instead of two, equal parts.

tritone: An interval made up of three whole tones or six semitones; an augmented fourth or diminished fifth. By some definitions, only an augmented fourth is a tritone, since only this spelling of the interval spans three whole steps.

turnaround: At the end of a blues progression, a V or V^7 chord to prepare for the repeat of the progression.

two-beat triplet: In simple meter, a division of a two-beat note into three equal notes (e.g., in $\frac{4}{4}$, a half note divided into three quarter notes).

U

unison: The interval size 1, or the distance from a pitch to itself. Voices or instruments that are performing the same melody with the same rhythm in the same octave are said to be playing "in unison."

upbeat: The beat that precedes a downbeat; named for the upward lift of the conductor's hand. Also known as an anacrusis.

V

variation: Repetition of a passage with changes to any number of basic musical features including the melody, cadences, rhythms, key, mode, length, texture, timbre, character, and style.

verse: A section of a song that returns with the same music but different text.

W

whole note: A stemless hollow notehead (**o**); its duration is equivalent to two half notes.

whole rest: A silence represented by ▬ hanging below the fourth staff line, equal in duration to a whole note.

whole step: An interval that spans two adjacent half steps.

whole tone: See *whole step*.

Appendix 4

The Overtone Series

Every musical pitch played by an instrument, or sung by a voice, is a complex tone, consisting of a fundamental (lowest) pitch plus a series of overtones that sound faintly above it. Example A4.1 shows an overtone series above C2. Overtones (also called partials) are naturally occurring phenomena, created by the vibrations of strings, vocal chords, or columns of air. Partials are often numbered: the fundamental is the first partial, the octave above is the second partial, and so on. The partials shown with black note heads sound out of tune compared to a piano.

EXAMPLE A4.1   Overtone series with C2 Fundamental

The characteristic timbre—or color—of an instrument is created by the different strengths (or amplitudes) of overtones, resulting from the shape of the instrument's resonating space. For example, a flute has a strong fundamental, a somewhat weaker second partial, and very weak higher partials. An oboe has more sound from higher overtones than from lower overtones.

The interval between the first and second partials (in Example A4.1, the octave from C2 to C3) may be represented by the ratio 1:2 (relating the frequencies of the two pitches). Throughout the series, each ratio between partial numbers represents the interval between the pitches; 2:1 is a perfect fifth (e.g., C3–G3, the second and third partials of C2), 4:3 is a perfect fourth (C3–C4), 5:4 is a major third (C4–E4), and so on. The intervals with smaller numbers tend to correspond to acoustic consonances, and higher numbers (e.g., 16:15, minor second) with dissonances. These ratios also represent the divisions of a string (e.g., on violin, guitar, or cello) where a performer would place his or her fingers to create these intervals, as Example A4.2 shows. If you play an open string, then divide it in half and play the string again, the second pitch is an octave above the first. For brass players, changing the valve combination or slide position changes the fundamental pitch; changing the air pressure and speed shifts the sound between pitches in the overtone series.

EXAMPLE A4.2   Divisions of a string to produce P8, P5, and P4

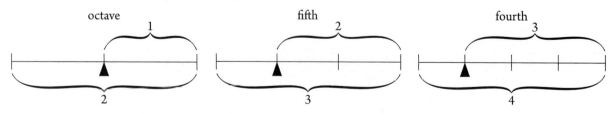

Appendix 5

The Diatonic Modes

Playing the seven white keys from C to C (with no sharps or flats) results in a C major scale, also known as the Ionian mode. Playing through the white keys starting on different notes (D to D, E to E, etc.) forms other diatonic modes, as shown in Example A5.1. There are six traditional diatonic modes (in order, from C): Ionian, Dorian, Phrygian, Lydian, Mixolydian, and Aeolian. (As a shortcut to learning the six mode names, think of a sentence that gives you the first letter of each mode, like "I don't particularly like magic acts.") A seventh mode, Locrian (Example A5.1g), was identified in the late Renaissance but deemed unusable; it was not used in composing music until the twentieth century. The traditional diatonic modes are found in twentieth- and twenty-first-century jazz, popular, and folk music, as well as in older styles of music.

EXAMPLE A5.1   The diatonic modes as rotations of the C major scale

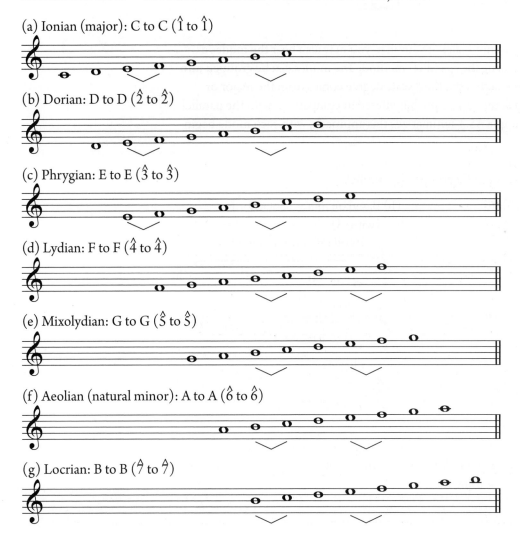

(a) Ionian (major): C to C ($\hat{1}$ to $\hat{1}$)

(b) Dorian: D to D ($\hat{2}$ to $\hat{2}$)

(c) Phrygian: E to E ($\hat{3}$ to $\hat{3}$)

(d) Lydian: F to F ($\hat{4}$ to $\hat{4}$)

(e) Mixolydian: G to G ($\hat{5}$ to $\hat{5}$)

(f) Aeolian (natural minor): A to A ($\hat{6}$ to $\hat{6}$)

(g) Locrian: B to B ($\hat{7}$ to $\hat{7}$)

One way to identify the mode of a piece is by the "relative" method: think of the major key associated with the work's key signature, then locate the most stable pitch in the melody and identify what scale degree that pitch would be, given the major key shown by the key signature. Major (Ionian) melodies rest on $\hat{1}$ of the major key as their most stable pitch, while minor (Aeolian) melodies rest on $\hat{6}$. If $\hat{2}$ of the major key seems to function as the most stable pitch, then a melody is in Dorian mode, as shown in Example A5.1. Look at "Greensleeves" (Example A5.2). The sharp in the key signature suggests G major, but $\hat{2}$ of that key (A) is the most stable pitch and the melody ends on A: the melody is Dorian. Occasionally modal melodies are altered at the cadence to insert a leading tone (as in harmonic minor); the G♯ in measure 7 is an example of this practice.

EXAMPLE A5.2 "Greensleeves," mm. 1–8

Because the major and minor scales are familiar, you may also hear the modes as alterations of these scales, using the "parallel" method. The modes can be grouped into two families, according to whether the third scale degree comes from the major or minor pentachord. For each mode, one pitch is altered in comparison with the parallel major or minor scale. Example A5.3 summarizes this approach, with each mode beginning on C.

EXAMPLE A5.3 Modes (on C) grouped by families

(a) Based on major pentachord
(with $\hat{3}$)

(b) Based on minor pentachord
(with ♭$\hat{3}$)

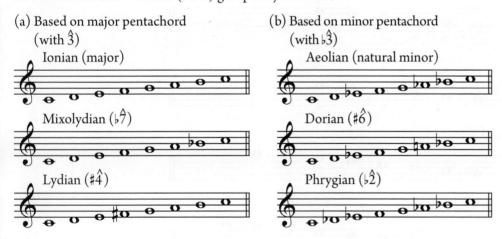

To write a mode beginning on any pitch, use either the relative or parallel method, as shown in Example A5.4. Both methods yield the same result; you can write the mode using one method and check it using the other.

To write a Dorian scale beginning on G:

A. Relative method (Example A5.4a)

1. Write note heads on the staff from G to G.
2. Remember that Dorian begins on $\hat{2}$ of a major scale; G is $\hat{2}$ in F major.
3. F major has one flat, so add a flat to B.

B. Parallel method (Example A5.4b)

1. Remember that Dorian sounds like natural minor with a raised sixth scale degree.
2. Write a G natural minor scale, with two flats (B♭ and E♭).
3. Raise ♭$\hat{6}$ by changing E♭ to E♮.

EXAMPLE A5.4   Relative and parallel methods of writing modes on any pitch

(a) Relative method:

1. and 2. Write pitches G to G, and think of the scale (F major) in which G is $\hat{2}$

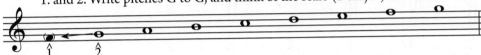

3. Add accidentals from key signature of F major.

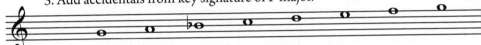

(b) Parallel method:

1. and 2. Write pitches and accidentals for G natural minor.

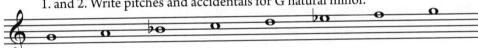

3. Raise ♭$\hat{6}$ to $\hat{6}$

Appendix 6

More on Seventh Chords

The quality of a seventh chord in a key depends on the scale degree of its root. The seventh chords built on each degree of the G major scale are given in Example A6.1 (with their quality of triad and seventh, chord quality names, Roman numerals within the key, and popular-music chord symbols).

EXAMPLE A6.1   Seventh chords built above the G major scale

	$\hat{1}$	$\hat{2}$	$\hat{3}$	$\hat{4}$	$\hat{5}$	$\hat{6}$	$\hat{7}$
Triad quality	M	m	m	M	M	m	d
7th quality	M	m	m	M	m	m	m
Full name	major-major 7th	minor-minor 7th	minor-minor 7th	major-major 7th	major-minor 7th	minor-minor 7th	diminished-minor 7th
Common name	major 7th	minor 7th	minor 7th	major 7th	dominant 7th	minor 7th	half-diminished 7th
Abbreviation	MM7	mm7	mm7	MM7	Mm7	mm7	$^{\varnothing}7$
Roman numeral	I^7	ii^7	iii^7	IV^7	V^7	vi^7	$vii^{\varnothing 7}$
Chord symbol	Gmaj7	Amin7	Bmin7	Cmaj7	D7	Emin7	F#min7 (♭5) or F#$^{\varnothing 7}$

Example A6.2 shows the seventh chords built on the G minor scale. Since ♭$\hat{7}$ is typically raised in minor, the chords on $\hat{5}$ and $\hat{7}$ are written with an F#; the chord on the leading tone in minor is therefore a diminished seventh, while the half-diminished seventh appears on $\hat{2}$.

While other types of seventh chords are possible, these are the most common.

EXAMPLE A6.2 Seventh chords built above the G minor scale

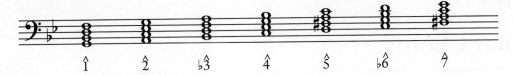

	$\hat{1}$	$\hat{2}$	$\flat\hat{3}$	$\hat{4}$	$\hat{5}$	$\flat\hat{6}$	$\hat{7}$
Triad quality	m	d	M	m	M	M	d
7th quality	m	m	M	m	m	M	d
Full name	minor-minor 7th	diminished-minor 7th	major-major 7th	minor-minor 7th	major-minor 7th	major-major 7th	fully diminished 7th
Common name	minor 7th	half-diminished 7th	major 7th	minor 7th	dominant 7th	major 7th	diminished 7th
Abbreviation	mm7	$^{\varnothing}7$	MM7	mm7	Mm7	MM7	$^{\circ}7$
Roman numeral	i^7	$ii^{\varnothing 7}$	III^7	iv^7	V^7	VI^7	$vii^{\circ 7}$
Chord symbol	Gmin7	Amin^7($\flat$5) or A$^{\varnothing 7}$	B$\flat$maj7	Cmin7	D7	E$\flat$maj7	F$\sharp$dim^7 or F$\sharp^{\circ 7}$

Appendix 7

Basic Guitar Chords

Guitar chords are often illustrated using fretboard diagrams—pictures showing where to place your fingers on the guitar to produce a particular chord. The six vertical lines on a diagram represent the six strings of the guitar, with the lowest-sounding string on the left and the highest-sounding on the right. The horizontal lines represent the frets (small raised bars that run perpendicular to the strings). In standard tuning, the open strings of a guitar produce E2, A2, D3, G3, B3, and E4, as shown in Example A7.1. These pitches are customarily written an octave higher, in treble clef, as shown.

EXAMPLE A7.1   Open strings on the guitar

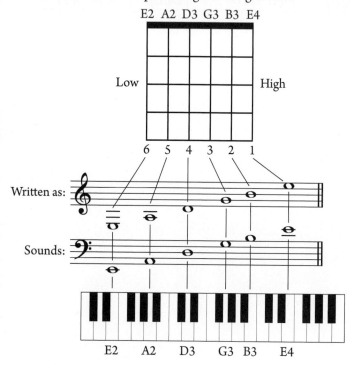

The placement of pitches on the guitar is shown in Example A7.2. To read this diagram, look at the low string in the illustration. The open string sounds E2; if you place your finger in the space before the first fret, you produce F2, the next note is F♯2 or G♭2, the next G2, and so on. You can continue up this string to E3 on the twelfth fret: fingering here sounds an octave above the open string. The diamonds shown in Example A7.2 represent marks that are traditionally used on guitars to help performers quickly locate frets: single diamonds for the third, fifth, seventh, and ninth frets, and a pair of diamonds for the twelfth fret. The bass guitar uses the same string arrangement as a standard guitar, but only has the four lowest strings, which are tuned to sound an octave below those on the six-string guitar (E1, A1, D2, G2).

EXAMPLE A7.2 Pitches on a guitar fretboard

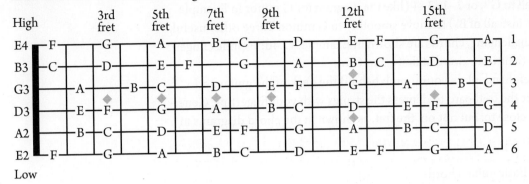

As an aid to performers, scores sometimes include fretboard diagrams, like the one shown in Example A7.3b, with chord symbols. A small o at the end of a string (shown at the top of the diagram) means that the string is played but not fingered; and an x in the same position means the string should not be played (it is not part of the chord). Black dots show you where to place your fingers on the fretboard.

EXAMPLE A7.3 How to read a fretboard diagram

(a) Finger indications

(b) Diagram

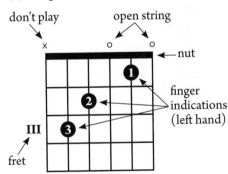

Each chord can be played in a variety of ways, but the basic chords shown in Example A7.4 are useful for beginners. Consult other resources (online or in the library) to build your repertoire of chords. The guitar chords often taught first are E, A, D, G, and C (Figure A7.4a) and Em, Am, and Dm (Figure A7.4c).

The letters below each symbol show the pitches played by each string (a dash means that a string is not played). Some basic fingerings are indicated by the finger numbers (1–4 from index finger to pinky) in this example. Guitarists often change these fingerings based on the chord progression. For example, an A major chord can be fingered 1–2–3 before a D major chord or 2–3–4 before an E major or A minor chord. The 2–1–3 fingering for A major shown in Example A7.4a connects well to the

A dominant seventh fingering shown in A7.4b. G major can be fingered 3–2–4 (as shown) to connect well to G7, or 2–1–3–4 (like the diagram for G minor in Example A7.4d, but with the B♮ instead of B♭) to move smoothly to G minor. Three other useful, but somewhat more challenging, chords are shown in Example A7.4d: F (index finger plays two strings), B7 (a little awkward at first), and Gm.

To position your left hand, place your thumb behind the neck of the guitar and curve your fingers over the fretboard to depress the strings with your fingertips. Generally place your fingers close to, but not on, the fret, as shown in the chord diagrams in Example A7.4.

EXAMPLE A7.4   Basic guitar chords

(a) Major chords

 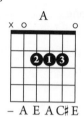 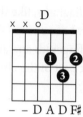 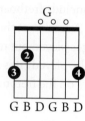 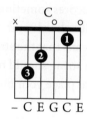

(b) Dominant seventh chords

 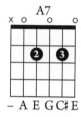 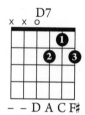 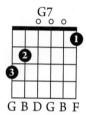

(c) Minor chords

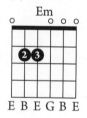 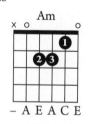 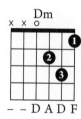 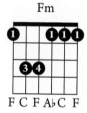 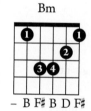

(d) F major, B7, and G minor

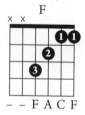 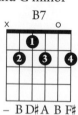 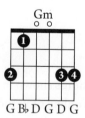

The chords in Example A7.4 can be combined to play basic phrase progressions in the keys of A, D, G, or C major, and in A and D minor, as shown in Example A7.5 and harmonic loops as shown in Example A7.6. You can also add ii and vi in C major (Dm and Am) and G major (Am and Em) and explore other combinations of these harmonies.

EXAMPLE A7.5   Basic chords in different keys

	I	IV	V	V^7
A major	A	D	E	E7
D major	D	G	A	A7
G major	G	C	D	D7
C major	C	F	G	G7

	i	iv	v	V	V^7
A minor	Am	Dm	Em	E	E7
D minor	Dm	Gm	Am	A	A7

EXAMPLE A7.6   Harmonic loops

(a)

	I	V	vi	IV
C major	C	G	Am	F
A major	A	E	F♯m	D
D major	D	A	Bm	G
G major	G	D	Em	C

(b)

	vi	IV	I	V
C major	Am	F	C	G
A major	F♯m	D	A	E
D major	Bm	G	D	A
G major	Em	C	G	D

(c)

	I	vi	IV	V
C major	C	Am	F	G
A major	A	F♯m	D	E
D major	D	Bm	G	A
G major	G	Em	C	D

(d)

	I	IV	vi	V
C major	C	F	Am	G
A major	A	D	F♯m	E
D major	D	G	Bm	A
G major	G	C	Em	D

To strum a guitar, use your thumb or the pick to sound all of the strings that are included in the chord (leave out any marked on the chord diagram with an ✗). Example A7.7 shows some basic strumming patterns.

EXAMPLE A7.7   Basic guitar strumming patterns

down up down up   down down up   down down up   up down up

For an arpeggiated accompaniment, you can pluck the strings of a chord one at a time, playing the lowest-pitched note first. Explore a variety of arpeggiated patterns by plucking the strings of a chord using different rhythms in a variety of meters.

Appendix 8

Piano Fingerings for Selected Scales

In this book, class activities have used scale fingerings that are very easy for locating pitches on a keyboard. If you are interested in studying piano further (or if your teacher directs), here are standard fingerings for the major and minor scales, where the thumb is 1 and the pinky is 5. Either hand may play in any octave; scales are often learned one hand at a time, then practiced with the hands one octave apart.

EXAMPLE A8.1 Major scales

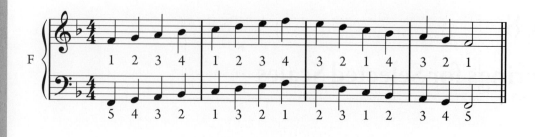

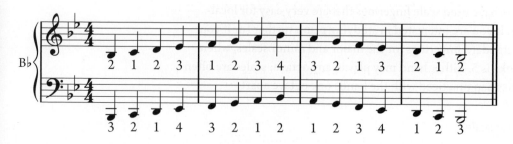

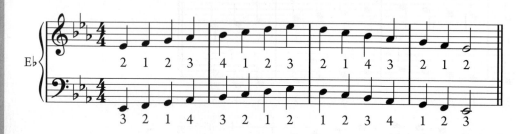

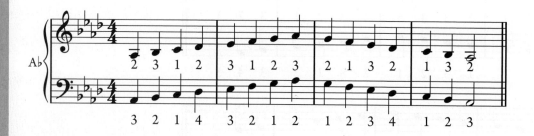

EXAMPLE A8.2 Harmonic minor scales

Appendix 9

Connecting Chords

General guidelines for connecting chords in SATB style (four-voice hymn style, with soprano, alto, tenor, and bass voices) follow. These basic principles may be adapted for keyboard and other styles. They are intended to create (1) smooth connections between chords, by step or common tone; (2) independence of voices, minimizing motion in the same direction; and (3) the correct resolution of tendency tones, such as $\hat{7}$ and chordal sevenths.

EXAMPLE A9.1 Chord connections in authentic cadences

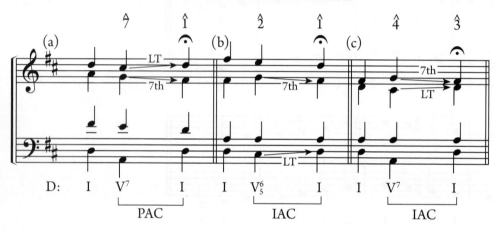

When you connect chords in SATB style:

1. If the chords have a pitch or pitches in common (called **common tones**) in one of the three upper voices, try to keep these common tones in the same voice part. (In Example A9.1b and c, A3 appears in the tenor in all three chords.)

2. When there is not a common tone, move the upper voices by step if possible. (In Example A9.1, the soprano and alto move by step.) The upper parts (soprano, alto, and tenor) are more likely to move by step or common tone than the bass, which sometimes skips between chord roots or inversions.

3. Tendency tones, such as the leading tone ($\hat{7}$) and the sevenths of chords, must move by step as marked in the example:

   • The leading tone moves up by step to $\hat{1}$.
   • Chordal sevenths move down by step.

4. Let some pairs of voices (soprano and alto, soprano and bass, tenor and alto, etc.) move in opposite directions, if possible. This is called **contrary motion**. (In Example A9.1a, the soprano and bass move up in the last two chords, while the alto and tenor move down. In c, the soprano/alto and soprano/bass pairs move in contrary motion.)

5. When pairs of voices move in the same direction, check the type of interval between them and adjust if necessary:

- If the voices move in the same direction but create two different intervals (called **similar motion**), the chord connection is acceptable.
- If the voices move in the same direction and create two intervals of the same size (called **parallel motion**), check the interval type:
  - Imperfect consonances (third to third or sixth to sixth) are acceptable. This is shown in the soprano and alto in the last two chords of Example A9.1b, both sixths.
  - **Parallel fifths** (P5 to P5), **parallel octaves** (P8 to P8), and **parallel unisons** (P11 to P11) are generally not found in SATB style though you may see them in popular music. If you find any in your writing, revise the chord connections.

Index of Musical Examples

"21 Guns" (Green Day), 336

"Agincourt Song," 135
"Ah, Belinda, I am prest," from *Dido and Aeneas* (Purcell), 190
"Ah, Poor Bird," 285
"All Because of You" (Bono and U2), 262
"Alleluia" (Mozart), 218
"All of Me" (Stephens and Gad), 332–34
"All Time High" (Barry and Rice), 33
"Amazing Grace" (Newton), 1, 24, 50, 52, 55, 171, 364
"American Pie" (McLean), 79, 126
"Am Flusse" (On the River) (Schubert), 218
Anonymous, Minuet in D Minor, from the Anna Magdalena Bach Notebook, 232
"Another Jig Will Do," 146
"Arfon," 254
Arlen, Harold, "We're Off to See the Wizard," from *The Wizard of Oz* (with Harburg), 143
Armstrong, Billie Joe, "Boulevard of Broken Dreams" (with Green Day), 124
"Ash Grove, The," 97, 98, 195, 303–4, 340–41
Ashman, Howard, "Beauty and the Beast" (with Menken), 295
"As Time Goes By" (Hupfeld), 111
"Aus meines Herzens Grunde" (Bach), 225
"Autumn Leaves" (Kosma), 219

Bach, Johann Sebastian
    "Aus meines Herzens Grunde," 225
    Chaconne, from Violin Partita No. 2, 181
    Invention in D Minor, 58, 161, 207, 342–43
    Minuet II, from Cello Suite No. 1, 65, 181
    "Musette," BWV Anh. 126, 113
    "O Haupt voll blut und Wunden," 65
    Passacaglia in C Minor, 61
    Prelude, from Cello Suite No. 2, 5
    Prelude in C Major, from *The Well-Tempered Clavier,* Book I, 51
    "Wachet auf," 190, 244, 272–73, 344–46
"Banana Boat Song," 217
Barry, John, "All Time High" (with Rice), 33
Bartók, Béla, "Bulgarian Rhythm," 137
Basie, Count, "Splanky," 315, 317
"Battle of New Orleans, The" (Driftwood), 251
Beatles, The
    "Eight Days a Week," 225
    "Hello, Goodbye," 20
    "Hey Jude," 52
    "Ticket to Ride," 325–26

"Beautiful Dreamer" (Foster), 129
"Beauty and the Beast" (Ashman and Menken), 295
Beethoven, Ludwig van
    Pathétique Sonata, 65
    Sonata for Violin and Piano, Op. 30, no. 2, first movement, 175
    Sonatina, WoO, 145
    String Quartet in F Major, Op. 18, No. 1, second movement, 151
"Before the Parade Passes By," from *Hello Dolly!* (Herman), 149
Blackwell, Ronald, "Lil' Red Riding Hood," 177
Bliss, Philip P., "Wonderful Words of Life," 145
"Blue Rondo à la Turk" (Brubeck), 138
"Blues for Norton" (Phillips), 6, 44, 56, 57, 94, 232, 314–15, 322
    full score, 366–68
    lead sheet, 365
Bono
    "All Because of You" (with U2), 262
    "Miracle Drug" (with U2), 71
    "One Step Closer" (with U2), 262
"Boulevard of Broken Dreams" (Armstrong and Green Day), 124
Brackett, Joseph, "Simple Gifts," 105, 193–94, 213, 347
Brahms, Johannes, Intermezzo, OP. 118, No. 2, 181
Brel, Jacques, "Seasons in the Sun," 64
"Broken" (Welgemoed), 179
Brubeck, Dave, "Blue Rondo à la Turk," 138
"Bulgarian Rhythm," from *Mikrokosmos* (Bartók), 137
Burleske (L. Mozart), 253
"Butterfly, The," 151
"By the Waters of Babylon" (Hayes), 286

Canon in D Major (Pachelbel), 266
"Can't Help Falling in Love," from *Blue Hawaii* (Weiss, Peretti, and Creatore), 88
Cerf, Christopher, "Dance Myself to Sleep," from *Sesame Street* (with Stiles), 130
Charnin, Martin, "Tomorrow" (with Strouse), 295
"Chartres," 274
Chopin, Fryderyk
    Nocturne, Op. 9, No. 2, 181
    Prelude in C Minor, Op. 28, No. 20, 61
"Circle of Life," from *The Lion King* (John and Rice), 9

Clarke, Jeremiah, *Trumpet Voluntary,* 190
"Come, Follow Me," 112
"Come, Ye Thankful People Come" (St. George's Windsor), 49, 52–53, 61, 236, 348
Corelli, Arcangelo, Allemanda, from Trio Sonata, Op. 4, No. 5, 165–66
Creatore, Luigi, "Can't Help Falling in Love," from *Blue Hawaii* (with Weiss and Peretti), 88
Credo, from *Messa Prima* (Leonarda), 87
Croce, Jim, "Time in a Bottle," 163–64
"Cruella de Vil" (Leven), 28, 31

"Dallas Blues" (Wand and Garrett), 76, 317, 372–75
"Dance Myself to Sleep," from *Sesame Street* (Cerf and Stiles), 130
Diamond, Neil, "Song Sung Blue," 252
"Dona nobis pacem," 287
"Down in the Valley," 307
Driftwood, Jimmy, "The Battle of New Orleans," 251

"Edelweiss," from *The Sound of Music* (Rodgers and Hammerstein), 295
Edwards, Clara, "Into the Night," 87
"Eight Days a Week" (Lennon and McCartney), 335
Ellington, Duke, "It Don't Mean a Thing" (with Mills), 318

"Fanny Power," 146
"For He's a Jolly Good Fellow," 275
Foster, Stephen
    "Beautiful Dreamer," 129
    "Jeanie with the Light Brown Hair," 24, 51, 230
    "Oh! Susanna!," 48, 49, 102, 105, 271, 303, 304–5, 349
Frasier, theme from (Miller), 44
Frog in the Bog, The" (Loomis), 112
"Funeral March of a Marionette" (Gounod), 179

Gad, Toby, "All of Me" (with Stephens), 332–34
Garrett, Lloyd, "Dallas Blues" (with Wand), 76, 317, 372–75
Gershwin, George, "They Can't Take That Away from Me," 252

Gilmore, Patrick, "When Johnny Comes Marching Home," 127, 128, 159, 310, 350
"Girl from Ipanema, The" (Jobim), 94
"Girls on the Beach" (Wilson and Love), 80
"Go Down, Moses," 276, 277
Gottwald, Lukasz, "Roar" (with Perry, Martin, McKee, and Walter), 326–28, 331
Gounod, Charles, "Funeral March of a Marionette," 179
"Green, Green Grass of Home" (Putman), 64
Green Day
    "21 Guns," 336
    "Boulevard of Broken Dreams" (with Armstrong), 124
"Greensleeves," 194, 211, 301–2, 351–52, A30

"Halting March, The," 178
Hammerstein, Oscar, II
    "Edelweiss" (with Rodgers), 295
    "If I Loved You" (with Rodgers), 71
    "The Sound of Music" (with Rodgers), 126
Handel, George Frideric
    "How Beautiful Are the Feet of Them," from Messiah, 154
    "Rejoice Greatly," from Messiah, 152
"Hanukkah Song," 300
Harburg, E. Y., "We're Off to See the Wizard," from The Wizard of Oz (with Arlen), 143
Harline, Leigh, "Hi-Diddle-Dee-Dee," from Pinocchio (with Washington), 149
Haydn, Joseph
    Piano Sonata No. 9, Scherzo, 175
    Seven German Dances, No. 6, 252
Hayes, Philip, "By the Waters of Babylon," 286
"Hello, Goodbye" (Lennon and McCartney), 20
Hensel, Fanny Mendelssohn
    "Schwanenlied," 151
    "Waldeinsam," 175
Herman, Jerry, "Before the Parade Passes By," from Hello Dolly!, 149
"Hey Jude" (Lennon and McCartney), 52
"Hi-Diddle-Dee-Dee," from Pinocchio (Harline and Washington), 149
Holst, Gustav, Second Suite in F for Military Band, "Song of the Blacksmith," 138, 181
"Home on the Range," 131–32, 135–36, 274, 276, 353
Horner, James
    "My Heart Will Go On," 67
    "Somewhere Out There" (with Mann and Weil), 94
"How Beautiful Are the Feet of Them," from Messiah (Handel), 154
"How Can I Keep from Singing" (Lowry), 218, 295
Hupfeld, Hubert, "As Time Goes By," 111

"I Guess That's Why They Call It the Blues" (John, Taupin, and Johnstone), 134, 153
"I Had a Little Nut Tree," 251
"I Like It Like That" (Kenner), 86
"I Need Your Love Tonight" (Wayne), 87
"I Will Always Love You" (Parton), 82
"If I Loved You" (Rodgers and Hammerstein), 71
"Imagine" (Lennon), 5
"Imperial March," from The Empire Strikes Back (Williams), 44
"Into the Night" (Edwards), 87
"It Don't Mean a Thing" (Ellington and Mills), 318
"It Takes Two," from Hairspray (Shaiman and Wittman), 153

Jacquet de la Guerre, Elisabeth, Gigue, from Suite No. 3 in A Minor, 136, 155
"Jeanie with the Light Brown Hair" (Foster), 24, 51, 230
Jobim, Antônio Carlos, "The Girl from Ipanema," 94
Joel, Billy, "Piano Man," 24
John, Sir Elton
    "Circle of Life," from The Lion King (with Rice), 9
    "I Guess That's Why They Call It the Blues" (with Taupin and Johnstone), 134, 153
    "Your Song" (with Taupin), 67
Johnstone, Davey, "I Guess That's Why They Call It the Blues" (with John and Taupin), 134, 153
Joplin, Scott
    "Pine Apple Rag," 44, 78
    "Ragtime Dance," 178
    "Solace," 8, 25–26, 27, 65, 75, 354–56

Kabalevsky, Dmitry, Toccatina, 253
Kander, John, Theme from New York, New York, 80
Kenner, Chris, "I Like It Like that," 86
Kern, Jerome, "Look for the Silver Lining," 81
"Kerry Cow, The," 254
King, Carole, "You've Got a Friend," 94
King's Row, Theme from (Korngold), 86
Korngold, Erich, Theme from King's Row, 86
Kosma, Joseph, "Autumn Leaves," 219

"Lacrymosa," from Requiem (Mozart), 130
"Land of the Silver Birch," 307–8
Larson, Jonathan, "Seasons of Love," from Rent, 67
Lennon, John
    "Eight Days a Week" (with McCartney), 335
    "Hello, Goodbye" (with McCartney), 20
    "Hey Jude" (with McCartney), 52
    "Imagine," 5
Leonarda, Isabella, Credo, from Messa Prima, 87

Lerner, Alan Jay, "Wand'rin' Star," from Paint Your Wagon (with Loewe), 86
Leven, Mel, "Cruella de Vil," 28, 31
"Lil' Red Riding Hood" (Blackwell), 177
Lloyd Webber, Andrew, "Memory," from Cats, 153
Loesser, Frank, "Luck Be a Lady," from Guys and Dolls, 95
Loewe, Frederick, "Wand'rin' Star," from Paint Your Wagon (with Lerner), 86
"Loftus Jones" (O'Carolan), 113
"Look for the Silver Lining" (Kern), 81
Loomis, Harvey Worthington, "The Frog in the Bog," 112
Love, Mike, "Girls on the Beach" (with Wilson), 80
"Love Me Tender" (Presley), 124
Lowry, Robert, "How Can I Keep from Singing," 218, 295
"Luck Be a Lady," from Guys and Dolls (Loesser), 95

Mann, Barry, "Somewhere Out There" (with Horner and Weil), 94
Martin, Max, "Roar" (with Perry, Gottwald, McKee, and Walter), 326–28, 331
Martini, Jean-Paul-Égide, "The Pleasure of Love" (Plaisir d'amour), 145
McCartney, Paul
    "Eight Days a Week" (with Lennon), 335
    "Hello, Goodbye" (with Lennon), 20
    "Hey Jude" (with Lennon), 52
McDaid, Johnny, "Photograph" (with Sheeran), 29
McKee, Bonnie, "Roar" (with Perry, Gottwald, Martin, and Walter), 326–28, 331
McLean, Don, "American Pie," 79, 126
Meistersinger, Die, Prelude to Act 3 (Wagner), 111
"Memory," from Cats (Lloyd Webber), 153
Menken, Alan, "Beauty and the Beast" (with Ashman), 295
"Merrily We Roll Along," 282
"Michael Finnegan," 61
"Midnight Train to Georgia" (Weatherly), 95
Miller, Bruce, Frasier, theme from, 44
Mills, Irving, "It Don't Mean a Thing" (with Ellington), 318
Minstrel Theme from Tannhäuser (Wagner), 178
"Miracle Drug" (Bono and U2), 71
Mission Impossible, Theme from (Schifrin), 8, 137–38
Mozart, Leopold, Burleske, 253
Mozart, Wolfgang Amadeus
    "Alleluia," 218
    "Lacrymosa," from Requiem, 130
    Piano Sonata in C Major, K. 545, 53, 225, 298

Mozart, Wolfgang Amadeus (*Continued*)
    String Quartet in D Minor, K. 421, third
        movement, 61, 357–59
    "Sull'aria," from *The Marriage of Figaro,*
        152
    Variations on "Ah, vous dirai-je Maman,"
        22, 52–53, 73–74, 157–58, 163, 232,
        360–62
    Variations on "Lison dormait," 63
"Musette," BWV Anh. 126 (Bach), 113
"Music Alone Shall Live," 219, 286
"Music for a While" (Purcell), 181
"My Country, 'Tis of Thee," 48, 49,
    233–34, 241, 242, 245, 248, 267–68,
    273, 363
"My Heart Will Go On" (Horner), 67
"My Paddle's Keen and Bright," 178

Nelson, Willie, "On the Road Again," 32
Newton, John, "Amazing Grace," 1, 24, 50, 52,
    55, 171, 364
New York, New York, Theme from (Kander),
    80
"Nun danket," 296

O'Carolan, Turlough, "Loftus Jones," 113
"O Haupt voll blut und Wunden" (Bach),
    65
"Oh! Susanna!" (Foster), 48, 49, 102, 105,
    271, 303, 304–5, 349
"Old Hundredth," 260
"O magnum mysterium" (Victoria), 190
"Once More My Soul," 177
"One Step Closer" (Bono and U2), 262
"On the Road Again" (Nelson), 32
"On Top of Old Smokey," 306

Pachelbel, Johann, Canon in D Major, 266
Parton, Dolly, "I Will Always Love You," 82
Pathétique Sonata (Beethoven), 65
Peretti, Hugo, "Can't Help Falling in Love,"
    from *Blue Hawaii* (with Weiss and
    Creatore), 88
Perry, Katy, "Roar" (with Gottwald, Martin,
    McKee, and Walter), 326–28, 331
Phillips, Joel
    "Blues for Norton," 6, 44, 56, 57, 94, 232,
        314–15, 322, 365–68
    "Rock around the Corner," 320
    "Tired of Work'in' Blues," 319
"Photograph" (Sheeran and McDaid), 29
"Piano Man" (Joel), 24
"Pine Apple Rag" (Joplin), 44, 78
"Pleasure of Love, The" (*Plaisir d'amour*)
    (Martini), 145
Presley, Elvis, "Love Me Tender," 124
Purcell, Henry
    "Ah, Belinda, I am prest," from *Dido and
        Aeneas,* 190
    "Music for a While," 181
Putman, Curly, "Green, Green Grass of
    Home," 64

"Ragtime Dance" (Joplin), 178
"Red Is the Rose," 146
Reichardt, Louise, "Spring Flowers"
    (*Frühlingsblumen*), 144
"Rejoice Greatly," from *Messiah* (Handel),
    152
Rice, Tim
    "All Time High" (with Barry), 33
    "Circle of Life," from *The Lion King* (with
        John), 9
Richie, Lionel, "Three Times a Lady," 71
"Roar" (Perry, Gottwald, Martin, McKee, and
    Walter), 326–28, 331
Robinson, Smokey, "You've Really Got a
    Hold on Me," 133
"Rock around the Corner" (Phillips), 320
Rodgers, Richard
    "Edelweiss" (with Hammerstein), 295
    "If I Loved You" (with Hammerstein), 71
    "The Sound of Music" (with
        Hammerstein), 126
Root, George F., "There's Music in the Air,"
    218
"Rosa Mystica," 274
Rose, Liz, "Teardrops on My Guitar" (with
    Swift), 330

"St. George's Windsor." *See* "Come, Ye
    Thankful People Come"
"St. James Infirmary," 254
Schifrin, Lalo, Theme from *Mission Impossible,*
    8, 137–38
Schubert, Franz
    Allegretto, D. 915, 175
    "Am Flusse" (On the River), 218
    Waltz in B Minor, 65, 160, 269, 270, 283,
        369–70
    Wanderer Fantasy, Op. 15, Adagio, 175
Schumann, Clara, *Three Romances,* Op. 11,
    No. 3, 113
Schumann, Robert
    "Trällerliedchen," 181
    "Wild Rider," 170, 297, 371
"Schwanenlied" (Hensel), 151
"Seasons in the Sun" (Brel), 64
"Seasons of Love," from *Rent* (Larson), 67
Second Suite in F for Military Band, "Song of
    the Blacksmith" (Holst), 138, 181
Seeger, Pete, "Turn, Turn, Turn," 64
Seven German Dances, No. 6 (Haydn), 252
Shaiman, Marc, "It Takes Two," from
    Hairspray (with Wittman), 153
"Shalom, Chaverim," 124
Sheeran, Ed
    "Photograph" (with McDaid), 29
    "Thinking Out Loud" (with Wadge), 330,
        331
"Shenandoah," 217
"Shut Up and Dance" (Walk the Moon), 124
"Simple Gifts" (Brackett), 105, 193–94, 213,
    347
"Solace" (Joplin), 8, 25–26, 27, 65, 75, 354–56

"Somewhere Out There" (Horner, Mann, and
    Weil), 94
"Song Sung Blue" (Diamond), 252
"Sound of Music, The" (Rodgers and
    Hammerstein), 126
Sousa, John Philip, "The Stars and Stripes
    Forever," 44, 54, 108, 298
"Spinning Wheel, The," 144
"Splanky" (Basie), 315, 317
"Spring Flowers" (*Frühlingsblumen*)
    (Reichardt), 144
"Stars and Stripes Forever, The" (Sousa), 44,
    54, 108, 298
"Stay" (Williams), 88
Stephens, John, "All of Me" (with Gad), 332–34
Stiles, Norman, "Dance Myself to Sleep,"
    from *Sesame Street* (with Cerf), 130
Strouse, Charles, "Tomorrow" (with
    Charnin), 295
"Sull'aria," from *The Marriage of Figaro*
    (Mozart), 152
"Sweet Betsy from Pike," 306
Swift, Taylor, "Teardrops on My Guitar"
    (with Rose), 330

Taupin, Bernie
    "I Guess That's Why They Call It the
        Blues" (with John and Johnstone),
        134, 153
    "Your Song" (with John), 67
"Teardrops on My Guitar" (Swift and Rose),
    330
"There's Music in the Air" (Root), 218
"They Can't Take That Away from Me"
    (Gershwin), 252
"Thinking Out Loud" (Sheeran and Wadge),
    330, 331
Three Romances, Op. 11, No. 3 (C.
    Schumann), 113
"Three Times a Lady" (Richie), 71
"Ticket to Ride" (Lennon and McCartney),
    325–26
"Time in a Bottle" (Croce), 163
"Tired of Work'in' Blues" (Phillips), 319
"Tomorrow" (Charnin and Strouse), 295
"Trällerliedchen" (Schumann), 181
Trumpet Voluntary (Clarke), 190
"Turn, Turn, Turn" (Seeger), 64
Twain, Shania, "You're Still the One," 94
"Twinkle, Twinkle, Little Star," 98–99

U2
    "All Because of You" (with Bono), 262
    "Miracle Drug" (with Bono), 71
    "One Step Closer" (with Bono), 262

Variations on "Ah, vous dirai-je Maman"
    (Mozart), 22, 52–53, 73–74, 157–58,
    163, 232, 360–62
Variations on "Lison dormait" (Mozart), 63
Victoria, Tomás Luis de, "O magnum
    mysterium," 190

"Wachet auf" (Bach), 190, 244, 272–73, 344–46

"Wade in the Water," 299, 318–19

Wadge, Amy, "Thinking Out Loud" (with Sheeran), 330, 331

Wagner, Richard
Die Meistersinger, Prelude to Act 3, 111
Minstrel Theme from *Tannhauser,* 178

"Waldeinsam" (Hensel), 175

Walk the Moon, "Shut Up and Dance," 124

Walter, Henry, "Roar" (with Perry, Gottwald, Martin, and McKee), 326–28, 331

Wand, Hart A., "Dallas Blues" (with Garrett), 76, 317, 372–75

Wanderer Fantasy, Op. 15, Adagio (Schubert), 175

"Wand'rin' Star," from *Paint Your Wagon* (Lerner and Loewe), 86

Washington, Ned, "Hi-Diddle-Dee-Dee," from *Pinocchio* (with Harline), 149

"Wayfaring Stranger," 172, 277, 278

Wayne, Sid, "I Need Your Love Tonight," 87

Weatherly, Jim, "Midnight Train to Georgia," 95

Weil, Cynthia, "Somewhere Out There" (with Horner and Mann), 94

Weiss, George David, "Can't Help Falling in Love," from *Blue Hawaii* (with Peretti and Creatore), 88

Welgemoed, Shaun (Shaun Morgan), "Broken," 179

"We're Off to See the Wizard," from *The Wizard of Oz* (Arlen and Harburg), 143

"When Johnny Comes Marching Home" (Gilmore), 127, 128, 159, 310, 350

"When the Saints Go marching In," 63

"Whoopee Ti-Yi-Yo," 144

"Wild Rider" (Schumann), 170, 297, 371

Williams, John, "Imperial March," from *The Empire Strikes Back,* 44

Williams, Maurice, "Stay," 88

Wilson, Brian, "Girls on the Beach" (with Love), 80

Wittman, Scott, "It Takes Two," from *Hairspray* (with Shaiman), 153

Wonder, Stevie, "You Are the Sunshine of My Life," 20

"Wonderful Words of Life" (Bliss), 145

"Yankee Doodle," 299, 309

"You Are the Sunshine of My Life," (Wonder), 20

"You're Still the One" (Twain), 94

"Your Song" (John and Taupin), 67

"You've Got a Friend" (King), 94

"You've Really Got a Hold on Me" (Robinson), 133

Index of Terms and Concepts

12-bar blues, 316–17
32-bar song form, 303–4

accelerando, 48
accents
    displaced, 77–79
    metrical, 49
accidentals, 25–29
    double flats, 32–33
    double sharps, 32–33
    flats, 25–27
    naturals, 25–27
    sharps, 25–27
adagio, 48
Aeolian mode, A29–A31
alla breve, 53
allegretto, 48
allegro, 48
alto, 234
anacrusis, 52, 55
andante, 48
andantino, 48
antecedent phrase, 302
Arne, Thomas, 248
arpeggio, 282
arrangements, keyboard, 279–83
ascending contour, 2
asymmetrical meter(s), 137
augmented intervals, 207–9, 212
augmented second, 161
augmented triads, 236, 237
authentic cadence, 272–73, 275, A42

bar lines, 2, 50
bar(s), 50
basic phrase, 271–72
    subdominant in, 274–75
bass, 234
bass clef, 5–6
    drawing a, 10
    ledger lines and, 7–8
beam(s), 50
    in compound meters, 131, 132
    notating, 50
    for rhythmic patterns, 75–76
beat division, 47, 54–56, 129
beat subdivisions, 73–77
    in compound meters, 131–33
beat unit(s), 52, 53
    in compound meters, 128, 129, 135–36
beat(s), 47
    strong, 49
    weak, 49

blue notes, 316
blues scale, 313–16
blues songs, writing, 313–17
Brackett, Joseph, 213
bridge (in 32-bar song form), 304
bridge (in later popular music), 325
build, 327

C clefs, 12–13
cadence(s), 270
    authentic, 272–73, 275, A42
    deceptive, 272–73
    half, 272–73
    imperfect authentic, 272–73
    inconclusive, 272
    perfect authentic, 272–73
    types of, 272–74
Cage, John, 59
call-and-response, 315
change of mode, 158
changes, 316
changing meter(s), 138
chord connection, 280, A42–A43
chord members, 234, 240
    fifth, 234, 240
    root, 234, 240
    seventh, 234
    third, 234, 240
chord progressions, 271
    keyboard arrangements of, 279–81
    writing, 279–81
chord(s), 234. *See also* dominant seventh
        chord; seventh chord(s); triad(s)
chorus, 305, 325
chromatic half steps, 30, 101, 107–8
chromatic scale, 107–8
circle of fifths, 106–7
    minor key signatures and, 169–70
clave rhythm pattern, 77
clef(s), 4–6
    bass, 5–6
    C clefs, 12–13
    rhythm, 55–56
    treble, 4–5
climax, 305
coda, 280
combo, 316
common time, 53. *See also* quadruple meter
common tones, A42
compound intervals, 210–11
compound meter(s), 127–39
    compound duple, 127–28, 135–36
    compound quadruple, 129–30, 135–36

compound triple, 129, 135–36
    meter signatures for, 129–30, 135–36
    other, 134–37
    subdivisions, 131–33
    syncopation in, 133–34
conducting patterns, 48–49
conjunct motion, 304
consequent phrase, 302
consonance, 317
consonant intervals, 211–12
contour, musical, 1–2
contrary motion, A42
contrasting period, 302
Copland, Aaron, 213
cut time, 53, 77

deceptive cadence, 272–73
deceptive resolution, 273
descending contour, 1–2
diatonic half steps, 30, 98
diatonic modes, A29–A31
diatonic scales, 98
diminished intervals, 207–9, 212
diminished seventh chord, 247, A32–A33
diminished triads, 235, 237
disjunct motion, 304
dissonance, 317
dissonant intervals, 211–12
dominant, 99–100
dominant seventh chord, 244–46
    inversion, 245–46
    in major keys, 267–68
    melody harmonization with, 267–70,
        276–78
    in minor keys, 268–69, 276–78
    spelling, 244–45
dominant triad, 235, 325
    in major keys, 267–68
    melody harmonization with, 267–70, 275,
        276–78
    in minor keys, 268–69
Dorian mode, A29–A31
dot, 52–53, 56
dotted notes, 52–53
dotted rests, 56
dotted-half note beat unit, 129
dotted-quarter beat unit, 128, 302
double flats, 32–33, 208
double sharps, 32–33, 161–62, 208
doubling (in chords), 234
doubly augmented intervals, 212
doubly diminished intervals, 212
downbeat, 49

drop, 327
duple meter, 47–48, 52–53
    compound, 127–28
duplets, 133–34
duration, 50
dynamic levels, 49

eighth note(s), 50, 51
eighth rest, 57
embellishing tones, 276
    neighbor tones, 276
    passing tones, 276
enharmonic spellings, 26–27, 33, 34–35
    for augmented and diminished intervals,
        209

F-clef. *See* bass clef
fifth (of chord), 234, 240
figures, 242
first-inversion chords, 241–43, 245–46
fixed-*do* solfège, 99
flags, 50
flats, 25–27
flatted fifth, 314
folk songs, writing, 301–12
form, 301–12
    32-bar song form, 303–4
    in later popular music, 325–29
    period, 302
    quaternary song form, 301–4
forte, 49
fortissimo, 49
four-phrase song form, 301–4

G-clef. *See* treble clef
Graham, Martha, 213
grand staff, 7–9
grave, 48
Guido of Arezzo, 108
Guidonian hand, 108
guitar fretboard diagrams, 271, A34–A38

half cadence, 272–73
half note(s), 50, 51
half rest(s), 51
half step(s), 26, 29–32
    chromatic, 30, 101, 107–8
    diatonic, 30, 98
    hearing, 32
half-diminished seventh chord, 247,
    A32–A33
harmonic intervals, 194–95
harmonic loops, 327–29
harmonic minor, 160–62, 164
    piano fingerings for, A40–A41
harmonic progressions, 271–72
harmonic rhythm, 271
harmonization, 270–71
head, 317
hexachord(s), 108
homophonic texture, 234
hook, 326

Houston, Whitney, 81
hymn style, 233–34, A42–A43

imperfect authentic cadence, 272–73
improvisation, 80–81
inconclusive cadence, 272
interval inversion, 201–3
interval quality, 193, 195–207
    augmented, 207–9, 212
    diminished, 207–9, 212
    doubly augmented, 212
    doubly diminished, 212
    major, 195–207, 211–12
    minor, 195–207, 211–12
    perfect, 196, 198, 204, 211
interval(s), 193–213
    compound, 210–11
    consonant, 211–12
    dissonant, 211–12
    enharmonic spellings, 34–35
    enharmonically equivalent, 209
    half step, 26, 29–32
    harmonic, 194–95
    melodic, 194
    simple, 210
    sizes, 193–95
    spelling methods for, 197–207
    spelling triads by, 237, 240–41
    unisons, 194
    whole step, 29–32
intro, 326
introduction, 280
inverted chords, 241–43, 245–46
inverting intervals, 201–3
Ionian mode, A29–A31

John, Sir Elton, 13
Joplin, Scott, 35

key signature(s), 102
    determining, 104
    identifying key from score,
        170–71
    for major keys, 102–5
    for minor keys, 168–70
    spelling intervals from, 205–6
    spelling triads by, 237–38
keyboard, piano
    half and whole steps on, 30
    ledger lines and, 6–9
    naming white keys on, 3, 26
    with octave numbers, 6
keyboard arrangements, 279–83
    styles of, 281–83
keyboard style, 243

larghetto, 48
largo, 48
lead sheet(s), 315
leading tone, 100, 161, 237
leading-tone triad, 235
leaps, melodic, 279, 304

ledger lines, 6–9
    drawing, 10–11
    landmarks for, 7
letter names, pitch, 2–3, 26–27
Locrian mode, A29–A31
Lydian mode, A29–A31

major intervals, 195–207, 211–12
major key(s)
    melody harmonization in, 267–68, 276
    seventh chords in, A32–A33
    signatures for, 102–5
major pentatonic scale, 171–73
major scale(s), 98–99, 164
    piano fingerings for, A39–A40
    spelling triads by, 237, 239–40
    writing, 100–102
major seventh chord, 247, A32–A33
major tetrachord, 100
major triad(s), 234, 235, 236
measure(s), 2, 50
mediant, 99–100
mediant triad, 235
melodic intervals, 194
melodic minor, 162–64
melodies, writing, 304–5
melody, 1–2
melody and accompaniment texture, 269
melody harmonization
    with basic phrase model, 270–71, 274–75,
        276–78
    embellishments, 276
    with triads and dominant seventh chord,
        267–70
meter signature(s), 52–54
    for compound meters, 129–30, 135–36
    for simple meters, 52–54
meter(s)
    asymmetrical, 137
    changing, 138
    compound, 127–39
    duple, 47–48, 52–53
    with eighth or sixteenth-note beat units,
        57–59
    quadruple, 47–48, 52–53
    simple, 47–59
    symmetrical, 137
    triple, 47–48, 283
metrical accents, 49
mezzo forte, 49
mezzo piano, 49
middle C, 3
minor dominant seventh chord, 276–78
minor intervals, 195–207, 211–12
minor mode, 157
minor pentatonic scale, 171–73
minor scales and keys, 157–73
    harmonic minor, 160–62, 164
    identifying from score, 170–71
    melodic minor, 162–64
    melody harmonization in, 268–69, 276–78
    natural minor, 159–60, 164, 314

minor scales and keys (*Continued*)
    parallel keys, 157–58
    seventh chords in, A32–A33
    signatures for, 168–70
minor seventh chord, 247–48, A32–A33
minor triad(s), 234, 235, 236
Mixolydian mode, A29–A31
modal scale degrees, 159
moderato, 48
modulation, 166
motives, 304
movable-*do* solfège, 99
Mozart, Wolfgang Amadeus, 173
Mozart family, 173
musical alphabet, 2
musical contour, 1–2

natural minor, 159–60, 164, 314
    relative, 167
naturals, 25–27
neighbor tones, 276
notation guidelines
    beaming of rhythmic patterns, 75–76
    beams and flags, 50
    beams in compound meters, 131,
        132
    clefs, 10, 12
    for duplets, 133–34
    ledger lines, 10–11
    note heads, 3–4
    notes and stems, 10
    unisons and seconds with stems,
        197–98
note heads, drawing, 3–4, 10
note(s), 1
    eighth, 50, 51
    half, 50, 51
    quarter, 50, 51
    sixteenth, 51
    whole, 51

octave equivalence, 2
octave numbers, naming pitches with, 6
octave(s), 2, 194, 211
outro, 326
overtone series, A28

parallel fifths, A43
parallel keys, 157–58
    parallel major, 158
    parallel minor, 158
parallel motion, A43
parallel octaves, A43
parallel period, 302
parallel unisons, A43
Parton, Dolly, 81
passing tones, 276
pentatonic scales, 171–73
    major pentatonic, 171–73
    minor pentatonic, 171–73
perfect authentic cadence, 272–73
perfect intervals, 196, 198, 204, 211

period(s), 302
    contrasting, 302
    parallel, 302
phrase(s), 270
    antecedent, 302
    consequent, 302
    keyboard arrangements of, 279–81
    paired, 301–2
Phrygian mode, A29–A31
pianissimo, 49
piano (dynamic), 49
piano fingerings for selected scales, A39–A41
piano keyboard
    half and whole steps on, 30
    ledger lines and, 6–9
    naming white keys on, 3, 26
pickup, 52, 55
pitch, 1
pitch notation, 1–13
    ledger lines for, 6–9
    letter names, 2–3, 26–27
    naming with octave numbers, 6
    staff, 3–4
    treble and bass clefs, 4–6
    writing pitches in score, 9–11
    writing pitches with accidentals, 28–29
postchorus, 326
prechorus, 326
prestissimo, 48
presto, 48

quadruple meter, 47–48, 52–53
quality (of triad), 234
quarter note(s), 50, 51
quarter rest, 57
quarter-note beat, rhythmic subdivisions of, 74
quaternary song form, 301–4

raised submediant, 164
refrain, 326
register, 9
relative keys, 165–68
    relative major, 166, 168
    relative minor, 166, 167
resolution, 212
rest(s), 56–57
    in compound meters, 132
    eighth, 57
    half, 51
    quarter, 57
    sixteenth, 57
    whole, 56–57
rhythm, 50
    counting in simple meters, 54–56
rhythm clef, 55–56
rhythmic motive, 304
rhythmic notation, 50–52
    dots in, 52–53
rhythmic variations in performance, 80–81
riffs, 315
ritardando, 48
Robinson, Smokey, 139

Roman numerals, 235, 237
root (of chord), 234, 240
root-position chords, 240, 241–43, 245–46

SATB, 233–34, A42–A43
scale degree(s), 98–100
    dominant, 99–100
    leading tone, 100
    mediant, 99–100
    in minor, 164
    modal, 159
    raised submediant, 164
    subdominant, 99–100
    submediant, 100
    subtonic, 164
    supertonic, 99–100
    tonic, 99–100
scale step(s). *See* scale degree(s)
scale(s), 97–102
    blues, 313–16
    chromatic, 107–8
    comparing, 164–65
    diatonic, 98
    harmonic minor, 160–62, 164
    major, 98–99, 164
    melodic minor, 162–64
    natural minor, 159–60, 164
    pentatonic, 171–73
    spelling intervals from, 203–5
score, 1
    writing music in a, 9–11
second-inversion chords, 241–43, 245–46
semitone. *See* half step
seventh chord positions and inversions,
        245–46
    first inversion, 245–46
    root position, 245–46
    second inversion, 245–46
    third inversion, 245–46
seventh chord(s), 246–48, A32–A33
    in blues, 317
    diminished, 247, A32–A33
    dominant, 244–46
    half-diminished, 247, A32–A33
    major, 247, A32–A33
    minor, 247–48, A32–A33
    spelling, 247
    symbols for, 247
seventh (of chord), 234
Shakers, 213
sharps, 25–27
similar motion, A43
simple intervals, 210
simple meters, 47–59
    counting rhythms in, 54–56
    duple, 47–48, 52–53
    meter signatures for, 52–54
    quadruple, 47–48, 52–53
    triple, 47–48, 283
single meters, 47
sixteenth note(s), 51
sixteenth rest, 57

skips, melodic, 279, 304
slurs, 77
solfège, 99, 108
  fixed-*do*, 99
  movable-*do*, 99
soprano, 234
staff notation, 3–4
staff (staves), 1
  grand staff, 7–9
  ledger lines and, 6–9
stem(s), 1
  drawing, 10
stepwise motion, 29
strong beat, 49
subdominant, 99–100
subdominant triad, 235
  in basic phrase model, 274–75
  in major keys, 267–68
  melody harmonization with, 267–70, 276–78
  in minor keys, 268–69
submediant, 100
submediant triad, 235
subtonic, 164
supertonic, 99–100
supertonic triad, 235
swung eighths, 81
symmetrical meter(s), 137
syncopation, 77–79, 81
  in compound meters, 133–34

"tacet," 59
tempo, 48
tempo markings, 48
tendency tone, 100
tenor, 234
tetrachord(s), 100
  major, 100
texture, 233
  homophonic, 234
  melody and accompaniment, 269
third (of chord), 234, 240
third-inversion chords, 245–46
ties, 76
tonic, 99–100
tonic triad, 235
  in major keys, 267–68
  melody harmonization with, 267–70, 276–78
  in minor keys, 268–69
transpose, 98
treble clef, 4–5
  drawing a, 10
  ledger lines and, 6–7, 7–8
triad positions and inversions, 241–43
  first inversion, 241–43
  root position, 240, 241–43
  second inversion, 241–43
triad qualities, 234
  augmented, 236
  diminished, 235, 236

  major, 235, 236
  in major keys, 234–36
  minor, 235, 236
  in minor keys, 236–37
triad(s), 233–43
  melody harmonization with, 267–70
  names of, 235–36
  spelling, 237–40
triple meter, 47–48, 283
triplets, 79–80
tritone, 208
turnaround, 316
two-beat triplets, 80

unison, 194
upbeat, 49, 52, 55

verse (in 32-bar song form), 305
verse (in later popular music), 325
vivace, 48

waltz, 283
weak beat, 49
whole note(s), 51
whole rest(s), 56–57
whole step(s), 29–32
  hearing, 32
whole tone. *See* whole step
writing music in a score, 9–11
writing pitches with accidentals, 28–29